*F*orensic Investigation of Animal Cruelty

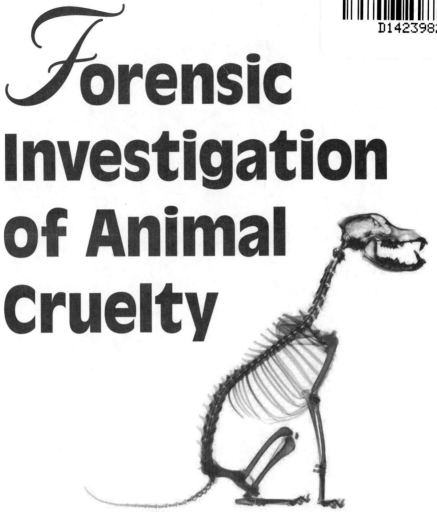

A GUIDE FOR VETERINARY AND LAW ENFORCEMENT PROFESSIONALS

by
Leslie Sinclair, D.V.M.
Melinda Merck, D.V.M.
Randall Lockwood, Ph.D.

Humane Society Press
an affiliate of

THE HUMANE SOCIETY OF THE UNITED STATES

Panel of Reviewers

K. Paige Carmichael, D.V.M., Ph.D., DipACVP
Pathologist and Professor of Pathology
Department of Pathology
College of Veterinary Medicine
University of Georgia
Athens, Georgia

Charlotte A. Lacroix, D.V.M., Esq.
CEO, Veterinary Business Advisors, Inc.
Whitehouse Station, New Jersey

Lila Miller, D.V.M.
Vice President, Veterinary Outreach
American Society for the Prevention of Cruelty to Animals
New York, New York

Janice Sojka, V.M.D.
School of Veterinary Medicine
Purdue University
West Lafayette, Indiana

First edition
ISBN 0-9748400-6-8

Library of Congress Cataloging-in-Publication Data

Sinclair, Leslie.
    Forensic investigation of animal cruelty : a guide for veterinary and law enforcement professionals / by
Leslie Sinclair, Melinda Merck, and Randall Lockwood. — 1st ed.
        p. cm.
    Includes bibliographical references and index.
    ISBN 0-9748400-6-8
  1. Veterinary jurisprudence—United States. 2. Animal welfare—Law and legislation—United States. 3.
Veterinary medicine. I. Merck, Melinda II. Lockwood, Randall, 1948- III. Title.
    KF8964.S54 2006
    363.25'987–dc22

                                                        2006008355

Printed in the United States of America on 100% post-consumer recycled paper, processed chlorine free
and FSC certified, with soy-based ink.

Contents

Author's Notes

Tables

Figures

Plates *(all appear on pages inserted between pages 70 and 71)*

Author's Note

There's no worse feeling than realizing you could have done more for one of your patients and the owner who cared for him. On a late afternoon in September of 1993, at the end of a busy day of surgery, exams, and treatments at the Houston SPCA, I was presented with the dead body of a young black domestic shorthair cat. His fur was wet, and his story was painful. A young woman's estranged husband had called her earlier that day and threatened to strangle her cat, who was still living at their house with him. Two hours later he threw the cat's body—lifeless and thoroughly wet—into the yard of the home where she was staying.

I had been working as the staff veterinarian for this large nonprofit animal shelter for a little over a year, and had already examined hundreds of victims—both living and deceased—of horrendous cruelty and neglect. Every case was a struggle, and I'd found few written resources to prepare me for this task. I was a new graduate, but my recent education had never mentioned this aspect of veterinary practice. This was my first case in which drowning was a suspected cause of death. I performed a physical examination on the dead cat, finding him to be in good condition with no obvious abnormalities. I believed that histologic examination of the lung tissue might be our only hope for a definitive cause of death and performed only enough of a necropsy to remove that tissue for submission. The report arrived a week later and read:

> Multiple sections of lung are examined microscopically. In two of these, no lesions are noted. In one there is alveolar capillary congestion with alveolar edema. Pulmonary edema may reflect acute congestive heart failure.
> The definitive cause of death cannot be determined.

I can't remember how much information our humane investigators were able to gather, but I do remember that those last words—"the definitive cause of death cannot be determined"—made them feel that they could not successfully pursue the case. Years later, armed with the knowledge of more experienced veterinary investigators and of human forensic scientists, I look back painfully on that case and realize how much more I could have done. I could not have revived the cat, but I could have vindicated his death. I could not have given that woman back her pet, but I could have played a significant role in protecting her from a man who quite possibly could have done to her what he did to her cat. I wonder if she is alive and unharmed today, and I'm sorry I didn't know enough then to help her.

Although much information has come to light about the insidious connection between violence toward animals and violence toward humans, scarce resources exist for veterinarians who become involved in the issue. The veterinary community is potentially the group most able to address violent crimes against animals, yet its power is largely untapped. Little information is available for the veterinarian who is called upon to assist in the investigation and prosecution of an act of animal cruelty. The topic has not been taught in veterinary colleges, it is not often presented in veterinary education forums, and little has been written in either the scientific or clinical literature of the veterinary profession. Most veterinarians are unfamiliar with anti-cruelty statutes and confused about issues of liability and confidentiality. They are rightfully worried about their personal safety and their reputation within their communities.

Veterinarians are an inherently compassionate group of people. In addition to the concerns cited above, the distress of becoming involved in the aftermath of an act of animal cruelty can be difficult to bear. As with any medical procedure, becoming highly knowledgeable about the task at hand makes it all the easier to perform. Although no textbook can remove the sting of witnessing the evidence of a heinous act of violence, an informed and clinical approach to addressing such an act may reduce the measure of pain it causes to the veterinarian, to the victim's owner, and to the community in which the act occurred.

Forensic Investigation of Animal Cruelty is meant to be a clinical and comprehensive guide for veterinarians who are faced—either voluntarily or inadvertently—with the task of initiating or participating in an animal-cruelty investigation. This book will define acts of cruelty to animals, introduce the legal processes of investigation and prosecution, orient the veterinarian to the task of gathering evidence and creating documents and presenting them properly to the legal system, outline procedures for examining victims, and illustrate the most common clinical presentations of both living and deceased victims.

The text focuses primarily on dogs and cats because they are the species most often affected by the types of cruelty discussed here, but much of this information can be easily applied to other domestic mammalian species. Although the types of cruelty that may accompany the commercial breeding and sales of dogs and cats are not directly addressed, some of the circumstances of those types of cruelty do appear here, particularly in the chapter on neglect. Because most veterinary practitioners are more experienced and comfortable with the examination of living animals and because there already exists more literature addressing evaluation of injuries to surviving patients, greater emphasis has been placed on post-mortem than pre-mortem findings.

The variety of acts of cruelty to animals is as limitless as the human imagination. You will not find an exact protocol for evaluating each complex case here, but you will find step-by-step procedures for examining the animal victim, evaluating her injuries, documenting your findings, preserving the evidence, and presenting the case to the legal system in a manner that will ensure that you have made a qualified effort to address a horrendous criminal act.

I hope that you will have no need for this book in your veterinary career, but I doubt that will be the case. I believe you will find it to be one of the most useful tools you possess to ensure that you have done everything you can for your patient and for the owner who cares for him.

Leslie Sinclair, D.V.M.
Columbia, Maryland

Author's Note

My involvement with cruelty to animals began during my second year of practice. An indoors-only, eight-week-old kitten presented comatose with unilateral hemothorax and epistaxis (bleeding in one side of the chest and nose). The owners said he fell off the kitchen counter. I knew differently. The officers agreed. The owners confessed and then fled the state. The kitten survived and was placed in a new home.

This incident taught me several things. The first thing I learned was that the outcome is not always what we want. Though the people were never brought to justice, the kitten survived—which is the most important outcome, after all. The second thing I learned is that if the symptoms do not match the history of the injury, you have to trust your judgment and act accordingly. We as veterinarians are knowledgeable investigators and have the ability to recognize when something is "not right." Statistics show that all veterinarians will see at least one case of cruelty to animals in their career. It is our duty to society and to the animals we swore an oath to protect to investigate and report these cases.

The success of the investigation and prosecution of cruelty to animals relies on animal-control officers, law enforcement, prosecutors, and veterinary findings. It is my hope that this book will provide resources for all those connected with the investigation and prosecution of animal cruelty to ultimately lead to justice for the animals and protection of society.

Melinda Merck, D.V.M.
Roswell, Georgia

Author's Note

The archives of the American Society for the Prevention of Cruelty to Animals (ASPCA), the nation's first animal protection organization, contain several calling cards from Dr. Alexandre Liautard, editor of the *American Veterinary Review*. These cards document visits by this prominent veterinarian to Henry Bergh, the organization's founder and president. Liautard consulted with Bergh on many issues, including animal-cruelty cases, helping him document the animal suffering the ASPCA and its agents had been empowered to investigate and prosecute (Unti 2002).

Since the earliest days of animal protection, veterinarians have played a central role in working with humane investigators and law enforcement authorities to help tell the story of animals who have suffered or died as a result of human abuse or neglect. Although it has a long history, *veterinary forensics*—the application of veterinary knowledge and skills to the law—is a new and emerging discipline. Expertise in this area has never been more important than it is today.

Animal-cruelty cases are being taken far more seriously than at any time in the past. As of this writing, more than forty states have new laws that define certain instances of cruelty to animals as serious, felony-level crimes that can result in substantial fines and/or prison sentences. Most of these laws have been passed within the last ten years in response to growing public concern about animal abuse and the nature of those who perpetrate such crimes. A December 1996 survey of more than one thousand representative households indicated that 81 percent of those surveyed favored strengthening laws against cruelty to animals and 71 percent favored making some forms of cruelty a felony offense (Penn and Schoen Associates 1997).

Even as recently as the year 2000, it was unusual to find a district attorney who had ever prosecuted an animal-cruelty case. In the training I regularly conduct for the American Prosecutors Research Institute it is now common to find that, even among prosecutors with less than two years of experience, more than half have already prosecuted such cases.

Why the change? We can point to several factors.

Stronger scientific support for the connection between cruelty to animals and violence against human beings. These connections have slowly attracted mainstream scientific interest, and there has been a gradual growth in academic and scientific support for these concepts (Lockwood and Ascione 1998). Much of this literature existed well before 1980, but appeared to have had little impact on public opinion or policy until the last decade.

Overall growth of the animal welfare, animal protection, and animal rights movements. Some of the societal shift in concern about animal abuse may be attributed to the overall growth of animal advocacy as a social movement. Even among those who may reject many of the concerns of animal rights or animal protection, opposition to the intentional infliction of pain and suffering may represent one piece of the message that they can accept without conflict.

Specific campaigns of animal advocacy groups. During the last decade, there have been major campaigns by several national animal protection and animal advocacy organizations to educate the public and professionals to the connections between cruelty to animals and other forms of violence. These have included well-crafted campaigns, publications, and workshops conducted by The Humane Society of the United States (HSUS), the American Humane Association, the Latham Foundation, and others, as well as efforts by local humane societies, including the Washington (D.C.) Humane Society, Michigan Humane Society, and Toledo Humane Society. Such efforts have created a climate in which the public has clearly been sensitized to the problems of animal abuse and to its relevance to the larger issues of crime and violence in society (Lockwood 1999).

Societal concern about violence. Public interest in cruelty to animals and its connections to other forms of human violence is a natural corollary of the much greater concern about violence in society. Concerns about the proliferation of crime, family violence, and other forms of antisocial behavior are, in a sense, the new environmental movement, as society seeks to locate, prevent, and correct the sources of "social toxicity" in our world. Attention to animal cruelty offers possible tools for the early identification of victims and perpetrators of this toxicity.

Practical validity. A final reason for growing public recognition of the violence connections is that attention to these connections works! It helps professionals confronting violence do their jobs better. Law enforcement officers benefit by taking the actions of animal abusers seriously. Social workers and other mental health professionals get useful information by paying attention to the treatment of animals in the home. Therapists seeking interventions that will build empathy and diffuse violence see the benefits of fostering compassion for animals. Veterinarians who become involved in responding to violence against animals and people not only help address the needs of individual animals who may suffer, but also take on the much larger task of addressing the ills of a violent society.

All of these factors have created a climate of unprecedented concern about cruelty to animals and other forms of human violence. Social change proceeds when society at large changes its attitudes toward the level of injustice and harm it will tolerate. Animals continue to be used, exploited, and harmed in many ways that society regards as acceptable. But that tolerance is undergoing change, and growing outrage at intentional harm is an important step in that change. Veterinary professionals will continue to play a key role in recognizing and responding to animal abuse and neglect. We hope that this volume will provide them with useful tools and techniques in this important endeavor.

Randall Lockwood, Ph.D.
Falls Church, Virginia

What is Cruelty to Animals?

Legal and Legislative Definitions

A sixteen-week-old puppy urinates on the floor in front of his owner. Frustrated with this "housebreaking" failure, his owner swings him up into the air by his collar. The puppy is presented to a veterinary hospital later that evening with bloodshot eyes. Two men club a pair of cats to death with a baseball bat. A veterinarian examines the cats and determines that they died almost instantly from blows to the brain.

A five-year-old Labrador retriever mix lives tied up on a chain in a backyard in a suburban neighborhood. He receives just enough water and generic brand dog food to sustain him, and a leaky wooden doghouse provides him with some protection from the weather. The fence is high enough that he cannot see out of the yard. He has less than five minutes of contact with his owner each day and no contact with other dogs or people.

A five-month-old puppy wanders out from under the house where he lives and into the street, where he is hit by an oncoming car. He staggers back into the ditch at the edge of the yard and lies there for three days before dying. The owner notices the puppy (there are six other dogs living under the house) but does not seek veterinary care because he believes he cannot afford it.

What *is* cruelty to animals? It would seem to be an easy question to answer. "Cruelty to animals" is any act that, by intention or by neglect, causes an animal "unnecessary" pain or suffering. The term is easily applied to an act so heinous and deliberate that society deems it unacceptable. But often the acceptability of an act is not clear. Each of us has his or her own personal definition of cruelty to animals, based on our unique experiences, our sociocultural background, our spiritual beliefs, our experiences with animals and with humans, and other variables. Our personal definitions are organic, too, growing and changing with time and experience.

For some, it is helpful to define different types of harm to animals (neglect, abuse, cruelty) and to rank them on a scale of severity or acceptability. *Neglect* has been defined as the unintentional lack of care that comes from ignorance, *abuse* as more willful knowledge of failing to provide care or the awareness of doing something harmful, and *cruelty* as the deliberate infliction of pain on an animal from which the abuser derives enjoyment or amusement (King 1998). While clear definitions (especially those that clarify intent) are important in the legal arena, veterinarians may be hindered by those same definitions. Neglect can also fall under the category of abuse and/or cruelty. The terms themselves are misused and have been overused to describe a broad range of behaviors and motivational states (Rowan 1993). A proposed typology—a categorization of types of companion animal abuse—has been offered based on a review of cases presented to the Royal Society for the Prevention of Cruelty to Animals in South Africa (Vermeulen and Odendaal 1993) (Table 1.1). Note that this typology includes a category of "mental abuse," which is not currently specifically recognized in any anti-cruelty statutes in the United States.

Table 1.1—Typology of Companion Animal Abuse

Physical Abuse (intentional or unintentional)		Active maltreatment
		Assault
		Burning
		Poisoning
		Shooting
		Mutilation
		Drowning
		Suffocation
		Abandonment
		Restriction of movement
		Incorrect training methods
		Inbreeding
		Trapping
		Abusive transportation
		Fireworks
		Bestiality
	Passive Neglect or Ignorance	Lack of food or water
		Lack of shelter
		Lack of veterinary care
		Lack of sanitation
		General neglect
	Commercial Exploitation	Labor (draft animal)
		Fighting
		Overbreeding
		Sport
		Experimentation
Mental Abuse (intentional or unintentional)	Active Maltreatment	Instilling fear and anxiety
		Isolation
	Passive Neglect	Deprivation of love and affection, lack of recreational stimuli

Source: Vermuelen and Odendaal 1993.

In common usage, the term "cruelty to animals" encompasses a range of behaviors harmful to animals, from unintentional neglect to malicious killing, and it is difficult to arrange these assaults against animals along a scale of acceptability. We may be able to place some acts at one end of the scale or the other, but too many of them fall somewhere in between, making the scale of little use to us. A more effective "scoring system" is necessary. As a society we define objectionable acts through our legal system. The laws we enact and enforce demonstrate our tolerance or intolerance of specified acts against animals. Our laws are a cumulative expression of many points of view, however, and they rarely represent the opinions of any one person. Instead, they are a compromise of many differing views about what is cruel, abusive, neglectful, or justifiable treatment of an animal and about whether and when animals deserve protection against such treatment.

Criminal Laws and Civil Laws against Cruelty to Animals

There are two primary types of laws in the United States (Wilson 1988). Criminal law defines the boundaries of the relationship between the individual and society. Acts that are harmful to people and those that disrupt the order of society are criminal acts and are classified as either misdemeanor or felony offenses, depending on society's view of the severity of the offense. Criminal laws also dictate the procedures by which a crime is investigated and the suspect is arrested and prosecuted and by which punishment is determined and administered. When a violation of criminal law occurs, American society brings action against the perpetrator by acting through a district or state attorney at the local and state level or the U.S. Attorney General at the national level.

Civil law pertains to the relationships among individuals within a society. Types of civil law include contract law and tort law. Contract law deals with duties established by individuals as the result of contractual agreements. Tort law deals with duties of individuals toward other people as established by law. Tort laws cover such circumstances as negligence, product liability, libel and slander, invasion of privacy, assault, and nuisance.

The response to neglect and cruelty toward animals may take the form of criminal actions, as determined by local, state, and federal laws. However, civil actions may be involved in criminal cases as well. Perhaps the most famous examples of this are the cases of the 1994 murders of Nicole Simpson and Ronald Goldman, in which the defendant, former football star O.J. Simpson, was found not guilty in the criminal case but liable for wrongful death in a corresponding civil case. Similarly, a person who commits an act of cruelty toward an animal may be charged in a criminal action for committing a wrong against society. The owner of the animal can file a civil lawsuit against the attacker in an attempt to receive compensation for the harm done to the animal. Animal-control and law enforcement officers often use a combination of criminal and civil charges when dealing with severe abuse cases. For example, a citizen who has ten starving dogs chained in her backyard could potentially be charged with failure to provide food, care, and shelter (violation of a state's criminal statutes, a criminal offense) as well as failure to license the animals properly (violation of a local ordinance, a civil offense).

Historically, and in most modern circumstances, animals are considered to be the property of their owners, regardless of whether the owner considers the animal to be a "member of the family." Early U.S. anti-cruelty laws were based on the premise that animals of commercial value (such as draft horses) should be protected from cruel acts because of the damage done to the owner's property and the resulting possible loss of income from the use of that animal (Favre and Tsang 1993). Animals who were mere companions were not protected by the law until well after protection was provided to those who had commercial value. Although many anti-cruelty laws are basically property-crime laws, some courts now recognize that a companion animal is more than property and that companion animals have some of the attributes of a member of the family with respect to compensation to the owner (Hannah 1999; Wise 1999). In rare cases, pet owners have been allowed to recover awards for emotional distress or loss of companionship as a result of the death of their companion animals under distressful circumstances, and this trend is likely to continue as courts attach greater significance to the human-animal bond.

The Language of Anti-Cruelty Laws

Despite recent advances, anti-cruelty laws can often hinder attempts to address an animal-cruelty crime. In state laws, "cruelty to animals" is used generically to describe a broad range of mistreatment, from malicious killing of an animal to a temporary lapse in providing proper care. Many state anti-cruelty laws still contain the original and somewhat antiquated language, developed a century ago, which prohibited the "overdriving and overloading" of a work animal (Donley, Patronek, and Luke 1999). The language of anti-cruelty laws varies tremendously, from Wisconsin's brief anti-cruelty statute, which declares, "No person may treat any animal, whether belonging to the person or another, in a cruel manner" (Wisconsin Statutes. Crimes. Chapter 951. Crimes against animals. §951.02. Mistreating animals), to Connecticut's dizzying, 251-word, single-sentence statute:

> Any person who overdrives, drives when overloaded, overworks, tortures, deprives of necessary sustenance, mutilates or cruelly beats or kills or unjustifiably injures any animal, or who, having impounded or confined any animal, fails to give such animal proper care or neglects to cage or restrain any such animal from doing injury to itself or to another animal or fails to supply any such animal with wholesome air, food and water, or unjustifiably

administers any poisonous or noxious drug or substance to any domestic animal or unjustifiably exposes any such drug or substance, with intent that the same shall be taken by an animal, or causes it to be done, or, having charge or custody of any animal, inflicts cruelty upon it or fails to provide it with proper food, drink, or protection from the weather or abandons it or carries it or causes it to be carried in a cruel manner, or sets on foot, instigates, promotes, or carries on or performs any act as assistant, umpire or principal in, or is a witness of, or in any way aids in or engages in the furtherance of, any fight between cocks or other birds, dogs, or other animals, premeditated by any person owning, or having custody of, such birds or animals, or fights with or baits, harasses, or worries any animal for the purpose of making it perform for amusement, diversion, or exhibition, shall be fined not more than one thousand dollars or imprisoned not more than one year or both. (Connecticut General Statutes, Title 53. Crimes Chapter 945. Offenses against humanity and morality. §53-247 Cruelty to Animals)

Some states provide a greater degree of specificity in defining acts or omissions that may constitute cruelty. Idaho state veterinary regulations include in the definition of cruelty "withholding of appropriate pain medications or levels of pain medications and the administration of unnecessary procedures and treatments" (Idaho Statute Title 44-2115—Grounds for Discipline).

Each state may or may not also define what it means by the term "animal" in its anti-cruelty statute. Many states provide no definition, leaving open to question which animals are protected. Other states specify which animals are included or excluded from protection. This widespread variation can produce uncertainty about which animals are protected by anti-cruelty legislation. Alaska states that the term "animal" means "a vertebrate living creature not a human being, but does not include fish." Arizona's statute refers to "animals and poultry" in all instances. The Delaware Criminal Code is careful to point out that the definition of animal "shall not include fish, crustacea, or molluska." The Indiana Code uses the phrase "vertebrate animal" throughout its anti-cruelty statute. Missouri excludes many species by applying its statute only to mammals. Louisiana declares that "fowl shall not be defined as animals," but goes on to identify birds of the order Psittaciformes (such as parrots, parakeets, and lovebirds) and Passeriformes (including canaries, starlings, and sparrows) as "animals," thereby providing protection for only these specified avian species. Other states have widely inclusive definitions (Table 1.2).

Although most prosecution of animal cruelty has involved crimes against mammals or birds, prosecutions involving reptile, amphibian, and even invertebrate victims have been successful. Marquis (1996) describes the prosecution of a man who stole Victor, a twenty-six-pound lobster, from Oregon's Seaside Aquarium. The man threw Victor to the ground during his escape, fatally injuring the creature. The offender, who had previous arrests for child abuse and shooting a police dog, was convicted of theft and cruelty to animals.

Misdemeanor and Felony Offenses

Although all fifty states deem some form of animal cruelty to be at least a misdemeanor offense, as of mid-2005, forty-one states and the District of Columbia had felony penalty provisions for specific animal-cruelty offenses (Mississippi's felony law applies only to livestock, and South Dakota currently has felony provisions only for bestiality), with most of those states enacting their felony provisions since 1993 (Table 1.3). Most apply on a first offense; others apply only upon a second, third, or fourth offense. Forty-eight states have laws that specifically make dogfighting a felony offense. Maximum sentences range from only six months (Mississippi, Ohio) to as long as ten years (Louisiana). Maximum fines for perpetrators of animal cruelty may be as high as $150,000 (Arizona) (Table 1.3).

Felony anti-cruelty laws vary widely from state to state. In Missouri cruelty to animals is not a felony unless the defendant has been found guilty of cruelty previously or the animal was tortured while alive. In Montana, Pennsylvania, and Indiana, only second and subsequent offenses of deliberate cruelty are felonies. In New Hampshire second and subsequent offenses or certain acts, as well as a first offense of beating and torturing, are felonies. In Texas and Nevada, a third cruelty offense is a felony. In Vermont aggravated cruelty to animals is a felony only if the sentence is over two years long; anything less than two years is a misdemeanor. The Pennsylvania felony provision applies only to dogs and cats; the New York felony provisions only apply to dogs, cats, and other companion animals.

Knowing Where and What the Law Is

Such drastic differences in the wording and application of anti-cruelty laws from one state to another make the use and interpretation of these laws more difficult, but anti-cruelty statutes are a common characteristic of the laws of our fifty self-governing states and the District of Columbia. Criminal anti-cruelty laws are found in the criminal (or "penal") portion of a state's statutes (often called the "state code"). Other laws in the criminal code may also apply, such as when a person who set an animal

Table 1.2—Definitions of "Animal" in State Anti-Cruelty Laws

State	Definition of "Animal"
Alabama	Dog or cat shall mean any domesticated member of the dog or cat family
Alaska	A vertebrate living creature not a human being, but does not include fish
Arizona	A mammal, bird, reptile, or amphibian
Arkansas	Every living creature
California	Every dumb creature
Colorado	Any living dumb creature
Connecticut	All brute creatures and birds
Delaware	Does not include fish, crustacea, or molluska
District of Columbia	All living and sentient creatures (human beings excepted)
Florida	Not defined
Georgia	Shall not include any fish nor shall such term include any pest that might be exterminated
Hawaii	Not defined
Idaho	Any vertebrate member of the animal kingdom, except man
Illinois	Every living creature, domestic or wild, but does not include man
Indiana	Does not include a human being
Iowa	A nonhuman vertebrate, but does not include livestock, any game, fur-bearing animal, fish, reptile, or amphibian
Kansas	Every living vertebrate except a human being
Kentucky	Every warm-blooded living creature except a human being
Louisiana	Fowl shall not be defined as animals except orders Psittaciformes and Passeriformes
Maine	Every living, sentient creature not a human being
Maryland	Not defined
Massachusetts	Not defined
Michigan	Vertebrates other than a human being
Minnesota	Includes any animal owned, possessed by, cared for, or controlled by a person for the present or future enjoyment of that person or another as a pet or companion, or any stray pet or stray companion animal
Mississippi	Any feline, exotic animal, canine, horse, mule, jack or jennet

Continued on page 6

Continued from page 5

Table 1.2—Definitions of "Animal" in State Anti-Cruelty Laws

State	Definition of "Animal"
Missouri	Every living vertebrate except a human being
Montana	Not defined
Nebraska	Any vertebrate member of the animal kingdom
Nevada	Does not include the human race, but includes every other living creature
New Hampshire	A domestic animal, a household pet or a wild animal in captivity
New Jersey	Includes the whole brute creation
New Mexico	Does not include insects or reptiles
North Carolina	Every living vertebrate in the classes amphibia, reptilia, aves, and mammalia except human being
North Dakota	Every living animal except the human race
Ohio	Any animal that is kept inside a residential dwelling and any dog or cat regardless of where it is kept. Companion animal does not include livestock or any wild animal
Oklahoma	No definition
Oregon	Any nonhuman mammal, bird, reptile, amphibian, or fish
Pennsylvania	Domestic animal: Any dog, cat, equine animal, bovine animal, sheep, goat, or porcine animal
Rhode Island	Every living creature except a human being
South Carolina	All living vertebrate creatures except homo sapiens
South Dakota	Any mammal, bird, reptile, amphibian, or fish, except humans
Tennessee	A domesticated living creature or a wild creature previously captured
Texas	A domesticated living creature and wild living creature previously captured
Utah	A live, nonhuman vertebrate creature
Vermont	All living sentient creatures not human beings
Virginia	The word animal shall be construed to include birds and fowl
Washington	Nonhuman mammal, bird, reptile, or amphibian
West Virginia	No definition
Wisconsin	No definition
Wyoming	No definition

Source: HSUS.

on fire is charged with criminal arson as well as cruelty to animals. Civil offenses are found in a city or county's local ordinances.

Finding and being knowledgeable about laws regarding cruelty to animals can be a daunting task for humane officers, animal-control officials, and veterinarians, especially for private practitioners who may only encounter a few cases of cruelty to animals in their careers. As it has for most informational tasks, the Internet has simplified the process. Each state has a website through which citizens can access the text of their state laws. Most of theses texts can be searched for applicable keywords, such as "animal" and "cruelty," to find portions that apply to animal neglect or abuse. In several states the state humane federation or animal-control association has published all animal-related laws in a single handbook. Interested parties can contact their local humane society, animal-care and -control agency, or Humane Society of the United States (HSUS) regional office to learn if such a publication is available in a particular state. States that had produced such resources as of 2005 included California, Connecticut, Maine, Massachusetts, New Hampshire, Ohio, Virginia, and Pennsylvania.

Federal Anti-Cruelty Laws

Most anti-cruelty laws are state laws, but there are also federal laws to protect animals against neglect and abuse. The Animal Welfare Act (AWA), for example, was enacted in 1966. While its original intent was to regulate the care and use of animals in the laboratory, it has become the only federal law in the United States that regulates the

Table 1.3—State Animal Anti-Cruelty Law Provisions—July 2005

Forty-one states, the District of Columbia, Puerto Rico, and the Virgin Islands have laws making certain types of animal cruelty a felony offense.

State	Statute Number of Cruelty Law	Felony	Classification of Crime/ Maximum Level of Penalty	Maximum Fine	Maximum Jail Time	Psychological Counseling	Year Enacted into a Felony	Other Significant Circumstances or Penalties
Alabama	§13A-11-241	Yes	Class C felony on the first offense (cruelty in the first degree)	$5,000	10 yrs.		2000	"Cruelty to a dog or a cat"—only felony
	§13A-11-14	No	Class B misdemeanor					All other animals
Alaska	AS 11.61.140	No	Class A misdemeanor	$5,000	1 yr.			The court may prohibit ownership of animals for up to 10 yrs.
Arizona	§13-2910	Yes	Class 6 felony on the first offense	$150,000	1 yr.		1999	Cruel neglect or abandonment resulting in serious physical injury or cruel mistreatment is a felony
Arkansas	A.C.A. §5-62-101	No	Class A misdemeanor	$1,000	1 yr.	May order (2001)		Misdemeanor includes all animals
California	§597	Yes	Felony can apply on first conviction	$20,000	1–3 yrs.	Mandatory	1988	
Colorado	§18-9-202	Yes	Aggravated cruelty is a Class 6 felony and any subsequent offense would be a Class 5 felony	Minimum $1,000 Maximum $100,000	Class 6: min. 1 yr., max. 18 mos.; Class 5: min. 1 yr., max. 3 yrs.	*May* order an evaluation or anger management treatment on the 1st offense, *shall* order on the 2nd offense	2002	Details of the felony and punishment can be found at: §18-1-105
Connecticut	§53-247	Yes		$5,000	5 yrs.	May order animal-cruelty prevention or counseling and education program	1996	
Delaware	§1325	Yes	Class F felony	$5,000	3 yrs.		1994	Cruelty to animals; Class A misdemeanor; Class F felony; with felony conviction, may not own animals for 15 yrs.
District of Columbia	D.C. Code §22-1001	Yes	Felony	$25,000	5 yrs.		2001	Does not apply to rats, bats, or snakes

Continued on page 8

Continued from page 7

Table 1.3—State Animal Anti-Cruelty Law Provisions—July 2005

State	Statute Number of Cruelty Law	Felony	Classification of Crime/ Maximum Level of Penalty	Maximum Fine	Maximum Jail Time	Psychological Counseling	Year Enacted into a Felony	Other Significant Circumstances or Penalties
Florida	§828.12	Yes	Felony of the 3rd degree	$10,000	5 yrs.	Psychological counseling/ anger management treatment is mandatory for acts of intentional torture/ torment	1989	Defendants found guilty of "intentional" cruelty must pay a minimum fine of $2,500
Georgia	16-12-4 (b) (c)		1st offense— misdemeanor	Up to $1,000	Up to 1 yr.	Sentencing judge may require psychological evaluation and shall consider the entire criminal record of the offender	2000	Causing death or unjustifiable physical pain or suffering to any animal, by act, omission, or willful neglect
			2nd offense— misdemeanor for unjustifiable pain/ suffering	Up to $5,000	Up to 1 yr.			
			2nd offense of causing death is a high aggravated misdemeanor	Up to $10,000	3 mos.– 1 yr.			
		Yes	1st offense	$15,000	1–5 ys.			Knowingly and maliciously causing death or rendering part of the animal useless or disfiguring the animal
			2nd offense	$100,000				
Hawaii	§711-1109	No	Misdemeanor	$2,000			1999	Other than insects, vermin, or other pests
Idaho	§25-304 Penalties: §25-3520A Definitions: 25-3502	No	3 stages of misdemeanor	$5,000–$9,000	6 mos.– 1 yr.			Exception for poisoning —jail: state maximum of 3 yrs., county maximum of I yr. Maximum fine of $5,000
Illinois	510 §3.02 and 510 70/4.01 and 70/16	Yes	Class 3 felony for torture on 1st offense. Class 4 felony for aggravated cruelty	$50,000	3–5 yrs. 1–3 yrs.	May order	1999	Felony applies to torture. Those convicted or anyone residing in the same household may not adopt any forfeited animals

Table 1.3—State Animal Anti-Cruelty Law Provisions—July 2005

State	Statute Number of Cruelty Law	Felony	Classification of Crime/ Maximum Level of Penalty	Maximum Fine	Maximum Jail Time	Psychological Counseling	Year Enacted into a Felony	Other Significant Circumstances or Penalties
Indiana	IC 35-46-3-12	Yes	Class D felony on the 1st conviction of torture or mutilation	$10,000	3 yrs.	Mandatory evaluation and treatment	1998; in 2002 felony on the first	A person who knowingly or intentionally beats a vertebrate animal commits cruelty to an animal, a Class A misdemeanor. §35-50-2-7 Fixed term 1 1/2 yrs., with not more than 1 1/2 yrs. added for aggravating circumstances or not more than 1 yr. subtracted for mitigating circumstances
Iowa	717B.3A —Animal torture 717B.1 717B.2	Yes	2nd offense committed is a Class D felony	$7,500	5 yrs.	Shall order	2000	Injury to animals other than livestock and does not apply to any game, fur-bearing animal, fish, reptile, or amphibian. Injury to an animal belonging to another person. Animal abuse is an aggravated misdemeanor
Kansas	21-4310	No	Class A non-person misdemeanor	$2,500	1 yr.			
Kentucky	525.135 525.130 Class A misdemeanor	Yes	1st offense of torture is a Class A misdemeanor Subsequent offenses are Class D felonies	$1,000–$10,000 for felony $500—for misdemeanor	1–5 yrs. for felony 1 yr.— for misdemeanor		2003	Felony only applies to torture of a dog or a cat
Louisiana	La. R.S. 14:102.1 (2004)	Yes		$25,000	10 yrs.		1995	Felony applies to all animals except chickens. Community service and a fine of up to $1,000 shall be ordered for the misdemeanor offenses

Continued on page 10

Continued from page 9

Table 1.3—State Animal Anti-Cruelty Law Provisions—July 2005

State	Statute Number of Cruelty Law	Felony	Classification of Crime/ Maximum Level of Penalty	Maximum Fine	Maximum Jail Time	Psychological Counseling	Year Enacted into a Felony	Other Significant Circumstances or Penalties
Maine	§7-4011 Civil	No	A 2nd offense of civil or criminal animal cruelty is a felony or maximum fine is charged	$5,000	Not ordered in civil prosecution	Shall order if juvenile; may order for all others	2001	If someone kills or tortures an animal to frighten or intimidate a person or forces a person to injure or kill an animal the perpetrator is guilty of a Class D crime. If convicted the court shall prohibit the defendant from owning or having animals on his/her property permanently
	§17-1031 Criminal	Yes	Felony penalty for the 1st violation of aggravated animal cruelty	$10,000	5 yrs.			
Massachusetts	272 §77 and 266 §112	Yes	1st conviction is a felony	$2,500	5 yrs. in the state prison or 2½ in the house of correction		1804; increased penalties in 2004	It is a felony if time is served in the state prison
Maryland	Criminal Law, §10-606	Yes	1st conviction of aggravated cruelty is a felony	$5,000	3 yrs.	May order	2001	2002 court case—man was also ordered not to own any dogs in the future
Michigan	750 §50b	Yes	Felony	$5,000	4 yrs.	May order	1931	May also order up to 500 hours of community service. The court may as a condition of probation order the defendant not to own or possess animal for a period of time not to exceed the period of probation; [for] a second conviction the court may order the defendant to permanently relinquish animal ownership
Minnesota	343.21	Yes	Felony	$10,000	2 yrs.	May order	2001	Felony only on cruelty to a pet. Court may limit the possession of pets or probation with no control of a pet

Table 1.3—State Animal Anti-Cruelty Law Provisions—July 2005

State	Statute Number of Cruelty Law	Felony	Classification of Crime/ Maximum Level of Penalty	Maximum Fine	Maximum Jail Time	Psychological Counseling	Year Enacted into a Felony	Other Significant Circumstances or Penalties
Mississippi	§97-41-16	No		$1,000	6 mos.			§97-41-16—Was found unconstitution-ally vague; it lacked words of intent §94-41-23—Kill or injure a public service animal—felony—$5,000 and/or up to 5 yrs. in jail
	§97-41-1	No		$1,000	6 mos.			97-41-16—Kill, maim, or wound a dog
	§97-41-15	Yes Live-stock only	Special—felony for livestock (does not include companion animals or wildlife)	$1,500–$10,000	1–5 yrs.			97-41-15—Maliciously, mischievously kills, maims, or wounds, injures any live-stock—felony penalties listed
Missouri	§578.012	Yes	Class D felony (first offense of torture or mutilation)	$5,000	5 yrs.		1994	Animal abuse is a Class A misdemeanor, but the 2nd offense of animal abuse is a felony
Montana	§45-8-210	Yes	First offense of aggravated cruelty is a felony	$2,500	2 yrs. (Dept. of Corrections)		1993	Deliberate cruelty The court may prohibit ownership of animals for any period of time. Misdemeanor: §45-8-211—$1,000 and 2 yrs. in Dept. of Corrections
Nebraska	§28-1009	Yes	First conviction of torture, beating, or mutilation is a IV-degree felony	$10,000	5 yrs.		2002— 2nd offense, 2003— 1st offense	It is a Class I misde-meanor for 2nd of-fense of abandonment or cruel neglect
Nevada	Rev. Stat. §574.100	Yes	The third offense committed is a felony	$10,000	5 yrs.	Mandatory for juveniles	1999	Specific exemptions for rodeo and ranching

Continued on page 12

Continued from page 11

Table 1.3—State Animal Anti-Cruelty Law Provisions—July 2005

State	Statute Number of Cruelty Law	Felony	Classification of Crime/ Maximum Level of Penalty	Maximum Fine	Maximum Jail Time	Psychological Counseling	Year Enacted into a Felony	Other Significant Circumstances or Penalties
New Hampshire	RSA 644:8	Yes	1st offense of beating or torturing	$4,000	7 yrs.		1994	2nd offense of certain acts is a felony. Court may also prohibit future ownership of other animals for any period or may impose other restrictions
New Jersey	4:22–17	Yes	Crime of the 4th degree on the 1st offense (felony equivalent)	$15,000	3–5 yrs.	Shall order juveniles for certain animal-cruelty offenses	2001	A 2nd offense is a crime of the 3rd degree. The court may also sentence the convicted to community service and bonding requirements
New Mexico	§30-18-1	Yes	"Extreme cruelty to ...animals"...is a felony in the 1st offense. 4th offense committed of "cruelty to animals" is a felony	$5,000	18 mos.	May order Shall order for juveniles	1999	Court may order an animal-cruelty prevention program
New York	§353-a 55.10 penal law	Yes	Class E felony	$5,000 (§80)	4 yrs. (§70)		1999	Felony applies only to dogs, cats, and companion animals
North Carolina	§14-360	Yes	1st offense of cruelly beating, mutilating, torturing, poisoning, or killing any animal is a Class I felony	$1,000	6 mos.		1998	Basic animal cruelty is a Class 1 misdemeanor; it is a Class 1 misdemeanor to instigate or promote animal cruelty
North Dakota	§§36 – 21.1-02	No	Class A misdemeanor	$2,000	1 yr.			
Ohio	§959.13	Yes	2nd offense committed is a 5th degree felony	$2,000	1 yr.	May order	2002	Felony only applies to companion animals and on the 2nd offense 1st offense is a Class 1 misdemeanor, with a maximum 6 mos. in jail and a $1,000 fine. In 2004 enacting the offense of "harassing a service dog or police dog" is a felony of the 3rd degree and the offender must pay resulting veterinary, replacement, and training costs

Table 1.3—State Animal Anti-Cruelty Law Provisions—July 2005

State	Statute Number of Cruelty Law	Felony	Classification of Crime/ Maximum Level of Penalty	Maximum Fine	Maximum Jail Time	Psychological Counseling	Year Enacted into a Felony	Other Significant Circumstances or Penalties
Ohio (continued)	§959.02	No	1st degree misdemeanor	$1,000	180 days			1st degree is ordered for "injuring" an animal whose value is more than $300; this applies to the property of another
Oklahoma	§21 Okl. ST. §1685	Yes	Felony on 1st offense committed	$5,000	5 yrs. in state jail; 1 yr. in a county jail		1887	Aggravated animal abuse in the 1st degree
Oregon	ORS §167.322	Yes	Class C felony on the 1st offense	$100,000	5 yrs.	May order	1995	
Pennsyl-vania	Pa. C.S. §18-5511 §18-1101 §18-1103	Yes	The 2nd offense committed on a dog or cat is a felony of the 3rd degree 1st offense committed on a zoo animal is a felony of the 3rd degree	$15,000	7 yrs.	May order (the court may order a presentence mental evalua-tion)	1995	The maximum fine only applies to zoo animals (1st offense) and dogs and cats (on the 2nd offense) based on deliberate cruelty. 1st offense is a misdemeanor of the 1st degree
Rhode Island	Gen. Laws §4-1-3 84-1-4	Yes Yes	1st offense committed is a felony	$1,000 $1,000	2 yrs.	§4-1-36—May order an evaluation	1896	Dismembering any animal maliciously or killing any animal or poisoning any animal: 10 hrs. of community restitution.
South Carolina	S.C. C.A. §47-1-40	Yes	1st offense is a felony	$5,000	5 yrs.		2000	
South Dakota	§40-1-21 & §40-1-27	No No Yes, for bestiali-ty only	Class 1 misdemeanor	$1,000	1 yr.			40-1-21—Killing the animal of another 406-1-27—Treating one's own animal inhumanely 406-22-42—Bestiality. Class 6 felony; 2nd offense is a Class 5 felony. 40-1-2.2—Unjustifiable or unreasonable phys-ical pain or suffering is caused 40-1-20—Poisoning animal of another 40-1.2.4

Continued on page 14

Continued from page 13

Table 1.3—State Animal Anti-Cruelty Law Provisions—July 2005

State	Statute Number of Cruelty Law	Felony	Classification of Crime/ Maximum Level of Penalty	Maximum Fine	Maximum Jail Time	Psychological Counseling	Year Enacted into a Felony	Other Significant Circumstances or Penalties
Tennessee	39-14-202 39-14-212	Yes	1st offense of aggravated cruelty is a felony	2001	9-mo. minimum (mandatory); no suspended sentence or probation until 9 mos. are served	Shall order	2001 2002 Felony on the 1st offense was passed in 2004	1st offense of aggravated cruelty to a pet is a felony. Includes failure to provide food/water and creating a substantial risk of death. Court may order forfeiture of any owned companion animals, and limit ownership in the future
Texas	Sec. 42.09 Sec. 12.21 Sec. 12.35	Yes	Felony of the 3rd degree if the person has been convicted two times prior. The 1st offense is a lesser felony	$10,000	2 yrs.	Mandatory for juveniles	1997	State jail felony on the 1st offense of most egregious; 3rd degree felony on 2nd. It is not illegal to kill one's own animal, no matter how cruelly or by what means
Utah	Code Ann. §76-9-301	No	Class A misdemeanor	$5,000	1 yr.	Mandatory for juveniles		The court may order the defendant to no longer possess or retain custody of any animal during the period of probation, parole, or other
Vermont	§352	Yes	1st act of cruelty committed is a felony	$7,500	5 yrs.	May order	1998, improved 2004	Felony applies to acts of aggravated cruelty. Any sentence less than 2 yrs. is a misdemeanor. Defendant may have forfeited the right to ever own animals again
Virginia	§3.1-796.122	Yes	1st offense committed is a felony	$2,500	5 yrs.	May order	1999— felony; upgraded in 2002	The animal must die as a result of his/her injuries for the felony to apply. Any person convicted of violating this section may be prohibited from possession or ownership of companion animals
Washington	§61.52.205	Yes	1st offense committed is a class C felony	$10,000	5 yrs.	May order	1994	

Forensic Investigation of Animal Cruelty: A Guide for Veterinary and Law Enforcement Professionals

Table 1.3—State Animal Anti-Cruelty Law Provisions—July 2005

State	Statute Number of Cruelty Law	Felony	Classification of Crime/ Maximum Level of Penalty	Maximum Fine	Maximum Jail Time	Psychological Counseling	Year Enacted into a Felony	Other Significant Circumstances or Penalties
West Virginia	61-8-19	Yes	1st offense committed is a felony	$1,000–$5,000	1–3 yrs.	Shall order an evaluation	2003	§61-8-19—A court shall prohibit those convicted from possessing, owning, or residing with any animal or type of animal for 5 yrs. (if misdemeanor) and for 15 yrs. (for a felony). For misdemeanor, maximum fine is $2,000 and one yr.
	For livestock §61-3-27	Yes	Felony only applies to animals with "value" over $100					Felony if the animal's value exceeds $100, but does not include dogs
Wisconsin	§951.18	Yes	Felony	$10,000	5 yrs.		2004	For aggravated cruelty or animal fighting. A court may order that the violator may not own, possess, or train any animal or species for up to 5 yrs.
	951.02 mistreating						1986	
Wyoming	§6-3-203	Yes	Felony	$5,000	2 yrs.		2003	The court may prohibit or limit the defendant's ownership, possession, or custody of animals
Puerto Rico	S.B. 2702 Law 439 Amends 67	Yes	Grave offense in the 4th degree				2004	Animal abuse is a felony offense
Virgin Islands	§181	Yes	Felony	$2,000–$5,000	2 yrs.		2005	Excludes "pests"

Source: HSUS 2005.

treatment of animals in research, exhibition, and transport and by dealers.[1] The AWA, enforced by the U.S. Department of Agriculture, is often applied to the care of animals in commercial breeding facilities, particularly those that are often referred to as "puppy mills," which produce puppies for wholesale distribution to retail pet stores.

Several states single out the killing of a service or police animal (horse or dog) as a felony offense, and attacking a federal law enforcement animal is now also a federal offense. The 1999 Federal Law Enforcement Animal Protection Act authorizes fines and mandatory jail time of up to ten years for those who willfully assault, disfigure, maim, or kill a federal law enforcement animal.

The ubiquity of the Internet has led to at least one federal law that addresses a specific form of cruelty to animals. In 1999 Title 18, Section 48 was added to the U.S. Code making it a federal crime to knowingly create, sell, or possess a depiction of animal cruelty with the intention of placing that depiction in interstate or foreign commerce for commercial gain. The term "depiction of animal cruelty" means any visual or auditory depiction, including any photograph, motion-picture film, video recording, electronic image, or sound recording of conduct in which a living animal is intentionally maimed, mutilated, tortured, wounded, or killed, if such conduct is illegal under federal law or the law of the state in which the creation, sale, or possession takes place, regardless of whether the maiming, mutilation, torture, wounding, or killing took place in the state. This law was enacted specifically to address the proliferation of Internet sales of "crush videos," in which various small animals were stepped on or killed by other methods, often by scantily clad women. The law has recently been applied successfully in prosecuting alleged dogfighters for the sale and distribution of training and fight promotion videos.

The AWA also prohibits interstate transport of animals for the purposes of fighting. When federal animal-fighting laws were initially enacted in 1976, no states made animal fighting a felony. Dogfighting is now a felony offense in forty-eight states, and cockfighting is a felony in thirty-one states. Existing federal laws dealing with these blood sports are considerably weaker than nearly all state laws, so they are rarely applied in such cruelty cases. As of 2005 federal legislation had been introduced that would bring federal penalties in line with state felony laws and would also prohibit interstate and foreign commerce in knives and gaffs designed for cockfighting.

A Law Is Not Enough

Although each of us may define cruelty to animals for ourselves, only as a society can we define those acts that may be addressed through our legal system. This is often a difficult concept for the general public, or even for ourselves, to grasp. A citizen may believe her neighbor's dog is being cruelly neglected. But if the owner can prove that he has met the minimal requirements of his state's anti-cruelty law, a criminal act has not been committed, regardless of the dog's quality of life. In terms of legal redress, it is important to understand that it is not enough that an animal is harmed; much more is necessary. There must be a law that makes the act a crime. There must be someone with law enforcement authority who is willing to charge the suspect with the crime; someone who will investigate the crime; and evidence that the crime has taken place; and such evidence must be collected, preserved, and presented in such as way as to convince a deciding body. There must be witnesses who will testify to the events of the crime or to their evaluation of the evidence associated with it; a member of the district or state attorney's office or the office of the attorney general who is willing to try the case before a court of law; and an adjudicating body—a judge and/or a jury—that determines from the evidence presented that a crime has been committed, as indicated by existing law. These requirements—the law, the enforcement authority, the investigator, the evidence, the witnesses, the prosecutor, and the adjudicating body—may be thought of as the blocks necessary to build a case that determines that an act constitutes cruelty to animals.

Assembling enough blocks to convict a person of cruelty to animals is a rare occurrence. Even those agencies that investigate thousands of incidents of suspected animal cruelty each year only pursue prosecution of a small percentage of them. Even fewer cases result in criminal charges and still fewer in convictions.

A case may not be investigated or pursued for many reasons. The primary one is that most cases of cruelty to animals are the result of benign or ignorant neglect (Donley, Patronek, and Luke 1999). Investigative and law enforcement agencies primarily deal with these situations by attempting to educate the offender. Offenders can choose either to provide the care required for the animal or to admit that they are unable to provide care and relinquish the animal to an animal-sheltering agency or another home. When an offender refuses to provide proper care or to relinquish the animal, the investigator still has the opportunity to use other measures to resolve the case. Such flexibility in addressing cases of mild or apparently ignorant neglect allows law enforcement and animal protection agencies to use their resources in the most efficient manner possible, especially when they are faced with resolving hundreds or thousands of cases annually (Vermeulen and Odendaal 1993).

Another reason that incidents of neglect are usually dealt with by means other than criminal charges is that it is more difficult to legally address acts of omission (such as neglecting to provide an animal with food) than acts of commission (those that are intentionally committed, such as beating an animal with an implement). While it is possible that some people may intentionally neglect an animal, perhaps as a means of punishing the animal for some perceived misdeed or of intimidating another person in the household (an abused spouse or child), this scenario is less common. In cases of severe neglect, there comes a point where the suffering of the animal is so obvious that the owner's failure to act can often be considered intentional. In some cases of severe animal neglect, such as animal hoarding (see chapter 17), the situation may be further complicated by questions of the mental health status of the alleged offender.

Educating those who neglect animals is considered the most effective approach to dealing with the majority of cases of mild to moderate neglect. The existence of a law mandating proper care of animals, regardless of whether it is ever used, is an effective educational tool. Many who neglect animals will own animals in the future. Educating them about the proper needs of an animal and their legal responsibility to provide for those needs may improve the quality of care they provide for generations of animals to come. While it is true that the punishment meted out to some people convicted of animal cruelty has included court-ordered prohibition of animal ownership, these punishments are rare and can only be enforced if law enforcement and animal protection authorities have the resources and manpower to monitor the convicted abuser for the rest of his life. Few agencies do. In the majority of cases, educational efforts are more likely to have a permanent effect.

Another reason cases are not pursued is that there is often little or no *usable* evidence. Better education of investigators and expanded implementation of investigative techniques used in human assault and negligence cases will continue to enhance the collection and presentation of evidence in animal-cruelty cases, but in some cases, evidence simply cannot be established. Witnesses are often nonexistent or uncooperative. They may not believe that addressing an act of cruelty to animals is worthwhile, they may refuse to "get involved," or they may fear for their own safety. In October 1993 an apparently abandoned young male red Chow Chow-type dog was captured by two men, who tied him to a tree behind a manufacturing plant in Houston, Texas, and then shot off the rostral portion of his muzzle with a shotgun. Despite the violent and public nature of the crime and the offer of a significant monetary reward for information leading to the identification and arrest of the two men, no witnesses ever came forward. The dog initially survived the assault but was euthanized by the agency that took him in due to the severity of his injuries.

Animal-cruelty cases may not be pursued due to a lack of knowledge or motivation on behalf of the investigating agency. Animal protection agencies may know how to care for the animal victims and may be motivated to rescue and aid them, but they may not know how to investigate a case and present it to a district attorney. They may feel that their efforts and resources are better spent in caring for the animals than in engaging in the difficult pursuit of an animal-cruelty conviction for the offender. Law enforcement agencies and their officers may be hesitant to fully pursue cases because they have neither the knowledge nor the resources to care for the animals involved. Although all law enforcement officers receive training in criminal investigative techniques, they may not realize that those same techniques can be applied to crimes involving animal victims. They may not realize the information veterinarians can provide from an examination of the animal can parallel that of the human medical examiner. In some cases, attending veterinarians may be unfamiliar with the emerging array of forensic techniques that are available and may tell humane or law enforcement officials that no usable information can be gathered from the animal evidence collected at the crime scene. Law enforcement agencies may be unaware of the well-documented connection between violent and neglectful acts toward animals and those toward humans. Having dealt with many higher crimes, such as homicide, they may fail to see the relevance of pursuing a case involving a fatal assault on an animal. It is hoped that increased awareness, greater availability of training, and more resources will help both of these types of agencies to overcome these obstacles to addressing animal-cruelty crimes in the future.

Because of the extensive effort and resources required to try an offender on criminal charges of cruelty to animals, all parties involved must be certain that the case cannot be resolved effectively any other way. Investigators and prosecutors must also reserve their efforts for the most meaningful cases. Communities plagued by violent crime are reluctant to commit resources to addressing animal-cruelty crimes. In these situations it may be prudent to respect the demands made on a community's legal system and to present only those cases that are well documented, well researched, and heinous enough to warrant criminal conviction. Many communities must also weigh their financial ability to address such cases through prosecution. Cases involving large numbers or animals or animals requiring expensive care (horses or exotic animals, for example) may cost tens of thousands of dollars as they make their slow way through the court system, and a city or county may find itself at the end of its budget before the case has come to a legal end.

To alleviate this cost of care, and for the protection of the animal, it is important that forfeiture of the animal is obtained. Every state has a different way of obtaining relinquishment of the animal. Animal-control officers, police, and, in some cases, the veterinarian may request forfeiture of the animal. The prosecutor also may ask for forfeiture as a condition of bond. This allows the animal to be treated and placed in a permanent home instead of being held in a cage until the case is resolved.

Another Approach

The phenomenon of animal hoarding, or "collecting," is a good example of how prosecution may or may not be used to resolve an animal-cruelty case. Historically, animal-control agencies have acted alone in addressing hoarding cases (see chapter 17). Because the social service and mental health communities were largely unaware of the phenomenon and had not evaluated its psychological component, animal-control agencies were forced to deal with animal hoarders by viewing them as criminal animal abusers. Education about how to provide proper care for hoarder-owned animals was rarely successful, due to the nature of the disorder. Animal-control agencies were forced to prosecute animal-hoarding offenders, and the punishment meted out in such cases—fines, jail time, community service—did little to address the hoarder's affliction. Today we realize that there is a psychological component to animal hoarding. Cases are often addressed jointly by animal-control agencies, social service providers, mental health experts, and other community service agencies. While prosecution may still be necessary in some cases, it is used as a last resort and as a means to remove ill or at-risk animals or to secure court-mandated psychological evaluation and counseling for the animal hoarder.

The Prevalence of Cruelty to Animals

How common is cruelty to animals? There is currently no national database of statistics related to animal-cruelty crimes. If there were, it would be necessary to define the information to be collected. Statistics might include (1) the total number of prosecuted cases of animal cruelty, (2) the number of prosecuted cases in which a conviction was obtained, (3) the number of cases that met certain criteria but were not necessarily prosecuted, and (4) the number of complaints from the public regarding animal abuse and neglect. Some of these data have been collected and published for specific agencies, communities, or circumstances. For example, it has been estimated that in Massachusetts in 1996 there were 9.3 reported cases of cruelty to animals involving dogs per 1,000 dog-owning households in that state, and 2.3 reported cases of cruelty to animals involving cats per 1,000 cat-owning households in that state (Donley, Patronek, and Luke 1999). A recent study estimated that between 700 and 2,000 cases of animal hoarding (as defined by the study) occur annually in the United States (Patronek 1999). Those who might want to collect statistics based on the number of cases prosecuted would need to clearly define which cases were to be included.

Some cases of cruelty to animals are prosecuted using laws that are not specifically related to animal cruelty. For example, due to the lack of strong anti-cruelty laws, prosecutors may choose to charge perpetrators with crimes other than cruelty to animals. This was the case when three young men broke into a cat shelter in Fairfield, Iowa, in 1997 and bludgeoned to death sixteen cats with baseball bats. Prosecutors charged the three with third-degree burglary and with "trespassing into and breaking and entering into an animal facility." They were not charged with cruelty to animals (a misdemeanor offense in Iowa at that time) because prosecutors hoped to convict them of a felony offense.[2] In June 1997 four young men in Kansas City, Kansas, tortured, burned, and killed a small Yorkshire terrier named Scruffy. Kansas did not have any felony anti-cruelty provisions, and prosecutors felt that the existing misdemeanor provisions would not provide for the necessary supervision and intervention the offenders needed. Thus the four were charged with, and convicted of, felony arson. (Had Scruffy's owner not been located, he would have been considered "unowned property," and a felony arson charge would not have been possible.)

Conclusion

Acts of cruelty to animals are not easily defined or addressed. Understanding the nuances of the laws and the language that pertain to cruelty to animals will assist those who wish to address a specific incident. Anti-cruelty laws vary enormously from state to state in their language, location, application, and intent. While it is helpful for veterinarians and other animal-care professionals to be familiar with their own state's anti-cruelty laws, it also helps to be somewhat knowledgeable about the variations in these laws among states and even among communities.

Understanding why most cases of cruelty to animals are not addressed by legal means will help veterinarians and others to assist their communities in creating and implementing more nonlegal interventions and in successfully addressing those cases in which legal redress is the best approach.

Notes

[1]The Act, which has been amended four times (1970, 1976, 1985, 1990), can be found in *United States Code*, Title 7, Sections 2131 to 2156.

[2]There were two ironic twists to the approach used in this particular case. The first is that the law under which the three men were charged was passed originally to punish animal rights activists who entered animal research facilities. The second is that the approach was unsuccessful. For the men to be convicted of felony offenses on those charges, the prosecution had to prove that the fair market value of the property that was destroyed—the cats themselves—was greater than $500. The prosecution was unsuccessful in convincing the jury that the lives of twenty-three previously abandoned cats were worth that amount of money (jury members did not consider the thousands of dollars' worth of veterinary care provided to the cats who initially survived the attack to be applicable, as they determined that the cats could just as easily have been euthanized as treated). Instead, two of the men—both of whom pled guilty to the crime—were found guilty of two aggravated misdemeanors and one serious misdemeanor. They were sentenced to twenty-three days in a local jail, three years' probation, and four years in the state penitentiary. The prison time was suspended pending their successful completion of a rigorous youthful offenders program. The third man, who cooperated by testifying against the other two, was also required to attend the program.

2 Investigators and Prosecutors of Cruelty to Animals

O f all the factors complicating the pursuit and prosecution of animal-cruelty crimes, perhaps the most disruptive is the confusion over who is responsible for doing so. There is substantial variation in the type, number, and competency of agencies and individuals responsible for investigating complaints of animal mistreatment at both the state and local levels (Donley, Patronek, and Luke 1999). Within each community and state, a number of agencies may be able to address an assault against an animal or there may be no agency capable of, or interested in, doing so.

Although every state has a statute defining the crime of cruelty to animals, 1aw enforcement agencies and their officers often do not understand or accept their role in addressing such crimes. Some agencies do not have adequate training or information about animal protection laws and animal-cruelty crimes, or they may not have adequate staffing or resources to deal with cruelty to animals. In a community where law enforcement officers are overwhelmed by other types of crime—homicide and drug trafficking, for example—cruelty to animals may receive little attention. Fortunately, this is changing, and there has been growing law enforcement interest in the investigation and prosecution of crimes against animals (Ascione and Lockwood 2001). As cruelty to animals becomes recognized as a serious concern in the community, law enforcement agencies are increasingly assigning one or more officers to full-time duty specializing in animal abuse and neglect cases. The Broward County, Florida, sheriff's department created a Special Victims and Family Crimes section in May 2000 to investigate and respond specifically to crimes against animals, children, people with disabilities, and the infirm elderly. This unit was the first to establish a specific unit specially trained to recognize the interconnectedness of these different forms of victimization. Similarly, animal-cruelty investigators from the Humane Society of the Pikes Peak Region in Colorado Springs, Colorado, have been assigned part time to the staff of the Domestic Violence Enhanced Response Team of the Colorado Springs Police Department to assist with investigations of animal abuse that commonly occurs within the context of domestic violence.

Before looking at who is responsible for addressing cruelty to animals in a community, it may be helpful to examine the structure of different types of animal-sheltering agencies. The phrase "animal shelter" is a generic term, but it is most often used to refer to either a private, nonprofit animal protection agency or a government (city- or county-operated) animal-control agency.

Private, nonprofit animal shelters are governed by a self-elected board of directors and are free to determine the extent and the limits of their own mission. Private, nonprofit animal-sheltering agencies may or may not have physical facilities for their operations. Generally, their goals include protecting, sheltering, and finding adoptive homes for unwanted, homeless, and abused companion animals. "Humane society" is a generic term as well. Any private, nonprofit animal-sheltering agency may refer to itself as a "humane society," an "animal rescue league," a "society for the prevention of cruelty to animals" (SP-CA), or any other moniker. The use of these terms does not necessarily signify that different organizations are related. For example, the Massachusetts SPCA is unrelated to the Houston SPCA or the Maryland SPCA and does not have direct ties to the American SP-CA. Likewise, the Connecticut Humane Society is not affiliated with the Humane Society of Baltimore County and has no legal or organizational affiliation with The Humane Society of the United States.

Government animal-control agencies are arms of city and county governments. Responsible municipalities provide animal-control services to protect the health and safety of the humans and animals in their communities. Government animal-control agencies may fall under the jurisdiction of a city or county public health department, law enforcement department, or environmental services department or within some other branch of city services. Government animal-control agencies may also refer to themselves by the term they prefer, using such phrases as "animal care and control," "animal regulation," and "animal services" in their formal names. Most government animal-control agencies have physical facilities for their operations, but smaller cities and counties may contract with local veterinarians or adjacent cities and counties to provide housing and quarantine of animals when such measures become necessary.

The resources of government animal-control agencies vary tremendously from one agency to the next. In rural areas there may only be a part-time animal-control officer with little training and equipment. In large metropolitan areas, there may be a squad of officers—with a fleet of animal-control vehicles—who have received extensive training, including completion of a police academy. Animal-control officers have whatever powers their local government has vested in them. They may only be able to issue citations for violation of ordinances, or they may be armed officers with full law enforcement powers, able to arrest violators of their state's anti-cruelty laws. For example, the Massachusetts SPCA (MSPCA) has its own law enforcement department. MSPCA officers possess the same authority and receive the same training as do other Massachusetts state police officers, except that they are restricted to the enforcement of animal protection laws. They are empowered by the state of Massachusetts with this law enforcement authority.

In many cases, animal-control operations in a city or county are provided by a hybrid agency: a private, nonprofit animal-sheltering agency provides animal-control services to a city or county government on a contract basis. For example, the Washington (D.C.) Humane Society (WHS) is a private, nonprofit organization that operates its own animal shelter, adoption agency, and sterilization clinic. WHS also provides municipal animal-control services to the jurisdiction of the District of Columbia, based on a contract with the District and operating in that capacity as the D.C. animal-control agency. This agency is also designated by its congressional charter as the entity to enforce the city's anti-cruelty laws. Due to the District of Columbia's unique legislative status, serious animal-cruelty cases in that jurisdiction are prosecuted by the U.S. Attorney's Office. This hybrid of a nonprofit and a municipal agency is found in many communities in the United States.

When an act of cruelty to animals occurs in a community, whose responsibility is it to address that act? Herein lies the confusion: it depends. Ideally, a city or county takes responsibility for this task, and reports of animal neglect and cruelty are addressed by the governmental animal-care and -control agency. A private, nonprofit animal-sheltering agency may also take the task upon itself, appointing its own "humane investigators" and accepting and evaluating reports. While such an agency does not have legal or government authority to issue citations or charge individuals with criminal acts, careful investigation, documentation, and presentation of animal crimes to a community's law enforcement agencies by a private, nonprofit animal-sheltering agency may result in action. Many animal-sheltering agencies have active investigation departments that have forged strong relationships with law enforcement and prosecutorial arms of their city's government and so are able to successfully address criminal acts of animal cruelty and neglect in their communities.

Just like these private, nonprofit animal-sheltering agencies, private individuals in a community and professionals, such as groomers, trainers, kennel operators, and veterinarians, may present evidence of animal cruelty and neglect to law enforcement authorities. For this method to be successful, any such evidence must be obtained by legal means, and the law enforcement agency must be willing to address the case.

It is important also to recognize the role of the concerned citizen in animal-cruelty scenarios. No matter how well organized or well funded the corps of humane investigators in a community is, it cannot be everywhere at once. It must depend on the citizens in a community to be its eyes and ears. Complainants who wish to remain anonymous must be respected: only they can gauge their personal safety in such a situation. It is possible that anonymity is related to the seriousness—and dangerousness—of the complaint, and anonymous complaints are often the most serious.

Lack of proper shelter; inadequate food, water, and veterinary care; and chronic tethering of dogs are common examples of neglect, and they account for a majority of complaints received by most humane agencies. For humane groups, the challenge is figuring out how to translate anti-cruelty laws into meaningful interventions to solve such problems.

Violent acts of cruelty *always* warrant investigation and prosecution, and cases involving animals in severe distress should be handled with the goal of relieving suffering as quickly as possible. However, for the vast majority of cases, the fundamental decision to be made is whether education or prosecution takes priority. In misdemeanor offenses, prosecution, fines, and jail time or probation can serve as a deterrent to future acts of cruelty. Felony prosecution itself can be considered an extreme form of education that should be appropriate to the extreme suffering of the animal and the heinous act committed. It is always the hope of investigators, prosecutors, and society that successful prosecution and punishment will change the future behavior of offenders.

The next chapter specifically addresses the special role the veterinary professional can play in recognizing and responding to animal abuse and neglect.

The Veterinarian as an Investigator of Cruelty to Animals

Thirty-three fighting dogs, emaciated and suffering from dehydration, have been confiscated from their owner during a search for marijuana plants. Your rural community employs one part-time animal-control officer, and this is the first case he has attempted to present for prosecution. He calls you to ask for assistance in examining and caring for the dogs.

A client brings you her Pomeranian puppy with the third fracture she has suffered in the last six weeks. From the radiographs the dog's bones appear to be growing normally and healing properly. The dog's history of repeated trauma and the owner's nervous attitude raise your suspicion that the puppy is being assaulted by someone in the household. Is it possible the woman's husband, who has appeared intoxicated and intimidating in your office during two prior visits, is injuring the dog to intimidate his wife?

Whether they wish to or not, most veterinarians become involved in an animal-cruelty case at some time during their career. Of 110 Massachusetts veterinarians surveyed in 1999, 79 percent reported having seen at least one patient during their career with injuries they suspected were inflicted by the client or another member of the household. Nearly half (47 percent) were positive or very sure they had seen injuries that were deliberate, and one-third (34 percent) indicated that a client admitted to causing injury to the pet. Most (81 percent) reported they had observed neglected or abused animals in their community (Donley, Patronek, and Luke 1999).

In another survey of small-animal practitioners, Sharpe (1999) estimated that the average practitioner saw 5.6 cases of animal abuse per thousand patients, regardless of location in a rural, urban, or suburban practice. She reported that only 8 percent of the 368 respondents felt that they had received adequate training in general abuse prevention, and less than 44 percent thought they adequately understood their rights and responsibilities when responding to suspected animal or human abuse.

Landau (1999) surveyed the deans of thirty-one American and Canadian schools of veterinary medicine. Of these, 97 percent agreed that veterinarians would encounter instances of intentional animal abuse, and 63 percent agreed that veterinary professionals would encounter cases of cruelty to animals associated with family violence. Thirty-one percent of deans reported that their schools had a policy requiring reporting suspected animal abuse, and two of these policies have been discussed in the literature (Rollin 1994; Arkow 1999). However, many veterinary students feel that their training does not address the issue adequately. This is consistent with Landau's finding that only 17 percent of deans reported that students are explicitly made aware of policies on responding to suspected abuse and her estimate that the average veterinary curriculum spends only *eight minutes* on the issue of cruelty to animals as it relates to other forms of human violence.

In general, there are four ways by which a veterinary practitioner may be presented with an animal-cruelty case (Yoffe-Sharp and Sinclair 1998).

A client-owned animal may be presented by the client after having been abused or neglected by the client or a member of the household. While it seems unreasonable that someone would abuse his pet and then seek veterinary care for her, it does happen. The abuser may be remorseful or may be attempting to show an abused spouse that he is remorseful. Or the abused spouse may be the one who seeks veterinary care, usually a day or so after the injury has occurred. A child may intentionally injure a pet, who is then presented by a parent for veterinary care. Those who intentionally cause their dogs to fight may also seek occasional veterinary care, during which it may be obvious that the animal has scars and injuries consistent with having been used for fighting (see chapter 20).

A client-owned animal may be presented by the client after having been abused or neglected by another party. This is the case when a client's pet is poisoned or shot by a neighbor or some other assailant. It can also occur if a pet is being boarded or trained by a third party, who subsequently neglects or abuses the animal.

An animal owned by someone who is not a client, having been abused or neglected by the owner or a member of the owner's household, may be presented by a third party. An investigator may confiscate the owned animal and then ask the veterinarian to examine him.

An unowned or abandoned animal attacked by a person who has no relationship to the animal may then be rescued by an individual or an organization. "Stray" dogs, cats, and other animals, as well as wildlife, are frequent targets of animal abusers.

The most important step a veterinarian can take to assure a good outcome in these inevitable situations is to prepare beforehand for their possibility. The first and most important aspect of such preparation is to obtain, read, and understand the applicable laws regarding animal care, control, and cruelty. (See chapter 1 for details about resources for this information.) Most laws and ordinances are organic, constantly growing and changing. One experienced animal-control director cautions her staff against rote memorization of the laws and ordinances they are authorized to enforce, because changes occur frequently and often with little public notice (Ratliff 2000). Instead, she advises her officers to pull out their latest copy of the laws and ordinances when they are investigating a neglect or abuse situation and to read through the laws to determine whether they apply. As animal professionals, it is imperative that veterinarians be very familiar with all of the laws regarding animals in their community and their state and with the methods by which those laws are applied.

The second preparatory step is to determine which person(s) or agency(ies) in a community accepts reports of neglect and abuse, and what its procedure is for processing those reports (see chapter 2). As much information as possible should be gained about the agencies. An ideal situation is one in which the veterinarian personally visits the agency and introduces herself, acquiring firsthand knowledge about its staff, facilities, and procedures.

The third preparatory step for the veterinarian is to carefully consider what constitutes actionable animal neglect or abuse and what her response to such an event might be. Specific language for discussing with a client her neglect of a pet's care is available (Wilson, Rollin, and Garbe 1993). The creation of a policy for the entire veterinary hospital further clarifies what actions will not be tolerated and what steps will be taken when abuse or neglect of a patient is suspected. One such policy has been created for the teaching hospital of the School of Veterinary Medicine at the University of Pennsylvania, with input from area humane organizations and animal-control agencies (Arkow 1999). That policy states that signs suggestive of abuse or neglect include:

■ Lameness or other injuries without histories supporting the severity of the clinical signs, injuries to pets where owners describe ongoing toilet training "accidents."

- Multiple bite wounds in patients with numerous scars around the head and legs from previous injuries.
- Severely matted animals where the animal's condition is not consistent with its pleasant disposition and/or temperament.
- Severe malnutrition from underfeeding.
- Chronic, infected, untreated wounds, often present in pets where grooming has been neglected (maggots may or may not be present).
- Chains and collars that have cut through the skin and into the musculature of the neck; often related to rapidly growing, medium- to large-breed dogs with inadequate owner attention.
- Aggressive, defensive, or other abnormal animal behavior—with the caveat that reports should be made only when other evidence of abuse is also present.
- Unexplained chemical or thermal skin burns.
- Stupor from possible drug or alcohol ingestion.

Despite such preparation, it is likely that veterinarians will still have questions when a case of suspected neglect or abuse does present itself, and they may be unprepared to address the situation (Tremayne 2005). Common questions that may arise include:

How do I determine whether this constitutes animal cruelty?

Veterinarians are widely considered to be the experts in all matters relating to animals. It is therefore not surprising that they often mistakenly believe they must assume the roles of investigator, prosecutor, judge, and jury with respect to animal-cruelty cases. It is important for veterinarians to understand that their report of suspected neglect or abuse is only the first step in evaluating a case, and that other experts and legal authorities will play roles that are just as important in determining the true circumstances behind an animal's injured or diseased condition. Keep in mind that a report of suspected abuse or cruelty does not necessarily lead to prosecution and conviction of the perpetrator. Particularly in cases of neglect in which the animal's life is not immediately threatened, reports to an investigative agency usually allow the agency the opportunity to formally educate pet owners about their legal responsibility to care for the animal.

How confidential is my relationship with the client? Am I liable if I say I believe that cruelty has occurred, and the legal system finds otherwise?

Liability and confidentiality are understandable concerns for the veterinary practitioner. In today's litigious society, the average veterinarian's day is fraught with opportunities for legal entanglement, from the client who slips in a puddle of urine to the hospitalized dog who manages to escape out the back door. Worrying about liability for protecting one's patients from abuse and neglect should not be part of that burden, but in many states it is. The answer to the question of whether the relationship between veterinarians and their clients is confidential varies from state to state. Some may liken the situation to that of a pediatrician, who would never be expected to keep quiet about suspicions of child abuse due to the confidentiality of the doctor's relationship with the child's parent. Legally, however, animals are not children, and the law most often views them as the property of their owners, rather than as family members with innate rights to protection from abuse. A summary of statutes and rules pertaining to client confidentiality demonstrates that fewer than half of the states explicitly regulate the confidentiality of the veterinarian-client relationship (Table 3.1). Some of them make exceptions in the case of a threat to the animal's health or suspected cruelty.

The most recent American Veterinary Medical Association (AVMA) position statement on animal cruelty (2005) notes:

Table 3.1—State Regulation of Confidentiality of Veterinary Records

State	Reference	Summary of Cited References
Alabama	930-X-1-11(15)	A veterinarian shall not violate the confidential relationship between himself or herself and his or her client.
Alaska	12 AAC 68.910 (d)	Patient medical records may not be released to a third party without written consent of the owner.
Delaware	24 Ch. 3313 (1)	Prohibits willful violation of any privileged communication.
Georgia	24-9-29	No veterinarian shall be required to disclose any information concerning the veterinarian's care of any animal, except on written authorization or other waiver by the veterinarian's client of an appropriate court order or subpoena.
	50-18-17 (a)	Medical or veterinary or similar files, the disclosure of which would be an invasion of privacy, are considered confidential.
Idaho	IDAPA 46-013	Incorporates by reference the AVMA Principles of Veterinary Medical Ethics*
Illinois	225 ILLCS	No veterinarian shall be required to disclose any information concerning the veterinarian's care of any animal, except on written authorization or other waiver by the veterinarian's client or an appropriate court order or subpoena
	115/25/17	….When communicable disease laws, cruelty to animals laws, or laws providing for public health or safety are involved, this privilege is waived.
Kansas	47-839	No veterinarian…shall be required to disclose any information concerning the veterinarian's care of an animal, except on written authorization or other waiver by the veterinarian's client or an appropriate court order or subpoena.
Kentucky	201 KAR 16:010 Sec. 23	A veterinarian shall maintain a confidential relationship with his client, except as otherwise provided by law, or required by considerations related to public health or animal health.
Massachusetts	256 CMR: 7.01 (15)	A veterinarian shall maintain a confidential relationship with his/her clients, except as otherwise provided by law or required by considerations related to public health and/or animal health.
Minnesota	156.081 2 (14)	Prohibits revealing a privileged communication from or relating to a client, except when otherwise required or permitted by law.
Montana	37-1-316 (9)	Unprofessional conduct to reveal confidential information obtained as a result of a professional relationship without the prior consent of the recipient of services, except as authorized or required by law.
New Hampshire	501.01	Incorporates by reference the AVMA Principles of Veterinary Medical Ethics*
Nebraska	71-148 (9)	Unprofessional conduct to willfully betray a professional secret except as otherwise provided by law.
Oklahoma	10-5-15	A licensed veterinarian shall not violate the confidential relations between himself and his client.
Pennsylvania	49 OE 31.21 Principle 7 (c)	Veterinarians and their staff shall protect the personal privacy of clients, unless the veterinarians are required by law to reveal the confidences or it becomes necessary to reveal the confidences to protect the health and welfare of an individual, the animal, or others whose health and welfare may be endangered.

Table 3.1—State Regulation of Confidentiality of Veterinary Records

State	Reference	Summary of Cited References
Tennessee	1730-1.13 (6)	It is unprofessional conduct to reveal without written permission knowledge obtained in a professional capacity about animals or owners. Exceptions (b) are to other law enforcement agencies.
Virginia	150-20-140.4	Unprofessional conduct shall include violating the confidential relationship between a veterinarian and his client.
	150-20-170	Unprofessional conduct includes compromising the confidentiality of the doctor/client relationship.
West Virginia	26-4-2.14	A licensed veterinarian shall not violate his or her confidential relationship with the client
Wyoming	Ch. 4, Sec 1(b)	Incorporates by reference the AVMA Principles of Veterinary Medical Ethics*
	Ch. 4, Sec 3 d vi	Contents of medical records shall be kept confidential and not released to third parties unless authorized by the client or required by law.

*Veterinarians and their associates should protect the personal privacy of patients and clients. Veterinarians should not reveal confidences unless required to by law or unless it becomes necessary to protect the health and welfare of other individuals or animals (AVMA 2000).

Source: HSUS.

The AVMA recognizes that veterinarians may observe cases of animal abuse or neglect as defined by federal or state laws, or local ordinances. When these situations cannot be resolved through education, the AVMA considers it the responsibility of the veterinarian to report such cases to appropriate authorities. Disclosure may be necessary to protect the health and welfare of animals and people. Veterinarians should be aware that accurate record keeping and documentation of these cases are invaluable. (*http://www.avma.org/policies/animalwelfare.asp#abuse*)

The AVMA encourages those who regulate veterinary matters in each state to respect the confidentiality of the veterinarian-client relationship but to allow exceptions when the health or welfare of the animal *or other people* might be endangered.

Recently, the American Animal Hospital Association (AAHA) adopted a policy on reporting of suspected animal abuse that goes beyond the mandates provided by the AVMA. Its October 2003 policy states:

Since veterinarians have a responsibility to the welfare of animals and the public and can be the first to detect animal abuse in a family, they should take an active role in detecting, preventing and reporting animal abuse. While some states and provinces do not require veterinarians to report animal abuse, the association supports the adoption of laws requiring, under certain circumstances, veterinarians to report suspected cases of animal abuse. Reporting should only be required when client education has failed, when there is no likelihood that client education will be successful, or in situations in which immediate intervention is indicated and only when the law exempts veterinarians from civil and criminal liability for reporting.

In order to encourage veterinarians and practice team members to be responsible leaders in their communities and to assist in the detection and reporting of animal abuse, the profession should educate its members to recognize, document and report animal abuse, develop forensic models, promote legislation concerning reporting by veterinarians, and collaborate with other animal and human welfare groups and professionals within communities to eliminate the incidence of animal abuse. (American Animal Hospital Association 2003)

In contrast to those states mandating confidentiality, several states have passed laws specifically protecting veterinarians from liability with regard to reporting suspected cruelty to animals. Other states have gone one step further by making veterinarians legally responsible for reporting animal cruelty (Table 3.2).

Am I qualified to evaluate this case with respect to cruelty or neglect?

The veterinary community has devoted little attention to the clinical characteristics of abused and neglected animals. Scarce information is available in the scientific literature; what information does exist must often be gleaned from reports of other conditions. Studies of feline hepatic lipidosis, for example, give some idea of the metabolic processes that occur during starvation in cats (Biourge et al. 1994; Dimski and Taboada 1995). While much of the human forensic literature can be extrapolated for application to veterinary patients, some of it cannot. Veterinarians who wish to evaluate a neglected or abused animal find little informational literature to guide them or to support their findings and conclusions. And although veterinary pathology is a well-developed and specialized field, there is as yet no specialized training for veterinary pathologists whose focus is *forensic* pathology.

Due to this deficit of knowledge and attention from the veterinary community, and because abused or neglected animals may present a wide range of clinical pictures, the veterinary practitioner, with a range of expertise and experience that is typically quite broad, is well suited to evaluate animal-cruelty victims with the support of other veterinary and forensic experts.

Occasionally, characteristics of a particular case may cause veterinarians to question whether they are the appropriate person to assist with the investigation. Veterinarians who assist with animal-cruelty investigations need many talents, including knowledge of the species, good examination and investigation skills, good communicative skills for developing written reports and testifying in court, and the ability to deal effectively with the tasks and details that distinguish a forensic case from the usual case that is focused only on diagnostics and therapeutics.

In cases involving less common species or unusual circumstances, veterinarians may be especially inclined to doubt their suitability to participate in the case. While it is essential that veterinarians carefully consider whether their skills, knowledge, and abilities closely match the needs of those who are performing the investigation, they should also realize that there may not be many veterinarians who are willing and able to do the job. For example: a mid-size suburban animal shelter admits five or six iguanas annually, and a local iguana rescue organization assists the shelter in rehabilitating and rehoming them, so the shelter's veterinarian is rarely called on to provide medical care for iguanas. Then the shelter's investigators confiscate fifteen iguanas in poor condition from a local would-be breeder. Ideally, the animals would be examined and cared for by a veterinarian who specializes in reptile medicine, who has extensive knowledge of forensic matters, whose fee is affordable to the investigative agency or to the city or county government, and whose time to devote to

Table 3.2—Veterinarian Reporting Laws for Animal Cruelty and Animal Fighting April 2005

State	Required Reporting	Voluntary Reporting	Required in State Criminal Code	Required under State Practice Act	To Report Suspected Animal Fighting	To Report Suspected Cruelty or Abuse	Citation, Date, or Additional Information
Arizona	Yes			Yes	Yes		Section 1. Section 32-2239, Arizona Revised Statutes (2001)
California	Yes				Yes ONLY		California Business and Professional Code §4830.5
Colorado					Yes		C.R.S. 12-64-121 (2004)
Georgia	No	Veterinarian "may" report			Yes	Yes	Title 4 of the Official Code of Georgia Annotated §4-11-17
Idaho	No	Veterinarian immunity if reported				Yes— immunity if sued	Idaho Code §25-3514A
Illinois	Yes (fighting, cruelty added in 2003)				Yes— in writing	Yes— in writing	State Practice Act and 225 ILCS 115/25/GG
Kansas	Yes					Yes	Administrative Regs. §70-8-1, failing to report to the proper authorities cruel or inhumane treatment to animals, if the veterinarian has direct knowledge of the cruel or inhumane treatment
Maine	No	Veterinarian "may" report				Yes	LD 1170 SB 356 Provides civil and criminal immunity for veterinarians reporting alleged animal cruelty. Signed into law 6/18/01, P.L. No. 425.
Maryland	No	Veterinarians are encouraged to report	Statute says the State Board must promulgate regulations to encourage reporting	Yes	Yes	Yes	State Practice Act (2002) and Statute §2-304 COMAR 15.14.15.03
Massa-chusetts	No	Veterinarian immunity if reported					Mass. Ann. Laws ch. 112, §58b

Continued on page 32

Continued from page 31

Table 3.2—Veterinarian Reporting Laws for Animal Cruelty and Animal Fighting April 2005

State	Required Reporting	Voluntary Reporting	Required in State Criminal Code	Required under State Practice Act	To Report Suspected Animal Fighting	To Report Suspected Cruelty or Abuse	Citation, Date, or Additional Information
Michigan	No	Veterinarian immunity if reported					(2000) §333.18827
Minnesota	Yes		Yes			Yes	§346.37 Reports of abuse, cruelty or neglect ***346.37. General provisions—2. Good samaritans. A person is not liable for rendering humane assistance to an injured pet or companion animal
New York	Law officers must report, no mention of veterinarians	Veterinarians are immune if they report				Yes	NYCLS §6714
Oklahoma				Yes			
Oregon	Yes	Veterinarians have immunity if they report					(1997) ORS §686.445 (2003 Required and fine imposed
Rhode Island	No	Veterinarians have immunity if they report					Gen. Laws §4-1-37
Vermont	No	A veterinarian who reports cruelty shall face no monetary liability for his actions					Sec. 12. 26 V.S.A. §2404. Enacted in 2003
Virginia		Veterinarians have immunity if they report					§3.1-796.76
West Virginia	Yes		Yes			Yes	W. Va. Code §7-10-4a
Wisconsin	Yes				Yes		Wis. Stat. §173.12 Shall report in writing

Source: HSUS (2005).

the court proceedings of the case is unlimited. In reality, such an ideal situation is rare, and the shelter's own staff veterinarian may be the best choice for the job.

Another option is for the expert on reptiles and the shelter veterinarian, who has forensic experience, to work together. The reptile veterinarian can examine the animal and note all pathology while the shelter veterinarian determines the medico-legal significance and proper application for the investigation.

When veterinarians agree to participate in investigations involving a species or situation with which they are not entirely familiar, they must make a series of commitments. They must be committed to quickly and carefully learning as much as possible about the species and the situation; committed to seeking out, consulting with, and relying on expert advisers to assist them; and committed to meeting the forensic needs of the case. Finally, they must be prepared to be challenged in court regarding their expertise in the matter (see chapter 4).

What will my responsibilities be if I decide to participate in the investigation and/or prosecution of this case?

Before becoming involved as a coinvestigator in an animal-cruelty case, veterinarians should understand and carefully consider what their responsibilities will be. Those responsibilities may include, but are not limited to:

- Examination of the crime scene, collecting evidence there, and possibly assisting other investigators and law enforcement officers in recreating the events of the crime.
- Collecting the bodies of the victims and carefully transporting them for examination or necropsy.
- Maintaining the chain of custody of the evidence at all times (see chapter 6).
- Properly storing the evidence until it is no longer needed.
- Performing careful, methodic, detailed examinations of the victim(s) and recording all normal and abnormal findings in a manner that will be effective and presentable in a court of law.
- Advising on or possibly even providing care for surviving animals who have been confiscated.
- Advising the investigator, prosecutor, and those providing short- and long-term care for surviving animals regarding veterinary matters in the case.
- Attending court proceedings.
- Testifying in court as a witness to the facts and as an expert witness.
- Assisting the investigative organization in preparing educational materials related to the case for the media's use.
- Providing euthanasia for victims who are severely ill or injured, and possibly even for healthy animals, as ordered by the court (i.e., a judge may order euthanasia of a group of confiscated fighting dogs, having determined that adopting them into new homes would pose a threat to the community).

These duties and more may be the responsibility of participating veterinarians. Careful discussion with the agency conducting the investigation and, ideally, with the prosecutor is necessary before making a commitment to being involved in the case.

Occasionally veterinarians will offer to assist with only a portion of the investigation. They may agree to perform the initial examination of a victim but decline to testify in court. The veterinary findings are the cornerstone of any animal-cruelty investigation. If the veterinarian is not willing to be fully involved, then efforts should be made to find someone who is. Failure to do so may result in a poor initial assessment and/or loss of evidence, and ultimately it will compromise the case. A partial commitment may be helpful to an agency that cannot find a veterinarian who will help in any other way. Veterinarians should understand that, having examined the victim(s) or any other evidence associated with the case, they will likely be called on by the prosecutor or the defending attorney to testify as witnesses to the facts of the case. If necessary, a court subpoena may be issued to coerce the veterinarian's participation, and refusal may result in contempt of court charges. (It is important to note that often a plea bargain between the parties is reached, and the case never goes to trial.)

What will my time commitment to this case be?

Depending on the charges filed, the need for veterinary testimony will vary. In misdemeanor or ordinance violation cases, veterinarians' presence may be needed for only a single court appearance. If the charges are at the felony level, veterinarians may or may not be needed to testify before a grand jury. If they are subpoenaed to testify at trial, they may be on call and have to appear within a few hours' notice. The prosecutor usually makes every effort to have a planned time for veterinarians' testimony to accommodate their work schedules. Often, their discussions with the prosecutor and their presence in the courtroom result in the individual charged agreeing to a plea bargain. Veterinarians may spend one to several hours in court, depending on the case. In all situations, they should have received ample notification from the prosecutor or investigator for them to make arrangements to appear. The court will make efforts to accommodate schedule demands of expert witnesses, but it is important to let the prosecutor know of any special schedule demands.

What will my financial commitment to this case be?

Veterinarians are wise to consider the financial commitment they may be making to a case. Whenever veterinarians are voluntary participants in the investigation and prosecution of a case, they are entitled to compensation. Veterinarians should make clear at the outset what their fees will be, provide an estimate of the cost of services (as would be done for any other client), and clarify exactly who is hiring them and who will be responsible for paying for the services rendered. In general, veterinarians charge the investigating agency by the hour, since there is no way to foresee complications that may require more time spent on the case, and because court proceedings are notoriously unpredictable in duration.

In high-profile animal abuse and neglect cases, the public has often been sensitive to the high costs associated with providing quality care for the victims and bringing the perpetrators to justice. Special funds may be created by local humane societies or animal-care and -control agencies to pay for these special costs. Frequently such appeals generate more than enough response to cover the expenses associated with the case. In certain cases, the prosecutor may request restitution from the defendant as a part of the sentence.

Will my personal safety be jeopardized by participation in this case?

Depending on the circumstances of the case and the nature of the perpetrator, veterinarians may have legitimate concerns about becoming involved in an animal-cruelty case. One veterinarian described the dilemma she faced when she was presented with a number of dogs she suspected had been used in organized fighting. As a single mother and one of only a few veterinarians in her small rural town, she feared reporting the clients as dog fighters for fear they might retaliate against her or her family. One method for dealing with such a scenario is to build a team of expert witnesses who may collectively accuse a suspect of cruelty. A veterinary radiologist could examine radiographs of healing bones; a dermatologist could examine healing skin lacerations and infections; specialists at the nearest diagnostic laboratory could evaluate samples taken from the dogs. The investigator could find neighbors who had witnessed suspicious activity at the owner's home or property. These and other measures could help to prevent the veterinarian from being singled out as the one who pointed the finger of suspicion at the perpetrator(s).

What effect will my participation have on my business?

Whether veterinarians are the practice owners or the associates, they may be legitimately concerned about the effect their participation may have on their livelihood. The public demands action on animal abuse cases. Clients, as pet owners, will be the strongest supporters of such action. Clients like to align themselves with veterinarians who not only practice medicine but are also willing to take action to protect a helpless victim. The clients develop a sense of pride in their veterinarians and the practice. A successfully prosecuted case that receives favorable media attention may paint the veterinarian in a favorable light in the view of his clients and other pet owners in the community. But cases do not always go smoothly, and there is always the possibility that veterinarians may receive negative attention from the media or the community with regard to the case. Veterinarians must weigh this possibility against the opportunity to assist the animal victim.

What might the final outcome of the case be?

Before becoming involved in a case, veterinarians should know what might lie ahead. Many cases are never fully prosecuted. Suspects may plea bargain. A judge may determine there is insufficient evidence for a trial. In animal-hoarding cases, suspects often may be declared mentally unfit for trial or may voluntarily seek commitment to a mental health facility for evaluation and therapy. Those cases that do go to trial may drag out seemingly interminably and may eventually be dismissed due to their duration. It is a common—and often effective—defense tactic to seek every possible delay. Even a successfully prosecuted case may have an unfavorable outcome. Suspects may be convicted but given light sentences. Animals may be returned by the court to their abusers despite a conviction. Even when custody of the animals is retained by the investigating agency, the animal victims may be poor candidates for rehabilitation. Common examples of this are dangerous dogs who have been trained to fight and animals associated with a hoarding case, for whom physical rehabilitation would be slow, difficult, and expensive, and behavioral rehabilitation might not be possible at all. In such cases, the judge often mandates euthanasia of the victims.

The answers to these questions and others will determine whether veterinarians choose to participate in a particular case. A well-prepared veterinarian will be a greater ally to the investigative agency and to the prosecutor and will be more likely to play a significant part in a successful outcome.

4 Testifying in Court

Interest in prosecuting serious animal-cruelty cases is increasing, and more such cases are being brought before courts across the country. Veterinarians and veterinary technicians will be called on to provide testimony in these cases, and they will play an important role in providing the substance of a story of animals who have suffered and/or died.

Most people, even highly trained professionals, are unprepared for the process of standing by their actions and opinions in a court of law. The process of serving as a witness in a criminal prosecution involving animal cruelty can be daunting to even the most confident veterinary professionals.

In general, there are two types of witnesses who testify in criminal proceedings, factual witnesses and expert witnesses. Factual witnesses testify only to what they saw, heard, felt, smelled, tasted, or did in association with an event. Factual witnesses are not generally allowed to tell what others have said (hearsay) or to offer opinions or responses to hypothetical questions.

Veterinarians who have examined a victim of animal cruelty can testify as witnesses to the facts. In addition, any veterinarians associated with a case will likely be considered *expert* witnesses, capable of rendering an opinion on the evidence that falls within their area of expertise. Any testimony they may give based on review of evidence collected by others, such as another veterinarian, police officer, or a cruelty investigator, will also be considered expert testimony.

Veterinarians may become *involuntarily* involved as witnesses in the prosecution of an animal-cruelty case, particularly if they examined at any time the animal who was the victim, even before the onset of abuse or neglect. For example, if a pet owner has been charged with starving his dog to death (criminal neglect), either the prosecution team or the defense may choose to subpoena any veterinarian who has previously examined that animal to attest to the level of care the dog was receiving at that time. In most cases, veterinarians are asked by either the prosecution or the defense to act as expert witnesses voluntarily and may choose to be paid a reasonable professional fee for their involvement in a case.

Expert testimony has come under much closer scrutiny in recent years as courts have tried to deal with accusations of expert testimony based on "junk science" or unqualified experts. Most states regulate such testimony under rules based on the Federal Rules of Evidence, specifically Rule 702, which defines who is qualified to give expert testimony, and Rule 703, which identifies on what the testimony may be based. However, states can vary in their application and interpretation of these rules, so it is important that potential veterinary witnesses discuss these issues with the legal professionals who have retained their services.

The judge or jury is the sole independent finder of fact. Although experts may have opinions of the guilt or innocence of those accused, the rules of evidence stipulate that the role of expert witnesses is "to assist the trier of fact to understand the evidence, or to determine a fact in issue" (Federal Rules of Evidence 2004, Rule 702). In general, one qualifies as an expert through "knowledge, skill, experience, training, or education." As modified by Congress in 2000, Rule 702 stipulates that a person may testify in the form of an opinion or otherwise if:

- the testimony is based upon sufficient facts or data,
- the testimony is the product of reliable principles and methods, and
- the witness has applied the principles and methods reliably to the facts of the case.

In animal-cruelty cases, experts may include not only veterinarians, but also veterinary technicians, cruelty investigators, animal-control officers, animal behaviorists, trainers, breeders, groomers, law enforcement officers, and other technical experts. The proliferation of many self-styled "experts" on companion animal care, training, and handling has created a climate in which the courts are increasingly concerned about the qualifications of those who might testify.

In some cases, veterinarians may be asked to provide testimony on topics outside the basic common practice of veterinary medicine. For example, they may testify regarding analysis of bite wounds, on toxicological or serological evidence, or on issues of animal behavior. Other animal-related professionals may provide testimony in areas, such as dog training, that do not have a well-defined body of scientific literature. Since veterinary forensic pathology is a relatively new discipline, the application of forensic techniques to animal-cruelty cases may face closer scrutiny than would testimony dealing solely with the practice of conventional veterinary medicine. In cases of novel or unfamiliar applications of expertise, the court is viewed as having a gatekeeping role to insure that any such testimony be on "good grounds." The accepted standards for admissibility of expert opinions was established by the U.S. Supreme Court in *Daubert v. Merrill Doe Pharmaceuticals* (U.S. 579, 593–94 [1993]), a case that relied heavily on expert testimony regarding the possibility that birth defects were caused by the morning sickness drug Bendectin.

Testimony based on novel application of forensic techniques to an animal-cruelty prosecution is likely to be subjected to a Daubert test. Under Daubert, a court should consider:

- whether the expert's hypothesis can be and has been tested;
- whether the expert's methodology has been subjected to peer review and publications;
- how often the methodology yields erroneous results;
- whether controls over the methodology exist and are maintained; and
- whether the scientific community has accepted the methodology.

In a more recent case (*Kumho Tire Co. v. Carmichael*, PICS Case No. 99-0550, U.S. [1999]), the U.S. Supreme Court ruled that the Daubert standard should be extended from purely scientific testimony to include technical and specialized-knowledge testimony as well.

In general, scientific testimony has a disproportionate impact on jurors. Veterinarians and others who care for animals may benefit from a halo effect associated with their positive image as protectors of animal well-being, which can give them credibility outside their immediate area of expertise (Lockwood 1985). Some judges, to guard against any bias this might produce, may set a higher standard for testimony from such professionals. The expert's remarks should always be probative (i.e., they must address the truth of points being raised) and nonprejudicial (i.e., they cannot be motivated by an attempt to place a suspect in a bad light). When testifying in cases of alleged cruelty to animals, it is vital to refrain from offering any opinions of the character of the defendant. Instead, the expert should evaluate the care or treatment of the animals against what you would consider to be a reasonable standard that you might expect from your clients or community.

Preparing to Testify

As in all phases of animal-cruelty investigation, successful courtroom performance requires good record-keeping. The bulk of veterinary testimony will be based on case records. In addition to recording all clinical procedures, treatments, tests, and analyses, those caring for or examining animal victims should log all contacts with investigators, law enforcement agencies, and prosecutors in the case.

Before testifying witnesses should compile and review records, paying attention to timetables and the history of contacts regarding professional involvement in the case. Witnesses will not be expected to have all of this in memory and will be allowed to refer to these records when testifying, but any written work product that may be entered into evidence can be reviewed by opposing counsel. Witnesses should review any prior testimony (e.g., depositions) they may have given in earlier proceedings to refresh their memory about what was already said. If conclusions or interpretations have changed since the earlier prior testimony, counsel should be advised of these changes and the reasons why the witnesses' interpretation may have changed.

It is important to dress professionally for these court appearances, in traditional business attire, not scrubs or other work clothes. Veterinarians should bring all files related to the case, several copies of any reports and lab work results, enlarged photographs, camera memory cards or negatives, all evidence, references, diagrams, radiographs and radiographic viewer, or pictures of the radiographs. In some cases, with the court's approval, the animal survivor may be brought to court to show the dramatic improvement in the animal's condition. However, judges are usually resistant to any procedures that may disrupt court decorum.

It is important to prepare counsel for using expert testimony effectively. Witnesses should provide an up-to-date curriculum vitae and copies of relevant professional publications. They should reveal their professional strengths and disclose to the prosecutor or other counsel any lack of experience or other weakness (e.g., "This is the first gunshot wound I have seen"). Make sure counsel understands any arguments that need to be made and has sufficient understanding of the underlying principles to be able to ask questions in a way that will help inform the judge or jury of the significance of these facts.

In working with a prosecutor, expert witnesses must remember that this individual, although an ally, is not *their* attorney, so discussions and correspondence are not protected by attorney-client privilege. If experts have concerns about participation in this process, they should consult with their own attorney. There is always the possibility that a defendant may take legal action against those who have testified against him, even when such testimony is clearly protected from such action by law. This should not discourage veterinary professionals from participating.

Testimony from experts is generally first introduced through the process of direct examination by the counsel who retained their services. In criminal prosecutions this will usually be the prosecuting attorney. There should be few surprises during this process, but witnesses should be sure they understand each question and pause briefly before answering. Statements should be made with confidence but should not appear rehearsed.

For most professionals, the most stressful part of the courtroom experience is cross-examination by opposing counsel. This is the essence of the adversarial nature of the U.S. legal system. It is the opposing attorney's job to call into question the testimony of expert witnesses. Common tactics used to accomplish this task include attacking the witnesses' education, background, experience, expertise, the manner in which they processed the animal(s) involved in the case, and the information contained in documents they created.

Opposing counsel will try to uncover any ethical violations by the expert, including:

- misrepresenting academic credentials
- falsifying or altering data
- ignoring evidence helpful to his client
- improperly handling evidence
- testifying outside the expert's area of competence
- reaching conclusions before research or testing was completed
- accepting payment based on the *results* of examination, rather than on the time or effort expended

It is also common for attorneys to try to characterize experts as "hired guns." It is reasonable to expect payment for rendering professional services, but witnesses should be prepared to testify that any fees they have or will receive are consistent with what they may expect in other contexts, and that these fees are *not* contingent on the nature or outcome of the testimony.

Expert witnesses in animal-cruelty cases, particularly veterinarians, are often surprised by attacks on their expertise. Opposing counsel will attempt to characterize experts as less than thorough, even incompetent. Since the standard for prosecution in serious felony cases is usually proof beyond reasonable doubt, opposing counsel's role will often be to suggest that the evidence presented should be seen as not meeting this standard—to exploit normal professional caution and make it appear as *doubt.* Opposing counsel may point to a lack of special training in the area in question; relevant experience with the species involved; or *direct* knowledge of the animal, suspect, or circumstances involved (e.g., "You never actually *saw* my client break the cat's leg, did you?").

Even if expert witnesses' testimony cannot be tarnished by examination, it may be damaged if opposing counsel can simply unnerve them by such examination. It may help witnesses to remain calm by keeping in mind that the opposing attorney is simply doing her job; it is not a personal attack, although it may feel as though it is. Attorneys who are needlessly harsh in cross-examination run the risk of alienating juries that are often predisposed to respect witnesses who have cared for an animal. However, if witnesses feel they are being treated unfairly, their counsel or the judge may intervene. Witnesses should not argue with opposing counsel, nor should they appear arrogant or sarcastic. Integrity, accuracy, and a professional demeanor are the best tools for effectively presenting evidence.

This professional approach should continue outside the courtroom as well. The media will often be eager for details of a witness's findings or photographs or clinical details about an injured animal. These inquiries should be referred to the prosecuting attorney, who should be given an opportunity to review any reports that might be released. Veterinary experts should be particularly cautious about releasing photographs or videos of injured animals before legal action. Such publicity may be considered prejudicial and may affect the later admissibility of this evidence. The pictures are considered evidence and should be protected as such.

The experience of providing testimony can be stressful and unnerving for anyone, regardless of experience and professional expertise. When the result is a just verdict that may prevent future animal or human suffering, the experience can also be deeply satisfying.

CHAPTER 5

Collecting, Preserving, and Presenting the Findings

Humans are sensual beings, and nothing makes more sense to us than something we can see, hear, smell, touch, or taste. The evidence of cruelty that a veterinarian or humane investigator gathers will speak volumes about a case, so it must be properly collected, preserved, and presented to those who must decide the outcome of the case based on it. Any item that helps to prove the existence or nonexistence of a fact may be considered as evidence. Legal counsel for both the plaintiff and the defendant will try to introduce into the judicial process all relevant evidence that helps to prove their contentions in a case (Wilson, Rollin, and Garbe 1993).

The collection, preservation, and analysis of evidence is a science unto itself. In human forensics, the collection and analysis of specific types of evidence, such as human fingerprints, has spawned entire professions, with experts who do nothing else. In veterinary medicine, there are also experts who are uniquely qualified to evaluate specific types of evidence: radiologists, toxicologists, pathologists, and the like.

Despite the existence of these experts for analysis of some types of forensic evidence, the veterinary general practitioner is the person most likely to be responsible for collecting, preserving, and presenting much of the veterinary evidence of the majority of animal-cruelty crimes. Before collecting any evidence, whether at the scene of the crime or during examination or necropsy of the victim, the veterinarian must first use a system for documenting the collection of each specimen and tracking its whereabouts, from the moment it is collected until the moment it is presented in court.

If the scene of a crime is being searched and examined pursuant to a search warrant, the law enforcement officer in charge of executing the warrant is responsible for completing a receipt that lists all property seized. The items on the receipt include animals (dead and alive) and any other evidence related to the commission of a crime on that property. The receipt should be specific, indicating the number of animals removed as well as each animal's species, breed or breed type, sex, color, and coat pattern. It should also give somewhat detailed descriptions of other seized property; for example, "one 10-foot by 6-inch length of x-inch-diameter cotton rope, bloodstained." If the object has a specific name, that name alone may be used as the object's description; however, the more specific the description, the better. For example: "one baseball bat" is a sufficient description, but "one aluminum 'Louisville Omaha Gold' baseball bat" is a better description.

The officer in charge is responsible for leaving a copy of the receipt with the owner of the property being searched or, if the owner is not present, in a prominent place on the property. Another copy of the receipt is filed with the court that issued the warrant. The officer keeps a third copy of the receipt. He may choose to provide the assisting veterinarian with a photocopy of the receipt, and this photocopy may appropriately serve as the veterinarian's log of evidence taken from the scene of the crime, or it may be used as supporting information for the veterinarian's own log. Care should be taken that no item appears in the veterinarian's log that was not also included on the officer's receipt.

After the seizure and in all other circumstances, the veterinarian should keep a log of any evidence collected that is related to an animal-cruelty case. The animal is part of the crime scene, and anything collected from the animal is considered evidence. This includes trace evidence, blood samples, swabs, collars, projectiles, and so on. This log should list the case number, the date and time of collection, the item's name and description, the location of the item when it was discovered, the name of the investigator who discovered or obtained the item (usually the veterinarian), and the names of any witnesses to the discovery or collection of the item of evidence. This log is a medical record; in fact, it is often presented as an addendum to the animal's medical record. It can and will be used in court as evidence, so it should be written carefully and kept safe (Figure 5.1).

Some items of evidence should appear in other logs kept in the veterinary practice, as well. Radiographs taken of a cruelty victim, for example, should be logged not only in the evidence log for that particular case but also in the hospital's radiology log. Some state boards of veterinary examiners actually require that a radiology log be maintained as part of a practice's medical records, and the American Animal Hospital Association (AAHA) requires the use of radiology logs in accredited hospitals. The use of a radiology log is not only good hospital procedure, but it also helps to authenticate the radiographs. Conversely, if veterinarians present in court radiographs taken at their hospital of an animal who is the subject of an animal-cruelty case but a record of those radiographs is not found in the hospital's radiology log, the authenticity of the radiographs will be challenged by the opposing attorney and their use as evidence in the case may be barred.

It is imperative that all evidence be handled in such a manner that any person who has custody of it at any time, from the moment of collection until the moment of presentation in court, can be identified. This is known as the "chain of custody of the evidence," the "chain of possession," or simply the "chain of evidence." Every person who is part of the chain of evidence may potentially be called on to testify in court that the evidence has not been tampered with, contaminated, or replaced. A chain of custody form (Figure 5.2) should accompany each item of evidence at all times, and any person handling the evidence—even delivery people—must sign the form, attesting to his personal responsibility for the evidence. When the evidence is finally presented to the court, it should be accompanied by this chain of custody form.

It is crucial that any person handling, storing, or transporting the evidence be aware of the necessary procedure for maintaining the chain of custody and be willing to participate in its maintenance. Couriers should be used only if necessary; they should be trustworthy and use package tracking methods that will stand up to the scrutiny of the defense. The defense will use any break in the chain of custody in an attempt to disqualify the evidence.

Human laboratories that deal with forensic cases have a system in place to properly handle samples preserving chain of custody. The receiving party signs for the sample and records the time and date of receipt. A record is made of the condition of the sample, a description of the contents, and the packing material to show the sample has not been tampered with. Most veterinary laboratories do not have a similar standard operating procedure to handle these cases, which can cause their findings to be inadmissible in court. The veterinarian needs to fill out a Cruelty Case Samples Packaging Record (Figure 5.3) recording the condition of the sample to be sent for testing. Along with this, a Sam-

Figure 5.1—Evidence Log

Evidence Log

Agency: _____

Case number: _____ Animal description: _____

Notes: _____

_____

_____

Items of Evidence	Collector's Name	Date Collected	Disposition

Figure 5.2—Chain of Custody Form

Chain of Custody Form

Agency:_____

Case number: _____ Animal description: _____

Notes: _____

_____

Item:_____	Transferred to: _____
Received from: _____	By: _____
Date:_____	Time: _____

Item:_____	Transferred to: _____
Received from: _____	By: _____
Date:_____	Time: _____

Item:_____	Transferred to: _____
Received from: _____	By: _____
Date:_____	Time: _____

Item:_____	Transferred to: _____
Received from: _____	By: _____
Date:_____	Time: _____

Final disposition of item(s):

_____

_____

NAME OF FACILITY
ADDRESS
PHONE NUMBER

Figure 5.3—Cruelty Case Samples Packaging Record

Cruelty Case Samples Packaging Record

These samples are part of an animal-cruelty investigation.

Agency: _____

Case number: _____

Animal ID number: _____

Date packaged: _____ Time: _____

By whom (print & sign)_____

Carrier: _____ Date Sent: _____

Tracking number: _____

Shipment destination: _____

Samples included in this shipment: _____

_____

_____

_____

_____

How samples are packaged (be as detailed as possible, including size and color of any sample containers, ice pack(s) included, in baggies, what type of box used, quantity of each item placed in package, how box was sealed, signature across seal, etc.): _____

_____

_____

_____

_____

NAME OF FACILITY
ADDRESS
PHONE NUMBER

Figure 5.4—Cruelty Case Samples Receipt Record

Cruelty Case Samples Receipt Record

To whomever receives and opens this package: Chain of custody is a priority with these samples. To ensure samples have not been tampered with, please fill out this form, fax it back to us, and keep the original on file. Thank you for your help and cooperation.

Agency: _____

Case number: _____

Animal ID number: _____

Time received: _____ Date received: _____

Received from: Sender _____

               Carrier _____

Carrier: _____ Date Sent: _____

Tracking number: _____

Shipment destination: _____

Samples included in this shipment: _____

_____

_____

_____

Package description [be as detailed as possible, including size and color of any sample containers, ice pack(s) included, in baggies, what type of box used, quantity of each item placed in package, was the box open or sealed, if samples were cool, warm or hot, etc.]: _____

_____

_____

_____

NAME OF FACILITY
ADDRESS
PHONE NUMBER

---

ples Receipt Record (Figure 5.4) must be sent for the receiving laboratory to fill out and fax back to the veterinarian. This will show that the chain of custody was intact and the sample arrived without being compromised.

As already defined, evidence is anything that helps to prove the existence or nonexistence of a fact. In animal-cruelty crimes, the type of evidence most frequently collected and presented in court is photographic evidence of the scene of the crime, of any objects used as tools in the commission of the crime, and of the victim(s). Usually, radiographic evidence is also created and used. Veterinary evidence obtained and analyzed pursuant to examination of a surviving or deceased animal victim—samples of tissue, blood, urine, feces, and skin debris—is also a common feature of the investigations of animal-cruelty crimes. Objects found in or on the body, such as a noose used to hang an animal, duct tape used to bind the animal's mouth shut, or a bullet or arrow retrieved from within a muscle, are also considered evidence in such cases.

Evidence of a more delicate nature, such as fingerprints, hair and fibers, and blood spatters found at the scene of a crime, are frequent features of human assault and homicide cases, but are not yet widely used in animal-cruelty cases. Nevertheless, the technology for doing so exists, and veterinarians and other investigators who are involved in animal-cruelty cases will benefit from knowledge about how such samples are collected and analyzed. Evidence of this type may be used in those higher-profile cases in which an assault on an animal is coupled with a crime against a human.

Photographic Evidence

A picture is indeed worth a thousand words, and by far the most convincing evidence ever presented in a court of law is a photograph that demonstrates the extent of a criminal act. In cases of cruelty to animals, photographs are the items of evidence most frequently used to portray the crime, and their value in such cases cannot be overlooked or overestimated. General guidelines for creating photographic evidence of cruelty to animals are presented in this chapter. (For more specific guidance about photographing the crime scene and the victim[s], see chapters 6 and 7.)

Ideally, photographs taken at the scene of an animal-cruelty crime or during the examination of evidence or victims should be taken by a professional photographer or at least by someone who is a skilled photographer. Although one does not need to be an expert in photography to take crime scene photographs that will be admitted in a court of law, a skillful photographer is more likely to be able to take clear, accurate, useful photographs of a scene with minimal effort. If at all possible, a law enforcement agency's crime scene photographer should be used for this purpose. For those agencies that frequently investigate animal-cruelty cases, it is ideal if members of the investigative team develop the necessary photography skills.

Like all other aspects of the investigation, the photography should be carefully documented. A photography log must be kept, and it should include the date and time the photographs are taken; the case number; the name of the photographer; a detailed description of the scene, item, or victim being photographed and any associated identification numbers; the type of film being used; the identifying number of the roll of film; and the site at which the photograph is being taken, as well as any witnesses present during photography.

Three major points of qualification are usually considered by courts when determining whether a photograph may be used in court proceedings. The object pictured must be material or relevant to the point in issue, the photograph must be free from distortion and must not misrepresent the scene or the object it purports to reproduce, and the photograph must not appeal to the emotions or tend to prejudice the court or jury (Staggs 1997).

This last point deserves careful attention. While the unpleasant nature of a crime should not be disguised, a photographer should take care not to use photographic techniques to add to the gruesome nature of a crime scene or a victim's body. If a judge or jury is unable to view a photograph objectively because it is exceedingly gory, these individuals will be unable to carefully consider the evidence it is intended to document. While the investigator's desire to demonstrate the offensiveness of a crime is understood, overly offensive photographs might not be useful or even admissible in the courtroom. It must be kept in mind that the average person is not as comfortable viewing a severely injured or necropsied animal body as is the veterinarian or animal-cruelty investigator. Like children, animals are considered among the most defenseless members of our society, and jury members may be particularly appalled at the gruesome results of cruelty to animals. The photographer should carefully photograph all aspects of a scene, giving the prosecutor the ability to choose from a number of photographs when he tries to determine how best to present the photographic evidence.

Photographs of victims are taken for two primary reasons: to identify the victim and to document the victim's physical condition. Photographs of the crime scene are taken for a number of reasons: to document (1) the appearance of the scene of the crime at the time of arrival of the photographer; (2) the existence and original placement of items of evidence; and (3) the initial condition of evidence, and to provide investigators and others with a permanent visual record of the crime scene for later use and evaluation.

Photographic identification of the victim is a step investigators too frequently overlook. If the animal is deceased or is confined in some manner when found, several photographs of the animal in situ should be taken whenever possible. Each such photo should include a handheld or otherwise visible card that indicates the case number, the date, and an identification number assigned to the victim. This step should be taken *even in the case of a deceased and severely decomposed animal.* Imagine a human victim in similar circumstances: forensic examiners would not neglect to provide identification for the body simply because the victim was badly decomposed, and investigators of animal-cruelty crimes should not either. Close-up photos that clearly show the victim, as well as panoramic photos sequentially panning around the scene to show the conditions in which the victim was found, are warranted. After being photographed, the animal is removed and follow-up photographs are taken during the examination or necropsy procedure.

Unless absolutely necessary, investigators and other law enforcement, animal-control, or animal-care staff assisting with photography of a scene or a victim should not be included in photographs. More than one study has shown that the presence of an animal in a photo of a person significantly influences the perception other people have of that person (Lockwood 1985; Budge et al. 1996). It is reasonable to assume that including a person in a photograph of an animal victim may unnecessarily influence the viewer's response to the animal as well. In case they must be photographed, those assisting with an investigation should be neatly and professionally dressed, without excessive makeup or jewelry, and with hair neatly arranged. Care should be taken that any portion of a person that appears in a photograph of an animal victim appears highly professional. An investigation scene is often exciting. Despite the gruesome nature of the crime, people may react in an inappropriate manner due to this excitement, perhaps smiling, laughing, or talking too loudly. Such actions can unduly influence a judge or jurors when captured in a photograph or on a videotape, especially when accompanied by sound.

Instant and 35 mm Photography

The choice of an appropriate camera may be difficult, as there are many thousands of cameras and features from which to select. Instant photography (e.g., Polaroid) is expensive and has the drawback of poorer image resolution and poor color documentation. Instant photos cannot be easily copied, enlarged, cropped, or made into slides. They degrade over time, sometimes even before a case is brought to trial. Instant photos do, however, provide assurance that the photo has been obtained and that it represents the evidence as it was intended to, eliminating worry about whether a roll of film will turn out well or will be lost or destroyed before or during development. The advantages of instant photography have been almost entirely replaced by the availability of relatively low-cost, high-quality digital photography (see below). If instant photography is used, it is advisable to scan instant photo images on a good-quality computer scanner as soon as possible after they are obtained. The scanned images can then be stored on a computer's hard drive or a floppy disk or they can be burned onto a compact disc for future use.

An automatic, even disposable, 35 mm camera is inexpensive, easy to operate, and can be used to document the overall scene of a crime. Automatic cameras have a fixed-focus lens, however, and have limited close-up capability. The flash feature of disposable cameras may also be very slow to recharge, making them less than ideal for use in any darkened area.

A 35 mm camera with adjustable focus length, shutter speed, and lens aperture is the tool of choice for documenting the scene of the crime, items of evidence taken from it, and victims' injuries. In addition to the camera, it is useful to have normal, wide-angle, and close-up lenses as well as filters, an electronic flash attachment, a light meter, and a tripod (Figure 5.5).

The use of 35 mm color slide film has been advocated for forensic photography. Slides are easy to store and can be made into color photographs easily and with little image distortion. Color slide or print film with a film speed rating of 100 or 200 ISO (International Standards Organization) provides greater sharpness with a minimum amount of grain and blurring (U.S. Department of Justice 1996). When shooting indoors with daylight film, a flash should always be used. A flash with a quick recharge is desirable.

Digital Photography

Digital cameras have greatly improved in quality and decreased in price during the past few years, making them a viable option for use in forensic photography. They offer the advantage of allowing for immediate viewing of a photograph, ensuring the photographer that the picture taken accurately represents the condition of the scene or the victim in front of him. Although photo storage

Figure 5.5—Suggested Crime Scene Photography Kit

- Camera
- Normal lens (a 50mm lens is considered a normal lens for a 35mm camera); wide angle lens (28mm or similar for a 35mm camera)
- Close-up lenses or accessories (e.g., macro lens, 1:1 adapter, extension tubes, bellows, reversing ring, or close up filters)
- Filters (red, orange, yellow, blue, and green)
- Electronic flash
- Remote sync cord for electronic flash (to operate flash when not mounted on camera)
- Extra camera and flash batteries
- Locking cable release
- Tripod
- Film (color and black and white print film)
- Owner's manuals for camera and flash
- Notebook and pen
- Rulers
- Gray card (to aid in getting accurate exposures)
- Index cards and felt pen
- Flashlight

Source: Staggs (1997).

capabilities vary by camera, most digital cameras use floppy disks or memory cards or sticks. One study of the use of a digital camera for photodocumentation of domestic violence scenes found that digital cameras have significant advantages over instant film technology and recommended that they replace instant photograph cameras in forensic settings (Blitzer and Jacobia 1997).

Despite concern about the ease of alteration of digital images, they are successfully admitted in court proceedings when a photographer is willing to testify that the images accurately represent the scene at the time the photos were taken and when the images are properly handled between the time they are taken and the time they are presented in court. Guidelines for handling digital images and other digital evidence in a manner that will ensure their admissibility in a court of law are undergoing development and revision (Scientific Working Group on Digital Evidence 2000). The veterinarian, or the investigators with whom the veterinarian works, should check their state's rules of evidence for specifics on the admissibility of digital photographs. Most states are developing laws that apply to digital evidence.

The California Evidence Code (Section 1500.6[a] [Admissibility of Printed Representation of Images Stored on Video or Digital Media to Prove Existence and Content of Image]) states:

> [A] printed representation of an image stored on video or digital media shall be admissible to prove the existence and content of the image stored on the video or digital media. Images stored on video or digital media, or copies of images stored on video or digital media, shall not be rendered inadmissible by the best evidence rule. Printed representation of images stored on video or digital media shall be presumed to be accurate representations of the images that they purport to represent.

This regulation reflects the rapid gain in acceptance of digital images as admissible evidence.

Videography

Videography is an important additional format for creating images of a crime scene or a victim. Guidelines discussed above for other types of photography should be followed during videography as well. One important aspect of videography that is not included in other types of photography is the audio portion of a videotape. In some cases an audio track is helpful. The investigator or veterinarian may want to narrate the scene or offer a running commentary on the procedures being carried out. It may also be important to record an animal's vocalizations during a behavioral assessment or physical examination to document pain responses or other behaviors that may provide evidence of pain and distress. However, microphones can also pick up conversations and sounds that are not desirable in a courtroom presentation, including extraneous conversations or emotional or inappropriate comments made by participants or bystanders. All members of the investigative team should be aware that audio information as well as video information is being collected when a video camera is used. In most instances, it is advisable to adjust the audio recorder, if possible, so that audio is muted after a brief voice-over at the start of the tape to identify the date, time, and place of the video; the camera operator; and other investigators or witnesses who are present.

Radiography

Another common imaging modality that is frequently used in animal-cruelty investigations is radiography of the victim. As in all other instances, radiographs should contain some form of permanent identification legibly exposed in the film emulsion that includes the hospital or clinic name and/or the veterinarian's name, client identification, patient identification, date, and left/right indicators. A radiograph taken of an alleged animal-cruelty victim should also include the case number and the animal's identification number (Wilson, Rollin, and Garbe 1993).

Collection and Preservation of Evidence

It is important to be prepared for the detection, collection, and preservation of all types of evidence. Certain items are needed for proper collection and preservation of evidence, most of which are inexpensive and can be purchased from a variety of on-line crime scene investigation suppliers (see appendix B). Evidence tape is needed to place on all containers of evidence. Chain of custody stickers can also be placed on containers. A variety of paper envelope and bag sizes is needed to collect and transport evidence. Plastic bags should never be used to hold evidence because moisture may accumulate, which may then cause corrosion and compromise the integrity of the evidence. If an item is wet, it may be placed in a plastic bag for transport for a maximum of two hours. Then it must be removed, allowed to dry, and placed in a paper bag. Special tweezers are available to collect fine pieces of evidence. Trace-lifting tape with or without cardboard holders is useful for collecting and submitting trace evidence. An ultraviolet light is used to detect certain types of fluid and trace evidence. An alternative light source, such as a flashlight, held at an angle is also useful to detect small items of evidence. A block of Styrofoam™ or a wooden block with drilled holes is needed to hold swabs for drying. This block should be divided into identifying categories such as blood, skin, genital, anal, oral, skin/fur, and so on. Some type of magnifying device is also helpful during the examination. To record findings as the veterinarian conducts his examination, it is helpful to have a voice-activated cassette or digital recorder.

Biological Specimens

Biological specimens are usually taken during examination or necropsy of the victim, but they may also be collected at the crime scene, often in the form of trace evidence. Bits of fur, skin, or blood may be found on a weapon or smeared on a surface near the scene of the attack. Biological specimens may consist of a victim's dismembered body parts.

One prosecutor experienced in the presentation of cases of animal cruelty recommends collection of samples of significant debris (e.g., a section of floor tile and the layer of feces that covers it) for preservation and later presentation to the judge and jury (Campbell 2000). In another case, an investigator wanted to demonstrate the extent of matting of the haircoat of a neglected dog, so he had the eight-inch-thick mat shaved from the dog's back in one piece and stored it in a freezer. He carried it to the courthouse in an ice chest, prepared to present it as evidence in the case.

Bloodstained materials should be allowed to dry as much as possible then placed in a paper bag or envelope. If a bloodstained item cannot be collected, the item should be carefully photographed, then the dried blood scraped from it using a new razor blade or scalpel blade. The scrapings should be folded in a piece of clean paper and secured in a paper envelope.

Animal DNA

There are three categories of DNA evidence that might be useful in animal-cruelty cases: DNA associated with the animal as the victim, DNA linked to the perpetrator, and DNA from other people or animals that might be needed to exclude certain evidence, such as bloodstains unrelated to the suspected cruelty. Sources of DNA include blood, saliva, urine, feces, hair, semen, bones, teeth, organ tissue, muscle, and skin. DNA may also be obtained from toys, bedding, brushes, bowls, or any related property to help identify a particular animal. During the commission of a crime, animal DNA can be transferred directly or indirectly from an animal to the crime scene or onto another person.

A few laboratories in the United States specialize in animal DNA testing (appendix A). In addition to having a large database of animal DNA results, they have developed special techniques that recognize unique qualities of animal DNA, and they are better able to detect and provide accurate animal DNA results. Proper sampling technique is paramount for successful DNA determination and essential if the results are to stand up to scrutiny in court. Strict chain of custody must be followed. It is preferred that the original item be submitted. If that is not possible, however, then the item should be swabbed, avoiding contamination. The DNA laboratory often needs control samples, so the veterinarian should contact the laboratory for its sample requirements and submission guidelines.

DNA evidence can be used in animal-cruelty investigations in many different ways. It may provide proof that a particular sample came from a specific individual, either the victim or a suspect. It may also allow identification of a sample as having come from a particular species. For example, DNA extracted from saliva samples has been used to link wounds on animals to a particular predator species (Williams et al. 2003) and has also been used to connect bite wounds on human victims of fatal dog attacks to specific suspect animals (D. Parmer, D.V.M., personal communication with R.L., April 6, 2005).

DNA fingerprinting has been used more widely in forensic investigations of crimes involving wildlife. Guglich, Wilson, and White (1993) report on use of DNA fingerprinting in forty cases of hunting infractions involving white-tailed deer and moose. In most cases DNA probes were used to link animal remains found at illegal kill sites to blood and tissue samples of the animals associated with a suspect.

Trace Evidence

Edmond Locard (1877–1966), a Frenchman educated in both medicine and the law, was well known for solving criminal cases on the basis of trace evidence. He set forth the concept known as Locard's Exchange Principle, which states that a cross-transfer of evidence takes place whenever a criminal comes in contact with a victim, an object, or a crime scene (Nickell and Fischer 1999). For example, a criminal may leave a latent fingerprint and a strand of hair at the scene, while carrying away animal hairs and spattered blood from a canine victim.

If necessary to the case, trace evidence can be analyzed extensively by forensic laboratories. For example, although a strand of hair cannot be exclusively determined to originate from an individual (DNA testing of the hair itself cannot be carried out unless the sample includes a root with some attached tissue), analysts can obtain very specific information from a single human hair, including the part of the body from which it came; whether the hair was removed forcibly; whether it was cut and, if so, by what type of instrument; whether it had been dyed or bleached; and whether certain chemicals or drugs might have been ingested by the person from whom the hair was taken. With some limits, it can even determine a person's race. These very specific details can be used to compare a hair left at the scene of a crime to that of a suspect. Although such a comparison may not be accurate enough to determine the outcome of a case, it can be extremely important when taken into consideration along with other facts of the case.

Animal hairs are frequently transferred to perpetrators or human victims of crimes. A victim placed in a vehicle or held at a location where animals are routinely found often results in the transfer of animal hairs to the victim's clothing. Cat or dog hairs, for example, can be found on the adhesive portions of ransom and extortion notes prepared by pet owners (Deedrick 2000). In animal-cruelty cases involving contact with or proximity to the animal victim, some transfer of hair to the perpetrator is almost inevitable.

When animal hair is found in connection with a suspect, it may be identified as a particular type of animal and microscopically compared with a known hair sample from either an animal hair reference collection or a specific animal (Moore 1999). If the hair in question exhibits the same microscopic characteristics as the known hairs, it is concluded that the hair is *consistent with* originating from that animal. Even though sample hairs do not usually show enough individual microscopic characteristics to be associated with a particular animal to the exclusion of other similar animals, their analysis can still prove useful in investigations (Deedrick 2000; Deedrick and Koch 2004). If the animal victim has relatively unusual hair qualities related to breed or individual differences, it will make for a stronger indication that the animal in question was the source of the sample.

In some cases a single animal hair may provide key forensic evidence. The first such case occurred in Canada in 1996 when cat hairs on a bloodied jacket linked a man to the murder of his estranged wife on the basis of a DNA match made using a feline genetics database maintained by the National Cancer Institute. In 1998 two men murdered Elizabeth Ballard, wrapping her in plastic and leaving her body in a shallow grave in the New Mexico desert. When her body was discovered a month later, it had been scattered by coyotes. Investigators found a few dog hairs on her socks—one of which had a root. It was analyzed by the University of California/Davis Veterinary Genetics Laboratory and was found to match the DNA from a blood sample taken from the suspects' pit bull, aiding in their conviction (Boxall 2001).

Although such high-level investigation and evaluation of evidence is not routinely a feature of animal-cruelty cases, it is being used in some instances. For example, in one case of intentional poisoning of neighborhood cats, the perpetrator was positively identified by the presence of his fingerprints on a plastic dish containing cat food soaked in blue-green liquid. Law enforcement officers assisting the local humane society with the investigation of the case collected the dish and submitted it to their crime lab for fingerprint dusting and analysis. The contents of the dish were given to the humane society's investigators, who had their staff veterinarian submit a sample for toxicological testing; the results were positive for ethylene. The proper method of collection and preservation of trace evidence can vary, depending on the type of evidence. Trace evidence can often be combed from the fur of a victim. A roll of white paper should be placed on the examining table and the animal combed in a grid fashion. The paper should be examined with both an indirect light source and an ultraviolet light. Samples of evidence can be plucked with clean forceps from a variety of surfaces. Adhesive tape may be used to capture and hold very fine trace evidence for later examination. For high-level investigations, special vacuum collection systems are used to collect trace evidence from carpeting or fabric surfaces. Dry trace evidence can be stored in plastic containers or a paper bag, then sealed with evidence tape.

Cloth Materials

Cloth materials are often found associated with an animal-cruelty crime. Ropes used to bind, restrain, or hang animals may be stained with blood, urine, and feces. Perpetrators may attempt to clean their hands by wiping them on a towel, sheet or bedspread, or curtain. They may attempt to clean up the evidence of the crime with a towel, washcloth, or dishrag. Bits of cloth may be used as torches to ignite an animal. A pillow or towel may be used to smother an animal. Suspects may carry away bits of fiber from cloth materials associated with an act of cruelty to animals.

Cloth materials collected from a crime scene should be thoroughly dried before being stored as evidence. Storage in a paper envelope prevents molding and deterioration of the evidence. Large pieces should be folded carefully. Very large items, like a bloodstained mattress, can be packed in clean cardboard cartons from moving and storage supply retailers.

In lower-profile cases, these items can be presented in court without having been analyzed. A bloodstained rope, coupled with photographs of an animal who has been hung with it and testimony from an eyewitness to the hanging, is often enough to result in a successful outcome of an animal-cruelty case. In higher-profile cases, cloth items collected from the scene of a crime and from the clothing, car, or other belongings of a perpetrator can be analyzed by a crime laboratory to determine how they are related to the criminal act.

In any criminal case, evidence may be as important as or more so than the testimony of either factual or expert witnesses. But evidence is only useful when it is properly collected, preserved, and presented. The veterinary examiner's familiarity with different types of evidence and its proper handling are crucial to the outcome of the case.

Examination of the Crime Scene

Proper examination of the crime scene is essential to handling cases of human assault and homicide. Numerous texts have been written about the subject of crime scene investigation (see, for example, Eliopulos 1993; Geberth 1996; Nickell and Fischer 1999; Swanson, Chamelin, and Territo 1999; Fisher 2000). In animal-cruelty cases, however, thorough processing of the crime scene is often a neglected aspect of the investigation; it is rarely considered a necessary step. The scene of a crime involving an animal victim can, of course, yield the same crucial information leading to successful identification and prosecution of the assailant as the scene of a crime involving a human victim.

Veterinarians should assist in the processing of a crime scene but they are not often asked to be involved. In human homicide investigations, the scene is usually visited and examined by one or more crime scene technicians, the medical examiner, and the prosecuting attorney. In animal-cruelty crimes involving deceased victims, veterinarians should serve as the veterinary medical examiner, examining the body at the scene and inspecting the evidence surrounding it, as well as performing the necropsy examination once the body has been removed. Whether they visit the scene or not, veterinarians should be familiar with the techniques commonly used to process crime scenes and the evidence such techniques may yield. Armed with this knowledge, veterinarians may be the ones to instigate a crime scene investigation, convincing a reluctant law enforcement officer to process the scene or to call for a crime scene technician to do the job. Veterinarians may also advise and direct investigators about what to look for. In some cases, veterinarians may be the only ones willing or able to process the crime scene. Knowledge of proper crime scene investigation, processing of evidence, and interpretation of evidence is thus crucial for all veterinarians who are involved in animal-cruelty cases.

A crime scene may be associated with a live or deceased victim. For example, if a female victim of domestic violence brings in a pet who was also abused, the veterinarian's role may be primarily advisory in nature to the investigators and will less likely include visiting the home where the incident occurred. If a client's pet is found dead in his backyard with apparent injuries, ideally a veterinarian, accompanied by appropriate law enforcement authorities, will be asked to examine the scene and inspect the body before the scene is disturbed.

The initial step in any crime scene investigation is to determine and establish the perimeter of the scene. The area is roped off and secured, and one route in and out of the scene is designated. A law enforcement officer is appointed to guard the scene and record all persons coming and going. Because the court may request such a record, unnecessary visitors to the scene should be discouraged from entering. If there is considerable media interest in the case, the perimeter should be established in a manner that minimizes what camera lenses and audio recording equipment might be able to detect. It should then be determined who might have entered and contaminated the scene before it was processed.

Successfully obtaining and using evidence such as fingerprint information and footwear impressions often depends on as few people as possible handling evidence at and contaminating the scene. Crime scenes involving live animals are unique in that the "property" or evidence associated with the crime is living and mobile and may not stay in or near the area where the crime was committed. Thus it becomes even more important for veterinary examiners to be alert to trace evidence (e.g., vegetation embedded in fur) that may prove useful in documenting the actual scene of the crime.

The prosecuting attorney guides the investigative team in determining what evidence might be most useful in the case. Special personnel, such as a blood-spatter or fingerprint expert, might also prove useful. A crime scene photographer is perhaps the most important member of the team and will work with other investigators to be certain that the entire scene, as well as all pertinent evidence, is properly photographed. Ideally, the entire scene is photographed and videotaped before any further processing takes place. If it is night and the scene is dark, whether outdoors or in a building without lights, it will be necessary to bring in lighting or wait until daylight to photograph and process the scene. When weather conditions threaten to obliterate the scene before it can be processed, steps should be taken to erect a protective structure, if possible.

Survey photography and videography of the scene are the first order of business. All photography should conclusively establish the location of the scene and the identification of victims. Identification photos should clearly demonstrate the species, sex, breed type, color, and coat pattern of the victim, if the body is in a condition that will allow such determination. In situ photos should include close-up views of victims as well as panoramic photos showing how victims were found at the scene and the proximity of other evidence (e.g., a can of gasoline found a few feet away from a burned animal). The photographs should also be inclusive enough to record information about terrain and vegetation in the area that might have concealed perpetrators or that might provide useful additional information. For example, photographs of an investigation of a mutilation of cats revealed the proximity of stands of tall pine trees that were favored habitat for great horned owls, who are capable of inflicting the kinds of wounds found on the victims.

Each in situ photograph should include a card on which the date, case number, and victim identification numbers are written. Photographs of the scene should provide conclusive identification of the house, building, or site that constitutes the crime scene. If an address for the location is visible on a mailbox, street sign, or street curb, a photograph will be convincing if the defense team questions where the photographs were taken. The photographer can also testify in court about the location where the photographs were taken.

Once initial photography and videography have been completed, the crime scene investigation should shift to initial examination of the body of the deceased victim(s), if present. Examiners should be careful to describe at this point only what they actually see rather than attempt to draw conclusions based on the evidence. A general description of the body should be written, followed by a description of visible wounds and any tools or implements applied to the animal (duct tape binding a dog's muzzle, for example). Identification worn by the victim (a collar and/or identification tags, for instance) should be examined and photographed. All bodies should be scanned for a microchip. Blood evidence should be photographed and described. Samples of all blood found at the scene should be taken. Several texts have been written specifically about bloodstain pattern analysis and its admissibility in the courtroom (Bevel and Gardner 1997; James 1998; James, Eckert, and Eckert 1998), and the subject has been covered in most crime scene investigation references. The location, pattern, direction of flow, and degree of coagulation of any visible blood should be noted. Photographs should be taken, including rulers showing the height and distance of all bloodstains, and a diagram drawn. Bloodstain pattern details may portray the choreography of the crime.

The position and location of the deceased animal may tell much about her death. A painful or frightened animal may seek shelter and be found hidden in a small space, huddled under a bed or in a doghouse. A long trail of smeared blood or blood drops may indicate a slow death and lead to the original scene of the crime. Upturned earth or disturbed furniture may indicate a struggle as the animal was dying. Voided feces and urine, especially when slung in a wide circle, are signs that the animal was extremely fearful and trying to get away. Material found under the claws or nails of an animal may yield clues about the events of the last few moments of the animal's life. Cats are likely to have scratched their attacker if possible, and close examination of their claws may yield material suitable for DNA analysis or contain fibers that link a suspect to the crime.

Consider the example of a dog hung by his owner over a balcony against the wall of a building, suspended by a chain attached to the dog's collar. Although the dog may be dead and his body retrieved by his owner before investigators arrive, the red paint embedded beneath his toenails matches the deep scratches in the wall against which his body swung in his death struggle. It also corroborates the story told by eyewitnesses and helps document the slow and inhumane nature of the animal's death. Should investigators not notice the paint and fail to carefully photograph its source while examining the scene of the crime, a significant and convincing aspect of this criminal story could be lost. Alternatively, the veterinary exam could reveal the paint and direct investigators to go back and retrieve paint samples to be presented in court.

The presence and degree of rigor mortis of the body(ies) should be noted at the scene as well as the presence and pattern of livor mortis (see chapter 8). If a body has been mutilated, the proximity (or absence) of the severed body parts should be noted, and body parts should be measured and photographed. The rectal or liver temperature of the body should be determined, as should the temperature of the soil or ground surface at various points beneath the body. Samples of urine, feces, vomitus, or other bodily fluids found on or near the victim should be obtained and carefully preserved. Any entomological evidence present on or near the body should be collected. Such specimens should be designated as having been collected from three different areas: on the body, directly under or in close proximity to the body (three feet or less), or from the surrounding area (up to twenty feet from the body). A more extensive description of methods for collecting entomological evidence, including a death scene case study form, is available in Haskell and Williams (1990). The air temperature, wind velocity and direction, and relative humidity at the scene or at the nearest weather station will be necessary in the analysis of entomological evidence and should be obtained. Such data will also be necessary in cases of death by exposure to extremes of weather.

The area immediately surrounding the body should then be examined. There are various methods by which crime scenes are searched (Eliopulos 1993).

The sector or zone search is used primarily when there are no more than a few rooms to be searched. The entire sector is searched by one person and then, ideally, by a second person.

In the ever-widening circle search, the searcher begins at the center of an area (the center usually being the body of a victim) and searches in ever-widening circles for evidence. Ideally, a second investigator repeats this method.

The straight line search is usually used for large outdoor scenes. A number of people stand side by side and advance in a line. Each person is responsible for searching only the width of his area.

When only one or a few people are available to search a large area, the strip search method is employed. Searchers search a small strip (usually their arms' width) for a short distance, then turn and search the same width in the opposite direction, resulting in a search of short, parallel strips of area. In a grid search, one searcher searches an area in parallel strips, then the same searcher or another searcher searches the same area in parallel strips that run perpendicular to the original searcher's direction of search.

At assault scenes, careful search may reveal bloodstain or arson evidence, projectile damage to walls or other surrounding structures, or signs of a struggle such as broken items or disturbed earth. At scenes of criminal animal neglect, the investigator should note the absence or presence and quality of food and water (samples should be taken of both); the presence and suitability of shelter; the presence or evidence of insects and vermin such as flies, maggots, mosquitoes, spiders (often attracted to fly-infested areas), rats, and mice; and the presence or absence of organic material (decomposing food or deceased animals, feces, garbage, urine). Hazardous conditions caused by weather should be noted; for example, unshoveled snowfall, or standing water or mud. If ambient temperature and humidity are thought to have contributed to the animal's injuries or death, current weather conditions as well as weather conditions for the preceding thirty to sixty days should be determined. It may be advisable to remain at the scene of the crime throughout the time of day the animal's death was thought to occur to determine how weather conditions might have affected the victim. For example, a dog may have what appears to be adequate shelter from the sun on a hot day, but observation of the angle of the sun throughout the day may indicate that there is a significant time during which the existing shelter offered the animal inadequate shade.

The hazards presented by other debris, such as falling fences, dilapidated buildings, rusting automobiles, discarded auto tires, and improperly stored or leaking chemicals or pesticides, should be assessed, documented, and photographed.

The scene of the crime should also be examined to determine who might have had access to or visual contact with a victim. If an animal is assaulted within a home, the assault must have involved either a member of the household or someone who had access to the home. If there is no suspect within the household, investigators must determine how someone else might have gained access. Doors and windows are examined for signs of entry. Neighbors or others who might have had visual access to the scene (such as a mail carrier) at the estimated time of the incident should be interviewed.

Victims of animal assault are often targets because they are left unsupervised, either tied or fenced in a yard or allowed to roam freely. Free-roaming animals are at greatest risk, for their mere presence or actions, albeit normal for the animal, may offend neighbors and instigate an assault on them. Cats seem to be the most common victims of such attacks, although dogs also suffer. When such an assault occurs on the owner's property, investigators should evaluate possible routes of access to the animal. For example, could antifreeze-laced hamburger meat have been tossed over a backyard fence? Could it have been done without any of the neighbors having seen the act? Would it be possible for someone to shoot an animal with a rifle in the middle of the day? Who might have heard the rifle shot? If there appears to be no easy access to the animal, investigators must look for a site in the fence or on the property at which someone might have gained access (by picking the lock on a rear gate, for example).

In the case of projectile injuries, investigators will want to attempt to reconstruct the trajectory of the projectile(s) while the victim is still in place. In cases where the victim died quickly, it may be possible to determine from which direction the animal was struck and to then evaluate the access the assailant had to the victim from that direction. In some cases, this information leads investigators directly to a suspect. If an arrow shot through a dog lying in his own backyard could only have come from the neighbor's raised backyard deck, for example, then the field of possible assailants is narrowed to those who have access to that deck. If a witness states that the teenage son of that neighbor was seen conducting archery practice from the deck at or around the time of suspected death of the animal, then the reconstruction exercise has identified a likely suspect.

As with any crime scene investigation, footprint evidence may prove useful. Samples of the type of earth, landscape material or flooring (carpet fibers, for example) should be taken and compared to the footwear of a suspect, if and when one is identified. Debris carried to the crime scene by the footwear of an assailant can also be a unique clue.

The scene should be searched for the presence of weapons. Projectiles found in the animal, such as bullets, air pellets, or arrows, will be removed during the forensic examination. But others may be found in fences, trees, walls, and surrounding structures, even in the earth beneath the animal. These projectiles may provide the best clue to the assailant's route of access to the animal, since the victim may have walked around or moved about after having been shot, thereby obscuring the evidence of the projectile's trajectory.

The crime scene should be examined for any signs of attempts to hide the evidence of a crime. Tools used during the perpetration of a crime, such as a knife or gun, a container of gasoline and box of matches, or a length of rope, may have been discarded hastily into a nearby trash container, deep foliage, or a sewer drain. The assailant may have cleaned up blood and other organic matter, perhaps leaving bloodstained cleaning supplies or clothing in a sink, laundry area, or trash can. Just as in the movies, crime scene investigators can use a variety of substances—the most popular of which is the chemical reagent luminol—to detect telltale traces of blood, even when an attempt has been made to clean it from floor and wall surfaces, clothing, and other items at the scene.

Some evidence may be left in plain sight because the assailant believes there will be no way to prove it was used as a tool in the crime. For example, an assailant may believe there is no need to hide a baseball bat used to beat an animal to death, simply because there is a legitimate and noncriminal reason to own a baseball bat, and many people own one like his. He does not realize that evidence of a crime can be both identified and individualized. A veterinary examiner may be able to identify a wound on a victim as having been inflicted with a baseball bat, based on the size and shape of the impression. With the help of other forensic specialists, it may also be possible to determine that the wound could only have come from the specific bat found in the home of the assailant, a process called individualization. Individualization is made possible by the fact that no two things in the universe are *exactly* the same (Nickell and Fischer 1999). Any item has unique characteristics, the result of the manner of construction or manufacture and the wear and tear an item has experienced. There may be characteristics (such as a fleck of aluminum, a chip of paint, or a divot in the pattern of the wound) that individualize the weapon used to create the wound, diminishing or eliminating the possibility that any other baseball bat— even one that is the same model and color—could have been used as the weapon of assault. Understanding the process of identification and individualization allows crime scene investigators to avoid the mistake of ruling out obvious evidence present at the scene, based on the false assumption that it could never be conclusively linked to the crime.

The scene of the crime may yield important clues about the time frame of the incident. Body temperature, rigor mortis, environmental conditions, and entomological evidence, as discussed above, may prove valuable indicators of the chronological sequence of events. Other items of evidence may also help. Newspapers and postmarked mail are often useful because they indicate the most recent date on which an event may have occurred. For example, a deceased animal wrapped in a very bloody newspaper could not have been killed before the date on which the paper was published; any veterinarian could confidently testify in court that the fluidity of the blood is quickly quelled by the clotting cascade, so that unless the animal suffered from an inherited or acquired disorder of the clotting cascade, the body is unlikely to bleed profusely even a few hours after death. If an animal were wrapped in a bloodied newspaper, the animal must have been killed on or after the date of that paper's publication.

Newspapers and mail may also suggest the last date on which an owner visited an abandoned animal. Pet animals are too often abandoned in vacated homes and apartments by owners who intend to continue providing care for them and to retrieve them eventually. When the owner visits the animal to provide care, she is likely to pick up any mail or newspapers that have been delivered to the residence. The postmark of mail left in the box may suggest the date of an owner's last visit and, therefore, the date on which the animal was finally abandoned. Conversely, when investigators try to determine the most recent date on which abandoned animals have received care, the date on a recent newspaper used to cover the floor or line a cage proves that care was provided at least as recently as that date.

Before leaving the scene of the crime, investigators should write down license tags of vehicles in the area. As in crimes involving human victims, they should canvass the neighborhood, carefully documenting all interviews and establishing rapport with any persons who have been interviewed by leaving a name and number to be contacted should any further information become available. Investigators should consult with the prosecuting attorney(s) and veterinary examiner before releasing the scene.

The chain of evidence must be carefully preserved (see chapter 5). Ideally, one person is responsible for removing and recording evidence, precluding the necessity for evidence to be introduced in court by a long list of persons. At the least, the chain of custody should be minimized to the degree possible. A receipt for the evidence removed should be left by the investigating officer with the resident or owner at the scene or in a conspicuous place. This receipt should list the complete description, date, time, location of recovery, and by whom the evidence was recovered. The exact location in which each item was found should be recorded, as should its relationship to the incident. The investigator should specify whether a search warrant was used, giving details about how evidence was collected if a warrant was not issued.

Drawings, diagrams, and sketches of crime scenes are used to augment those areas in which a photograph is lacking. Specifically, a drawing is used to depict the relationship between certain items at the scene, without necessarily showing all of the details present in a photograph (Eliopulos 1993). A drawing should assist in presenting and clarifying investigative data (Figure 6.1). In addition to being presented in the courtroom, a drawing can be used while questioning persons in conjunction with the investigation and to supplement, clarify, and understand the prepared report of the investigation. The drawing may be made by a witness, an investigator, or some other person (perhaps by a neighbor familiar with the residence where an incident occurred), but it must be part of some qualified person's testimony to be admissible in court. Both rough sketches and finer drawings may be made. Rough sketches should be preserved and presented to the court, along with final drawings, in case the court seeks to determine whether there are any discrepancies between the two.

When making drawings, investigators use two general measurement techniques. With the coordinate method, the artist indicates the distance of each item from two fixed reference points, usually the walls of a room. For example, "the roll of duct tape was located 2 feet from the south wall of the room and 3.5 feet from the west wall." Using the triangulation method, a single reference point is chosen (such as the head or the body of the victim), and the distance from that point to another item or feature of the scene is noted. For example, the distance and direction from the victim's head to a knife is noted. The triangulation method is used more commonly outdoors, where there may be no walls from which to measure the distance to objects.

Figure 6.1—Sample Crime Scene Diagram

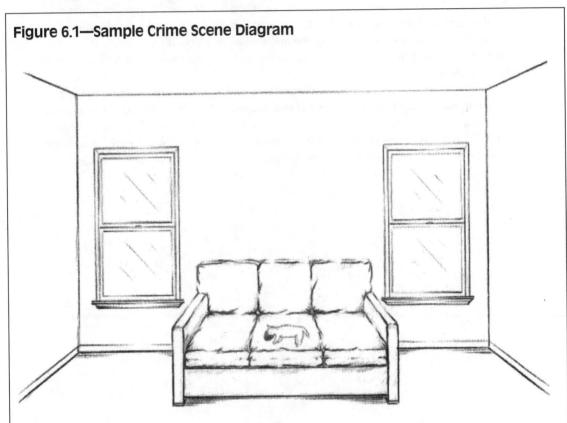

This is a diagram of a kitten who was found unconscious on the sofa one morning. The owner believed the cat had been attacked by the resident dog. The veterinary exam did not reveal any evidence that the kitten had been attacked by a dog. The kitten has blood coming from his mouth and nose and was comatose. The kitten eventually died. Necropsy findings revealed unilateral lung and kidney contusions and cerebral hemorrhage. At the home there was no blood trail or spatter; the only blood was pooled around the kitten's head. The kitten's location is unusual—an injured animal will crawl under or inside something to hide. Consider the following: the lack of blood at the scene, the absence of evidence of a dog attack, the findings of blunt force trauma to the head, chest, and abdomen and the fact that the severity of the kitten's injuries would have rapidly rendered him unable to ambulate. The first conclusion is that there is no supporting evidence of a dog attack. The second is that the kitten suffered from blunt force trauma to the head and body from a human action. Lastly, where the kitten was found was where he landed after the blunt force trauma events, possibly after being thrown against the wall.

In addition to using one of the measurement techniques mentioned above, each drawing must incorporate one of three views: a bird's-eye view, an exploded view, or a three-dimensional view. A bird's-eye, or floor plan, view is the one most commonly used. An exploded view is one in which the floor of a room is depicted, surrounded by the walls and ceiling, laid out flat. This type of view is used when investigators wish to show objects or evidence found on the walls or ceiling, such as blood splatters. Three-dimensional views are the most difficult to create, but they are useful when investigators wish to supplement photographs taken of the scene, assist witnesses in providing clear testimony, or represent the relative positions of critical evidence in a three-dimensional manner.

Any drawings used to depict the crime scene should include the artist's full name; the date, time, and case number of the crime; the full name of any person who assisted in taking measurements; the address of the crime scene, its position within a building (e.g., "sketch represents the downstairs bathroom of the address given"), and any landmarks for the scene and compass direction; the scale of the drawing if a scale has been used or a disclaimer if one has not been used; the major items of physical evidence and the measurements involving those items; and a legend or key to any symbols or abbreviations used in the drawing.

Although this text provides an introductory overview of the topic, further reading of cited references should prove both useful and interesting to those veterinarians who assist with investigation of animal-cruelty cases. An excellent free resource for all professionals involved in investigating crimes is *Crime Scene Investigation: A Guide for Law Enforcement* (2001), available on-line from the Office of Justice Publications at *www.ncjrs.org*.

Examination of the Surviving Victim

The examination of surviving victims of cruelty to animals can often be heart-wrenching. Depending on the nature and severity of the assault, veterinarians may have to deal with not only the animal's pain and suffering but also their own discomfort and distress. Rendering aid and pain relief to a suffering animal is, of course, the first priority. However, every effort should be made to collect any evidence as soon as possible and not ruin it with treatment. As veterinarians proceed with a case, they must keep in mind that to address the situation legally, they must handle the patient and the records in a manner that preserves the forensic evidence so that it may be presented in a court of law. Thorough and careful examination of all veterinary patients is a cornerstone of good medicine, but examination of a victim of cruelty to animals consists of more than just a good physical examination. Surviving victims can be difficult to examine, because in many cases they are fractious due to pain, psychological trauma, poor socialization, or feral nature. Since the condition of a surviving victim changes over time, either healing or deteriorating, those changes must be documented as well as the initial condition in which the animal was presented.

Before examining a surviving victim, the veterinarian should consider the safety risks to himself and those working with him. Zoonotic risks are the same as those encountered by those performing veterinary work in other arenas, although the risk may be more significant when dealing with animal-cruelty victims. The greatest risk is that of being bitten or scratched by an animal who is fearful, painful, or unsocialized to handling, as animal-cruelty victims often are. Animals associated with neglect or hoarding cases are often unsocialized. Ideally, persons handling animals associated with such an investigation should be knowledgeable about handling fractious, feral, and unsocialized animals and have available—and know how to use—specialized equipment for handling such animals. Chemical restraint should be used when necessary, although it may compromise the condition of the animal being examined, and the need for such restraint should be carefully documented. Rabies exposure is a real threat in many animal-cruelty situations, and people involved in examination of the victims should have received pre-exposure vaccination.

Sarcoptic mange and ringworm are the next most likely zoonotic risks associated with surviving victims. Good personal hygiene (frequent hand washing) and protective clothing can reduce the likelihood of exposure, but they are not always possible or completely protective. Fleas and ticks can be transmitted, causing dermatitis and discomfort and transmitting plague (in the southwestern United States) and Lyme disease. Handling flea-infested kittens may expose the handler to cat-scratch disease (*Bartonella henselae*). Leptospirosis can also be a threat, especially to those who must go into buildings or enclosures contaminated by dog and rat urine.

Psittacosis and histoplasmosis can be a concern for those involved in confiscating birds who are surviving victims of cruelty to animals. Sometimes zoonotic risks are unforeseen:

one California animal protection organization confiscated a herd of goats that was being neglected by a local goat breeder only to have several staff members contract listeriosis ("Q fever") from handling and caring for the goats and their offspring.

Examination of the Victim

The veterinarian should begin by carefully determining the animal's species, sex, breed type, estimated age, color and coat pattern, and unique physical markings. Unless there is documentation to verify the animal's age and purebred status, records should indicate that the age documented for the animal is estimated and the breed is a "breed type." While such information is seemingly trivial, a defense attorney can attempt to use the variable nature of age and breed determination to attempt to discount a veterinarian's credibility to the judge and/or jury.

An identity is created for an animal by recording her characteristics and assigning to the animal both a case number and an individual number. Photographs of the animal, accompanied by a card on which the date, the case number, and an individual identification number assigned to that particular animal are legibly written, create an identity that should accompany the animal throughout the confiscation and examination process.

A victim who cannot be handled due to an aggressive or unsocialized nature should be described, photographed, and examined to the extent possible. Body weight can be determined by transferring the animal into an enclosure created around a weight scale or by transferring her into a container of known weight, such as a humane trap or transfer cage.

Veterinarians should be aware of their personal approach to physical examination and how they developed it. They should be prepared to explain to a judge or jury how they goes about performing a physical examination ("Regardless of the site of the injury or lesion, I always examine the patient from nose to tail, noting any additional abnormalities as well as the obvious injury or lesion. The body can be divided into eight body systems [digestive, respiratory, urogenital, musculoskeletal, cardiovascular, endocrine, neurologic, and integumentary], and I record my findings according to those eight systems"). Although it is likely that veterinarians will need to be more meticulous than usual, they should not adopt an entirely new physical examination method for examining a cruelty victim. They are likely to miss lesions that they would not otherwise and may not be able to assure a judge or jury that they examined the animal in a manner with which they were familiar. One of the best ways to prepare to evaluate a victim of cruelty to animals properly is to use good examination and record-keeping techniques for all patients.

When veterinarians provide emergency care to a victim, they collect and preserve evidence as they proceed. If possible, the animal should be weighed and her degree of dehydration assessed before providing water, or at the least the amount of water provided should be measured. Feces, urine, blood, and vomitus should be collected as early as possible during the course of treatment. If hair must be shaved from around a wound, it should be preserved for careful examination once the animal is stabilized rather than discarded, since it may contain trace evidence such as gunshot residue or tool or weapon fragments. A photographer should be available to take photographs at veterinarians' direction as they proceed to examine and provide care for the animal.

Animal abusers, unfortunately, are often creative in formulating their attack on an animal, and multiple causes of injury must be considered when evaluating a victim. In chapter 11 is a case in which a spurned boyfriend burned his former companion's two cats in her microwave oven. Before this assault, he had administered acetaminophen to them. It is not uncommon for an animal to be beaten, strangled, or shot before he is set afire. Animal victims have often been abused over an extended period of time. Full-body radiographs should be taken, regardless of the presenting injury, to look for evidence of past abuse. Multiple forms of trauma and injury must be considered and veterinarians' examination of the animal's injuries must always look for more than what meets the eye.

The Condition of a Surviving Victim

Whenever possible, accepted scales and scoring systems should be used to describe the extent of an animal's abnormalities. Examples of such scoring systems include those typically used to characterize heart murmurs, body condition, degree of dehydration, and fractures of growing bones.

Heart murmurs should be graded as I through VI and described as systolic, diastolic, or continuous. If possible, they should be localized to a specific anatomical area and described by their configuration: plateau, crescendo-decrescendo, or decrescendo (Smith and Hamlin 2000). The record should include a list of differential diagnoses for the type of murmur identified as well a list of those steps necessary to further characterize the animal's cardiac condition (chest radiography, electrocardiogram [ECG], echocardiography).

Most published body condition scoring systems for dogs and cats (Scarlett et al. 1994; Laflamme 1997a,b) are designed to characterize obesity in pet animals. A scale designed specifically to evaluate suspected starvation in neglected dogs (Patronek 1997) (appendix C) has been widely used in courtroom presentations involving dogs. Most leading pet food companies, including Hill's Pet Nutrition, Purina, and Iams, have developed canine and feline body scoring systems to allow veterinarians and pet owners to systematically assess and describe body conditions. Some employ a five-point scale, others a nine-point scale. Any of these systems may be employed, as long as they are used consistently throughout the treatment and recovery of all animals in the case.

Body condition scoring systems for large animals—horses and cattle—have long been available and are appropriate for characterizing emaciation and starvation in these animals. More information on emaciation and starvation is provided in chapter 16.

Any specific lesions present on a victim should be carefully described. The size and depth of the lesion should be determined and noted, using calipers and/or a medical evidence rule. A photo evidence scale should be included in a photograph of a lesion to provide a permanent record of the dimensions of the lesion. Subsequent measurements of a lesion will help to characterize the lesion's severity and the timeline of healing.

Diagrams and outlines that document the location and size of lesions are extremely useful. It is not necessary to create a diagram or recording system from scratch; veterinary medical stationery suppliers sell forms and medical records stickers designed to make the task of documenting the location, nature, and size of a lesion easier, and these products can easily and significantly improve the quality of information recorded by veterinarians who are examining an animal-cruelty victim. Excellent sample forms for recording the results of physical examination of living or dead animals are shown in Miller and Zawistowski (2004) and may be obtained directly from the ASPCA (New York, New York).

Specific characteristics of any lesion should be carefully documented. Is there fresh blood evident on the lesion's margins? Purulent material? Granulation tissue and contraction? Entomological evidence? Gunpowder or any evidence of burning that would indicate gunshot? Foreign material in the wound?

Care should be taken to identify and remove any evidence that might be traced back to the perpetrator. Obvious examples of this are projectiles, such as arrows and bullets, and bindings, such as rope or duct tape. Less obvious might be hair, blood, glass, or clothing fibers belonging to the perpetrator. Materials poured or splashed on the victim, such as lye, gasoline, or paint, should be carefully sampled and preserved for further analysis by a crime lab, which may be able to match them to their source.

Bone fractures have many characteristics that should be considered and documented. Is the fracture closed (no skin breakage) or open (more likely to be contaminated, infected, and further injured)? Is the fracture complete (total disruption of the bone, usually accompanied by marked displacement) or hairline? Is the bone stable or unstable (displaced)? How long ago did the fracture occur?

Are there any clinical signs associated with the fracture? These may include pain or localized tenderness, abnormal angulation of the limb, abnormal gait or loss of function (either non-weight-bearing lameness or inability to use the limb due to pain or loss of functional anatomy), or local swelling (this may appear almost immediately or be delayed for up to ten days due to disturbed blood and lymph flow) (Brinker, Piermattei, and Flo 2000). If the fracture involves a growth plate in a young animal, the fracture should be classified anatomically according to the Salter-Harris system, which classifies separations or fracture-separations involving a growth plate and the adjacent metaphysis and epiphysis. Older fractures may show evidence of healing or callus formation; poor healing may result in a limb malformation that should be carefully described and documented. The age of the fractures should be estimated based on all the exam findings.

Laboratory Tests

Laboratory testing can provide significant useful information to characterize the physical condition of an animal-cruelty victim. Several factors determine whether and which laboratory tests are performed. Availability of samples is one: it may be difficult and dangerous to obtain a blood sample from an unsocialized or fractious animal or one whose condition is so fragile that the stress of restraint may lead to death. Financial considerations may also come into play; while some laboratory tests can be performed easily with a minimum of equipment (such as a fecal flotation to examine a patient for the presence of the eggs of intestinal worms), others (such as a serum biochemistry profile) are more costly. The costs of laboratory tests can usually be covered by the investigative unit, other humane organizations, or special funds. Regardless, any tests that can help in the investigation or the treatment of the animal should be conducted. Which particular tests are performed on a victim depends on the nature of the injury or illness with which the animal is affected. The heartworm status of a dog who has been set on fire is not necessarily pertinent information to identifying the perpetrator and prosecuting the crime, unless the perpetrator is also the dog's owner and neglect has also been alleged.

In multiple-victim cases, finances may not allow extensive sampling and testing of scores or hundreds of victims, although extensive laboratory evaluation of the victims in the worst condition is useful. If only a few animals can be evaluated in detail, it is also important to examine one or more of the healthiest animals found at the scene. Such information can demonstrate the level of care that could have been provided to the animals in the worst condition and might strengthen the argument the the condition of the worst animals was the consequence of a willful act.

In cases of neglect, a minimum analysis should consist of a fecal flotation, determination of packed cell volume and serum total protein value, urinalysis, and a skin scraping of those animals with dermatitis suggestive of external parasitism. These tests require a minimum of analytical equipment (microscope, hematocrit centrifuge, refractometer), yet provide a significant amount of information about the animal's health status when coupled with physical examination findings. A Woods light should also be used for a basic analysis of skin lesions, particularly to screen for ringworm, which is important to note for purposes of documenting the animal's condition, but also to be alert for possible zoonotic conditions that may be transferred to staff handling the animals. (Wood's light screening alone is limited in its effectiveness and is not a definitive diagnostic test.)

One doesn't often think of entomological evidence associated with surviving victims of cruelty to animals, but maggot infestation is a common component of injuries, especially in warmer climates or seasons. Collection and analysis of fly larvae or pupae associated with an injury caused by trauma or neglect can help to provide a timeline for the presence of that injury and attest to the length of suffering.

Evaluation of the Surviving Animal: Behavior

Forensic evaluation of animal behavior has been important in the development of cases in which the animals have been alleged to be agents or instruments in the commission of a crime. This has generally been limited to fatal or severe dog attacks that have resulted in charges of assault or manslaughter against the animals' owners (Borchelt et al. 1983; Wright and Lockwood 1987). However, thus far, behavioral studies have rarely been used as part of the assessment of animals who are the *victims* of abuse or neglect.

Behavioral assessment of animals who have been the victims of cruelty can serve several purposes. First, such an evaluation helps to provide an overall picture of the animal's health, with an emphasis on determining behavioral health, rather than the presence of a specific behavior problem (Hetts and Estep 2000, 2002). Such an assessment can be helpful in evaluating the consistency of accounts explaining the animal's injuries. For example, an allegation that a dog was struck or kicked because she responded aggressively when gently petted would be called into question if the animal responded nonaggressively to handling by a variety of people. Evidence that an animal can be easily handled and groomed would strengthen the argument that a matted and unkempt coat was the result of neglect rather than of the owner's inability to restrain the animal.

Second, such an assessment can help evaluate the likelihood that the animal will be able to recover behaviorally, as well as physically, from the effects of abuse. This may be necessary in cases where many animals have been seized from an animal hoarder, puppy mill, or dogfighting situation. If suitable housing for the animals is limited, behavioral assessment may need to be part of the triage procedure for deciding which animals would benefit most from limited resources to attempt to rehabilitate and rehome them.

Several authors have proposed consistent approaches for trying to assess and document the behavioral health of dogs. Overall (1997) provides a comprehensive client questionnaire used in a behavioral clinic that can serve a template for documenting a general behavioral profile for dogs and cats as well as a canine aggression screen, which notes the response of dogs to common situations that might elicit aggression. Van der Borg, Neto, and Planta (1991); Hetts and Estep (2000); and Sternberg (2002) provide descriptions of systematic procedures to be used to assess the behavior of dogs in an animal shelter.

These approaches evaluate the dog's response to common situations that are likely to occur in the life of a companion animal, such as encounters with a variety of strangers, novel objects, auditory stimuli, and other animals. A similar approach is used by the American Kennel Club in its Canine Good Citizen Test (described at *www.akc.org*) and the Temperament Test of the American Temperament Test Society Inc. (*www.atts.org*).

It should be noted that, in general, behavioral assessment cannot be used to prove or disprove the allegation that the irregularities in an animal's behavior (such as unusual fear or aggression) are the result of abuse, nor can such an assessment conclusively demonstrate that an animal's response to a particular individual or class of individuals proves or disproves that the animal was victimized by such a person. There is a strong tendency for people to attribute fear or aggression in dogs and cats to earlier abuse, particularly in animals obtained from shelters, whose early experiences are unknown. Dogs who are timid or "hand-shy" or who display defensive threats to certain people (e.g., men with beards) are routinely characterized as having suffered from abuse. People may be inclined to make such attributions because they give their companion animals a history, even if it is incorrect. They also reinforce their feeling that they have "rescued" their pet and provide a ready excuse for failing to correct problem behaviors (Lockwood 1997).

Although dogs, cats, and other animals can exhibit long-standing behavioral changes as a consequence of physical or psychological trauma, these reactions show a high degree of individual variation. Animals vary widely in their resiliency or sensitivity to stressful or traumatic situations. The kinds of behaviors we might associate with such trauma, such as fearful or aggressive behavior, can be the end result of many different factors, including genetic variation in temperament (Murphree, Dykman, and Peters 1967), social isolation (Melzack 1968), degree of socialization to a variety of people and animals, physical health and maturity, conditioned fears, accidents, or intentional abuse.

Few studies have attempted to systematically characterize behavioral differences between animals who experienced cruelty and those who had not. Marder and Engle (1998) looked at a small sample (N = 17) of dogs seized by the ASPCA's Humane Law Enforcement (HLE) Division for reasons of physical abuse, neglect, or abandonment. These HLE dogs were compared with eighteen owner-relinquished (OR) dogs on ninety different scores in response to situations such as novel objects and environments, friendly and threatening approaches by men and women, and interactions with other dogs and cats. There were few consistent differences. Both groups were likely to show signs of fear in some situations, with no consistent pattern. HLE dogs were more likely to show fearful responses to petting or reprimand, OR dogs showed more fear of an opening umbrella or when brushed. There was a slight but statistically insignificant tendency for more HLE dogs to exhibit aggression when threatened and to show distress when left alone.

An animal's behavior alone cannot prove that he has been abused or, if so, by whom. The friendly reception given by a dog to the animal's allegedly abusive owner does not demonstrate that the abuse did not occur. An animal's fear of or threats to a particular person do not prove a history of traumatic encounters. However, accurate descriptions of an animal's response to a variety of people and situations can still be an important component of the complete description of the physical and behavioral health of an animal who has survived abuse or neglect.

Euthanasia

In many states existing laws allow veterinarians to determine on behalf of law enforcement authorities that euthanasia is the most humane alternative for an animal-cruelty victim, and such euthanasia may take place before any hearing on the animal-cruelty charges has taken place. A good example of this is a burn victim who is severely injured but still clinging to life. Although supportive treatment could be offered, veterinarians could also offer the opinion that such treatment will prolong, but not save, the animal's life. There is ample evidence in the veterinary literature to support a poor prognosis for animals who are the victims of smoke inhalation or extensive burns. Similarly, veterinarians may opine that an animal's life could be saved but that he would suffer prolonged or chronic pain as a result of the assault or neglect. These victims should be identified, photographed, and examined to the extent that doing so is possible without significantly compounding their suffering. After euthanasia is performed, a complete and thorough necropsy should be performed and documented, as described in the next chapter. The examining veterinarian should be careful to list the cause of death in such cases as euthanasia, rather than the illness or injury the animal suffered that led to a decision to perform euthanasia.

It is not unusual for animal-cruelty victims to die after confiscation due to the severity of their injuries or the chronic nature of their illnesses, often compounded by the stress of confiscation, which is particularly significant for poorly socialized animals. Pregnant animals may abort their offspring, and mothers with newborns may neglect or even cannibalize them in response to the stress of confiscation, examination, and relocation. Careful documentation of the condition of victims before and after death is necessary to present the findings to the court.

Documentation of the Survivor's Examination

Like most other aspects of veterinary medicine, evaluation of a victim is an organic process, one that grows and changes over time. Completion of the initial physical examination of a victim is by no means the end of the process. Results of laboratory tests are often not available for a few hours to a few weeks after the animal is examined, and illnesses and injuries will change in character over time. Serial examination of alleged victims is often useful to prosecution of the case, especially in those cases (such as starvation or a burn injury) in which the progression of the injury or disease provides additional information about its nature and the timeline of infliction. However, time is often of the essence to successful investigation and prosecution of animal-cruelty cases. The results of initial examination of a suspected victim may be used to convince a judge to sign a confiscation order that allows other victims to be rescued in a timely manner. Results also may allow for confiscation of other evidence related to the case before it can be altered or destroyed or for the timely arrest of a suspect who might not otherwise be apprehended.

One method for dealing with the serial nature of the results of examination of an animal-cruelty victim is to issue a preliminary report or even a series of such reports. In a preliminary report, it is important to include only confirmed findings. It will be difficult to explain any retractions in a final report without providing a valid reason. When no further information related to the case can be obtained from the victim or from specimens or samples taken from the victim, a final report can be issued.

It is appropriate to use technical language and concepts to record findings when evaluating an animal-cruelty victim. While some would suggest that, because the record of a forensic examination is intended to be used as evidence in a court of law, it should be written in a form that does not embrace medical-ese, the reason veterinarians and other physicians use such terminology is that it provides a more accurate and descriptive form for communicating the characteristics of lesions or disease. Veterinarians should use proper veterinary terminology to describe the abnormalities they detect on physical examination as well as the treatment they provide for a victim. An additional, plain language description of the findings can be included in the summary of the examination/necropsy report. Testifying veterinarians will also, of course, have the opportunity to explain their findings in plain language, and to explain the background of any scales or scoring systems used to create an objective record of the animal's condition, in court.

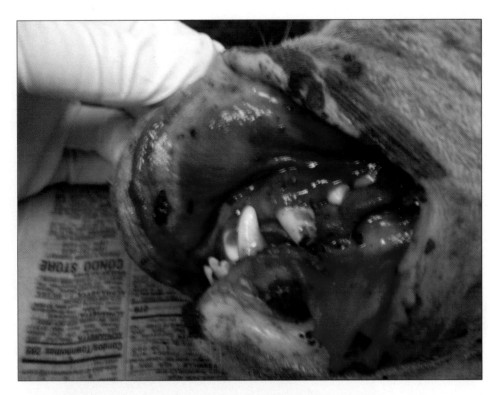

Plates 1A and 1B—Lividity present on the buccal mucosa (above) and the inner surface of the ear (below) of a dog

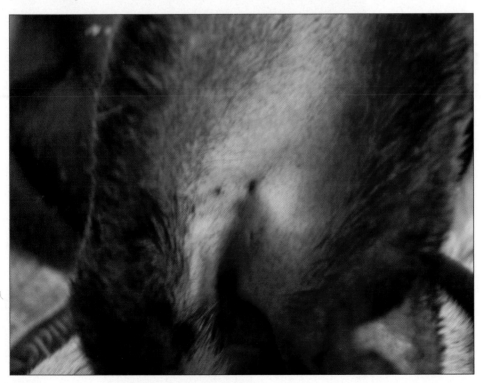

Plates 2A and 2B—Maggot eggs on a dog (above) and maggot larvae on a cat (below)

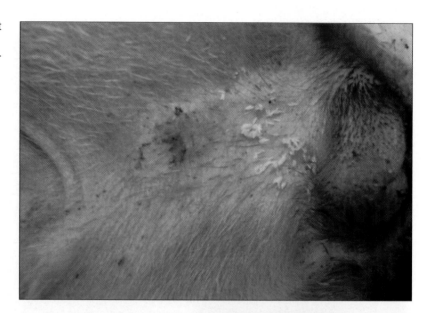

Plate 3—Tissue sloughing off a kitten's ears one week after he had been placed in a microwave oven for an unknown period of time

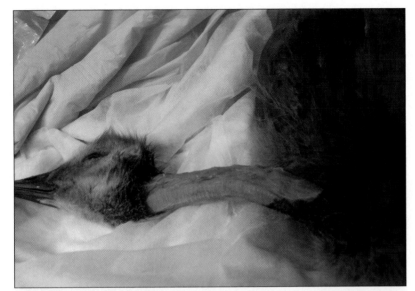

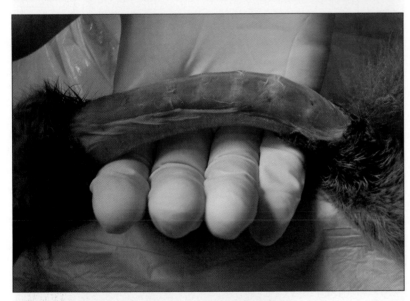

Plates 4A and 4B—A gosling who had been picked up by the neck and thrown into a lake. The skin was missing 360 degrees from around the neck, with irregular tears proximal and ventral to the wound

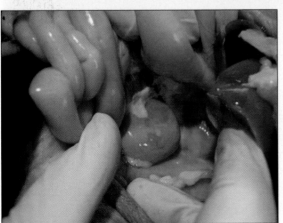

Plate 5—Bruising on a kidney due to blunt force trauma in a puppy

Plate 6—A contusion in the lung of a kitten due to blunt force trauma

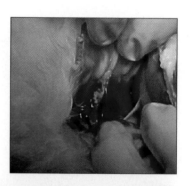

Plate 7—A dog beaten with a belt and hit with bricks. Bruises are visible after shaving the fur on the right lateral mandible and ventral mandible

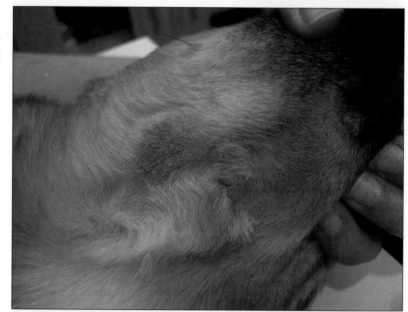

Plate 8—Old bruises turning brown, as seen in a cat

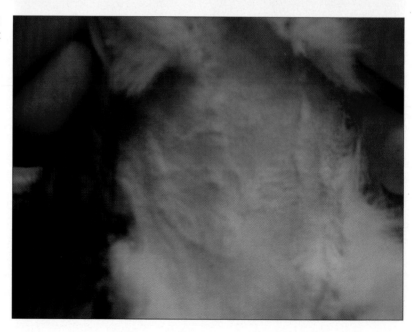

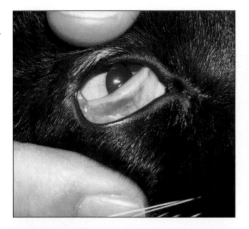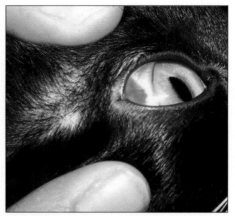

Plates 9A and 9B—Bruising of the third eyelid and conjunctiva (left) and scleral hemorrhage (right) in a cat due to blunt force head trauma

Plate 10—Petechial hemorrhages of right pinna (ear) of a cat caused by blunt force trauma to the head

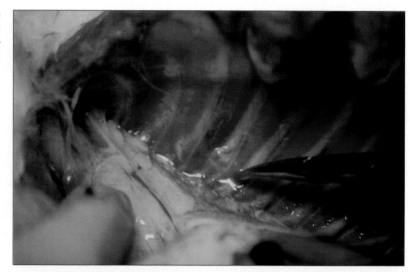

Plate 11—Older, healing rib fractures in a kitten who had been repeatedly physically abused

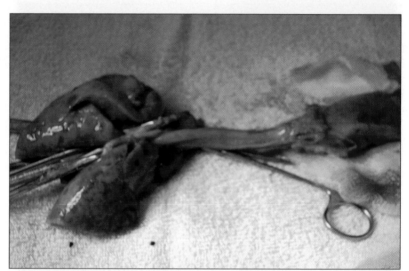

Plate 12—Removal of lungs, trachea, and tongue of a dog, for investigation of asphyxiation

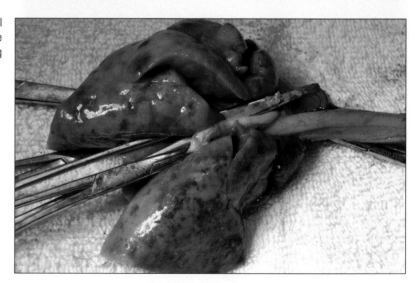

Plate 13—Petechial hemorrhages on the lung of a dog

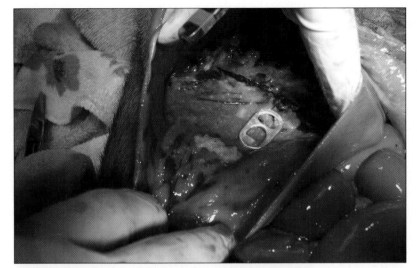

Plate 14—The stomach contents of a dog who died due to starvation. The dog had eaten a metal pull tab from a can, pieces of plastic and wood, and leaves. The interior lining of the stomach shows ulcerations, which can occur with starvation.

Plates 15A and 15B—A five-month-old puppy suffering from starvation

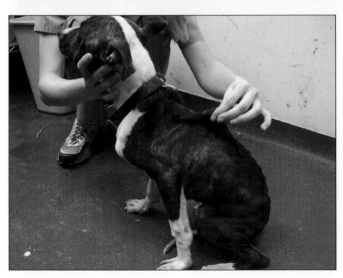

Plate 16—Bruising around the vulva and abrasions of the vulvar folds in a dog who was sexually assaulted. The bruising pattern around the anus is due to subcutaneous bleeding from coccygeal vertebra separation. The anal tissue is normal.

Plate 17—Bruising around the anus of a dog. Where there is proximal injury to the tail, such as separation of the coccygeal vertebrae, bleeding from the injury may dissect under the skin and around the anus. This bruising pattern does not necessarily indicate trauma to the anus or sexual assault.

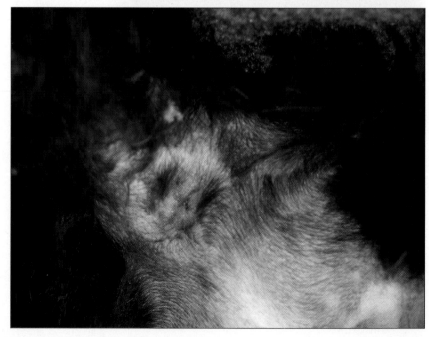

8 Examination of the Deceased Victim

O nce the crime scene (if there is one) has been examined and photographed (see chapter 5), the veterinarian's attention should turn to examining the body of the victim. The following steps in the examination of the deceased victim will not necessarily be undertaken in the order presented here, but they should all be considered in the process. Some steps may have one or more parts, each of which may be performed at a different place (e.g., the crime scene, the veterinary hospital, or the laboratory) and time. This chapter focuses primarily on the necropsy of small mammals (dogs, cats, and the like); therefore, some of the steps described here are not appropriate for all species. Reference is made in this chapter to published protocols for other species. Protection against zoonotic infection is essential for all parties involved in the handling and examination of deceased animal-cruelty victims.

Investigators should conduct an initial survey of the crime scene to determine how many deceased animals there are. Ideally, each animal should be carefully identified and examined and all, or most of them, should be necropsied. In cases involving multiple animals, it may not be feasible or necessary to necropsy each animal to build a case for prosecution. Each animal should nonetheless be carefully identified, photographed and retrieved, so the prosecutor can determine how many counts of cruelty to animals will be filed and which animals they will involve.

Each animal is given a unique identification number and carefully photographed in situ (see chapter 5). As soon as possible, veterinarians should be allowed to perform a cursory examination of the body, as it was found if possible. They should examine all photographs taken at the scene and inspect any evidence retrieved for clues surrounding the death.

Time of Death

Establishing time of death is not an exact science. Guidelines have been extrapolated from human medicine for animal application, but more research is needed. To establish time of death, the post mortem interval must be determined. It is imperative that certain elements are identified and documented at the scene as well as during the necropsy exam.

The temperature of the body should be quickly and carefully determined, either rectally or directly in or under the liver, by making a small incision in the skin. Algor mortis—the rate of body cooling—is most accurate in the first twenty-four hours after death. It can be affected by the body temperature before death, size of the body, dehydration, obesity, edema, body position (curled versus recumbent), haircoat, humidity, wind, cover, and water immersion. A special thermometer is needed to register low temperatures. An initial temperature plateau occurs in the first-thirty-minutes-to-five-hour period. The normal rate of cooling is 1.5 degrees Fahrenheit loss/hour (rectal) at 75 degree environmental temperature (Rauch 2003). It is important to take two readings in an hour to establish the rate of cooling and confirm that the initial plateau period has passed. The atmospheric temperature and humidity, as well as other temperatures relevant to entomological evidence (Haskell and Williams 1990), should be determined as well; this information is usually available from a nearby weather station.

Body and environmental temperature documentation is particularly important in cases where hyperthermia, or heat stroke, is the suspected cause of death. Intense heat causes muscle proteins to coagulate, which in turn causes muscle shortening. Heat stroke is characterized by a rigidity of the limbs, resembling rigor mortis. Rigor mortis, however, is a transient condition. Visceral congestion and petechial hemorrhages may also be seen during the necropsy exam.

The degree of rigor mortis present at the time the veterinarian first encounters the body should be assessed and documented. Following death, the muscles are initially flaccid, but they continue their metabolic activity of glycolysis for a short time after somatic death. Adenosine triphosphate (ATP) continues to be hydrolyzed to adenosine diphosphate (ADP). Lactic acid is also produced during this hydrolysis, lowering the cellular pH. The lack of ATP regeneration after death, coupled with increased acidity, results in the formation of locking chemical bridges between the two major muscle proteins, actin and myosin. Thus the muscles become stiff and fixed without becoming shortened (in contrast to the stiffening that occurs when a living muscle is flexed, and actin and myosin slide across each other into an interlocking pattern). As the proteins of the body decompose, the chemical bridges between actin and myosin break down and rigor mortis slowly subsides (Perper 1993).

Rigor mortis develops and disappears at a similar rate in all muscles of the body and affects the smaller muscle groups first. Because smaller muscles are composed of fewer muscle proteins, they become hardened and then soften at a faster rate than do larger muscles, a phenomenon that once led to the erroneous belief that rigor progresses from the head (where most of the muscles are quite small) to the lower parts of the body (where there are larger muscles) (Perper 1993). Rigor mortis can be forcibly broken with manipulation and will not recur unless it is broken before full development, so it is important to ask how the body was handled before the veterinarian receives it.

Table 8.1—Time of Death Estimates in Animals

Warm, not stiff	0–3 hours
Warm, stiff	3–8 hours
Cold, stiff	8–36 hours
Cold, not stiff	36 hours

Source: A. Rauch, Center for Animals and Public Policy
Tufts University School of Veterinary Medicine.

The development of rigor can help determine the time of death, taking into consideration other examination findings. The onset of rigor is faster and of shorter duration in animals who have the decreased glycogen levels seen with starvation, exhaustion, seizures, and sepsis, and in high environmental temperatures.

Livor mortis, or lividity, is the bluish-red staining or discoloration of the body caused by postmortem gravitational settling of blood within the dilated skin capillaries. Lividity is not often apparent on the external skin of dogs and cats unless the skin is light in color; it is more likely to be seen on the buccal mucosa, sclera, internal organs, and body walls (see Plates lA and lB). Lividity may appear within twenty minutes, but it usually becomes obvious one to two hours after death and is fixed (i.e., it cannot be pressed out of the tissues by manual manipulation) after twelve hours in one position (Strafuss 1988; Perper 1993). There may be pale areas within areas of lividity where the body was pressed against an object, such as a rock. The presence of lividity can be particularly useful in forensic examination because it indicates the position of the body during the time shortly after death. When compared to in situ photographs taken of the victim, the pattern of lividity may suggest the victim was moved some time after death occurred. In certain cases, it may be difficult to differentiate lividity from antemortem bruising. Since lividity consists of blood contained within the capillaries, and bruising is caused by blood that has been released from damaged capillaries into the tissues due to trauma, it may be possible to incise the area and allow the blood within the capillaries to drain out, thus ruling out a bruise (Perper 1993). Once decomposition begins, however, the capillaries begin to degrade and become permeable, and it may no longer be possible to differentiate the two conditions.

Entomological evidence can be important in several ways. Although physiological changes may provide indicators of time since death for a few days, after three days the most accurate methods of determining time elapsed since death involve insect evidence. Maggot larvae grow and molt at a certain rate, depending on the species and environmental conditions, and can be aged by an entomologist, who needs weather data as well as the length of time and temperature of where the body was stored before examination. Different kinds of beetles feed at different times postmortem. Insect evidence may also provide information about the presence and location of wounds in a decaying body. Insects typically colonize bodies in a pattern, starting with laying eggs in facial orifices. If there are wounds such as projectile injuries, insects will colonize these first. Maggot activity away from facial, oral, or genital orifices suggests the possibility of underlying wounds that should be investigated in detail. In addition to DNA, insects may bioaccumulate drugs or toxins and may be useful in determining drug presence in the absence of organ tissues that might usually be tested.

Insects can colonize wounds on an unclean area of a living victim, such as a dog with an embedded chain, in a process called cutaneous myiasis. The onset of maggot infestation can indicate the minimum length of time an animal has harbored an open wound.

In general, efforts should be made to collect samples of insects of all developmental stages (eggs, larvae, pupae, and adults) found on, in, or associated with the animal (see Plates 2A and 2B). Some should be preserved, and a sample should be kept alive for a forensic entomologist to develop for later identification. The following collection techniques are guidelines; a certified forensic entomologist should be contacted for her particular collection and submission guidelines.

Eggs can be collected with forceps or a paintbrush dipped in water. Half should be preserved in 50 percent isopropyl alcohol, the remainder placed in a vial with dampened tissue paper and sealed with paper toweling held with a rubber band.

Larvae or maggots should be collected from each site, with an emphasis on the larger (older) specimens. Preserve some by immersing them in hot water for a few minutes, then in alcohol. A sample of the living larvae should be placed in a vial with air and food (a small piece of beef liver) and sealed as above.

Pupae and empty pupal cases may be found attached to hair or in soil near the body. The presence of empty pupal cases indicates that at least one generation of insects has gone through an entire life cycle on the animal. Pupae are football-shaped and 2–20 mm in size. Empty cases are open at one end. Pupae that have not emerged should be placed in sealed vials, as with eggs.

Adult insects are less important, since they may have come to the animal as adults and their presence cannot indicate time since the animal was injured or killed. However, they can indicate the types of insects likely to develop from other evidence that has been collected. They should be netted or captured in inverted vials.

Insect evidence should be packed in a box with ample air. This evidence should be couriered or hand delivered to an entomologist as quickly as possible. Haskell and Williams (1990) provide greater detail regarding methods for collecting and preserving entomological evidence. Byrd and Castner (2000) provide a more detailed discussion of many aspects of forensic entomology, and Goff (2000) gives a more popularized review of the use of this evidence.

Gastric contents and emptying times are helpful in human medicine in determining time of death. When it is known what an animal has last eaten and when, it is possible to use that information to evaluate the gastric contents. Gastric emptying time is affected by many factors: solid or liquid food, caloric content, water intake, volume ingested, and whether the animal was fed meals or ate food at will (free choice). It can also be affected by the size of the animal. Recent research has shown that in cats, unlike humans, increased age does not affect gastric emptying times. The maximum time elapsed is important to establish the minimal post mortem interval and place it in context with other post-mortem findings.

Dogs: Solids 4.7–15 hours   Liquids 0.5–3.5 hours
Cats: Solids 4.7–12.5 hours   Liquids 1 hour
Average Normal: <14 hours

The Necropsy

Veterinarians should make careful notation of all they have done, including any procedures they performed at the scene, and should ascertain that photographs have been taken of all relevant evidence. If the owner of the deceased animal is not the party being charged with the assault (e.g., a dog owner who has found her dog poisoned in the backyard by an unknown assailant), the veterinarian should be certain that the owner has granted permission to remove, examine, and necropsy the victim. The owner should give signed consent on a written statement informing the owner that cremains will not be available until the case is closed and all possibilities for appeal have been exhausted. Only then should the veterinarian or investigator proceed to remove the body of an owned animal. The only exception to this procedure is when a law enforcement investigator has seized an animal and ordered a veterinary examination.

At this point, the body is prepared for transport. The animal's identification number, the case number, and the date should be affixed to the body before it is transported. "Tab band" collars are a good choice for this task. An inexpensive, handheld laser label printer, available from most office supply and discount department stores, can be used to make clearly legible identification labels quickly and easily. These labels can be affixed to a tab band-type collar. If the victim is small or there are amputated body parts to be identified, the label itself can be affixed around a narrow part of the small animal or body part. Such labeling clearly identifies bodies and body parts as they are prepared for transport.

The feet should be bagged with a paper bag and a zip-tie (a white plastic tie used as a closure or as hand-cuffs) or rubber band. Ideally, the body should be wrapped in a white sheet, and each body or body part should be placed in a separate bag for transport. Thick white trash bags are ideal for this, since it is easier to detect and remove any evidence remaining in the bag once the body is removed after transport. The bag should be sealed completely by twisting the neck of the bag and sealing it with strong adhesive tape. Simply tying the "tie handles" of a bag designed for household use may result in a small opening at the site of the tie through which evidence may be lost or contaminants introduced during transport and handling. Each bag should be labeled on the outside with the case number, identification number, and date to make handling of the carcasses easier once they arrive at the veterinary hospital.

Thought should be given to the method for transporting the body. The body should not be exposed to extremes of heat or cold, as might occur in the trunk of a car or the back of an open truck. Placement in a temperature-controlled transport cage (such as those found in animal-control vehicles) is ideal. It may be useful to place the bagged body(ies) inside a plastic thermal picnic cooler as well. Ideally, the body is kept at 39 degrees Fahrenheit (the temperature of most refrigerators) to prevent further decomposition. Ice packs can be placed around the body as long as they are not in direct contact with the bagged body, where they may cause tissue freezing and damage.

Once the body of the deceased victim has been removed from the scene and arrived at the veterinary hospital, the veterinarian and investigator should carefully consider who should perform the necropsy. Many diagnostic laboratories employ board-certified veterinary pathologists or experienced diagnosticians who perform necropsies on behalf of referring veterinarians. Using such services has two benefits: it allows a highly experienced specialist to perform the procedure, and it brings yet another expert witness on board to provide testimony during prosecution of the case. It is important first to verify that the pathologist is willing to perform a forensic examination and is willing to testify in court; some universities and laboratories are unwilling to do so. Additional drawbacks of using a diagnostic service are that it may significantly increase the costs associated with the case, and it will likely be necessary to educate the laboratory staff about the special procedures associated with a forensic case. It will also be more costly and difficult to transport the bodies of the deceased victims to a state or university laboratory than to a local veterinary hospital, and it will add several names to the list of people who must be called on to attest to the chain of custody of the evidence. Even if it is decided that the private practitioner will perform the necropsy procedure(s), he will likely want to consult with the diagnostic laboratory to which body tissues will be sent for further analysis, particularly if multiple animals are involved. The laboratory staff should be thoroughly advised of the forensic nature of the case, the need for photo documentation, and the importance of carefully handling and saving all samples.

The necropsy should be performed as soon as possible, although, due to the meticulous nature of a forensic necropsy, it is better to delay the procedure until the veterinarian is prepared and unhurried. The body should be kept chilled at refrigerator temperatures until the necropsy takes place. Freezing the body will cause damage to the tissues since ice crystals form within them, making histopathological evaluation difficult if not impossible (Petrites-Murphy 1998).

Regardless of who is chosen to perform the necropsy, the procedure should be formal and complete and should follow a prescribed order. It is important to note normal as well as abnormal findings. Many times veterinarians assisting with animal-cruelty cases make the mistake of only pursuing the obvious lesions during necropsy. They may retrieve the bullet but fail to notice the healing limb fractures or the evidence of starvation. A thorough necropsy should be performed and carefully documented in every case, even when the cause of death is easily discerned. A judge and jury will expect a high quality of work.

Consider this scenario: a veterinarian has been hired by a local investigative agency to perform a necropsy on a four-year-old male Dalmatian found dead in his owner's backyard. The veterinarian is able to quickly determine that the dog suffered a blunt force injury to the head, and he examines only the structures associated with that wound, deciding that the injury is the cause of death and writing a report to that effect. In court, the defense attorney cross-examines the veterinarian, and this exchange takes place:

Defense Attorney: Doctor, I'm looking at the necropsy report you've written and I don't see mention of any other orthopedic findings, other than the fractured skull. Did you detect abnormalities of any bones other than those of the skull in this dog?

Veterinarian: No, I did not.

Defense Attorney: None, Doctor?

Veterinarian: No, there was only the fracture of the skull, which I've described for the court.

Defense Attorney: Doctor, I have here the dog's veterinary records, which I obtained by subpoena from his regular veterinarian. These records indicate that this dog underwent a procedure called a femoral head ostectomy—an FHO—on his right hip when he was eleven months old to relieve the pain of arthritis caused by a congenital malformation of that hip. My understanding is that during this procedure the part of the rear leg that fits into the socket of the hip—the head of the femur bone—is entirely removed, and that there is a significant amount of scar formation in the hip after the surgery. Are you familiar with that procedure, Doctor?

Veterinarian: Yes.

Defense Attorney: Would you agree that a complete postmortem examination of this dog would reveal some evidence of that procedure? A piece of this dog's hip has been removed; wouldn't that be obvious if you performed a thorough examination, doctor?

Veterinarian: Yes.

Defense Attorney: Wouldn't you agree, Doctor, that if your examination missed this significant abnormality in this dog, it might have also missed some other abnormality, something that might have contributed to this dog's death?

Veterinarian: But I...I....

Defense Attorney: Thank you, Doctor. That's all I need from you.

Regardless of how the veterinarian may reply to this final question, his credibility as a competent examiner of this dog has been called into question in the minds of the members of the jury, even if nothing in the defense's questioning has negated the conclusion of blunt force trauma.

This scenario is imagined and seems straight from a courtroom television drama, but it underscores the necessity of a detailed, complete, well-documented examination for every animal who undergoes a forensic necropsy. The veterinarian must also realize that the defense team has the right to have the animal's remains examined by the veterinarian of its choice. No veterinarian relishes the thought of being shown up in court by a colleague who is more thorough. A final argument for a meticulous necropsy is that practice makes perfect. By performing a painstaking necropsy of every specimen, veterinarians sharpen their skills for those cases in which the lesions are subtle. At the same time, they become highly adept at documenting the results of the examination in a manner that will withstand the rigors and scrutiny of the court.

Another common mistake veterinarians make when performing a forensic necropsy is the failure to perform a rigorous examination of a severely decomposed victim. Never underestimate the amount of information that can be extracted in such cases. One of the authors (L.S.) once submitted the bodies of a Savannah monitor lizard and a reticulated python found in apparently mummified state, having been left on display for some time after their deaths in a crowded pet store. The diagnostic laboratory to which they were sent was able to issue a report verifying that both animals were emaciated due to starvation (defined as a lack of any contents of the stomach or intestines, coupled with poor body condition). The snake suffered from bacterial dermatitis and septicemia, and the lizard showed evidence of bacterial enteritis. The laboratory was even able to identify the specific bacterial pathogens affecting each animal. This case demonstrates the significant amount of information that may be obtained even from decomposing bodies and is intended to encourage readers to pursue the story that every animal victim, no matter how long dead, has to tell.

It is worth noting that even very old skeletal or mummified remains can be of forensic significance. Clutton-Brock (1993, 38) describes findings from the radiological study of fifty-five wrapped cat mummies collected by Egyptologist F. Petrie in 1907. She notes, "Contrary to the general belief that ancient Egyptians never killed their cats, many of these had 'broken necks.' This could be seen in the x-rays as markedly displaced vertebrae in the neck."

She notes that the mummies fell into two groups. Twenty were kittens one to four months old when they died or were killed, and 17 were nine to seventeen months old. Only two were older than two years old. She suggests that the cats were being specially bred to be mummified by the priests for sale as votive offerings, which could explain what appears to have been a mass market in mummified cats. This market was not without a hint of fraud. Some cat mummies from other sources appear to have been faked, wrapping a cat skull mounted atop fragments of human tibia and fibula.

In some cases, victims may be so decomposed that efforts to determine the species of animal are necessary. At any stage of decomposition, the remains should be carefully examined, photographed, weighed and measured, and described in a necropsy report that is as detailed as possible. Full-body radiographs should be performed on all bodies, from head to tail, looking for evidence of trauma or lodged projectiles. Just like other bodies, decomposed bodies should be carefully stored until a case has finally been disposed.

Another test that can be performed on a decomposed body is a bone marrow fat analysis which measures the percentage of bone marrow fat in a long bone. In cases of starvation, the bone marrow fat is the last to be depleted for nutrition. Normal bone marrow fat level is 60 percent and higher; in severe starvation the levels can be as low at 0–10 percent. The fat will only go rancid if exposed to warm temperatures for an extended period of time or if there is significant decomposition, and it can be preserved frozen for up to one year.

Once veterinarians are ready to proceed with the necropsy, they should be accompanied by a skilled photographer and, ideally, someone who will be able to take notes of the findings as the procedure is performed. It is impossible to dissect a carcass and make notes of one's findings at the same time. An alternative to a scribe is a tape recorder. Whichever method is used, it should be kept in mind that the contents of the notes or audiotape will be considered legal evidence and may be viewed or heard by the jury in a courtroom, so a professional demeanor should prevail during the necropsy. The notes and/or audiotape should be preserved with other materials related to the case.

The body of the victim is carefully removed from the bag used for transport, and any trace evidence (dirt, hair, feathers, fibers, vegetation, dried blood, or similar material) remaining in the bag is collected, examined, and preserved, along with the bag itself. Initial identification photographs are taken, and a careful physical examination of the body is performed. The entire body should be examined with an ultraviolet light. The veterinarian should palpate all portions of the body for abnormalities, taking care to note the condition of the orifices, lymph nodes, limbs, joints, and feet. Samples of contents of the orifices may be taken at this time: vomitus from the mouth; discharge from the nose, eyes, or reproductive tracts; fecal samples from the rectum. Ocular fluid may be obtained by inserting a twenty-two-gauge needle attached to a six ml syringe into the anterior chamber of the eye. In cases where bestiality is suspected or known, a swab of the vaginal cavity and anus should be taken at this time. The color of the mucous membranes and the presence of any signs of hemorrhage are noted.

The body should then be thoroughly combed with a fine-tooth comb in a grid fashion over a surface from which material may be easily collected. White roll paper from an office supply store or Tyvek®, the thick white plastic material supplied in rolls, used in home building, and available from building supply stores, provides an excellent surface for this portion of the examination (Leonard 1999). The material should be examined with an ultraviolet light and indirect light source. Dirt, insects, and foreign material should be collected and preserved. In cases of physical attack, dirt and other trace evidence found within the animal's fur could possibly link the victim's body to the attacker. The nails and feet should be inspected for embedded evidence. A decision should be made either to scrape the nails for microscopic evidence or to remove the nails entirely and place them in a paper envelope for crime lab analysis. Maggots and parasites encountered during combing should be collected and quantified, if at all possible (e.g., "twenty-five ticks, ranging in size from three to twelve millimeters in diameter, were removed from the body"). Careful combing will often also reveal bruises, wounds, and projectile entry and exit wounds that are otherwise difficult to discern.

After combing, any newly identified lesions are photographed. The body and any separate body parts are carefully weighed. Any instruments associated with the abuse of the animal, such as rope or duct tape used to bind the animal, an embedded collar, or a protruding arrow or knife, should be carefully photographed in situ, removed, weighed and measured, and photographed again as separate entities. None of these items should be discarded but rather carefully recorded as evidence and packaged accordingly for testing or storage.

The body is then measured and weighed. The girth is measured with a flexible measuring tape, then the animal's length is measured from the nose to the base of the tail. The animal should be photographed beside an appropriate measurement scale. For reptiles, the full length of the animal (including tail) should be measured and recorded as well as the snout-to-vent length (SVL). Small animals should be weighed on an appropriate scale, one that is accurate in ounces, if necessary. A dietary scale (one used to measure food portions) may be useful in such cases.

Ideally, full body radiographs of the victim should be taken, consisting of at least two views perpendicular to each other (lateral and ventrodorsal views, for example). This step often identifies previously undetected projectiles, metallic fragments within old projectile wounds, acute or healing fractures (especially in various stages of healing), enlarged or shrunken thoracic or abdominal organs, and other abnormalities. Each radiograph must bear legible permanent identification that includes the date, the name of the hospital where the radiograph was taken, the case number, and the animal's identification number. It is important that two views are taken, the body properly positioned with correct right and left markers, and that the radiograph is of good quality. A defense attorney may attempt to attack a veterinarian's credibility based on her inability to verify in court on which side of the animal a lesion is located.

Veterinarians employed by animal shelters must often rely on local veterinary hospitals to take radiographs of deceased animal-cruelty victims for them. It must be emphasized to the assisting hospital's staff that the radiographs will be inadmissible in court proceedings without relevant permanent identification (case number, animal identification number, date, and hospital name imprinted on the radiograph during the exposure). In such cases, hospital staff members often neglect to record the procedure in their radiology log, since the animal is not a regular patient of theirs. They must understand that such an omission may also render the radiographs inadmissible in court or, at the very least, cause the jury to doubt their authenticity.

The veterinary examiner should view the radiographs before proceeding with the necropsy. When an animal has been shot multiple times, the tracks of the fragments can be confusing. Studying whole body radiographs can tell examiners about the nature of the projectile injuries before they begin removing the fragments (Munro 1998). Radiographic images also give veterinarians a better idea of what lies ahead during the necropsy examination, allowing them to prepare for any special procedures. For example, if the radiograph indicates consolidated portions of the lung, they should be prepared to culture those tissues.

After radiography, the entire body is shaved with a number 40 blade (the type of blade used to prepare surgical sites, which effectively removes all of the hair from the skin surface). It may be necessary to use a coarser blade to remove thick or matted hair first, then finish with the finer blade. Although this may seem an arduous task, particularly if the victim's hair coat has been soaked in water or blood or is severely matted, shaving will reveal skin lesions, including bruises that otherwise might be easily missed and will allow all detectable lesions to be clearly photographed at this time. The hair itself should be collected and saved, along with the rest of the remains. If there is a great amount of hair, particularly if it is severely matted and/or wet, the body should be weighed again after shaving to determine the true body mass and the weight of the matted hair the animal was required to carry.

At this point, the veterinarian is ready to proceed with the dissection. The procedure for a detailed, step-by-step dissection is beyond the scope of this text; however, several such procedural descriptions are available (Strafuss 1988, 1997; Brown 1995; Sartin, Spano, and Hathcock 1999; King and Dodd 2000). Necropsy techniques for specific animals have also been published, including fish (Reimschuessel 2000), calves (Meuten 1985), cattle and pigs (Andrews, Van Alstine, and Schwartz 1986), reptiles (Dolensek 1971; Mader 1996), and avian species (Schwartz and Bickford 1986; Graham 1984).

During the course of the necropsy, the skin on all portions of the animal's body should be reflected and carefully examined for evidence of bruising that might not have been apparent on the epidermal side of the skin. Subtle bruises are often found in this manner. Any observed lesions should be described based on their proximity to landmark anatomic features, so the skin should be carefully examined as it is reflected.

Since the body will need to be preserved by freezing until the case is disposed (possibly months or even years into the future), a complete set of tissues must be obtained during this initial necropsy. At a minimum, fresh (frozen) and fixed samples of lymph nodes, intestines, lung, spleen, brain, heart, liver, and kidney (Rohrer 1996) should be taken as well as any tissues associated with lesions. A more exhaustive list of tissues, appropriate for forensic investigations, has been published (Brown 1995) (Figure 8.1). Although it may be cost-prohibitive to analyze all of these tissues, especially when there are obvious lesions and no apparent involvement of many of the tissues, it is advisable to collect them nonetheless so that they are available for future analysis by either the initial examiner or by another examiner designated by the defense team. University pathology services usually have a reasonable flat fee for multiple tissue sample analysis. Tissues that are not submitted for initial examination should be carefully labeled and stored as evidence until the case has been disposed.

Figure 8.1—Tissue Collection Checklist[1]

Primary Incision
Peripheral lymph node
Muscle

Thoracic Cavity
Thyroid glands with parathyroid gland
Esophagus (can be collected attached to trachea)
Upper trachea
Thymus
Bronchial lymph node (can be collected with section
   of trachea for identification purposes)
Lung
Right atrium
Right ventricle
Left ventricle

Abdominal Cavity
Liver with section of gallbladder attached
Kidney (the left kidney should be cut longitudinally
   and the right kidney transversely)
Adrenal glands
Spleen
Stomach
Duodenum[2] with pancreas attached
Jejunum[2] with mesenteric lymph node attached
Ileum[2] with cecum
Colon[2]
Urinary bladder
Ovary
Uterus
Testis

Other
Brain with hypophysis
Femoral bone marrow

Optional
Eyes
Tonsil
Prostate
Spinal cord

[1]Any tissue with a lesion attached to adjacent normal tissue must be collected.
[2]The mucosa of samples submitted for examination must not be washed, scraped, or rubbed.

Source: From Brown 1995. Reprinted with permission.

Body fluids and other samples should be obtained. Urine may be obtained by cystocentesis of the bladder once the abdominal cavity has been opened. Contents of the esophagus, stomach, small intestine, and colon, if present, should be obtained. Depending on the time since death, blood may be collected from the major arteries or from the chambers of the heart. Clots within the heart may be spun down to obtain a serum sample for biochemical and/or toxicological analysis. Cerebrospinal fluid may be obtained before the spinal cord and brain are dissected.

Proper preservation, packaging, and shipping of necropsy specimens is essential, and several references provide guidelines for doing so correctly (Brown 1995; Rohrer 1996; Petrites-Murphy 1998). The laboratory test request form should be completed in as much detail as possible. A cruelty case submission form should be filled out completely and a receipt form sent along with the samples (see chapter 5). Withholding information from the diagnosticians will not cause them to be more diligent or more objective in evaluating the tissues (Petrites-Murphy 1998) but instead will make it more difficult for them to form an accurate opinion. The diagnosticians should be informed in writing that the tissues they are receiving are associated with a forensic case and that they may expect to be called on as witnesses in possible court proceedings.

All lesions should be accurately photographed and carefully described in the necropsy report. Measurements should be in metric units, although they should be converted to U.S. units as well in the final report, so that they may be more comprehensible to a judge or jury. Measurements should be related to specific anatomical reference points, and diagrams, no matter how crude or schematic, more accurately describe lesions when coupled with written descriptions. An appropriate scale should be available so that organs and other structures can be weighed; a dietary scale is easily obtained and usually suitable for this task. A human infant scale (found at larger baby supply stores) may also be useful. Weights should be recorded in grams and kilograms and later converted to ounces and pounds as well.

On completion of the necropsy, the body should be retained as evidence so a second postmortem examination can be conducted, if requested, by a veterinarian or veterinary pathologist chosen by the defense. The body should be stored in a manner that will preserve as many of the original features as possible. Freezing to –20 degrees Celsius (–4 degrees Fahrenheit) is recommended. A dedicated, locked freezer should be available to store evidence (Munro 1998), and the paperwork related to the case should include documentation of the location of the evidence.

A forensic necropsy is a very different procedure from the diagnostic necropsy more commonly performed on deceased animals. Each step and each finding must be carefully documented in a manner that will withstand rigorous examination. Veterinarians who agree to perform a forensic necropsy must be aware of these unique procedures and be willing to perform them in the most meticulous manner possible.

9 Thermal Injuries

Thirty-two-year-old William Scott Manciano of Oceanside, California, set fire to a one-year-old male brown tabby cat named Bob in October 1996, intending that the cat would run into Manciano's former girlfriend's house and set it on fire. When Bob ran in the other direction, the arsonist was forced to use another approach: he set the building ablaze by starting fires in a garage and a pile of debris near the house.

The house did go up in flames, but the inhabitants awakened and managed to escape without harm. Bob was not found until more than seventy-two hours later. Severely painful deep burns over the lower part of his body necessitated euthanasia. Manciano—who had an earlier manslaughter conviction for which he had served three years in prison and arrests for other violent crimes, including a barroom stabbing—was charged with three counts of attempted murder and one charge each of first-degree arson and maiming another person's animal.

During the preliminary hearing, a thirteen-year-old girl testified to having watched Manciano, dressed only in boxer shorts, hold a yowling cat by the scruff of his neck, dip him into a fluid-filled bucket, and fling him several feet into the yard of the house. Although Manciano told investigators he hadn't been outside the house and was never near the bucket, the girl identified the polka-dot pattern of the shorts he wore, and his fingerprints were lifted from the bucket.

During the trial, a veterinarian was called on to testify that a cat would not voluntarily run into a burning house, so the cat's condition could not be accidental. A jury convicted Manciano of all charges. The judge sentenced him to ten to forty-six years in prison and ordered him to pay $77,000 in restitution. Nearly nine years after the incident occurred, the Nevada Supreme Court upheld Manciano's convictions (Associated Press 2005).

Manciano apparently attacked this cat for utilitarian purposes, using him as a tool for setting a house on fire. But intentional burning of animals is not uncommon; newspapers around the country chronicle daily events in which people set animals on fire or throw them into fires, whether for "entertainment," out of spite, or for other malicious reasons.

Crimes of this type present unique challenges to cruelty investigators, veterinarians, and prosecutors. Such acts can be classified as acts of animal cruelty, arson, or both. The nature of the evidence required to document these two kinds of crimes may be different. In general, arson is viewed as a property crime, and the victim is the property owner (e.g., the owner of an animal who is killed or injured). Yet, when the "property" is a living creature, anti-cruelty laws give weight to the pain and suffering experienced by the true victim.

In general, to establish a criminal intent with arson, the main requirement is to document the intent or purpose to start a fire, even if there is no clear intent to burn a structure or otherwise destroy property. Since arson is a crime against possession, it is generally possible for persons to be charged with committing arson against themselves.

Acts of cruelty involving the intentional burning of animals are receiving greater attention from law enforcement agencies and are increasingly seen as serious offenses that may predict the potential for other violent acts. The close connection between firesetting and cruelty to animals has been recognized for some time. A triad of juvenile symptoms considered predictive of adult crime was advanced by Hellman and Blackman (1966). The triad consisted of cruelty to animals, firesetting, and enuresis (bedwetting) persisting past the age of five years. This triad was more common for prisoners convicted of violent crime (45 percent) than it was for those with nonaggressive offenses (13 percent), leading to the suggestion that detection and early management of children with such a combination of symptoms could prevent careers of violent crime.

The importance of the triad was confirmed in a later detailed study (Wax and Haddox 1973), but an additional study of a large sample of children in a psychiatric outpatient clinic (Heath, Hardesty, and Goldfine 1984) suggested that the relationship between the different elements of the triad is not straightforward and uniform. There are clear parallels between individuals likely to be involved in firesetting and those generally implicated in serious and intentional cruelty to animals. Both offenses are more common in people under age eighteen, with cases involving adult perpetrators usually associated with revenge as a motive. Both generally involve male offenders (more than 90 percent). Usually offenders of both types have absent or abusive fathers, a history of emotional problems, problems at school, and a history of other property offenses (Icove and Estepp 1987; Ascione 1993).

Mental health and firefighting professionals recognize that acts of juvenile firesetting, like cruelty to animals, can fall into different categories and require different responses. Some acts of young children can be considered unintentional damage, motivated primarily by curiosity. Other fires may be set in response to a crisis situation, as a reaction to the perpetrator's own witnessing or experiencing abuse. Prosecution or other law enforcement intervention is most likely to take place in cases involving adolescent firesetters where the fire was an intentional criminal act or when the child has a history of other behavior disorders (DiMillo 1996; Lewchanin and Zimmerman 2000).

In the case of older adolescent and adult perpetrators, arson experts believe about 22 percent of fires are set for profit (e.g., insurance fraud or to conceal other crimes); about 41 percent are motivated by revenge; 30 percent by a need for excitement; and 7 percent in response to family disturbance or peer pressure (Icove and Estepp 1987). Firesetting involving animal victims is most likely to fall into one of these last three categories.

In addition to treating the injuries of surviving animals, the role of the veterinarian conducting a forensic examination of a burn victim is to thoroughly describe and document the nature of the animal's injuries and the manner in which they were likely to have been produced and to collect any evidence (e.g., contaminants on fur) that may be of significance in identifying the perpetrator.

Many methods are used to burn animals, several of which are discussed here. Animals are burned with heat sources other than flames, including hot implements, chemicals, scalding water, microwave ovens, and electrical appliances. Smoke inhalation usually accompanies exposure to flames but may occur without actual burning of the animal and without flames. Although ambient temperature injuries (heatstroke and frostbite) are rightly classified as thermal injuries, they are so often associated with neglectful circumstances that they are included in chapter 16.

In the case described at the beginning of this chapter, a witness was able to link the perpetrator to the cat who was burned. More often, animal burn victims are found unaccompanied by any clue to who has assaulted them or how, why, or even when the assault took place. If the animal was unconfined and survived the attack, even for a short time, he is likely to have fled the scene of the crime, and the only evidence to indicate what has occurred is the animal's physical condition. Evidence gained from examination of the victim, however, may corroborate the testimony of a witness or even lead investigators directly to a crime scene or suspect. Veterinarians investigating burn cases should be familiar with the clinical signs and syndromes associated with burn injuries and be able to classify the severity and extent of the injuries as well as analyze any clues the victim provides about the mechanism and perpetrator of the injuries.

Burning an animal may be only one aspect of a larger crime. Responsibility for investigation of a fire is usually split among many entities: representatives from law enforcement, fire, rescue, and emergency medical services; hazardous materials teams; utility company personnel; health and safety officers; and other public agency personnel. Animal-crime investigators, including veterinarians, must be prepared to participate as members of the large team that is assembled in cases involving both human and animal victims. The U.S. Department of Justice has published guidelines for public safety personnel who investigate fire and arson scenes that will help veterinarians to understand the commonly used investigative protocols (U.S. Department of Justice 2000).

Just as animal-crime investigators may become members of a team that investigates fire and arson crimes involving people, so should the members of the other agencies listed above be notified and involved when an animal has been burned. Too often, these events are seen only as crimes against animals. When appropriate authorities are involved, it is often possible to include property crime charges as well, making it even more likely that witnesses and investigators will pursue the perpetrator and that he will be successfully prosecuted. In general, most states consider arson to be a more serious crime than animal cruelty, so cruelty cases that involve firesetting are often easier to move through the criminal justice system.

Care and Treatment of the Burn Victim

Much of what is known about burn injuries to humans is the result of studies using animals as models. Pet dogs and cats can also become victims of residential fires, without animal abuse playing a part, and information has been gathered from these instances as well (Drobatz, Walker, and Hendricks 1999a,b). Therefore, many veterinary medical texts include fairly extensive chapters or portions detailing the evaluation and treatment of animals who have been burned in some manner or who have suffered from smoke inhalation, and this information should be carefully reviewed by any veterinarian who investigates an animal-cruelty case involving a burn victim (Saxon and Kirby 1992; Tams 1994).

When presented with a surviving victim of a burn injury, therapy for life-threatening injuries is the first order of business. At the same time, care should be taken to obtain and preserve evidence. The temptation to focus only on burn injuries should be avoided. Concurrent injuries—including gunshot wounds, poisoning effects, and restraint trauma—may also have been part of the assault on the animal and should be evaluated, documented, and addressed as well. Every burn pattern should be documented, since the pattern itself is a clue to the cause of the burn. The burned area and the body of the animal should be checked for any odors that could indicate the accelerant or type of chemical used. All burns and their surrounding areas should be swabbed for evidence.

Characterizing Burn Injuries

The extent and severity of the burn injuries must be thoroughly assessed and specifically documented. Burns are classified based on depth (of damage to skin and underlying tissues) and extent (percent of the total body surface area affected). In humans, the depth of burn injuries is related to the degree of blistering of the skin. Although some veterinarians and veterinary pathologists use this system of classification to describe some animal burns (Swaim 1990), it is usually not applied to veterinary patients, in whom blistering rarely occurs.[1] Nonetheless, it is useful to review the "first-, second-, and third-degree" system of classifying burn injuries to humans, because analogy to human injuries allows judges and juries to understand more easily the degree of damage an animal has suffered (Table 9.1).

Animal burns are more accurately characterized by the depth of injury to the skin. "Superficial" burns are comparable to first-degree burns in humans and are characterized by damage only to the epidermis and overlying haircoat. Erythema and moderate to severe pain accompany superficial burns in animals. Because only the epidermis is damaged, healing of a superficial burn may be quick and uncomplicated.

Table 9.1—Classification of Burn Wounds of Humans According to Depth of Tissue Destruction

■ **First-degree burns** of humans are superficial and do not cause any blistering of the skin, although peeling of the skin may follow later. The burned area is generally inflamed (erythemic and edematous) and often significantly painful.

■ **Second-degree burns** of humans typically result in blisters, and the upper layers of the skin are destroyed. Second-degree burns in humans are less painful than first-degree burns.

■ **Third-degree burns** of humans involve the entire thickness of the skin, with damage to both the epidermis and dermis. Pain is usually absent because nerve endings are destroyed.

■ **More severe thermal injury** in humans is referred to as charring or fourth-degree burning, and is characterized by complete destruction of the skin and underlying tissues, including the bones in some cases.

"Partial-thickness" burns affect both the epidermis and dermis of animals. A superficial partial-thickness burn is comparable to a second-degree burn in humans. It affects the epidermis and mid-dermis, is characterized by erythema and subcutaneous edema, and is moderately painful. Because incomplete destruction of the skin has occurred, healing of a superficial partial-thickness burn by re-epithelialization from the edges of the wound and from small epithelial remnants is possible. Body fluid loss and secondary bacterial infection become significant concerns with burns of this magnitude.

A deep partial-thickness burn, like a third-degree burn in a human, fully destroys the epidermis and partially destroys the dermis. It is characterized by severe inflammation and a dry surface that does not blanch when touched. It may only be moderately painful or even painless if nerve endings in the skin and underlying tissues are completely destroyed. Because healing can only occur from the edges of the injury, scarring is common and skin grafting is usually necessary to cover the resulting defect. Life-threatening complications almost always accompany deep partial-thickness burns.

Burn Injury Extent

The extent of burn injury to an animal must be determined and documented. It is expressed as a percentage of the animal's total body surface area, or TBSA. TBSA is calculated as follows:

TBSA (in centimeters squared) = $K \times W^{2/3}$, where K is a constant (10.1 for dogs and 10.0 for cats) and W is the animal's weight in kilograms.

Consulting a conversion table of body weight to surface area for dogs and cats eliminates the need for this cumbersome calculation (Table 9.2).

Once an animal's TBSA is known, the extent of burn injury is determined by measuring the area of the burn injury with a metric ruler, dividing that area by the TBSA of the

Table 9.2—Body Weight to Surface Area Conversion for Dogs and Cats

Wt kgm	Sq m	Wt kgm	Sq m	Wt kgm	Sq m	Wt kgm	Sq m	Wt kgm	Sq m	Wt kgm	Sq m
1	0.10	11	0.49	21	0.76	31	0.98	41	1.19	51	1.37
2	0.15	12	0.52	22	0.78	32	1.00	42	1.20	52	1.39
3	0.20	13	0.55	23	0.80	33	1.02	43	1.22	53	1.41
4	0.25	14	0.58	24	0.83	34	1.05	44	1.24	54	1.43
5	0.29	15	0.60	25	0.85	35	1.07	45	1.26	55	1.44
6	0.33	16	0.63	26	0.87	36	1.09	46	1.28	56	1.46
7	0.36	17	0.66	27	0.90	37	1.11	47	1.30	57	1.48
8	0.40	18	0.68	28	0.92	38	1.13	48	1.32	58	1.49
9	0.43	19	0.71	29	0.94	39	1.15	49	1.34	59	1.51
10	0.46	20	0.73	30	0.96	40	1.17	50	1.35	60	1.53

Source: http://petcancervet.co.uk/.

animal, and multiplying by 100. For example, the extent of a burn injury to a 16 kg dog (whose total body surface area is calculated to be 6,413 square cm) with a burn area of approximately 8 cm by 8 cm (64 square cm) is 1 percent (64/6,413 x 100).

The Rule of Nines

In humans, the extent of burn injuries is often conveniently estimated using the "rule of nines." Although historical information on the development of the rule of nines is scant, it is presented in many human medical texts and is believed to be widely used as a method of estimation of affected body surface area in humans. Using this rule, the human head is considered to account for 9 percent of TBSA, each arm accounts for 9 percent, the front of the torso is 18 percent, the back of the torso is 18 percent, each leg is 18 percent (9 percent on the front surface and 9 percent on the back), and the genital area comprises the final 1 percent of the TBSA. For human infants, whose heads are much larger in comparison to the rest of their bodies, the head area is considered to account for 18 percent of the body surface area, and each leg is estimated at 13.5 percent, with the remaining body surface areas estimated to be the same as that of an adult.

The rule of nines has been applied by veterinary authors to animal patients (Duckett 1995), and this may be a useful approach for initial estimation of the extent of injuries or estimation under extenuating circumstances. However, actual measurement of wounds and comparison to calculated TBSA is a more accurate and defensible approach for presentation in written medical records and for court testimony. In infant animals, as with infant humans, the rule of nines is skewed somewhat by the comparatively larger size of the head and the shorter extremities. Dogs with neotenic features—Lhaso apso or Pekingese dogs, for example—may also conform more closely to the method for estimating infant TBSA.

Documentation

Well-written documentation of the extent and depth of a burn injury is essential, for example:

> Careful examination reveals an approximately 8 cm by 8 cm burn injury on the left lateral abdomen, comprising 1 percent of the total body surface area of this 16 kg dog. All portions of the wound appear to be superficial partial-thickness in depth, with damage to both the epidermis and dermis.

Clear photographs of the burn wound must accompany the examination report.

Further Characterization

Besides extent and depth, the location of burn wounds should be considered when determining their severity (Saxon and Kirby 1992). Burns to the perineum, face, ears, and eyes may cause greater pain than other injuries and are accompanied by potential loss of function. A severe burn to one limb may allow amputation, a condition to which many animals respond well, but amputation of more than one limb due to severe burns obviously carries with it a poorer prognosis for ongoing quality of life.

An eschar, the residue of hair and skin elements that have been coagulated by the heat of a burn injury, is composed almost entirely of tough denatured collagen fibers, and it is sometimes left on to function as a bandage until granulation tissue and new epidermis has formed underneath it (about two to four weeks after the burn has occurred). More superficial burns may develop only a scab, which contains dead cells and flimsy fibrin. It is not a strong protective covering like an eschar.

Whether covered by a thick haircoat, a scab, or an eschar, burn wounds are sometimes hidden from casual observation. An observer may be able to determine only that an animal is experiencing pain, and in some cases the condition does not become noticeable at all until several days after the burn has occurred. When the animal is finally presented to the veterinarian for examination and treatment, the skin is often hard and dry. Infection may result in a purulent discharge accompanied by an unpleasant odor. Large areas of necrotic skin may eventually slough and reveal a deep, suppurating wound. All of these changes can make it difficult to determine that the original traumatic insult was a burn, particularly if there is no remaining accompanying evidence such as singed hair or the presence of gasoline or other fuel. The diagnosis is easy if burning of the animal is witnessed; without a witness, however, a burn injury can present as a diagnostic challenge.

Assessment of the physical effects of an animal's burn injuries might be the easiest part of the evaluation. Most burn victims suffer involvement of more than 25 percent of the body, and systemic manifestations are usually involved. These can include septicemia, shock, renal failure, anemia, and respiratory difficulty. Fluid loss, infection, pain, closure, and metabolic maintenance are all considerations in the evaluation and clinical management of a burned animal. Treatment recommendations for burn patients are described in some of the references mentioned above.

Fire Burns

Setting animals on fire appears, anecdotally, to be the method of choice for burning them. Doing so often requires the use of an accelerant. Solid accelerants may be paper, wood chips, or other flammable materials as well as gunpowder and other solid explosive materials. Liquid accelerants, the most commonly encountered, include petroleum products (gasoline, kerosene, fuel oil, etc.), alcohols, paint thinners and other solvents, and ether. Some gas accelerants are used, such as propane or natural gas. The contents of aerosol cans (such as those containing hairspray or deodorant) may be used as a lighted torch to burn an animal or ignite fur.

The extent and severity of any flame-induced injury depends on various factors, including:
- the amount of accelerant doused on the animal;
- the degree of contact of the ignition flame with the animal's fur;
- whether the animal is confined with or attached to solid, liquid, or gaseous accelerant materials (e.g., a cat tied within a burlap sack);
- the method of ignition (a match versus a butane torch, for example);
- the reaction of the animal. An animal who runs may unwittingly feed the fire with

oxygen, whereas an animal who rolls in pain may put the fire out; and

- the physical characteristics of the animal. For example, a thin tail or ears may burn off entirely; thick fur may insulate the skin, whereas thinner fur provides little, if any, protection.

Analysis of materials remaining on or around the victim can often identify a less-than-obvious accelerant. Gas chromatography is widely used to analyze liquid accelerants, commonly referred to as "ignitable liquid residue" by forensic chemists. It is possible to isolate traces of liquid accelerants from the skin of suspects and match them to substances found at the scene of a crime or on the body of a victim (Almirall et al. 2000). A thorough examination of the fire scene and the body of the victim should be conducted. Porous materials, such as unburned paper or cloth, are especially likely to contain accelerant residue. Some commonly used flammable fluids—such as deodorized kerosene, charcoal lighter fluids, and some alcohols—have no characteristic odor and might easily escape detection. Small samples of soil, wood, cloth, paper, etc., should be placed in small, clean metal cans (available from investigation supply companies, see appendix B) and sealed immediately to prevent loss of additional volatile components by evaporation. Large pieces of wood, upholstery, wallboard, etc., can be collected as well. Contact the analyzing laboratory to determine the best method for packaging and delivering larger evidence samples.

Eyewitness reports of a fire affecting an animal victim can provide some information about the characteristics of the fire. The color of the smoke from the fire can indicate the type of material or accelerant that is combusting (Table 9.3). The color of the fire's flame also indicates the temperature at which the fire burns (Table 9.4).

Table 9.3—Color of Smoke Indicates Type of Material Combusting

Color of Smoke	Material Combusting
Black	Acetone, kerosene, gasoline, rubber, tar, oil (lube), coal, plastic
Black to brown	Turpentine
Brownish black	Lacquer thinner
Brown to black	Naphtha
Brown	Cooking oil
Gray to brown	Wood, paper, cloth
Greenish-yellow	Chlorine gas
Yellow to brownish-yellow	Sulphur, nitric acid, gunpowder, hydrochloric acid
White to gray	Benzine
White	Phosphorous

Source: Eliopulos 1993. Reprinted with permission.

Table 9.4—Color of Flame Used to Estimate Temperature of Fire

Color of Flame	Estimated Temperature of Fire
Red	900–1650 degrees Fahrenheit
Orange	1725 degrees Fahrenheit
Yellow	1825–1975 degrees Fahrenheit
White	2200 degrees Fahrenheit
Blue-white	2550 degrees Fahrenheit

Source: From Eliopulos 1993. Reprinted with permission.

Inhalation of Smoke, Steam, and Heat

Fire burn injuries are commonly accompanied by smoke inhalation, although smoke inhalation without direct burn injury is also possible. Smoke inhalation is most serious when the animal is confined in an enclosed space or when the animal loses consciousness at the scene of a fire. The leading cause of death of human fire victims in the initial hours after the injury is smoke inhalation and hypoxia, which leads to respiratory failure. The same is true for animal victims.

The veterinary literature has addressed the effects and treatments of smoke inhalation injuries in dogs and cats (Saxon and Kirby 1992; Drobatz, Walker, and Hendricks 1999a,b; Peterson 2000). Heat injury is usually limited to the airway cranial to the larynx because of efficient heat dissipation mechanisms of the pharyngeal tissues, but smoke inhalation may result in damage anywhere along the respiratory tract. Abnormalities of the pulmonary system resulting from smoke inhalation may be attributable to various causes. Inflammation can result from inhalation of such irritants as aldehydes, acrolein, and ammonia, all by-products of flaming building and furniture materials.

Clinical signs of dogs examined immediately after smoke inhalation include coughing or gagging, respiratory difficulty, weakness or ataxia, foaming from the mouth (rarely), rubbing at the eyes, and bleeding from the nose. Clinical signs for cats include dyspnea, vocalization, coughing, open-mouth breathing, loss of consciousness, and lethargy. Other reported signs for cats are wheezing, gagging, mucoid nasal discharge, protrusion of the third eyelid, foaming from the mouth (rarely), laryngospasm, laryngeal edema, limp or flaccid body, blepharospasm, loud abnormal respiratory sounds, vomiting, stupor, and ataxia.

Steam contains four thousand times the heat capacity of air and readily injures the lower airway structures when inhaled. Steam or hot air inhaled by a burn victim may produce a severe tracheitis. Although a victim of steam inhalation may initially be asymptomatic, asphyxia can quickly follow when edematous swelling of the airways begins (Davis 1963; Spitz 1993b).

Differentiating Death Due to Fire from Death Due to Other Causes

Occasionally, veterinarians may be called on to determine whether exposure to fire or smoke is the cause of death of an animal or whether the animal was burned after death. As heinous as it may be to set the body of a dead animal on fire, it is not the same offense as burning the animal alive. Suspects in the death of animals may claim to have burned the body only after finding it dead. Juvenile boys have been known to hang, drag, burn, and otherwise mutilate animals they have found dead.

Much information is available in human forensic literature regarding the determination of whether a person burned to death in a fire or was burned after death (Spitz 1993b). A number of laboratory analyses may be used to determine whether a deceased animal was alive when exposed to a fire. A postmortem blood sample can be analyzed for the presence of carbon monoxide. Even a low level of carbon monoxide in the blood (10–30 percent) indicates that the living animal was exposed to the fire. The postmortem blood sample should be placed in a sodium fluoride anticoagulation tube for transport because sodium fluoride prevents bacterial production of carbon monoxide. This same sample can also be analyzed for the presence of cyanide, as many animals who die in fires die as the result of hydrogen cyanide poisoning. Frozen samples of liver and spleen can also be analyzed for the presence of carbon monoxide.

Another method for determining fire exposure is to seek evidence of smoke, soot, or other burned debris in the animal's tracheal and bronchial passages. Foam in the airway, at the nostrils, or in the mouth indicates the animal was breathing while the fire progressed and is caused by an accumulation of protein-rich fluid (edema) in the lungs as a result of irritation by smoke and of heart failure due to the asphyxiating effects of carboxyhemoglobin buildup. Histopathologic examination of lung tissue, even when there is no gross evidence of smoke or soot in the airways, is also warranted. Such analysis also creates an additional witness—the examining histopathologist—who can testify to fire exposure of the victim. While the absence of carbon monoxide in the blood, liver, or spleen and of soot or foam in the airways does not alone rule out the possibility that a victim died as the result of a fire rather than before it, the presence of these signs unequivocally establishes that the animal was alive when exposed to the fire.

Chemical Burns

On the evening of August 11, 1984, two Philadelphia men knocked on the door of the Willingboro, New Jersey, home of Edward Atwood. When Atwood, a disabled man who walked with the aid of a cane, answered the door, one of the two shot him with a shotgun, murdering him in full view of his wife, two children, and great-grandparents. A few weeks later, in Mount Airy, Pennsylvania, a half-dozen dogs in the community were attacked by perpetrators who threw a mixture of drain cleaner, bleach, and pancake mix over backyard fences onto the animals. Five dogs, including the pet of a city councilman, were so badly injured that they were eventually euthanized. The sixth dog survived with permanent injuries, including blindness in one eye.

Analysis of chemical residue found on the bodies of the victims led to the identification of three suspects who had purchased the commercial drain cleaner, leading to their arrest on animal-cruelty charges. When photos of the three were shown on television in connection with their arrest, Atwood's wife was watching. She identified one of the three as one of her husband's killers. A participant in both crimes, twenty-one-year-old Dwayne Wright, was eventually convicted of murdering Atwood and received a life sentence. Strangely, Atwood's death was also animal-related: prosecutors claimed that Wright and his partner were hired to kill Atwood by a neighbor against whom Atwood had filed a complaint for not providing proper care for a dog.

Burning animals with chemicals is a particularly violent offense. Drain cleaners contain high concentrations of lye (sodium hydroxide) and are a popular choice for this crime. They may be mixed with a thickening agent, such as flour, cornstarch, or pancake mix, to form a paste that will stick to an animal's fur and skin. Lewis Red Devil Lye®, a 100-percent sodium hydroxide preparation, is sold in many grocery, hardware, and discount department stores as a drain opener. In Canada, Gillett's Cleaning Products retails Gillett's 100-percent Lye® through many hardware stores. Lye is legitimately used in some types of cooking, as a paint remover by those who refurbish old metal appliances (antique tractors, for example), and by hobbyists who enjoy crafting homemade soaps. Lye is also used, however, in the illicit manufacture of methamphetamines, and those who are involved in this activity are often all too familiar with its caustic effects.

Chemical burns may also occur when an animal is doused with an accelerant, such as kerosene, gasoline, or turpentine, by someone who is preparing to set the animal on fire. Chemical burns may appear and progress similarly to flame burns but are not accompanied by singed hair, soot, or ashes. Analysis of samples of skin and fur will usually identify the chemical used. Skin and fur samples should be carefully obtained and preserved for such analysis.

Microwave Irradiation

With the advent of the microwave oven and its installation in seemingly every home in America during the 1980s came a new method of assaulting animals: microwave irradiation. Animal abusers have found it easy to place an animal in the microwave and press the timer, resulting in serious injury and even death.

In 1992 Bel Air, Maryland, attorney Stanley E. Protokowicz, Jr., pleaded guilty to one count each of breaking and entering and cruelty to animals after he and a client broke into a home where the client's estranged wife was living. The two men were intoxicated at the time; Protokowicz was representing his client in divorce proceedings, and the pair claimed to be looking for stock certificates that were part of the divorce case.

During the break-in, Protokowicz placed the wife's cat, Max, in the microwave oven "because it was underfoot," then turned the oven on, killing the cat. Protokowicz claimed to have been looking for the stove light. He faced up to three years in prison for the charge of breaking and entering and ninety days on the animal-cruelty charge (a misdemeanor); he received a fifteen-month suspended jail sentence and eighteen months of probation. He was also ordered to perform forty hours of community service, pay a $1,500 fine (the maximum fine allowable on the two counts), and seek treatment for alcoholism. The Maryland Attorney Grievance Commission later suspended Protokowicz from practicing and recommended that he be disbarred.

Other cases involving microwave irradiation of animals have been just as sensational. A Houston, Texas, man microwaved his former girlfriend's cats after he administered acetaminophen to them. Both cats later died, and the local newspaper and television stations gave great play to the events of this case.

In 1999 college student Chad Alvarez kidnapped and microwaved a fraternity brother's Quaker parrot. Alvarez's father, Barry, was the head coach of the University of Wisconsin football team (which had just won the Rose Bowl game), and Alvarez's attorney claimed his client faced unduly harsh prosecution due to his father's fame. The twenty-three-year-old had killed the bird in a dispute over an e-mail message from the bird's owner. Alvarez was convicted of two felony charges, theft of a domestic animal and mistreatment of an animal. He served ten days in jail and received nine years of probation. He was also ordered to undergo counseling, perform community service, and make a donation to the local humane society.

The response of the general public and of the legal system to these cases confirms that microwave irradiation of an animal is a particularly gruesome offense. Veterinarians should be well prepared to assist when such a case becomes a high-profile event in their own communities.

The 2000 report of the American Veterinary Medical Association's (AVMA) Panel on Euthanasia addresses the use of microwave irradiation as a means of euthanasia for laboratory animals (American Veterinary Medical Association 2001). The report explains that heating by microwave irradiation is used primarily by neurobiologists to fix brain metabolites in vivo while maintaining the anatomic integrity of the brain. Microwave instruments specifically designed for this purpose are used primarily on rats and mice. The report is careful to state that "only instruments that are designed for this use and have appropriate power and microwave distribution can be used. Microwave ovens designed for domestic and institutional kitchens are absolutely unacceptable for euthanasia." The AVMA report lists microwave irradiation as an "acceptable" method of euthanasia for mice and rats in the table "Agents and Methods of Euthanasia by Species" and in a second table, "Acceptable Agents of Euthanasia—Characteristics and Modes of Action." Both tables give the caveat that the procedure "requires training and highly specialized equipment."

Veterinarians who participate in cases involving microwave irradiation of animals should be thoroughly familiar with the panel report's statements on this method, so that a defense attorney cannot successfully represent to a judge or a jury the killing of an animal by irradiation in a household microwave oven as a euthanasia method deemed "acceptable" by the AVMA.

In 1987 a report in the journal *Pediatrics* described two separate incidents in which human infants suffered full-thickness burns as the result of placement within microwave ovens; child abuse was alleged in both cases (Surrell et al. 1987). These reports prompted a study of the effects of microwave radiation on living tissues, in which anesthetized piglets were subjected to radiation from a standard household microwave for periods of 90, 105, and 120 seconds, then euthanized without anesthetic recovery (Surrell et al. 1987). The study identified a unique and characteristic burn pattern, described as "relative layered tissue sparing," in which the skin and muscle are burned, with relatively unburned subcutaneous fat (compared to flame, contact, chemical, and electrical burns, which typically affect all layers of tissue). Resultant burns were sharply demarcated from unburned tissue and located on those parts of the body that were closest to the microwave-emitting device in the top of the oven. Experimental evidence obtained from this study also indicated that microwave irradiation may inflict serious burn damage to deep structures as well as to skin, and the authors admonished that surviving microwave irradiation victims should be closely monitored for any signs of complications due to acute visceral damage (such as bowel obstruction from a stenotic segment of burned bowel).

To understand how a microwave oven injures an animal, it is helpful to understand first how a microwave oven works. The source of waves is a high-powered vacuum tube called a magnetron. It emits a beam of radio waves whose frequency is roughly 2,450 megahertz (2.45 gigahertz). Radio waves of this frequency are absorbed by water to a great extent, and by fats, oils, and sugars to a lesser extent. Once absorbed, they are converted into atomic motion, resulting in the creation of heat. Radio waves in this frequency are not absorbed by most plastics, glass, or ceramic; however, metal reflects them.

Heating with microwaves differs from heating by other methods. In a regular oven, heat is transferred from the oven to its contents by convection (hot air) and/or conduction (direct contact with the heat source). Microwave irradiation does not require either convection or conduction for the transfer of heat; the molecules affected by the waves are excited all at one time. Microwaves generally produce even heating of all of the water molecules in a body, but it is possible for them to penetrate a very large mass unevenly or to create "hot spots" caused by interference of the waves with one another at certain spots within the oven. Microwave irradiation can be therapeutic: unenclosed microwave-emitting systems are used in some forms of medical therapy to provide deep warming to injured or diseased tissues (Pollard et al. 2001).

Exposure to a small amount of microwave irradiation results in warming of the body. The blood circulation normally dissipates this small amount of heat, resulting in little or no damage. The corneas of the eyes, however, have water content but no method of circulatory heat dissipation and may heat quickly enough to become permanently damaged with minimal exposure. Any other tissues with poor circulatory function are at similar risk.

While published veterinary scientific literature on this type of injury is lacking, veterinarians who have examined animals subjected to microwave irradiation have reported anecdotally clinical signs, including blistering and separation of the skin of the paw pads, blistering and ulceration of the tongue, and burning of other thin body areas, such as the tips of the ears (Plate 3). The extent of injury and the survival of the animal likely depend on the animal's body mass, the body water content, the amount of power emitted by the particular oven, and the length of time of irradiation. Juvenile animals have a higher body water content and would presumably be affected more quickly and more completely by microwaves than would adult animals. The prognosis for an immediately surviving animal who has been subjected to microwave irradiation depends on the degree and nature of injuries sustained.

An animal wearing a collar containing any type of metal may suffer an additional fate from microwave irradiation. Microwaves cause electrical currents to flow through any metal objects they encounter. Thick, smooth pieces of metal (like a spoon left in a coffee cup) generally are not much affected by microwaves, but thinner pieces of metal may become overheated (Ascione 1993; Almirall et al. 2000).

In addition, electrical currents may arc from sharp ends of metal pieces. For these reasons, an animal wearing a collar containing metal may be burned by the heat absorbed by the collar (if it is thin or if it is heated for a sufficient period of time) or may be set aflame by the arc of current emitted from a thin or sharp piece of metal (such as an identification tag) on the collar. When examining an animal who has been injured or killed in a microwave oven while wearing a collar, veterinarians should look closely for evidence of these additional injuries. It is theoretically possible that the involved tissues of an animal sustaining this type of electrical burn injury associated with microwave irradiation might paradoxically demonstrate on histopathological examination the microscopic nuclear streaming previously described as *not* being a typical feature of tissue obtained from microwave irradiation victims.

In microwave irradiation cases, preserving the oven itself may be useful. In the Houston case involving both acetaminophen administration and microwave irradiation, the oven—with tufts of cat hair still inside—was presented as evidence in court. If the animal has died while still in the oven, photographs taken of the body and body fluids within the oven should help to convince a judge and jurors of the violent nature of this crime.

Scalding

Scalding does not appear to be a common form of burning an animal, although animals may be dipped or submerged into hot liquids or splashed with them. Scald burns may be caused by any type of hot liquid, including water or coffee, or thicker liquids such as soup or grease. Fur may protect animals from burns when they are splashed with scalding water. There may be a spill/splash type of burn or an immersion burn, in which an animal is dipped into the hot liquid. Dipping often results in clean lines of demarcation between burned areas and unburned areas. An animal who is immersed in hot water will attempt to fold up, possibly creating "sparing" creases in the abdomen and groin areas. Stocking or glove-pattern burns on the limbs may occur when only these parts of the body are immersed. When documenting burn injuries that clearly show such distinctive patterns, make sure that photographs show sufficient detail and clarity to illustrate these characteristics.

Some form of restraint is usually necessary to immerse an animal in scalding liquid, resulting in bruising and injury to the body parts by which the animal was held. The animal may have been hung by a rope, causing bruising around the neck or around the front legs. Conversely, an animal may be enclosed entirely in a cloth or mesh bag or net, resulting in burns of even depth over most of the body.

The temperature of the water and the duration of exposure have much to do with the severity of a scalding burn. Only liquids at temperatures greater than 120 degrees Fahrenheit are capable of causing significant injury to skin and underlying tissues (although submersion in lower-temperature liquids for a significant period of time may induce hyperthermia). Liquids at higher temperatures produce burns with shorter duration of contact.

Most household water heaters are set between 120 and 140 degrees Fahrenheit but may be set as high as 160 degrees. At these higher temperatures, severe burns can be caused by exposure of only a few seconds.

Hot Implement Burns

Fur may also protect animals from much of the injury of hot implement burns. In rare burn cases, a "match" may be made between the burn and the implement that caused it. Contact burns may be caused by a curling iron, a clothing iron (which may also cause steam burns), a cigarette or cigarette lighter, a grill surface, or a heated implement, such as a kitchen or barbeque tool. The pattern of the object may be "branded" onto the animal, possibly allowing identification of the implement if it is found.

Electrical Burns and Injuries

Animals may receive electrical burns and injuries in a variety of ways. Large animals kept outdoors, particularly cattle and horses, may fall victim to lightning, especially if they seek shelter from electrical storms under trees. Lightning-related fatalities may be mistaken for predator kills or malicious killing (see chapter 19). Only about 20 percent of human victims of lightning strike die immediately as a result. Victims experience a wide range of injuries, including myocardial damage, pulmonary edema, spinal cord injury, burns and cutaneous markings, blunt trauma, tympanic membrane ruptures, corneal damage, and retinal abnormalities (Gourbiere 1999). No comparable data exist for animal victims, but it is likely that the survival rate may be equally high for large animals who may exhibit physiological or behavioral changes as a result, without clear external evidence of injury. Lightning generally produces "fern-shaped" burns, known as Lichtenberg figures, which might be one external indication that this should be considered as a possible cause when investigating such deaths.

The most common cases of electrical burn injuries to animals are those involving avian collisions with power lines or other high-voltage installations (California Energy Commission 1995). Many of the incidents documented in this report involved the deaths of between two hundred and a thousand birds at one time, often comprising a mixture of more than a dozen species.

In companion animals the most common electrical injuries are the result of biting into household electrical wiring. Intentional electrical burning of animals does not appear to be a common form of abuse, and few anecdotal reports of such injuries are available.

Electricity causes injury to animals either by generating heat that is destructive to tissue or by inducing physiological changes. Electrical injuries vary depending on whether the electricity passes through the tissues or the tissues are only very close to a very high-temperature arc flash (Davies 1997). Electric current causes injury in one of two ways: the electricity may be transformed into heat, causing protein coagulation as it passes through tissues or crosses an air gap, or it may disrupt electrophysical activity of various tissues, resulting in muscle spasms, ventricular fibrillation, unconsciousness, or apnea. Electrical burns are primarily the result of heat generated as current passes through the tissues. Dry skin offers high resistance to electrical current, but moisture significantly reduces resistance; oral burns due to electrical cords and burns to animals whose skin is wet when current is applied are therefore more severe than are those of dry surfaces. Resistance also decreases as the time of contact increases, so an electrical source that can be applied constantly can cause more injury than one that can be applied for only a few seconds (such as the pulse of electricity emitted by many static-shock training collars). Bone is the tissue most resistant to electrical current, followed by fat, tendon, skin, muscle, blood, and nerve. Blood offers low resistance to electrical flow, and low-voltage current often moves preferentially along blood vessels, causing damage that may lead to thrombosis and further tissue destruction. Pulmonary edema may be a life-threatening complication.

Low-voltage injuries, those most likely to be intentionally applied to an animal as a form of abuse, usually cause local injury but rarely create an exit wound. Electrical burns are usually small, gray, charred marks with a grayish white rim. Production of electrical burns depends on voltage of the electrical source, the amount of current flow, the size of the area of contact, and the duration of contact. An electrical burn may be severe enough to cause death without actually burning the skin or hair of the victim.

The most common form of electrical assault may likely be the abuse or misuse of electric shock-producing devices for restraint or control of an animal, including electric fences, electric prods, stun guns, and electric training collars.

Electrical stun guns, used by law enforcement personnel and by private citizens for personal protection purposes, are widely available despite being prohibited or restricted in many states, communities, and foreign countries. The type of stun device most commonly used by law enforcement personnel is the Taser®, manufactured by Taser® Industries, Inc., of Monrovia, California, and commercially available since 1974. It is a flashlight-size electric weapon designed to be a "stand-off" device that propels two darts into the victim using a small gunpowder or compressed air charge. Each dart is connected to a transformer in the device by an eighteen-foot wire. The operator transmits an incapacitating electrical shock into the victim by depressing a switch on the handheld portion of the device.

Similar devices resemble electric razors in size and weight. These require that the operator physically apply the weapon's electrodes directly to the victim. Both devices inject an electric current into the victim, inducing involuntary muscle contraction and incapacitation.

Stun guns and Tasers have gained popularity with law enforcement agencies around the country and have been credited with reducing injuries to officers and suspects (Meyer 1992). However, such devices have also been implicated in fatalities. One review of sixteen deaths associated with use of the Taser noted that all of the victims had a history of substance abuse and thirteen were under the influence of cocaine, PCP, or amphetamine. In only one case was the Taser use considered a possible contributing cause of death (Kornblum and Reddy 1991).

Law enforcement and animal-control agencies have shown interest in the possibility of using these devices against potentially dangerous animals. The manufacturer notes that "Taser is not specifically recommended for use against animals as its main function...[it] was created for 'human nervous systems' not animals...[and is] designed to hit a standing vertical target which most animals are not" (Taser International 2002). This report documents successful use of the device against aggressive dogs in several cases but notes that animals tend to recover from the effects of the Taser more quickly than humans do.

Despite the concerns and restrictions, stun guns and, to a lesser extent, Tasers, have become widely available to the public and may be used in the perpetration of crimes against people or animals, so it is important that veterinary and animal-care and -control professionals be familiar with their effects.

Veterinarians and humane investigators may receive complaints of abuse or misuse of electrical training devices, including containment fencing, training collars, and antibark collars. The output of these devices, when functioning properly, is relatively low compared to other sources (Figure 9.1). There is the potential for abuse through repeated application of aversive stimuli, but most of the recent devices prevent rapid repetition of shocks. External marks on the neck associated with electrical training collars are unlikely to be electrical burns. They are more likely to be abrasions caused by friction from a poorly fitted collar or chemical sensitivity to electrodes that have been in contact with the skin and weather for an unacceptably long time. In either case, such injuries may be more indicative of improper use than of malicious use or product malfunction.

Many different agents can produce burn-like injuries to animals. Proper attention to the details of the injury itself, and to the circumstances surrounding the injury, enables investigators to offer a more accurate interpretation of the circumstances underlying these injuries.

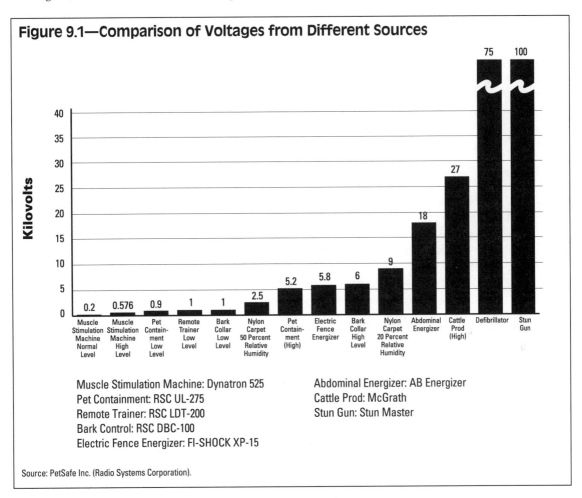

Figure 9.1—Comparison of Voltages from Different Sources

Muscle Stimulation Machine: Dynatron 525
Pet Containment: RSC UL-275
Remote Trainer: RSC LDT-200
Bark Control: RSC DBC-100
Electric Fence Energizer: FI-SHOCK XP-15

Abdominal Energizer: AB Energizer
Cattle Prod: McGrath
Stun Gun: Stun Master

Source: PetSafe Inc. (Radio Systems Corporation).

Note

[1]Human skin functions as a mechanism for cooling the body. A vast system of capillaries brings blood close to the surface of the skin, where it is cooled by the evaporation of sweat. Burn injuries extensive enough to cause significant damage to the endothelial cells lining these capillaries result in leakage of plasma-like fluid from them, resulting in the blisters that are so characteristic of second-degree burns in humans. Because the skin of dogs and cats functions more as insulation and therefore lacks the extensive capillary system of humans, blistering is much less likely to be associated with a burn wound, even one that causes identical damage to the layers of the skin as a second-degree burn injury in a human.

CHAPTER *10* Blunt Force Trauma

Blunt force injuries occur when an animal is beaten with or against a blunt object, falls against or is thrown against a hard surface, or is hit with a hard surface, such as the tire of an oncoming car. Blunt force can also include injuries from kicking, punching, stomping, or crushing. Skin manifestations of blunt force trauma are the most common clinical signs, but there may be many other forms of damage as well.

The skin manifestations of blunt force trauma differ depending on the nature of the impact (Spitz 1993a). Three basic injuries are recognized, contusion, abrasion, and laceration. Blunt force trauma may result in only one of these skin manifestations or in a combination of two or all three of them. The contusion, or "bruise," the most common form of injury, is the result of a blow forceful enough to crush the tissues and rupture the blood vessels beneath the skin, causing hemorrhage. It is much less common to see external bruising in animals than it is in humans due to animals' protective fur covering, skin thickness, and reduced blood supply to the skin. The pattern of a bruise is affected by many factors, including the tool used to cause the bruise (a hammer or the fingers of a hand, for example), force of the blow, site on the body, and proximity of other bruises. Quality photographs of the bruise, including a ruler, should be taken for a weapon specialist to analyze. When blunt force trauma is applied over a bony prominence, a bruise occurs due to the crushing of soft tissue between the bone and the object striking the body. Therefore, when a bruise is believed to involve a wide area of the body, it may be best detected by incising the skin over a bony prominence in the area. Bruising around the time of death has an inflammatory reaction but it is minimal. The pattern of contusions may be used to help reconstruct the circumstances of an injury, and most bruising is seen in the subcutaneous or deeper tissue.

In one case, the bodies of two dachshunds were found by the side of the road, apparently struck by a car. However, the position of the bodies and the absence of injuries usually associated with vehicular trauma raised suspicions. Necropsy revealed that both dogs had depressed circular skull fractures consistent with blows from a small hammer. Investigators hypothesized that the dogs had been killed during a burglary attempt, but no suspects were identified (personal communication, D. Skand, D.V.M., with R.L., June 10, 1985).

Munro (1999) notes that animals may be subjected to repeated bruising injuries in the same area, such as over the shoulder blades. Necropsy may reveal new bruising superimposed over areas of previous hemorrhage. Some bruises may have unique patterns, such as a weapon pattern, to raise suspicions of deliberate injury. Multiple bruising over the midrib area behind the shoulder blade may be indicative of intentional kicks or blows, particularly if there is no other evidence of a motor vehicle accident.

The second form of blunt trauma, an abrasion or scrape, occurs when superficial layers of skin are scraped and removed. Thin flaps of tissue may remain at the end of the abraded area, indicating the direction in which the abrasion occurred (toward the flaps). The surface of an abrasion is at first pink, then pale yellow-brown, and then dark brown or black. Bleeding is rare, unless the abrasion is quite deep, and an animal's thick fur can prevent or hide abrasions. Animals have thicker skin and thicker fur on the dorsal and lateral surfaces of their bodies, so abrasions are more common and more obvious on the ventral and medial surfaces. Abrasions are often more patterned than other types of injuries: they characteristically demonstrate the pattern of the material or object that created them. A threaded pipe, a rough board, or even the wood grain of a baseball bat can leave an abraded imprint on an animal's skin. An animal who is dragged over gravel or heavy brush may also have telltale abrasions.

A third skin manifestation of blunt force trauma is the laceration, tearing of the skin caused by a forceful blow. The appearance and depth of a laceration is determined by the force and direction of the trauma, which also determine whether there are associated underlying injuries, such as broken bones. It is possible to determine the direction in which an impact occurred by examining and undermining the edges of a laceration. Equal damage on all sides of the laceration indicates the impact occurred perpendicular to the surface of the skin (Plates 4A and 4B).

Within most lacerations, there is "tissue bridging": bits of underlying tissue are elastic enough to remain joined despite the laceration. Nerves, connective tissue fibers, and blood vessels bridge the width of the laceration, their strands running perpendicular to its length. Foreign bodies (gravel, plant material, fragments of glass or wood, or chips of paint) may be found within the depths of a laceration, offering significant clues to the mechanism of the injury.

In addition to these three effects on the skin, blunt force trauma can have other effects on the body, such as damage to skeletal structures and soft organs, including the brain and spinal cord (Plates 5 and 6). Most veterinarians are more comfortable assessing these types of injuries, which are often associated with accidents, such as motor vehicle impacts and falls from heights.

Evidence of Trauma in Surviving Victims

Evidence of blunt force trauma may be especially difficult to detect in surviving victims. Less severe injuries (contusions, abrasions, mild laceration, nondisplaced fractures) begin healing as soon as they occur and may disappear quickly, particularly in young, growing animals. Invasive methods used for detecting contusions in deceased animals (incision of the contusion site and shaving and skinning of the carcass) are unavailable for use in surviving victims. Although slight swelling or reddening of the skin may be apparent at the site of blunt force trauma, bruises may take hours or even days to become apparent on the skin of surviving victims. The color of a bruise changes from light bluish-red to dark purple, green, yellow, and brown with time (Spitz 1993a) (Plates 7 and 8). This may or may not be noticed on the surface of the skin depending on the color of the skin. Color changes may be more obvious in the subcutaneous tissues. The outer edges of a bruise are the first to darken after injury and the last to lighten as the bruise heals. Therefore, a bruise with dark edges and a light center may be very fresh or somewhat old (healing).

In head trauma, the animal may have epistaxis and mouth injuries such as fractured teeth, tongue lacerations, or even split hard palate. There may be hemorrhage or inflammation inside the eyes, luxated lens, and/or scleral and conjunctival bruising (Plate 9). Petechial hemorrhages may be visible on the external pinnae and preaural areas (Plate 10). There may be frank hemorrhage inside the ear canals from a ruptured tympanic membrane or middle ear hemorrhage. A unique injury to animals with blunt force trauma to the head is petechial bruising of the ear canal surface. This injury is not seen in humans with head trauma.

Some veterinarians have sought to verify physical trauma to an animal by measuring serum creatine phosphokinase (CPK, also referred to as creatine kinase, or CK). CPK is highly specific for muscle damage; there are three clinically important isoenzymes, one found in brain tissue and two found in cardiac and skeletal muscle. Transient, mild increases (<2000 IU per liter) are associated with restraint, physical activity, and muscle damage during venipuncture. Transient, moderate increases (>2000 IU per liter) are associated with trauma and episodes of seizure (Parent 1999). The magnitude of increased serum activity of this muscle enzyme does not correlate with the extent of muscle injury. Increased serum concentrations occur within a few hours after muscle injury, peak by twelve hours, and return to normal within twenty-four to forty-eight hours if there is no further trauma (Miller 2000). Evidence of transient, moderate CPK elevation in an animal may serve as supporting evidence of trauma wrought on a surviving victim, but unless such evidence is accompanied by other evidence such as bruises, broken bones, or eyewitness accounts of an assault on the victim, convincing a judge or jury that blunt force trauma has been inflicted is unlikely. Healthy puppies often have high levels of CPK in the absence of specific muscular injury; older dogs may have levels below normal reference ranges (Duncan and Prasse 1986).

There are many possible mechanisms by which blunt force trauma may be inflicted on an animal; several of them are discussed here.

Motor Vehicle Trauma

Motor vehicle trauma encompasses many forms of injury. The result of the impact of a motor vehicle on an animal depends on what part of the vehicle hit the animal, what part of the animal hit the vehicle, and whether the vehicle rolled over the animal or only delivered a glancing blow. The speed and size of the vehicle, the size of the animal, and the texture of the driving surface (smooth asphalt versus rough gravel) also play a role. One study has evaluated the frequency, extent, and severity of injuries inflicted by motor vehicles on dogs (Kolata and Johnston 1975). Of six hundred dogs studied, 31 percent demonstrated only superficial wounds. Of the remaining dogs, skeletal injury was diagnosed in 87 percent and soft organ injury in 27 percent. Thirty-six percent of the dogs had injuries to multiple regions of the body. The pelvis was the most frequently injured skeletal structure, and the liver was the most frequently injured soft organ. The overall fatality rate, including those animals euthanized due to the severity of their injuries, was 12.5 percent. The authors acknowledged that dogs who were more seriously injured likely died before they could be presented to the hospital and that the number of brain injuries seen and the fatality rate observed could be greater than that observed.

It is unlikely that a veterinary examiner will be able to determine whether a motor vehicle injury to an animal was intentional or accidental. The veterinarian must remain impartial to proving the driver's guilt or innocence and focus instead on reading the evidence and seeking the story it tells. The driver's intent, or lack thereof, will be discerned through the testimony of eyewitnesses or the driver's own confession. The results of the veterinary exam, however, can corroborate or disprove that testimony.

Bumper injuries to humans have been well described (Spitz 1993a). Contusions and abrasions often correlate closely with the physical characteristics of the bumper and can help to identify the specific car that hit an animal. The location of bumper injuries can tell something about the event. A dog with a bumper pattern on her left lateral body surface was traveling or standing with that side to the car at the time of impact. A dog with bruising of the caudal end and fractures of the spine and rear legs was running in front of the car at the time she was hit. A cat with tire tread-shaped bruises on the lateral thorax, accompanied by multiple rib fractures and contusions of the lung lobes, was completely run over by a car. Therefore, the veterinarian is able to testify in court that the animal's injuries are or are not consistent with the testimony of the suspect or of witnesses. Paint chips in lacerations and tire tread patterns on the body of an animal can point to a specific vehicle. Hair and blood, if found on the vehicle, are corroborative evidence.

Information on the characteristics of injuries to dogs caused by motor vehicle accidents has been described (Spackman et al. 1984). Dogs often have unilateral fractures and thoracic injuries on the same side of the body, the result of broadside impact of a motor vehicle. Due to the insubstantial nature of the dog's mediastinum, pneumothorax and hemothorax usually manifest as bilateral lesions, even in dogs with unilateral fractures and lung lobe contusions. Presumably, motor vehicle injuries have different effects on cats from their effects on dogs. A study of patterns of trauma in urban dogs and cats bolsters this theory, showing that cats are most likely to suffer injuries to the head in motor vehicle impacts, whereas dogs are more likely to suffer injuries to the extremities (Kolata, Kraut, and Johnston 1974). Further study is needed to more fully characterize the effects of motor vehicle impact on cats and dogs.

In motor vehicle impact cases where eyewitness testimony is strong and it seems that no further evidence is necessary, veterinary testimony may still prove valuable. By describing the extent and severity of the animal's injuries, a veterinarian helps the jury to understand the violent nature of the crime.

Another form of motor vehicle injury that inflicts blunt force trauma is dragging behind a vehicle. Numerous cases have arisen in which persons have dragged their own dogs, either accidentally (allegedly forgetting the dog was tied to the bumper) or as a means of "exercising" the dog. Intoxication often plays a role in such cases and, while most perpetrators are distraught and remorseful and law enforcement authorities do not charge them with the crime, is an indicator of negligence that may not be overlooked. Some defendants have claimed that dragging is a component of a training program for an animal.

In December 2000 Gary Filbeck of Webster County, Missouri, pled guilty to dragging a mule behind his truck, receiving a six-month suspended jail sentence, two years of probation, and a $500 fine for the misdemeanor offense. He also agreed to relinquish the mule (who survived despite critical injuries) and to refrain from owning another animal during his probation. Filbeck and a friend claimed to have been training the eighteen-month-old mule. They had also beaten him with a rope and kicked him numerous times, according to witness reports to law enforcement authorities.

Other cases involve dogs being transported while tied by a tether in a pickup truck who leap from the vehicle and are then dragged without the driver's knowledge. Prosecution of such cases may be pursued when negligence and/or intoxication are deemed to be contributing factors.

Injuries sustained during dragging depend on many variables, including how far the animal has been dragged, at what speed, and across what surface. Animals often have severely damaged paw pads or hooves, the result of their initial attempt to keep up with the motor vehicle. Injuries of the neck as occur with hanging and asphyxiation may be seen. Skeletal injuries are inflicted when the animal fails to keep up with the vehicle and falls into a recumbent position. Severe abrasions of the feet and surfaces of the body are characteristic. Dragged animals are often physically exhausted from attempting to keep up with the vehicle and, presumably, from the extreme fear incited by the situation. Shock, dehydration, and depletion of energy reserves may significantly contribute to the mortality rate of these victims.

"High-Rise Syndrome"

The term "high-rise syndrome" first appeared in the veterinary literature in 1976, in a report that examined a triad of clinical signs—epistaxis, split hard palate, and pneumothorax—exhibited by cats who had fallen out of windows in urban high-rise apartment buildings (Robinson 1976). Since then, the term has been widely used to refer to the effects of extreme vertical deceleration trauma on both dogs and cats who fall from a significant height (usually two or more stories; a story is typically twelve to fifteen feet). Two additional reports characterized the effects of high-rise trauma on cats (Whitney and Mehlhaff 1987) and on dogs (Gordon, Thacher, and Kapatkin 1993), manipulating the initial triad of injuries somewhat so that it is now considered to consist of thoracic injury, facial trauma, and extremity fractures.

While few of the animals who were the subjects of these reports were believed to have been shoved or thrown, familiarity with the general characteristics of high-rise syndrome will help veterinarians to evaluate cases in which intentional abuse is suspected. Because the effects of high-rise syndrome on dogs and cats are significantly and interestingly different, they are considered separately here.

Effects of High-Rise Syndrome on Dogs

Most dogs presented for veterinary examination after falling from heights are known to have jumped voluntarily while chasing other animals, toys, intruders, or owners driving away on the street below. A few dogs jump after being frightened by fireworks or thunderstorms, and a few others slip from windowsills and icy ledges. Only one dog in a published report was thought to have been thrown out of a window, by a child. Most dogs fall during summer evening hours, when windows are open and outdoor activity is at its height. While the cause of a fall, the surface on which a dog lands, and the weight of the dog have no apparent significant influence on the severity of injuries sustained, the height from which the fall occurs does. Dogs who fall from less than three stories are significantly less likely to sustain life-threatening injuries than are those who fall from greater heights. None of the dogs presented for treatment in the published report had fallen from higher than six stories, suggesting that few dogs, if any, survive such falls.

Thoracic trauma with pulmonary contusions and pneumothorax are the most common injuries sustained by dogs. Head injuries consist predominantly of minor soft tissue abrasions, although a scant number of cranial neurologic abnormalities have been observed. Multiple forelimb fractures, with or without hindlimb fractures and ligamentous injuries, are common. Injuries to the spine and spinal cord are occasionally seen, particularly in dogs who fall from a height of four stories or more. Rare injuries noted included hemoperitoneum secondary to splenic rupture (one reported case) and epistaxis of undetermined origin (one reported case).

Dogs who voluntarily jump sustain more head, thoracic, spinal, forelimb, and extremity soft tissue injuries than do those who fall accidentally, in whom hind limb and abdominal injuries are more common. A high initial survival rate has been reported, although it can be assumed that dogs who did not survive falls were not presented to a veterinary hospital. Long-term survival rates for dogs receiving treatment for high-rise trauma injuries are high.

Reports show that dogs suffer from the same types of injuries as cats, but in different proportions (Figure 10.1). Less serious head trauma in dogs than cats might be attributable to the larger size and strength of their limbs, which have a greater capacity to absorb the energy of impact, thus decreasing secondary impacts to the head. The high prevalence of forelimb ligamentous injuries (carpal hyperextension) and fractures in dogs as compared to cats also suggests more absorption of impact by the dogs' extremities.

Effects of High-Rise Syndrome on Cats

High-rise syndrome's effect on cats is interestingly different from its effect on dogs. Two studies have examined these effects. The majority of cats who have been the subjects of published reports were not seen to have fallen; they were assumed to have fallen or jumped based on the characteristics of their injuries and on their access to a point from which they could fall or jump. The few cats who were observed when falling were either attempting to turn on a narrow ledge or jumping after an insect.

The two published reports describe cats who fell between one and thirty-two stories. Most cats who are treated survive, even though many are critically injured. Deaths that occur in treated cats happen within twenty-four hours of initial examination; shock, stress, and respiratory distress secondary to thoracic trauma play significant roles in those deaths. The majority of high-rise trauma cats suffer thoracic injuries, pulmonary contusions, pneumothorax, or both. Fractures of one or more limbs are a common feature, with some cats suffering simultaneous fore- and hindlimb fractures. Because of the force associated with high-velocity impact, limb fractures are often highly comminuted, and open fractures are not uncommon. Most forelimb fractures occur distal to the elbow. Femoral fractures are most common in young cats (younger than one year) and are primarily growth plate-related. Traumatic luxations are also common. A small percentage of cats suffer fractures of the pelvis, ribs, or vertebrae.

It is not unexpected that the most common injuries are skin manifestations of blunt force trauma: abrasions, contusions, and lacerations, primarily to the face and head. Mandibular, dental, and hard palate fractures accompany skin wounds in many cats.

Abdominal soft organ damage is reportedly rare. A few cats suffer ruptured bladders. Investigators have hypothesized that cats may void their bladders while falling, therefore decreasing the risk of traumatic rupture on landing. Significant injuries to the liver, spleen, kidneys, or other abdominal organs are not reported. Traumatic abdominal hernias are rare, possibly because simultaneous increases in thoracic and abdominal pressures on impact minimize their occurrence.

The interesting aspect of high-rise injuries in cats is the effect of the distance fallen on the frequency and severity of injuries. The rate of injury is linear up to a distance fallen of approximately seven stories; above this height, injury rates do not increase and the fracture rates decrease. A cat who free-fell from thirty-two stories onto concrete, the subject of one of the published reports, suffered only mild pneumothorax and a chipped tooth and was released after forty-eight hours of observation.

The physics behind this phenomenon have been discussed (Whitney and Mehlhaff 1987). The cat's unique ability to right himself and attain a "feet first" presentation during free fall is legendary but has been described in detail in the veterinary behavioral literature (Beaver 1992). The average-size cat (about 4 kilograms, 8.8 pounds), in a horizontally outstretched position, achieves a terminal velocity of approximately sixty miles per hour after falling approximately five stories (not accounting for wind and other environmental factors). Cats falling from higher heights do not accelerate beyond this speed but continue to fall at terminal velocity. Investigators speculate that until cats achieve terminal velocity, they experience a feeling of acceleration and reflexively extend their limbs, making them more prone to injury. Once terminal velocity is reached, however, and the vestibular system is no longer stimulated by acceleration, cats might relax and orient their limbs more horizontally, much like a flying squirrel. This position allows the impact to be distributed more evenly throughout the body and provides some protection for the limbs, although it does not alleviate thoracic injury.

Because the force of impact is governed by the Newtonian equation $F = ma$, where F is the force at impact, m is the mass of the cat, and a is the acceleration (in this case, the deceleration at impact), larger cats can be expected to suffer more severe injuries. This relationship may also explain why dogs are unlikely to survive falls from great heights, in contrast to cats.

Figure 10.1—Comparison of Injuries in Dogs and Cats with High-Rise Syndrome

Injury	Percentage of 132 cats	Percentage of 104 cats (1–6 stories)	Percentage of 80 dogs
Thorax	90	80	63
Pulmonary contusions	68	52	37
Pneumothorax	63	43	25
Facial	57	NA	45
Hard palate fracture	17	NA	0
Dental fracture	17	19	14
Mandibular fracture	9	NA	3
Extremity Fractures	61	63	80
Forelimb	54	41	60
Hindlimb	46	28	41

NA = not available.

Source: Gordon, Thacher, and Kapatkin (1993, 118–122).

A variable that may have significant effect on the injuries sustained by a falling animal (dog, cat, or other) is the presence of a projection in the path of the fall, such as a fire escape, awning, or tree. Depending on its nature, a projection might help to prevent serious injury (such as the awning the stereotypical cartoon cat falls into). Conversely, a projection might increase the degree of injury due to direct impact with the falling animal or by altering the animal's landing position, so that his impact with the ground is more traumatic than it would have otherwise been.

Despite this significant body of knowledge about the effect of high-rise trauma on dogs and cats, there is little evidence to address the question of whether an animal has fallen from a height versus being thrown or pushed. The only clue is the finding that dogs who fall accidentally sustain injuries to the rear half of the body, while those who jump voluntarily sustain injuries to the front half. This correlation could be presented by an examining veterinarian to a judge or jury, allowing them to weigh it against all other evidence in a case when making their determination. Another possibility is that an animal may be pushed or thrown from a height as the final act in a history of abuse. In such cases a thorough necropsy may reveal past abuse in the form of healed fractures, embedded projectiles, or older bruises.

There is one additional consideration in cases in which an animal is suspected to have been thrown from a height. If the height is not great, it is possible that the force with which the animal is thrown could be additive to the force that is the product of the animal's mass times the acceleration of the animal's body as it falls. An animal thrown with extreme force might be expected to sustain more severe injuries than if the animal were to have fallen or been dropped without force. When this situation is suspected, it is advisable to solicit the assistance (and perhaps even testimony) of a professor of physics from a local university, who can estimate the force of deceleration with which the animal collided with the ground.

In all animal-cruelty cases, the veterinarian's job is to analyze all the evidence to make a determination of what occurred. In some cases it is not possible to do so until the investigation is completed by law enforcement and all the information is compiled and analyzed, together with the veterinarian's findings.

Binding

Binding is a common feature of attacks on animals. Rope, twine, tape, elastic bands, or wire is wrapped around their feet, body, neck, muzzle, or scrotum. While it may not seem that binding is a form of blunt force trauma, the crushing effects bindings exert on underlying tissues are the same: contusion, abrasion, laceration, and possibly damage to underlying structures.

The binding material may still be present at the time of veterinary examination, or it may have been removed before presentation. Even if it is removed, trace evidence associated with the binding material, such as sisal rope fibers or duct tape adhesive, may remain. Bindings often leave marks on the skin as well, depending on the makeup of the bindings, the amount of pressure they exert (tightness), how much the animal struggled against them, and the characteristics of the underlying anatomical structures. There may be patterns on the skin or wound that can identify the item used. Binding marks are more apparent over bony prominences around which they are wrapped, due to the pressure exerted by the bone against the binding. For example, a binding wrapped tightly around a dog's muzzle would leave the most visible bruise marks over the dorsal aspect of the muzzle (where the bony bridge of the nose lies closely under the skin) and over the ventral surfaces of the mandibles, where there is little soft tissue to absorb the pressure.

In deceased victims hemorrhage into the skin directly beneath bindings may be apparent on incision into bruised tissues. The absence of hemorrhage beneath bindings, however, does not prove that the animal was dead when bound. Some bindings are wide and smooth and do not cause bruising. If the bindings are somewhat loose, or if the animal does not struggle against them, little bruising may occur. Tight bindings or bindings left in place for a significant period may cause hair loss and/or edema of the underlying tissues. An animal's attempt to remove the binding material—a dog pawing at her bound muzzle, for example—may also cause trauma to adjacent and underlying tissues.

One form of binding that small-animal veterinarians have encountered is that of using a rubber band in an attempt to castrate a dog. When a man who adopted a male dog from a Midwest animal shelter had not returned required paperwork verifying that the dog had been neutered by a veterinarian on the specified date, the shelter staff was horrified when he reported that he had neutered the dog himself by placing a rubber band proximal to the testicles. Veterinarians may also encounter cases in which dog owners have attempted to dock the animal's tail using a rubber band. Such procedures are often unsuccessful, resulting in necrosis of the site of the rubber band and, in many cases, of the tissue distal to it (whether tail or testicles) as well.

The perpetrators of these actions, particularly of attempts to castrate by this method, often cite the use of rubber bands used to dock and castrate calves, lambs, and goat kids. This method, known as the "elastrator" or "banding" or "rubber ring" method has been used for such purposes in the United States and throughout the world. There has been discussion in the veterinary literature about the degree of pain and distress inflicted by this method on cattle, sheep, and goats (Molony, Kent, and Robertson 1993; Thornton and Waterman-Pearson 1999).

Another special form of binding or blunt force injury veterinarians commonly encounter is the damage associated with an animal's capture in a leghold trap or snare. Such wounds are usually seen on the neck (in the case of snares or large leghold traps) or legs or chest (in the case of "body-gripping" conibear traps). Snares cause deep skin depressions and broken hairs. Leghold and conibear traps cause extensive hemorrhage, bruising, and depression, often with broken bones at the point of impact (Spraker and Davies 1999). The HSUS has documented hundreds of instances in which companion animals have been injured or killed in illegally set or improperly monitored traps. Although forensic investigation is likely to focus on determining ownership and legality of use of the trap, veterinary testimony regarding the nature and severity of injuries may be important in helping to determine the nature of the charges that might be filed in such a case. If, for example, the nature of the animal's wounds and evidence from the scene suggest that the animal spent a prolonged period in the trap before being found, that might meet the legal definition of "torture or torment" and could be used to justify a more serious charge.

Binding is also sometimes associated with cases of asphyxia of animals (those in which the victim is strangled or hung by bindings around the neck), a subject that is further addressed in chapter 13.

Bite Injuries

Bite injuries typically involve characteristics of both blunt force trauma (crushing, bruising, and fractures) and sharp force injury (incised and puncture wounds), though it is possible to have blunt force trauma without penetration of the teeth. Accurate forensic documentation of such injuries should address both types of injury. Most bite wounds seen in the context of animal-cruelty investigations are dog or cat bites. (The special nature of bite injuries seen in the context of organized dogfighting is reviewed in chapter 20.)

The initial appearance of many bite wounds is deceptive, because most tissue damage occurs below the skin (Holt and Griffin 2000). Muscles and subcutaneous tissues are often crushed and damaged, leaving dead space within the tissues, and underlying bones are crushed and broken. Contusions and lacerations beneath the skin's surface may not be readily apparent once the skin has returned to its normal position.

A strong dog can inflict significant contusions and abrasions on another animal by pawing at or "pinning" the animal's body with a forelimb as well as by biting. This "forelimb stab" behavior has been described in the veterinary behavioral literature (Beaver 1999). It is evident in puppies as young as ten weeks of age, sometimes accompanied by a vertical leap, and is classified as predatory behavior.

Beating

More than forty years ago, a group of physicians published a landmark paper describing the "battered-child syndrome" (Kempe et al. 1962). They correlated their findings and those reported in many papers published before theirs and gave a name and a sense of urgency to a previously undefined but terrifying condition: that suffered by children who are beaten and battered, most often at the hands of an adult entrusted with their care. The references these authors cited included many that detailed the skeletal lesions suspected to be evidence of physical trauma, usually blunt force trauma.

For two reasons the battered-child syndrome, and its evidence and features, cannot be directly applied to battering of animals. One reason is that many of the skeletal changes that are considered evidence of trauma in children are evident because children have different physical and physiological characteristics from animals of the same size. The periosteal reaction of a growing bone (that of a child) to blunt force trauma is quite different from that of a completely ossified and no-longer-growing bone of an adult (albeit child-size) dog. And, while children are expected to be watched and protected at virtually all times, animals are typically left alone, sometimes for extended periods, with their caretaker having little way of knowing what their activities might have been during that time. Evidence of healing blunt force trauma to a dog is much more easily excused by saying, "It must have happened when the dog was unattended," than that of a child, for whom "unattendance" itself might be construed as neglect.

Munro (1999) and Munro and Thrusfield (2001a,b) have attempted to apply some of the principles used by Kempe et al. (1962) to injuries to cats and dogs. They describe some of the clinical signs and pathology that suggest that trauma may be the result of "non-accidental injury." They note that multiple fractures in various bones in different stages of healing should be cause for concern, particularly if the history offered is inconsistent with the nature of the injuries (Plate 11).

In one case, a puppy was presented with fractures to the femur, pelvis, and ribs, all about two to three weeks old, and a fracture to the tibia that appeared to be five to six weeks old. In addition, the animal had two large open wounds on the skin overlying the broken ribs. These were not consistent with the owner's claim that the dog had "fallen down the stairs."

In such instances of suspicious injuries, noting the attitude and behavior of the client may be as important as documenting the clinical pathology. Munro (1999) notes that these cases often demonstrate the following characteristics:

■ The account of the accident does not fit the observed injuries.
■ The owner refuses to comment on how the injury came about.
■ The owner shows a lack of concern for the animal's injuries.
■ There has been a significant delay in seeking veterinary treatment.

When these elements are present in the clinical history of an animal victim, appropriate notation should be made in the record, without framing such notations in the form of an accusation.

Perhaps the most common source of blunt force trauma to an animal is repetitive beating, whether it is a one-time occurrence or a chronically occurring event. The animal may be kicked; whipped with a belt or other tool; or beaten with a stick, baseball bat, or other object. Characteristics of injuries caused by kicking depend on the force of the kick, the characteristics of the foot (barefoot versus steel-toe or pointed leather boots), and the part of the body that is struck. The ribs are especially vulnerable to damage and fracture because they comprise a large portion of the surface area of the broad side of an animal. Multiple kicks may result in numerous coin-size bruises. Kicks to the head may, of course, result in fragmentation of the facial skeleton as well as damage to or fracture of the skull. The characteristics of skull fractures due to blunt force trauma in humans have been described in detail (Spitz 1993a).

As is evident from the variety of topics addressed in this chapter, blunt force trauma plays a significant role in many forms of intentional injury. The injuries this form of trauma causes are often general and do not always lend themselves to clear characterization of source of trauma. However, veterinarians who are knowledgeable about the manifestations of different types of blunt force trauma infliction are better able to assist in the investigation of cruelty to animals, better prepared for court testimony, and more confident on cross-examination.

Sharp Force Injuries

The world is full of sharp instruments that can inflict accidental or intentional injuries on animals or people. Such injuries may come from knives, axes, exposed metal, nails, glass, stones, and teeth. The challenge in forensic investigation of animal cruelty involving sharp force injury is often to associate a particular wound with a specific source and the source with a particular suspect and, if possible, to distinguish between accidental and nonaccidental injuries. Sharp force injuries can be classified into one of several categories:

- Stab wounds
- Chop wounds
- Puncture wounds
- Iatrogenic wounds
- Incised wounds
- Dicing wounds
- Bite wounds

Stab Wounds

In classic stab wounds, the track left by the weapon is usually deeper than the width of the wound on the skin. Stab wounds differ from blunt force lacerations in that they usually have clean, sharp margins without bruising at the edges and without the "bridging" deep in tissues seen in lacerations. Although it would seem reasonable that the size and shape of the weapon used would be reflected in the wounds that resulted, that is often not the case. Tissue can stretch, distorting entry wounds, and the path of a wound may be altered by fur, underlying bone, or other complicating forces. However, a dull knife is more likely to produce bruised or abraded margins, and a very dull implement will result in jagged, contused margins. Many knives have a sharp and a dull edge, resulting in entry wounds that may be cleaner and more pointed at one end. If the knife is partially withdrawn and another stab made, the wound will have a double point at one end. It is difficult to determine whether the blade was smooth or serrated unless there are superficial markings on the body. If the knife has a guard or thickened hilt, a powerful blow may produce a bruising pattern that matches the guard. This also indicates that there was full penetration, and the length of the blade can be determined from the wound. Multiple stab wounds can be more informative than a single wound. They provide a good sample of tracks, allowing a better estimate of the length and thickness of the weapon.

Incised Wounds

Incised wounds are cuts in which the track is shallower than the width of the wound. They may be the result of shallow knife, razor, or scissors cuts; falls onto or through glass; or slashes from teeth or claws.

In cases involving human victims, some stab or incised wound characteristics may also provide information about the motivation of the attacker and the attacker's relationship with the victim. Pathologists often characterize shallow, light cuts near a deeper injury as "hesitation" wounds. These are characteristic of wounds inflicted by an attacker who is inexperienced or somewhat reluctant to proceed with the attack. They are often seen in sharp force injuries associated with suicide. Conversely, emotion-charged attacks may often be reflected in multiple, deep wounds. In analyzing 316 sharp force homicides, Karlsson (1997) found that the number of injuries inflicted varied with the relationship between perpetrator and victim. Attacks with ten or more wounds were most often seen in spouses or family members. A similar pattern is likely to exist in sharp force attacks on animals. Multiple wounds may reflect a "personalization" of the attack on the animal associated with anger or a desire for revenge against an animal connected with a person close to the attacker.

A recent case in Louisiana reflects this pattern. An eighteen-year-old man was arrested for stealing and stabbing an eight-hundred-pound pet sow belonging to his girlfriend's mother. He admitted to the killing but alleged that he had taken the pig to slaughter for food. However, this account was inconsistent with the fact that the animal had been stabbed more than seventy times with a hunting knife, primarily in the genital area, and had been abandoned in a nearby yard. Prosecutors noted that the killing had taken place shortly after the mother had ridiculed the perpetrator for his lack of income. In recognition of both the brutality of the attack and the assessment of the potential danger to people, he was charged with and convicted of aggravated animal cruelty, which carries a minimum prison sentence of one year and a maximum of ten years.

Chop Wounds

Chop wounds are usually produced by heavier weapons with a sharp edge, including axes, hatchets, machetes, and cleavers. Rotating blades, such as propellers, mowers, or fans, may also produce chopping injuries. These injuries have characteristics of other sharp force wounds as well as elements of blunt force trauma. Chopping instruments incise tissues but, due to their weight and force, they also crush the margins of the tissue and can cut into or fracture underlying bone.

Dicing Injuries

Dicing injuries are a combination of abrasions and shallow incised injuries. They may result from the victim being dragged over a surface with sharp elements, such as gravel, or from being thrown through or against glass. Such wounds are often contaminated with the substrate, including gravel or glass shards, which might provide evidence of the circumstances of the injury.

Puncture Wounds

Punctures are special stab or incised wounds that are usually the product of a narrow instrument with a conical or wedge cross-section, such as a screwdriver, ice pick, dart, pen, pencil, or tooth. As with other stab wounds, the size and shape of the wound may or may not accurately reflect the nature of the instrument producing the injury. However, in some cases, the puncture wound reflects the cross-section of the source of the wound, particularly in punctures through strong but thin tissue such as mesentery or pericardium.

Such evidence proved important in a California case in which the body of a newborn infant mauled by a pit bull puppy had been found in a yard. The infant had allegedly been put in the neighbor's yard by his mother. He had received multiple puncture wounds, so investigators thought it possible that the infant had been stabbed with a knife or fork and put in the yard to try to hide the evidence. The defense argued that that the mentally handicapped mother had believed the infant was born dead and had disposed of the body out of fear. If the child's death had been the result of intentional stabbing, the mother could have been charged with first-degree murder, a capital offense. However, the child's autopsy revealed a puncture wound through the pericardium that matched the cross-section of the puppy's teeth, the likely direct cause of death. No injuries were consistent with stab wounds from any implements found in the home, and the mother was subsequently convicted of manslaughter rather than murder.

Bite Wounds

Bite wounds have come under increasing scrutiny in human forensic cases since homicides and sexual assaults are often associated with bite injuries inflicted by the victim in self-defense or by the perpetrator as part of the attack. Considerable attention has been given to developing the discipline of forensic odontology and to the standardization of methods for collecting, preserving, and interpreting bite mark evidence (Bowers and Bell 1995; Aksu and Gobetti 1996; Sweet and Bowers 1998).

In forensic cases involving animal victims, bite wound analysis may be important for:
- discriminating between bite injuries and other sharp force wounds;
- identifying the species of the animal causing the injuries; or
- identifying the individual animal responsible for the injuries, or ruling out a particular individual as the source of the injury

Analyses that seek to differentiate between bite wounds and other sources of injury have been particularly important in cases of alleged ritualistic killing of animals. A similar analysis proved important in the 1997–1998 investigation of the mutilation deaths of ten endangered sea turtles found washed ashore at Padre Island National Seashore, Texas, over a three-month period. Since the turtles competed with commercial shrimpers, it was feared that the killings were the malicious result of this competition. The National Marine Fisheries Service, Texas Parks and Wildlife, and the Texas Shrimp Association offered rewards for information leading to arrest or conviction of anyone responsible. Forensic analysis by the U.S. Fish and Wildlife Forensic Laboratory concluded that the wounds did not fit the pattern of sharp force injury associated with a knife or axe but were in fact typical of the crushing jaws and teeth of large sharks (National Oceanographic and Atmospheric Administration 1998).

Bite wound analysis has also been used in cases of killing or wounding of livestock to distinguish among injuries associated with different carnivore predators, including dogs, coyotes, wolves, and cougars, or damage resulting from postmortem scavenging or other sources of injury. In these investigations it is important to do a complete forensic investigation of the scene, not just of the victim's wounds. Different carnivores typically produce different kinds of wounds and may direct these attacks to different areas of the body. They leave secondary evidence such as tracks, scratch and scent marks, scat, and traces of fur (Schaefer, Andrews, and Dinsmore 1981; Wade and Browns 1985; U.S. Department of Agriculture 1994).

Bite mark analysis has also been used to identify individual wild animals involved in attacks on humans. Rollins and Spencer (1995) report on the bite mark study of imprints left on the chin of a female jogger killed by a mountain lion in California. Analysis of the bite allowed authorities to judge the age and gender of the attacking animal and subsequently to establish that the lion responsible for the attack had been removed from the area.

Bite mark analysis is rarely used in animal-cruelty cases to attempt to identify the individual human or animal responsible for inflicting wounds on an animal victim. However, there may be scenarios in which such an analysis would prove helpful, such as when it has been alleged that an individual has allowed or encouraged her dog to attack the victim, and the defendant argues that the wounds were inflicted by another dog. Veterinary professionals are more likely to become involved in holding and examining dogs or other animals who have been implicated in a fatal or severe attack on a person. In such cases they may be called on to assist in preparing dental casts from the suspect animal as well as collecting blood, saliva, and other evidence according to the procedures outlined below. Care should also be taken to collect items that link the dog to the victim (clothing fibers, victim's hair, blood) and that may help in recreating the actions of the dog (soil, grass). In addition, toxicology studies may be helpful in explaining the behavior (Lauridson and Myers 1993).

Iatrogenic Wounds

"Iatrogenic" wounds are caused by a medical practitioner, including sharp force injuries produced in the course of medical treatment (e.g., injection, intubation, incision) or at the time of autopsy or necropsy. This may also include unintentional damage caused during treatment or examination, such as enlargement of knife or projectile tracks while probing a wound. It is important that the examining veterinarian have a complete record of any procedures that were done on the victim to distinguish between those associated with the injury and those resulting from treatment or examination.

One case in which the authors were involved demonstrates the potential problems associated with iatrogenic wounds. There had been a long-standing controversy over whether a child's death had been the result of stab wounds to the groin or injuries from a dog attack. It was also possible that dogs had been given access to the child's body to try to destroy the evidence of a fatal assault. The parents were convicted of murder but were released when the evidence of accidental death by dog bite was reintroduced during the appeal. The child was exhumed six years after her death, but a second autopsy was inconclusive, since examiners were unable to definitively distinguish among possible knife wounds, bite wounds, or scalpel wounds caused by the original autopsy. The parents remained free when prosecutors decided that the evidence was too contaminated to warrant a retrial, due in part to the iatrogenic wounds.

Examination and Documentation of Sharp Force Injuries

The procedures for recording and preserving evidence from sharp force injuries are similar to those for projectile injuries. An excellent standard for this procedure is that established by the American Board of Forensic Odontology (regularly revised and available at *www.abfo.org*) for the documentation of bite wounds.

Before wounds are cleaned, swabbings of the site should be obtained whenever possible, particularly in the case of bite injuries. Samples should be taken of any obvious blood drops around the wound and blood found distant from the wound, especially blood that appears out of context with the injury. The perpetrator may have slipped and cut herself, leaving DNA. Material collected near the opening of a sharp force wound may include traces of oil, lubricants, or other material associated with the weapon. In the case of bite wounds, DNA analysis of saliva found near the wound may prove to be more valuable than bite mark analysis in identifying the species and individual that inflicted the wound. It is acceptable to use either cotton tip applicators or cigarette paper to gather this evidence. Control swabbings should be taken from other regions of the individual who was bitten.

The record of the injury examination should make note of the details of each wound, including:

■ description of the anatomical location;
■ description of the surface contour: flat, curved, or irregular;
■ description of the tissue characteristics and underlying structure (bone, cartilage, muscle, fat);
■ description of the shape and color of the wound; and
■ measurement of the vertical and horizontal dimensions of the wound in metric units.

Photographs of each wound should be taken before and after cleaning the area. In cases of multiple wounds, it is best to assign a number to each wound and describe the location with a measurement to an anatomical landmark such as the spine. When taking measurements you can also use a clock reference, identifying a landmark, such as the head, as twelve o'clock.

In cases where it is unclear whether wounds were inflicted by a tool or by teeth (e.g., predation), there should be careful examination of wound edges and surrounding fur or feathers. Carnivore carnassial teeth and the beaks of birds of prey can produce wounds that are superficially identical to those produced by tools, particularly after partial decomposition or cleaning by insects. However, blades are more likely to cut hairs as well as flesh, leaving distinctive shorter hairs near the wound. In addition, ends of smaller bones, such as ribs, cut with an instrument are more likely to appear clean, while those that have been bitten or chewed appear jagged or crushed, particularly on microscopic examination.

The record should also include high resolution photographs of each wound. These should include larger field-orienting photographs to show the overall location and pattern of wounds as well as close-up photos of each wound. Each close-up photo should be made with and without a scale in place adjacent to the bite. It is desirable to also include a circular reference (a paper disc or coin) to control for angular distortion if attempts are made to match the bite mark photos to dental impressions.

After the wounds have been photographed, they should be examined for contaminants (sand, gravel, ink, pencil lead). Radiographs may reveal any fragments of the weapon that might have broken off and become embedded in bone. The wounds should not be probed excessively, but any paths going into organs should be noted. As in the case of projectile injuries, it may be desirable to preserve the injury site by excising the tissue containing the wound and preserving it in 10 percent Formalin.

If it is necessary to collect photographic or dental impression evidence from an animal suspected of causing a bite injury, the veterinarian should work with a forensic odontologist referred by the local law enforcement agency to be sure that the procedures followed meet established guidelines.

As with many other injuries, carefully describing and documenting sharp force wounds is an important part of the process of telling the story of an animal who has suffered or died and may provide essential evidence that could prevent such violence against others.

CHAPTER 12 Projectile Injuries

Esther was a mixed-breed dog, about fifteen years old, owned by Nancy Davis. Like many other animal companions, she became a pawn in a tumultuous relationship. Davis broke off her relationship with one Eddie Knowles, and two days later, on June 23, 2001, Knowles broke into Davis's trailer near Columbus, Georgia, to await her return from work.

According to press reports (Houston 2001), neighbors heard a gunshot and the cries of a dog and then saw Esther pulling herself along the ground dragging her hind legs. Knowles told a neighbor that he had accidentally shot the dog and was taking her to the veterinarian, but witnesses saw no dog in the truck as he sped off. Neighbors followed a trail of blood to some shrubs and found the dog alive but in obvious pain. Davis took the dog to Auburn veterinarian Mark Freeman, who determined that the dog had been shot below the tail, directly into the anus. The shot was from such close range that the hot gases had cauterized the wound, preventing Esther from immediately bleeding to death. However, her injuries were so severe that she was euthanized.

Knowles originally pleaded not guilty to felony animal cruelty, claiming that he was drinking and playing with a twelve-gauge shotgun when it went off. He said that he then noticed that the gunshot had apparently hit the dog. Freeman's testimony about the closeness of the shot was supported by a Georgia Bureau of Investigations firearms expert, who testified that the no. 6 shot had to have been fired from closer than six inches and was probably fired from a distance of an inch or less.

After this forensic evidence was introduced, Knowles changed his plea to guilty, and he became the third person in Georgia to be convicted under that state's new aggravated felony animal anti-cruelty law. In December 2001 Knowles was sentenced to three years in prison, plus five years probation for being a convicted felon (for a 1973 burglary) in possession of a shotgun.

Shooting and other projectile injuries have become all too common to veterinarians and animal-cruelty investigators. The HSUS's survey of media accounts of major cruelty cases reported in 2001 revealed that 22 percent of the 740 cases of intentional injuries were due to gunshot or other projectiles. It is essential that the professionals who respond to these cases have a good grasp of the proper investigation of these violent acts.

Pavletic (1996) defines a projectile as "an object propelled by an external force that continues in motion by inertia." Common projectiles that produce injuries of forensic significance include bullets, shotgun pellets, BBs and airgun pellets, arrows, and darts.

Gunshot Injuries

Gunshot is the most common projectile injury seen in animal-cruelty cases. Although prosecution of these cases may often involve experts in firearms or ballistics, it is helpful for any professionals dealing with these injuries to have some knowledge of basic ballistics. Pavletic (1986 a,b) provides an excellent review of this subject.

Projectile weapons cause injury by transferring kinetic energy from the projectile to the target. The nature of the injury is related to the velocity, size, and mass of projectile; the flight pattern (tumble); and the composition of the bullet. Projectiles cause injuries in several different ways. Primary injuries are the result of direct crushing and tearing of tissue on contact with the projectile, its fragments, and/or fragmented bone. Additional injuries result from cavitation, the process by which the shock wave of the projectile causes soft tissue to balloon outward from the path of the projectile, creating a temporary cavity with crushing forces that can cause trauma to tissue and circulation. During cavitation a vacuum forms that can draw contaminants and debris into the wound.

Projectile-related injuries or fatalities to animals can occur in many situations (Green 1980), including the legal killing of meat animals, hunting wildlife in season, euthanasia, accidental killing, malicious killing of pets, and illegal killing or poaching of wildlife. Pavletic (1985) surveyed 121 gunshot injuries treated at Boston's Angell Memorial Animal Hospital during an eleven-year period. Victims included 111 dogs and 10 cats. Of these injuries, 86 percent were from handguns, 3 percent from high-velocity rifles, 5 percent from shotguns, and 15 percent from BB or pellet guns. It is significant that most of these had initially been misdiagnosed as vehicular trauma or bite wounds. Spraker and Davies (1999) note that projectile injuries are often confused with other sources of injury. Furlington and Otto (1996) review eighty-four cases of gunshot (82 dogs and 2 cats) treated at the University of Pennsylvania veterinary teaching hospital during a nine-year period. They note that 29 percent of the victims returned home with injuries, 21 percent were shot in the owner's yard, and 19 percent were shot by police.

Both of these surveys of animal gunshot victims show a low representation of cats—2.3 percent in Furlington and Otto (1996) and 8.3 percent in Pavletic (1985). The 2002 HSUS cruelty database noted that 31 of the 179 reported animal shootings (17.3 percent) involved cats. Given the preponderance of cats over dogs in the pet population, and the large number of cats who spend much or all of their time outdoors, it is likely that all of these studies underestimate the true incidence of shootings involving cats.

The Veterinarian's Role

Veterinarians will have several important tasks in responding to a projectile injury incident. In the case of animals who have survived, the primary task is treating the animal's injuries, while preserving and documenting evidence that can assist in the investigation. Other important steps in handling victims, either alive or dead, include:

- documenting the number and location of wounds and features of wounds and adjacent areas;
- recovering the projectile(s) and evidence that could aid in associating the projectile(s) with a particular suspect or weapon;
- determining weapon type and range;
- determining trajectory of projectile;
- documenting final cause of death, time of injury to death or presentation, how far the victim might have traveled, sequence of projectile injuries compared with other injuries, and overall "humaneness" of the killing.

Treatment

Pavletic (1985) notes that low velocity wounds are generally treated by local wound debridement, lavage, antibiotic therapy, and application of sterile dressing. Nonpenetrating and penetrating or perforating thoracic wounds are treated conservatively with medical support, and abdominal wounds generally have internal injury that justified exploratory laparotomy. Furlington and Otto (1996) report that conservative treatment is usually adequate for animals with limb injuries not associated with a fracture, but they concur with Pavletic that those with evidence of peritoneal penetration require exploratory laparotomy. Those with thoracic injuries could be managed with conservative treatment or thoracocentesis. Most dogs in these studies survived; however, those with vertebral column or abdominal wounds had a worse prognosis than did those with limb or thoracic injuries.

High velocity injuries, which are rare in the reports in the veterinary literature, may result in more extensive injuries due to cavitation, but Fackler (1988) disputes the dogma that such injuries must be treated by extensive excision of tissue around the missile path, unless there has been increased tissue disruption due to bullet fragmentation. Drawing on military studies of wound progression in anesthetized animals, he notes that high velocity bullet wounds generally show less lasting tissue damage than that estimated from observation of the wound in the first few hours after it was inflicted.

Examination of Projectile Injuries

The primary forensic concerns in examining a victim of projectile injury should be proper identification and recording of any objects removed from the animal and a complete and accurate description of any wounds and lesions present in the body. Injuries to the body should be mapped and recorded as described in chapters 6 and 7. Any specimens, including fragments, must be handled, recorded, and stored in a way that ensures continuity of the chain of evidence and in a manner that minimizes damage.

In documenting wound characteristics, it is important to try to distinguish between entrance and exit wounds. Animals have the advantage of their fur being forced in or out of a wound, thereby indicating the direction of the projectile. In general, exit wounds are round or irregular, with no grease, gas, or powder residue. They may be stellar, slit-like, circular, crescent-shaped, or completely irregular. Exit wounds through tight skin tend to be larger. Low velocity weapons (e.g., handguns) usually produce exit wounds slightly larger than entrance wounds, while high velocity weapons may produce exit wounds that are smaller than the entrance wounds (Green 1980). At close range, however, explosive gases released at the muzzle may cause an entry wound to balloon and enlarge. Entrance wounds may have abrasion rings where the bullet rubbed the edges of the hole. There may also be singed fur or skin around the wound. Entrance wounds may be smooth or have micro-tears at the edges. Contact wounds may have a star-shape appearance due to the bullet wobble when it exits the barrel of the gun (Di Maio 1999).

Green (1980) describes how wound appearance varies with the weapon, bullet, and firing distance. Since skin is flexible, entrance wounds may not accurately reflect the caliber of the weapon. One of the most important findings in a forensic investigation of gunshot is an estimate of the distance between the gun and the victim at the time of the shooting. Guns discharge not only projectiles but also hot gases, powder residue, and other components of the projectile (e.g., shotgun wadding) that produce very different effects on tissue at different distances.

Contact Wounds

These are point -blank injuries caused by holding the barrel of the gun against skin. If the weapon was perpendicular to the surface, these wounds are usually circular. The edge of the wound shows a thin band of contusion and hemorrhage and bruising in the subcutaneous tissue. Hair may be singed and gas bubbles may be found in the pannicular layer. If the shot is over bone, a slight tearing of the edges of the wound may occur. Contact wounds do not generally result in "tattooing" (i.e., impregnating powder residue under the skin).

Close-Range Wounds

These are wounds from weapons within 60 cm of the skin but not in actual contact with it. They show more effects of exposure to hot gases and residue. Tattooing is seen at a range of less than 60 cm. Smoke fouling of the hair or skin occurs at 30 cm and singeing at range of less than 15 cm.

Long-Range Wounds

These wounds are generally round or oval, with none of the signs of combustion seen in closer-range injuries. There may be some deposit of grease from the bullet at the edges of the wound. If the angle of fire is not perpendicular to the wound surface, there may be some abrasion at the edge of the wound nearest the line of fire.

Many animal shootings may involve shotguns. These produce more complex injuries due to the special nature of and variety of shotgun shells and pellets. The principles discussed above can be applied to estimating the range.

Sherman and Parrish (1963) offer a slightly different classification of shotgun injuries based on pattern of distribution, depth of penetration, and range. They designate Type I injuries as more distant wounds where subcutaneous tissue and deep fascia are penetrated. Type II wounds are at closer range and show perforation of structures beneath deep fascia. Type III injuries are point-blank wounds (which they designate as being from less than three yards), with an extensive central zone of destruction and a small peripheral halo of pellets.

In all of these cases, the investigator should photograph an area 15 cm around each lesion to show shot or propellant patterns. Each photograph should include a ruler to demonstrate scale.

Further Examination

In addition to photographing and describing the wounds in detail, a full-body radiograph of the animal should be made. This may be necessary to confirm location of bullets or pellets if excavation threatens to destroy the pathway. Radiographs also document related injuries and may reveal additional trauma not related to the gunshot. The presence of an exit wound does not necessarily mean the projectile has exited. It is possible for tissue and bone fragments to be propelled out, and the bullet can rebound back in (Di Maio 1999). Not all projectiles are necessarily related to the incident under investigation. Pavletic (1996) comments that embedded projectiles are a common incidental finding in radiographs. Dogs and cats may often be carrying BBs, pellets, and even bullets from earlier attacks. In the past unscrupulous and abusive dog trainers have even advocated using BB or pellet guns to discipline barking dogs, and many animals may exhibit the signs of such maltreatment. When multiple projectiles are removed, their original location should be recorded and referenced to the radiograph, and any projectiles that are clearly associated with prior assaults (e.g., scar tissue) should be noted.

In the case of a necropsy of a shooting victim, the skin surrounding the entrance hole should be removed in a 15 cm square, pinned to a piece of rigid material, and frozen to preserve the original size and any traces of propellant. A small section should be removed for histopathology prior to freezing the tissue. Green (1980) suggests photographing the inside of the skin after it is removed to show the shotgun's dispersion pattern.

Having identified and documented the entrance wound, the investigator should estimate the probable path of the bullet with a probe made of soft material such as an insemination pipette or hollow semiflexible tubing. A metal rod may be inserted inside the tubing and radiographs taken to show the trajectory path. Trajectory of the bullet can help determine from where the shot was fired and help recreate the crime scene. Care should be taken not to create false tracks or dislodge the projectile. A bullet path creates shearing, compression, and stretching that cause injuries far away from the path. This can cause fractures, usually of the ribs, without a direct hit (Di Maio 1999). With direct hits one should look for the bone beveling out and possible lead deposit on the bone. Hemorrhage, torn viscera, or ingesta in the body cavity may also suggest the path or location of bullet if a clear track is not defined. Once organs have been examined, the entrance and exit wounds and location of the projectile should be examined. If there are discrepancies, a check should be made for additional projectiles. When determining the trajectory, it is important to consider that the animal may have been in motion.

The projectile(s) should be photographed in place before removal. If forceps are used to recover bullets and/or copper jackets, they should be wrapped in tape or cotton or dipped in wax so as not to scratch the surface and remove rifling marks. These marks can be matched to the gun that fired the bullets. Fragments should be rinsed free of blood and tissue fragments, since these will become difficult to dislodge from the grooves when dry, then dipped in alcohol to dry and disinfect; air dried; wrapped loosely in facial tissue (not cotton); sealed in a jar, vial, pillbox, or film container; and marked according to procedures outlined in chapter 5.

In the case of shotgun wounds, as many pellets as possible should be recovered and placed in a suitable container. Efforts should be made to recover any wadding that may be associated with the wound, since composition varies widely with manufacturers and can be important in associating the wound with a specific stock of ammunition.

Any examination of a shooting victim should include a complete postmortem exam, as described in chapter 8. This is particularly important if the killing was allegedly described as "euthanasia" to deal with a sick or injured animal. In many states the "humane killing" of one's own pet is not a crime, but it still may be a matter of concern or police inquiry. It is important to address the injuries and the time between injury and death to help determine if the death was "humane." A very common scenario in cases of domestic violence or child abuse is killing a family pet in front of a spouse or child to demonstrate the perpetrator's ability to wield power and control (Ponder and Lockwood 2000, 2001). A perpetrator may "justify" such killing to investigators or others by claiming that the animal was sick or aggressive. Even if veterinary evidence does not support a clear ruling of inhumane or unjustified killing, prosecutors may wish to proceed with charges on other grounds, such as discharge of a firearm within a residential area, child endangerment, or domestic violence. Animal victims in such cases may show evidence of earlier assaults (e.g., old embedded projectiles, healed fractures, internal injuries) that might substantiate reports of a long history of nonfatal abuse of the pet within the context of family violence.

Although Green (1980) cautions against attempting any forensic interpretation of wound characteristics, noting certain characteristics of the victim, wound type, and location can be pertinent to determining the weapon used, range, and context of the injury. For example, Furlington and Otto (1996) comment that the majority of the gunshot victims they saw were young, sexually intact male dogs of breeds with aggressive reputations. They note that 18 percent were German shepherds, 13 percent pit bull types, 13 percent rottweilers, 10 percent Doberman pinschers, and 2 percent mastiffs. All of these breeds were over-represented compared with the general clinic population. There was a preponderance of forelimb vs. hindlimb injuries and thoracic vs. abdominal injuries, leading Furlington and Otto to suggest that most of these animals were facing the weapon or had their attention focused on the shooter at the time of the shooting. Such characteristics suggest a very different story from hindlimb injuries to a Labrador puppy with a trajectory indicating that the animal was fleeing when it was shot.

Pellets and BBs

BBs and pellets are lighter-weight projectiles usually propelled by compressed gas. BBs are spherical, usually .175 caliber (i.e., having a diameter of .175 inches), while pellets can be a variety of sizes and shapes, the most common being an hourglass shape ranging from .177 to .22 caliber. These are considered low-velocity weapons, with muzzle velocities in the range of 330–525 fps for common pneumatic pistols and 390–940 fps for pneumatic rifles. Because of the smaller size and lower velocity of these weapons, BB and pellet penetration is often limited to the hypodermis and underlying muscle. These weapons have been associated, however, with fatal injuries in animals and humans (Harris, Luterman, and Curreri 1983). It is important to note that discharging a pellet gun, and sometimes BB guns, within city limits or residential areas falls under the category of a firearm in most ordinances and is against the law.

In general, documentation and preservation of evidence in cases involving these weapons should proceed as discussed above. Radiographic evidence can be particularly important in these cases since it is likely that the victims may have been shot several times.

Other Projectiles—Darts and Arrows

Animals may fall victim to a wide variety of other projectiles. These can include small darts fired from BB or pellet pistols, larger darts from blowguns, and arrows from hunting, target, or crossbow weapons.

Wildlife officers routinely encounter attempts to disguise the nature of injuries to game. For example, animals may be shot during a "bow-only" hunting season and then have arrows inserted into the wound to make it appear they have been taken legally (Spraker and Davies 1999). Careful analysis of wounds using the procedures described above can distinguish among injuries from different kinds of weapons.

Deep puncture wounds from darts often retain the projectile. In these cases the projectile should be photographed in place, with surrounding wound tissue, as with bullet wounds. After removal, the projectile should be labeled and stored in an appropriate crush-proof container.

Wounds from arrows are classic puncture wounds with hemorrhaging around the wound. Wounds from broad-head arrows have lateral cuts, making an "X." A flathead arrow produces a slashing wound. Some hunting arrows are feathered to spin, resulting in a drilling wound that causes extensive hemorrhage as it passes through tissue (Green 1980). In the case of fresh wounds, the edges of the skin can be rejoined to approximate their appearance before penetration; however, this is more difficult in older wounds. Arrow wounds that do not show hemorrhaging along the edges occurred after the animal was dead. In cases where arrows have been inserted into bullet wounds, there is hemorrhaging at the center of the wound but not at the lateral edges where the arrow cut into dead tissue (Spraker and Davies 1999).

As with bullet wounds, the area surrounding arrow wounds should be clearly photographed, with particular attention paid to the size and shape of the wound. At necropsy, the inside surface of the skin should be photographed as well, and a 15 cm square of skin should be preserved as described above. This evidence may provide a key link to projectiles found near the victim or in the possession of a suspect.

13 Asphyxia

omicides due to asphyxia are relatively uncommon (Di Maio 2000). There are few data, however, on the frequency of asphyxiation in victims of cruelty to animals. A survey of more than 5,100 animal-cruelty cases reported in the media between 2001 and 2004 included reports of sixty-eight animal hangings (1.3 percent of the cases) and eighty-four instances of suffocation (1.6 percent of cases). About one-third of these cases involved cats as victims and two-thirds involved dogs.

Asphyxiation of animals can take many forms, including hanging, ligature strangulation, manual strangulation, suffocation, oxygen deprivation, carbon monoxide inhalation, carbon dioxide inhalation, and choking (aspiration of foreign material). (Drowning, another form of asphyxia, is discussed in chapter 14.)

When evaluating cases of cruelty to animals, it is important to be aware that multiple acts of abuse may have been committed on a single animal. The offender may attempt to asphyxiate an animal, successfully or unsuccessfully, in conjunction with inflicting other injuries. Investigational findings regarding the scene and circumstances of death are crucial to determining the cause of death.

The definition of asphyxia is loss of consciousness due to the lack of oxygen. An animal must be able to breathe to take in oxygen, transport it to tissues, and eliminate carbon dioxide. Interference in any of these components can result in asphyxiation. Restrictions of blood flow to the brain, as seen in neck compression or increased cerebral blood pressure caused by chest compression, are also categorized as asphyxia.

There are several categories of asphyxia, and characteristic findings may or may not be present in each category. Most commonly found are injuries to the external and internal neck structures. It is critical to recognize that the primary difference between animals and humans is the skin and musculature. The neck and chest muscles of animals are much thicker than those of humans, providing greater protection for the internal structures. The skin of animals also is much less susceptible to bruising, making detection of ligature patterns more difficult.

The causes of asphyxia can be broken down into the categories used in human medicine:

Mechanical Asphyxia
- Suffocation: vitiated atmosphere, internal airway, external airway
- Neck compression: hanging, strangulation
- Chest/abdominal compression

Chemical Asphyxia

- Interference with oxygen uptake: carbon monoxide
- Interference with oxygen utilization: cyanide

In all cases of suspicious death or possible asphyxia, the head and neck structures must be carefully examined. The fur and skin should be inspected for bruising and abrasions and the mouth for foreign material and soft tissue tears. Since an animal may bite the perpetrator, it is important to swab the lips and teeth of all victims of cruelty for possible blood, skin, or other sources of DNA. The animal also may scratch the perpetrator during a struggle, so the animal's feet should be placed in paper bags until they can be examined. They should be inspected for trace evidence and blood, and the nails should be removed for human DNA testing, preserving each foot sample in a separate envelope.

Petechial hemorrhages on the face and mouth are commonly seen in human asphyxia cases. These are caused by compression-release-compression of the major neck vessels. Petechiae may be seen in the sclera, conjunctiva, and periorbital tissue. These hemorrhages also may be found on the lips, oral mucosa, and soft palate. The presence of these hemorrhages is not necessarily pathognomonic for asphyxia. In humans it is also seen with seizures and cases of sudden infant death syndrome (SIDS). (It is important to note that the lack of petechiae does not rule out asphyxia as the cause of death.)

The skin and underlying subcutaneous tissue, muscles of the neck, blood vessels (including the jugular veins and carotid arteries), hyoid bones, thyroid cartilages, and cervical vertebrae are all structures susceptible to damage during one of these methods of asphyxia. Neck radiographs should be done before necropsy exam. The external neck should then be examined by first shaving the fur to look for bruises or abrasions. The internal neck exam should be performed after the chest contents have been removed and the blood drained to minimize artifact. The tongue and neck structures should be removed all together for examination by making an incision along the inside of the entire mandible (Plate 12). The neck should be dissected layer by layer looking for deep-tissue bruising and injuries to the neck structures.

Mechanical Asphyxia
Suffocation
Vitiated Atmosphere

A vitiated atmosphere is one that is lacking adequate oxygen. This can happen when oxygen is replaced by another gas such as methane or when oxygen is consumed and not replenished. This occurs most often in an enclosed space such as in a well sealed carton or refrigerator.

There are no characteristic physical findings of this type of suffocation. Diagnosis is predominantly made by the death scene findings.

Internal Airway: Choking

Choking is blockage of the posterior pharynx, larynx, trachea, and bronchi by foreign material. This can be accidental or intentional, depending on the object found lodged in the airway. The foreign material may be forcibly put in the animal's mouth, inhaled, or aspirated, as can occur in force-feeding. Not all material may be foreign, as with blood aspiration from head or neck injuries. The internal airway should be examined for foreign material. Aspiration of less discrete material may be found in the deeper airways.

Airway Swelling and Obstruction

Obstruction of the airway, caused by the swelling of tissues around or lining the airways, may be due to a variety of causes. The swelling may occur at the upper airway or in the deeper bronchioles. An obstruction can be due to a tumor, infection, or anaphylaxis. Inhalation of irritating substances, such as pepper spray, can cause swelling of the airway lining, a buildup of mucus, and bronchospasm effectively obstructing the airway. A blow to the neck can take minutes to hours to swell, resulting in external swelling and obstruction of the airway.

External Airway: Smothering

Smothering is characterized by blockage of the air passage due to the occlusion of the mouth and/or nose and the oropharynx. This occlusion can be caused by using a variety of objects, such as a plastic bag or pillow case and, less often, hands. It can also be caused by an object lodged at the oropharynx. The external and internal mouth area should be inspected for trace evidence of the material used.

The injuries seen with smothering are variable depending on the object used and how much the victim struggled. There may be abrasions or contusions on the face, oral mucosa, lips, and torn frenulums, and petechiae may or may not be found around the eyes or mouth.

Neck Compression

Asphyxia by neck compression, including hanging and strangulation, involves constriction of the jugular veins and carotid arteries and may or may not include compression of the airway. Loss of consciousness and death are due primarily to compression of the major blood vessels in the neck. Hanging, ligature strangulation, and manual strangulation have many characteristics in common, the most notable of which is that each of these methods of asphyxiation can, but does not always, result in damage to the physical structures of the neck.

Hanging

A significant body of scientific literature details the effects of hanging—accidental, suicidal, and homicidal—in humans, including literature on the effects of ligature or manual strangulation. In hanging, the force on the neck is from the weight of the body transmitted through a ligature suspending the animal. It requires very little pressure to compress the major blood vessels of the neck, so complete suspension may not be necessary.

In humans, the most common finding is a ligature mark. This may or may not occur in animals, depending on the density of fur, type of ligature, and length of time suspended. Most ligature marks bear the pattern of the ligature used. A wide variety of materials can be used to hang animals, including rope made of nylon, cotton, sisal, or other materials; heavy twine; wire; a leather belt; bedding; and clothing. Wide and soft ligatures can be difficult to identify because of the material's tendency to compress in some areas while remaining wide in others.

It is important to try and to determine if the ligature mark was made ante- or postmortem. True hanging must necessarily be differentiated from "faux hanging," which occurs when an already-deceased animal is hung. (In humans, the mark may be a yellow-tan color when the body was hung postmortem.)

The ligature usually causes an inverted "V" bruising pattern on the neck in humans. Because of the thickness of animals' skin, the bruising may be more evident in the subcutaneous tissues. There is usually minimal damage to the internal neck structures. Depending on where the point of pressure is applied, there may be deep hemorrhages, especially in the submandibular lymph nodes.

The face and structures above the ligature may be congested if the jugular veins were compressed before the carotid arteries. Petechiae may be seen on the eyes and in the mouth. Most often the compression completely occludes both major vessels and petechiae are absent. Livor mortis develops in the lower body. As all the blood pools in the lower body, the vessels can rupture, causing pseudohemorrhage, known as Tardieu's spots.

If the hanging involved a sharp drop before suspension, it is possible to see cervical intervertebral separation. Such a drop is more likely to cause damage to the internal neck structures. Fractures of the thyroid cartilage, hyoid bone, and/or cervical spine have been studied (Feigin 1999). Ligature width is not predictive of whether a neck organ fracture will occur; age appears to be the most important variable. Full suspension is not necessary to produce fractures.

It is important to know the position of the body before it is cut down. The ligature knot should be preserved as evidence; the inside of the knot may contain trace evidence or human DNA linked to the perpetrator.

Strangulation

Strangulation involves the use of outside force to exert pressure on the neck, which causes compression of the major blood vessels and/or the airway. The time for death to occur depends on how effectively, how extensively, and how quickly the pressure is applied. Compression must be maintained for a period of time before death occurs. If a struggle ensues, the compression may be released and reapplied, ultimately causing petechial hemorrhages on the face. The carotid sinus may be stimulated with the neck pressure and causes a vagal nerve response resulting in a lowered heart rate.

Manual Strangulation (Throttling)

Manual strangulation is defined by using hands to compress the neck. The external neck should be inspected for linear or oval bruises, abrasions, and fingernail marks. It is not always possible to tell if the person is left- or right-handed based on the bruising pattern unless it is determined the person was in front of or behind the animal.

Petechial hemorrhages are commonly seen in the eyes and mouth. Hemorrhage within the tongue is common in humans and can be detected by making multiple cross-wise slices of the tongue. Depending on the force of the struggle between the victim and the assailant, there may be substantial hemorrhaging of the soft tissues in the neck.

The deeper internal neck structures may be injured. Depending on the force and where it is applied, the hyoid bone may be damaged. (The hyoid bone is reportedly fractured in one-third of all human homicides by strangulation [Pollanen and Chiasson 1996], whereas approximately 9 percent of accidental and suicidal hangings exhibit neck organ fractures.) Since more cases lack hyoid fracture than feature it, the absence of this finding does not preclude strangulation. Whether a hyoid bone, thyroid cartilage, or other bony or cartilaginous neck structure fractures or not is determined by the nature and magnitude of force applied to the neck, the age of the victim, the nature of the strangulating instrument (rope, wire, hands), and the intrinsic anatomic features of the hyoid bone. In humans, fractured hyoid bones occur more commonly in older victims, and the age dependency of the occurrence correlates with the degree of ossification or fusion of the hyoid synchondroses. Seventy percent of all fractured hyoids are fused, while only 30 percent of non-fractured hyoids are fused (Pollanen and Chiasson 1996).

Ligature Strangulation (Garroting)

Garroting has characteristics of both hanging and manual strangulation. Ligature marks may or may not be present. If present, ligature marks are usually lower on the neck and have a more horizontal orientation. It is possible to see multiple marks or atypical marks as the perpetrator was trying to get a "grip" before tightening the ligature. Ligatures come in a variety of forms, and the nature of the ligature influences the presence of a telltale mark. A narrower and harder ligature produces a deeper furrow than one that is wide and soft. There may be material from the ligature embedded in the fur or in the ligature mark. The knot should be preserved as evidence.

Petechiae are often seen in the eyes and mouth. The internal neck structures may be injured, and there may or may not be soft tissue hemorrhaging. Fractures of the larynx may occur, depending on the point of compression. Hyoid fractures are not commonly found in human garroting victims (Dix, Graham, and Hanzlick 2000).

Yoking

Yoking is defined as compression of the anterior neck using a forearm or an object. External neck injury may be absent, depending on what is used to apply the pressure. If there is a forceful struggle, there may be external bruising or abrasions. Damage to the internal neck structures and soft tissue is also variable. Petechiae are often present in the eyes and mouth.

Chest/Abdominal Compression

Compression of the chest or upper abdomen causes increased intrathoracic pressure and/or hinders breathing, resulting in death. The increased intrathoracic pressure compromises the hemodynamics of the heart, lungs, and brain. Venous pressure is increased, causing congestion of the head and neck in humans. Petechiae are most common on the eyes and face and may also be seen on the surface of the chest and shoulder. The increase in venous pressure is transmitted to the brain, causing unconsciousness. Inhalation is hindered, and when compression is prolonged, death results. Marks may be seen on the surface of the chest or abdomen, and injuries to the ribs or internal organs may be present. Hemorrhages may be seen in the deep muscle attachments of the neck and chest. Compression with less pressure causes death primarily due to hindrance to breathing.

Chemical Asphyxia
Carbon Monoxide

When a chemical interferes with oxygen uptake, use, or transport it causes asphyxia. Carbon monoxide (CO) is a colorless and odorless gas that binds to hemoglobin. It has an affinity approximately 240 times that of oxygen, thereby inhibiting the uptake and use of oxygen (Dix, Graham, and Hanzlick 2000). Carbon monoxide also has greater affinity for myoglobin than oxygen does, and it interferes with certain respiratory processes with the cells. Most cases of human carbon monoxide poisoning are from smoke inhalation, car fumes in an enclosed space, or fumes from a faulty furnace or heater in the home.

Carbon monoxide is not absorbed or produced to any significant degree after death, so a carbon monoxide hemoglobin test accurately reflects the animal's level at the time of death.

Livor mortis in people who have died from CO poisoning has a characteristic cherry red or red-pink color. This is most visible on the nailbeds and the lips. The internal organs and blood are a lighter red than is usually seen. In humans the outer skin layers are separated from the underlying layers, resulting in epidermal slippage. This is normally seen as a postmortem phenomenon. The deeper layers may have red or gray-tan discoloration. The epidermal slippage is not specific to CO poisoning (Dix, Graham, and Hanzlick 2000).

Cyanide

Cyanide binds to and inhibits mitochondrial cytochrome oxidase, a cellular respiratory enzyme, which disrupts the cells' ability to use oxygen. The brain and heart are affected more rapidly and severely. Victims of cyanide poisoning also have a characteristic cherry red or red-pink coloring because of blood's high oxygen content. However, some victims of cyanide are cyanotic. An aroma of "bitter almonds" or "mustiness" is often associated with the body, although it is reported that not everyone can detect this aroma. Cyanide may be inhaled or ingested. The forms for ingestion are often corrosive, causing injuries to the oral cavity, esophagus, and/or stomach.

Although asphyxia is relatively uncommon in intentional animal cruelty, these cases deserve close attention. Hanging, strangulation, and suffocation can be extremely violent crimes and may be carried out with the specific intent to frighten and control those who care about the animal victim. The "intimacy" of these crimes and the necessity of having close contact with the victim can be associated with an increased potential for violence that may generalize to other nonhuman and human victims. The skills of veterinarians and cruelty investigators can help tell the story of what really transpired and help prevent future violence.

14 Drowning

Although drowning is a form of asphyxia, in which death occurs due to anoxia, the mechanisms involved in drowning may include factors other than asphyxia, and the physical findings differ somewhat from those found in other forms of asphyxia. The diagnosis of drowning is derived from information not found in typical asphyxial deaths. For these reasons, death by drowning is considered separately here from other forms of asphyxia.

Less than 1 percent of the 5,100 animal-cruelty cases in The HSUS's 2001–2004 database involved drowning. These were equally distributed between dogs and cats. Such cases are likely to go unreported unless they are witnessed or take place indoors (e.g., in a tub) or in a swimming pool. A search of current veterinary literature reveals only one publication that addresses either accidental or intentional drowning of a nonaquatic animal (Humber 1988). Even veterinary texts that discuss environmental trauma do not include drowning. This absence of literature suggests that drowning is an uncommon presentation in veterinary medicine. Intentional drowning as a form of animal cruelty, however, does occur, and generally takes one of two forms. The primary form is drowning "nuisance animals": wildlife (such as skunks) or unwanted offspring (newborn kittens, puppies, rabbits, and hamsters, for example) are drowned, sometimes in a misdirected attempt at euthanasia. This form of drowning may be termed "disposal drowning." A secondary form of intentional drowning is an act of punishment or attack, meant to frighten, intimidate, or abuse the animal victim, or—more often—a human victim who has an association with the animal. Here this form of drowning is referred to as "furious drowning." A third form of drowning may be categorized as "faux drowning," in which a perpetrator kills an animal by some noninvasive means, such as strangulation or a blow to the head, and then saturates the body with water or dumps the body in a container or body of water, to simulate drowning. Faux drowning can have two purposes: it may be used as a means of intimidation of another person (an abused spouse in a domestic violence situation, for example, as described in the author's note on page v), or it may be the result of a perpetrator's attempt to cover up an act of violence against an animal. For example, a teenage boy may kill the family cat in a fit of rage, then dump the cat's body in a swimming pool or pond and claim the animal has accidentally drowned.

Prosecutors may be reluctant to prosecute drowning cases as felony animal cruelty in the mistaken belief that such "disposal" is humane or socially acceptable. The *AVMA Report on Euthanasia* (2001, 696) clearly states: "Drowning is not a means of euthanasia and is inhumane." Investigation of drowning cases can often demonstrate that death was likely to have been slow, stressful, and painful and thus may be consistent with a definition of "torture," which may be necessary for a felony charge.

When a drowned or nearly drowned animal is presented to a veterinarian for examination, these questions must be considered:

- Did the animal actually drown or was the body wetted or submersed after death due to another cause?
- If death is attributed to drowning, why did the animal drown? Information about the mechanism of the animal's drowning may include details regarding a method used to restrain the animal as well as evidence of injuries that may have made the animal more susceptible to drowning.

Diagnosis of drowning is difficult and often elusive. Often, the determination that an animal has drowned or has been drowned is based on physical findings that correlate with investigative information, such as eyewitness testimony and evidence collected from the scene of the crime (the container of water that was used, for example). Although it is possible to drown an animal without complete submersion of the body, most intentional drowning uses submersion. Animals may be drowned in bodies of water (lakes, ponds, swimming pools, oceans), but buckets and other containers are often used. If the crime scene is known, it should be thoroughly processed for evidence to correlate with the findings of the victim's veterinary examination.

Disposal Drowning and Furious Drowning

Disposal drowning is a traditional method for dealing with unwanted animals. In the 1860s, unwanted dogs in New York City were routinely gathered into a wooden crate and drowned by dunking the crate into the East River, an event often cheered by a crowd of onlookers (Curtis 1984). Drowning has also been a traditional wildlife management technique, used for killing aquatic mammals such as beaver, muskrat, nutria, mink, and river otters, and for nonaquatic mammals such as raccoons, skunks, and opossums (Ludders et al. 1999). Disposal drowning to end the lives of feral cats has been used by animal-control personnel who have no access to or knowledge of methods, drugs, and restraint equipment necessary for providing humane deaths for these difficult-to-handle animals.

Proponents of disposal drowning have argued that animals being drowned are rendered unconscious by excessive accumulation of carbon dioxide in the blood stream (hypercarbia) early in the drowning process, which is said to produce a state of "narcosis," and that the animals are thus insensitive to the distress and pain associated with drowning. The often-cited study that proposed this theory monitored electroencephalographic (EEG) and electocardiographic (ECG) activity but did not actually measure carbon dioxide or oxygen levels in the blood of drowning animals (Gilbert and Gofton 1982).

The authors mentioned that carbon dioxide-induced narcosis could be a possible cause of death during drowning, but they also acknowledged that death could be due to anoxia. They did not present substantiating data (blood gas analyses) to support either hypothesis.

A recent review of relevant literature (including that published since 1982) disputes the occurrence of carbon dioxide-induced narcosis (Ludders et al. 1999). The review's authors cite several studies involving numerous animal species in which blood gases were measured to demonstrate that carbon dioxide levels in drowning animals do not become sufficiently high enough to induce narcosis before the induction of hypoxemia: drowning animals run out of oxygen long before they build up enough carbon dioxide to induce a narcotic state. The reviewers further concluded that drowning animals experience hypoxemia-induced discomfort and distress, based on cited studies that measured a surge of circulating catecholamines (epinephrine and norepinephrine) in anesthetized animals as they experienced drowning.

While disposal drowning may be a traditional method of eliminating unwanted animals, it is by no means a humane method. It may be particularly distressful to young animals such as newborn puppies and kittens. Because neonates are particularly resistant to the effects of hypoxia (AVMA 2001), death due to drowning may be especially slow in onset.

Furious drowning is a violent act often associated with domestic violence situations. The perpetrator must restrain the struggling animal manually—a difficult feat, except in the case of a very young puppy or kitten or an elderly or sick animal—or must use restraint equipment such as a rope or bag, an action that requires forethought and planning. Alternately, the animal is restrained by the effects of physical injury, usually strangulation or a blow to the head, before drowning.

A popular dog training book has recommended partial drowning as an effective method for training dogs who dig holes. Would-be dog trainers are instructed to fill the hole to the brim with water and "with the training collar and leash, bring the dog to the hole and shove his nose into the water; hold him there until he is sure he's drowning." The instructions are to perform this procedure for as many as six consecutive days, whether the dog continues digging or not, and readers are assured that it is not necessary to "catch the dog in the act" for such measures to be effective (Koehler 1986). Since some animal abuse cases arise out of situations in which disciplinary action is carried to the extreme, advice such as this may contribute to situations that result in drowning.

The Process of Drowning

Little is known about drowning in animals under natural circumstances, but most knowledge of the mechanisms and pathophysiology of drowning and the treatment of near-drowning in humans is the result of experimentation on dogs, rabbits, rats, and other animal species. The mechanism of drowning was first recorded by French physician P.C.H. Brouardel (1897), who described his observations of intentional drowning of several dogs. Brouardel identified five stages of drowning due to total submersion in fresh water:

- the stage of surprise, lasting for five to ten seconds;
- the first stage of respiratory arrest, lasting for about one minute and involving a struggle to reach the surface;
- the stage of deep respiration, lasting for about one minute; this was coupled with the formation of foam at the nose and mouth;
- the second stage of respiratory arrest, again lasting for about one minute, during which sensibility was lost and hypoxic convulsions occurred;
- terminal gasping, which constituted the last external signs of life.

The entire process of experimental drowning, as observed by Brouardel, took only three to four minutes. The onset of death may be slower if there is a prolonged struggle, which depends on the nature of the animal and the method of drowning. Humans are known to exhibit breath-holding, which lasts for variable lengths of time until accumulating carbon dioxide in the blood and tissues causes stimulation of the respiratory center in the brain and inevitable inhalation of large volumes of water (Spitz 1993c). This activity corresponds to the first stage of "respiratory arrest" observed by Brouardel. Inhaling water is accompanied by swallowing water; coughing, vomiting, and progressive loss of consciousness follow in rapid succession.

The Pathophysiology of Drowning
Dry Drowning
Not all of those who drown inhale water. True asphyxia, also referred to as "dry drowning," is thought to occur in 10–15 percent of human drowning deaths when closure of the larynx by a protective reflex (laryngospasm) seals the airway and prevents inhalation of water into deeper air passages (Spitz 1993c). Little is known about this form of drowning-associated asphyxia, so it is difficult to determine whether it might also occur in animals. Such cases present a forensic dilemma, since the laryngeal spasm subsides without a trace once the victim is dead. The typical physical findings of drowning, discussed below, are absent in dry drowning victims.

Wet Drowning: Fresh versus Saltwater Drowning
The majority of drowning victims, however, suffer from "wet drowning." They inhale water, which fills their lungs. The effect of water in the lungs differs dramatically, depending on its solute concentration. When an animal drowns in a hypotonic fluid—fresh or brackish (approximately 0.5 percent salinity) water—the blood volume is rapidly and largely diluted as water rushes into the circulation. Rapid hemolysis and dilution of blood constituents takes place, the heart is overburdened, and pulmonary edema quickly develops. In one study of cold freshwater drowning in anesthetized dogs (Conn et al. 1995), aspiration produced gross hemodilution with an average increase in body weight of 16.5 percent. Cardiac arrhythmia follows inhalation; ventricular tachycardia and fibrillation lead to death within a few minutes.

Seawater is hypertonic to blood, and when it fills the lungs of an animal, fluids are pulled out of the bloodstream rather than into it. The fluid shift is relatively small, compared to the large-volume fluid shift seen in freshwater drowning; during cold saltwater drowning, average body weight increases by only 6 percent, with hemoconcentration and a shrinkage of vascular volume (Conn et al. 1995). Severe pulmonary edema occurs in saltwater drowning, just as it does in freshwater drowning. Cardiac arrhythmias are rarely observed, so saltwater drowning takes longer than drowning in freshwater.

While it would seem that the effects of instillation of these hypotonic and hypertonic solutions into the lungs—significant hemodilution or hemoconcentration—would pose the greatest risk to the animal's well-being, it is simply the lack of oxygen—hypoxia/anoxia—that causes death in drowning victims (Orlowski, Abulleil, and Phillips 1989).

Hypothermia in Drowning
Hypothermia can play a significant role in the mechanism of drowning. Animals submersed in cold water develop tachypnea immediately, followed by aspiration of water with predictable effects. As long as circulation continues, aspirated cold water produces extremely rapid cooling of body core temperature, and the onset of death is accelerated. Several factors play a role in an animal's response to cold water: breed tolerance, acclimation, thickness and texture of the haircoat, and body surface area-to-mass ratio. Depending on these characteristics, some animals may be able to tread cold water, but all succumb eventually, and colder temperatures decrease the time of survival. Many humans suddenly exposed to cold water experience hyperventilation, a reflex activated through the cold receptors in the skin (Keatinge and Nadel 1965). This reflex appears to be largely uncontrollable and may enhance the risk of inhaling water. Presumably, some animals might also experience reflexive hyperventilation on sudden exposure to cold water.

The Physical Presentation of a Drowning Victim

The physical presentations of deceased drowning victims vary tremendously, depending on the physical condition of the animal before drowning and on the circumstances and mechanism of the drowning process. A complete physical examination of the victim, and the subsequent necropsy examination, should document all aspects of the animal's condition, in addition to those aspects that might be associated with the animal's drowning. There should be little in the way of conflicting evidence in a victim who has been drowned only a few minutes or a few hours previously. Examination becomes more difficult when the animal has been left in the drowning medium for some time, as decomposition often begins immediately after death. Decomposition is slower in water than in air, but it accelerates when the body is out of the water, so the necropsy should be performed as soon as possible (Dix, Graham, and Hanzlick 2000).

The presence of a characteristic "froth" exuding from the mouth and nose of a human drowning victim is considered by some to be pathognomonic for recent drowning (Giertsen 2000). The froth is produced by a mixture of mucus, proteins, and lung surfactant with the inhaled water during the violent respiratory movements of drowning. The froth may be blood-tinged due to alveolar capillary damage but is usually white and forms a mushroom-like cloud when discharged from the mouth and nose. It may persist for several days after death, reappear when wiped away (due to its abundance in the respiratory tract), and occur even in people who have remained submerged for several days after drowning. The respiratory tract (trachea, bronchi, and bronchioles) are filled with this material as well. While copious pulmonary foam may be seen in other conditions in which copious pulmonary edema is present (such as heroin overdose), in the absence of other potential causes, it is a strong indication that the victim inhaled water while still breathing (Dix, Graham, and Hanzlick 2000). It is presumed that this phenomenon occurs in animal victims of drowning as well, although necropsy findings of drowned animals have not been reported.

Pulmonary edema and aspirated water may fill the lungs of a drowning victim, so much so that in some cases they become characteristically heavy (Copeland 1985). Increased lung weight is a nonspecific indicator of drowning, but one that has been successfully used as supportive evidence of a diagnosis of drowning. The lungs may appear hyperexpanded due to the presence of entrapped water and air and bulge from the chest cavity when it is opened during examination. The lungs may exhibit indentation impressions from the ribs and their medial edges may meet at the center of the mediastinum ("kissing lungs"). The absence of pulmonary edema does not rule out drowning—that is, dry drowning.

Histological changes in the lungs of human drowning victims include *emphysema aquaosum*, expansion of the alveolar spaces, and *oedema aquaosum*, the presence of proteinaceous fluid in the alveoli. However, in fresh water drowning, *oedema aquaosum* may not be evident histologically due to the low protein content of the fluid in the alveoli. Petechial hemorrhages may be present on the pleura of the lungs (Dix, Graham, and Hanzlick 2000) as well as marked congestion (Plate 13).

The presence of water, sand, and mud in the trachea, bronchi, and bronchioles may be the result of water washing into the chest once the animal is dead and does not prove drowning. In the process of drowning, water is often swallowed, but water may enter passively postmortem. Though the presence of water and debris inside the airways or stomach does not confirm the diagnosis of drowning, it should raise the index of suspicion.

Complete descriptions of the physical findings associated with drowning in humans are available (Spitz 1993c; Pollanen 1998; Dix, Graham, and Hanzlick 2000).

Diagnosis of Drowning

There is no definitive test for drowning. Historically, many methods for diagnosis have been proposed, adopted by the medicolegal community, and then discarded as conflicting or disproving evidence has been subsequently presented (Spitz 1993c).

Recent Developments

Reports of Strontium

Strontium is a trace metal found in the crust of the earth. A quantification test of blood strontium levels in cases of drowning could aid in diagnosis. Strontium is widely present in seawater and in smaller amounts in fresh and domestic water. Because strontium has a naturally low concentration in plasma, the increase of strontium in the blood can support the diagnosis of drowning. The content of strontium in the water affects the blood level. Saltwater drowning has higher levels than in freshwater. In addition, aquatic decomposition reduces the level of detectable strontium (Pollanen 1998).

Forensic Diatomology

Diatoms are aquatic unicellular plants that have a distinguishing extracellular coat, or frustule, composed of silica. This frustule has unique patterns of symmetry and structure in the crystalline coat. There are a huge number—estimated at more than ten thousand——of morphologicially distinctive varieties of diatoms. These diatoms are found in naturally occurring bodies of water ranging from oceans to puddles. The populations even have monthly fluctuations in their concentrations in a particular body of water. Diatoms have become forensically important in the diagnosis of drowning. The foundation for this test is how diatoms are introduced into the body. In wet lung drownings, water is aspirated into the lungs. The diatoms perforate the alveolar-capillary barrier, enter the bloodstream through the heart, and then embolize to various organs, including the femoral bone marrow. If diatoms are detected in the bone marrow and the same diatoms are detected in the water that was inhaled or from the site of drowning:

- Drowning caused death or was a contributing factor to death.
- The individual was breathing upon entry into the water (Pollanen 1998).

Detection and testing for diatoms as confirmation of drowning have been used more in the United Kingdom, Europe, Japan, and South America. There has been controversy over this test in the United States. The main argument has been that diatoms may be found in nondrowning victims. This criticism has been successfully countered by using the "criterion of concordance," which demands that the diatoms recovered from tissue be comparable to the diatoms in the putative drowning medium (Pollanen 1998). This removes the ambiguity of the origin of the diatoms and proves the diatoms were introduced in the drowning process.

A sample of the drowning medium, approximately 500–1,000 mls, should be obtained from the scene at the exact site of body recovery and placed in a clean container. In circumstances where the drowning medium is not available or is unknown, samples may be taken from water in the stomach, sphenoid sinus, or tracheobronchial tree. Last, the femur should be removed for testing. The body and leg should be rinsed before removal to prevent contamination of the bone surface with exogenous diatoms. It is also important to change to clean gloves before removing the femur. The bone then can be frozen in a plastic bag prior to submission to the laboratory. Water taken from the scene may be refrigerated for several days to prevent microbe growth (Gruspier and Pollanen 2000).

Conclusion

Though drowning has been widely used as a traditional method of disposing of unwanted animals, it is not euthanasia. Drowning an animal with intent to hurt or "punish" the animal or to intimidate another person is a violent act and may demonstrate the perpetrator's dangerous nature. A wet or submersed animal is not necessarily a drowning victim, and veterinary examiners should perform a careful and complete examination that may rule in or out other possible causes of death or predrowning injuries that might have enhanced drowning. Animals may experience "dry drowning" as do humans, but the majority of drowning victims inhale large amounts of water. Despite the effect of inhaled hypotonic and hypertonic fluids on blood content and volume, lack of oxygen is the primary cause of death in cases of drowning. Animals may drown in freshwater, brackish water, saltwater, and various other liquids, and in relatively little volume.

Although some physical signs, including a characteristic froth exuding from the lungs and inflation of the lungs with water, are considered pathognomonic when observed in recently drowned victims, there are no diagnostic tests that clearly indicate drowning. Diatomology is the most promising method for diagnosis of drowning, but it has some well-recognized limitations. The sooner a victim is examined, the more likely an examiner is to be able to state confidently whether drowning has occurred. Because the diagnosis of drowning is difficult to make, it is highly important that veterinary examiners and criminal investigators work closely together to gather and analyze all available evidence and to make a strong case.

15 Poisoning

Poisoning is a method humans rarely use to cause intentional harm to other humans, despite the prevalence of this method in crime fiction. Only about .15 percent of all homicides involve poisoning (Evans 1996). Intentional poisonings usually fall within the context of chemical submission (so-called date rape druggings), altruistic suicide (usually distraught individuals who attempt to kill their children and then themselves), compassionate homicide ("mercy killing," or euthanasia), and chemical pranks in the workplace (Bismuth, Pierlot, and Borron 2000). Human-to-human poisoning is rarely an act of domestic violence: "In the conflict-filled domestic setting, the stereotype is that the husband beats, while the wife poisons" (Bismuth, Pierlot, and Borron 2000).

Poisoning animals, however, appears to be common. Humans have been using toxins to intentionally kill animals for centuries. European naturalists in the sixteenth century described the use of curare in hunting by indigenous people in South America. Hieronymus Bosch, in his 1577 *Herbal (Kreutterbuch)*, describes use of rotenone and other plant substances to kill fleas, lice, mites, and flies (in Martinez and Lohs 1987).

Motivations for poisoning in the context of cruelty to animals include "pest" abatement, retaliation (against the animal or the animal's owners), and sadistic cruelty. Recklessly negligent poisoning also occurs, such as when a dog is given access to alcohol or prescription or recreational drugs.

Investigation of animal poisoning is complicated by the fact that animals frequently encounter a variety of naturally occurring toxins (e.g., poisonous plants, venomous animals, microbial toxins in spoiled food). They may actually seek out medicinal and even toxic levels of a variety of substances with psychoactive, emetic, or other physiological properties (Siegel 1989; Samorini 2002). Animals may also come in contact with poisons that were not intended to cause them harm, including rodenticides, insecticides, and herbicides.

The most common topical poisons are petroleum fuels, lye (concentrated sodium hydroxide), and bleach (sodium hypochlorite); because these poisons cause chemical burns, they are discussed in chapter 9. Other common poisons discussed here include ethylene glycol (the primary component of most forms of antifreeze), alcohol, illicit drugs, over-the-counter and prescription drugs, pesticides (rodenticides), and snail and slug baits containing metaldehyde.

Dogs, in particular, have been largely used as models for studying the effects and treatment of drugs of intoxication, including cocaine and alcohol, so a significant amount of scientific literature on the administration of such drugs under experimental conditions is available and may be useful in particular cases of animal cruelty. It should be noted that there are significant differences between dogs and cats in their metabolism and physiologic responses to various poisons. In some cases minute quantities can be a lethal dose in felines, while the equivalent dose in dogs may have little effect.

Because poisoning cases can easily be classified once the toxin is identified, and because both human and animal poison control centers keep data on animal-poisoning cases reported to them, poisoning is one form of animal abuse for which some statistical information exists. The American Association of Poison Control Centers has published several summary reports of poisoning in animals, exhibiting increasing interest in collecting and classifying intentional and malicious poisoning of animals (Hornfeldt and Murphy 1992, 1997, 1998; Khan et al. 1999). The ASPCA Animal Poison Control Center offers the AnTox™ Veterinary Toxicology Consulting Program and maintains a database of more than 600,000 animal product/substance exposures (see appendix B).

Investigation of Animal Poisoning: General Considerations

Veterinarians can play a central role in supplementing other investigative activities to help tell the story of an animal who has been poisoned. Just as the challenge in investigating many injuries is to distinguish between accidental and nonaccidental injury, the challenge in poisoning cases is to collect and evaluate evidence that can distinguish between accidental and intentional exposure to toxins. Veterinary evaluation of the evidence can be valuable in a number of ways:

- Identifying the toxin and the possible route of administration or method of delivery
- Helping to estimate the time of exposure to the poison, based on the progression of physical symptoms and physiological changes
- Helping to identify evidence that might be associated with intentional poisoning, for example, remains of bait or unusual food items found in stomach contents or vomitus
- Helping to exclude possible natural or accidental sources of poisoning (toxic plants, snakes, insects, etc.)
- Possible commentary on pain and suffering potentially associated with a particular poison, which may be necessary to meet the legal requirement for bringing cruelty charges against the perpetrator
- Direct forensic investigation of the crime scene to retrieve evidence of poisoning.

In all suspected poisoning cases, whether the victim is living or dead, it is helpful to obtain as complete a health and behavioral history as possible. When was the animal last healthy? Is there a history of illness or injury? What was the animal's daily routine? When, where, and what was the animal fed? Did the animal have any unusual food habits (e.g., routinely raiding garbage, eating large quantities of unusual foods such as chocolate, grapes, or raisins)? Were there any potential toxins in the home (including pesticides, herbicides, or prescription or other drugs)? Was the animal allowed out in the yard or permitted to roam freely? Did the animal have access to the garage, storage sheds, or areas where toxic substances might be encountered? Had the owner been working on his car recently? Was there a history of problems with neighbors, their pets, or the pets of the owner?

The poisoning may not have been acute. In some cases of cruelty to animals, poisoning has been deliberate and slow, occurring over a long period, possibly with increasing doses. This could result in confusing laboratory data with evidence of chronic organ damage and acute symptoms.

If the source of poisoning is suspected to be illegal drugs, veterinarians have to structure their line of questioning carefully to obtain an honest response. If there is more than one person living on the premises, it may be helpful to talk with the owner alone. Veterinarians should emphasize that their only concern is to save the pet, and the importance of knowing the source of the problem will allow them to treat the animal appropriately.

Examination of Surviving Victims

Certain symptoms and clues should raise veterinarians' index of suspicion that an animal has been poisoned. A thorough documentation of all findings and a full laboratory workup are needed to help determine the source of the poison. Any animal who exhibits unexplained neurological signs, muscular abnormalities, acute organ failure, spontaneous bleeding, oral mucosal irritation, bowel mucosal sloughing, and/or body temperature abnormalities should be considered a possible victim of poisoning. The animal's heart rate, respiration, blood pressure, and temperature should be recorded and monitored for changes. A full neurological exam should be performed, including a fundic exam, and any vomiting, diarrhea, or urine output should be noted. Close attention should be paid to any odors from the mouth or gastric contents. Some poisons have characteristic odors: a garlic odor has been described in cases of exposure to arsenic, organophosphates, thallium, and zinc phosphide (which can also can smell like acetylene). Cyanide smells like bitter almonds. An acetone-like odor has been described with aspirin and other salicylates as well as toluene, xylene, pine tar, creosote, benzene, phenols, and isopropyl alcohol. Metaldehyde can smell like formaldehyde but the odor quickly dissipates from the stomach contents (Gfeller and Messonnier 2004).

In an animal-cruelty investigation it is important to determine the amount of poison the animal has ingested, which can be estimated from the known minimum toxic dose for the animal. A more accurate estimate can be established with laboratory testing on the food, stomach contents, urine, and/or blood. Whenever identifying tests are conducted, the veterinarian should always request quantification.

All samples of vomit, stomach contents, and diarrhea should be saved. They should be inspected for evidence of the source of poisoning, such as pill capsules, dyes (which could be linked with a certain brand of poison), plant material, illegal drugs, inert material associated with garbage, foreign objects, or candy wrappers. It is important to know what type and brand of food the animal is normally fed and compare it with the stomach contents. The animal's mouth should be inspected for clues, the outside as well as the inside, paying close attention to items lodged in the teeth. These areas should be swabbed and the swabs placed in a sterile container. Urine should be saved for testing as the kidneys excrete many illegal drugs.

Special laboratory tests can be performed on blood as well as on the saved urine or stomach contents. Specific in-house tests are available for vitamin K antagonist rat poisons (PIVKA test, Accurate Chemical and Scientific Corporation), coagulation cascade tests (SCA 2000, Synbiotics; ACT cartridge for the I-Stat analyzer, Heska), and an ethylene glycol test (PRN Pharmacal, Inc.). Veterinary toxicology laboratories can perform various toxicology screens. Local human commercial laboratories can run various screens as well and usually provide results more quickly, depending on the location. They also have the capacity to test for specific toxins. It is important to contact the lab before submitting samples to discuss the content of its screen and determine its sampling and submission guidelines. Human over-the-counter (OTC) commercial drug-testing kits are available; however, research is needed to determine their sensitivity with animals. With most toxicology screening, a negative result does not rule out the possibility of poisoning.

Once intentional poisoning is suspected, it is important to involve a cruelty investigator. Any findings should be communicated to the investigator and the investigator assisted in what evidence to look for at the crime scene. All samples should be saved and chain of custody preserved to ensure their admissibility in court.

Special Considerations in Necropsy of Poison Victims

Gross necropsy findings of most poisoning victims are, unfortunately, normal. Some specific indicators are covered under the specific poison discussions in this chapter. The odor of the gastric contents when the stomach is first opened should be noted, and all of the contents should be retrieved for testing and inspected for clues to the source of poison. Swab samples of the oral cavity, the teeth, and the outside of the mouth should be taken. If the toxin is known, the laboratory should be contacted for the specific samples that are needed to confirm diagnosis, the extent of injury (to address suffering), and the cause of death. If the toxin is unknown, as is often the case, it is important to include fixed and unfixed tissue samples.

Histopathological evaluation can determine the type of poison or narrow the list of possibilities. Each unfixed specimen should be placed in a separate container, wrapped in foil, and placed in a sealable plastic bag. It is important to submit large samples of liver and kidney as well as urine. Samples should not be mixed together. The laboratory should be contacted to discuss the quantity of samples needed, what tests to request, and submission guidelines. All items should be shipped using a courier with tracking to maintain chain of custody.

General Sampling Requirements

Toxicology Samples (unfixed): stomach contents, vomitus, intestinal contents, liver, kidney, brain, urine (frozen); blood with EDTA, serum or plasma (refrigerated); 3" x 8" section of skin for pesticide; water, soil, food, or forage and the fat and tissue around an injection site.

Toxicology Samples (fixed): heart, liver, lung, spleen, kidney, brain, and lesions.

Poisons: An Overview
Ethylene Glycol

By far, ethylene glycol (EG) appears to be the toxicant of choice for intentional poisoning of animals, no doubt because its effects are well known, it is cheaply and easily obtained, and it is usually readily consumed by the victim. The most common source is automotive antifreeze solution, but other sources include industrial solvents, rust removers, and color film processing fluids. Of 510 reports of EG exposure compiled by the ASPCA Animal Poison Control Center from July 1995 to December 1997, 3.0 percent were known to be intentional, while 33 percent were of unknown cause (by contrast, 16 percent were from engine leaks, 14 percent were from EG container spills, and 9 percent occurred during flushing of engines).

There are "safe" antifreezes (Sierra, ARCO) containing propylene glycol, which are flavored to make them distasteful to animals, thereby preventing ingestion. These antifreezes do not cause the problems related to EG; however, they may cause Heinz body anemia.

EG is technically easy to use because it is often readily consumed by dogs and cats and is easily mixed with another palatable substance such as raw hamburger meat or canned pet food. The minimum toxic dose of undiluted EG in dogs is 6.6 ml/kg bw, with a mortality of 59–70 percent (Connally et al. 1996). In cats, the reported minimum toxic dose of undiluted EG is even less, and more effective: 1.5 ml/kg bw with mortality up to 100 percent (Beasley and Buck 1980; Barton and Oehme 1981). Most common automotive antifreeze products contain approximately 95 percent EG (Gaynor and Dhupa 1999), so ingestion of 31.6 milliliters (ml) (little more than an ounce) is likely to be fatal to a ten-pound dog, while 7.2 ml (less than half a tablespoon) is fatal to a ten-pound cat.

Sometimes accidental exposure can occur gradually over an extended period. In one case a cat was poisoned from chronic exposure to antifreeze. His litterbox was in the garage, and the car had a radiator leak directly in the pathway to the litterbox. The cat exhibited mild lethargy for ten days before developing renal failure and other signs related to EG poisoning.

EG is rapidly absorbed from the gastrointestinal tract and readily distributed throughout all body tissues. Although ingestion with food may delay absorption, serum EG levels rise rapidly by one hour after ingestion and are highest at three hours after ingestion in both dog and cats. These levels remain significantly elevated for at least twelve hours and are usually undetectable forty-eight hours after ingestion. EG itself is relatively nontoxic; it has narcotic or euphoric effects similar to alcohol but is not lethal. However, EG is rapidly metabolized to glycolic acid, causing metabolic acidosis, then further metabolized to glyoxylic acid, which forms glycine, oxalic acid (the precursor to calcium oxalate), and formic acid. The exact action of the metabolites of EG is unknown; depending on the species, 0.05–3.79 percent of ingested EG is excreted in urine as oxalate, and cats are thought to produce more oxalate than other species do. Oxalate combines with calcium in the blood to form a soluble calcium oxalate complex that precipitates in the renal tubules and, to a lesser extent, in the vasculature of the brain, heart, and other organs. Some investigators believe that renal tubular epithelial damage and subsequent renal failure may result from the precipitation of calcium oxalate crystals per se, whereas others believe that nephrotoxicosis is caused by direct cytotoxic effects of either oxalate or the other metabolites of EG. The exact mechanism of renal tubular epithelial necrosis and failure remains unknown.

Understanding the three stages of the clinical syndrome of EG intoxication is valuable in assessing an animal who has ingested EG. Knowledge of the time sequence of symptoms of EG toxicity can also be important in determining the possible timeline of the animal's exposure to this toxin. It is important to note that there may be considerable overlap between these stages, some animals will not experience each stage, and death can occur at any stage. The first stage occurs thirty minutes to twelve hours after ingestion and is associated with central nervous system (CNS) disorders. This stage may pass very quickly and go undetected by the owner or veterinary staff. Signs may resemble those of alcohol intoxication and include CNS depression and lack of coordination that progresses to ataxia and paresis, somnolence, and sometimes—especially with large-volume ingestion—to focal or generalized seizures, coma, and death. Cats may become unresponsive within nine hours after ingestion. Other less common signs include muscle fasciculation, head tremors, and nystagmus. Hypothermia is a common finding, especially in cats, and may be secondary to CNS depression, hypoperfusion, and any exposure to low ambient temperatures. Vomiting is also seen frequently and may be secondary to direct gastric mucosal irritation from EG or the acute rise in serum osmolality. After the initial CNS depression, many animals seem to recover but then rapidly deteriorate due to severe metabolic acidosis. Intoxicated dogs, but not cats, exhibit marked and progressive polydipsia within one hour of EG ingestion that is thought to result from stimulation of the thirst mechanism by the acute rise in serum osmolality. Severe polyuria is common in both species and can lead to serious dehydration and hypoperfusion.

Stage 2 begins when cardiac and pulmonary manifestations occur, twelve to twenty-four hours after EG ingestion. Tachypnea and tachycardia are fairly common signs in dogs and may also be noted in cats; these signs may be partially attributable to severe metabolic acidosis. Congestive heart failure has not been reported in dogs and cats (although it is present in some human victims of EG intoxication), but pulmonary edema and congestion are fairly common postmortem findings in small animals.

Stage 3, the onset of oliguric renal failure, generally occurs twenty-four to seventy-two hours after ingestion of EG in dogs but may be seen as early as twelve to twenty-four hours after ingestion in cats. Most cats and dogs are presented at this stage of intoxication, when most of the EG has already been metabolized. Manifestations include depression, anorexia, vomiting, azotemia and/or uremia, and minimal urine output, with low to fixed specific gravity. Complete anuria often develops by seventy-two to ninety-six hours after ingestion. Flank pain is a common finding on abdominal palpation, especially in cats, and oral ulcerations and seizures may be seen secondary to uremia.

Calcium oxalate crystalluria is a consistent finding in EG intoxication in all species that have been studied, appearing in urine as early as three hours after ingestion in cats and by four to six hours after ingestion in dogs. Although the well-known dihydrate (weddelite) octahedral or envelope-shaped form may be seen, the monohydrate (whewellite) form—similar in appearance to and often misidentified as hippurate crystals—is much more commonly observed in cases of EG intoxication, although often misidentified. The absence of crystalluria does not rule out EG toxicity (Gwaltney-Brant and Richardson 2002a).

Laboratory findings associated with EG toxicity include increased osmolality, increased osmol gap, high anion gap, metabolic acidosis, high BUN, high creatinine, hyperglycemia, +/- hyperkalemia, hyperphosphatemia (if EG contained rust inhibitors), +/- hypocalcemia, low urine specific gravity, +/- calcium oxalate crystalluria, renal tubular casts.

Necropsy findings include pale, tan, swollen kidneys. Yellow birefringent, rosette-shaped oxalate crystals in renal tubules, are seen under polarizing light. Without polarized light, crystals can still be seen but the renal epithelial cells appear as tan- to gray-colored amorphous blobs.

The appropriate method for diagnosis of EG intoxication depends on the stage of intoxication during which the animal is presented. Any animal suspected of EG intoxication should be examined as quickly as possible. The Ethylene Glycol Test™ kit, manufactured by PRN Pharmacal, is an on-site test designed to detect EG in dogs one to twelve hours after ingestion, before the EG is excreted or metabolized (since cats can develop toxicosis at lower levels, commercial kits may not be sensitive enough to effect diagnosis). This test can cross-react with propylene glycol and other chemicals, so it is important to perform it before undertaking any treatment. Fluorescein dye, added to radiator fluid to help identify the source of a leak, is excreted in urine, so the urine of an animal who has ingested EG may fluoresce under ultraviolet light. A Wood's lamp may also be used to inspect the animal's mouth, paws, stomach contents, or food retrieved from the scene. Crystalluria in the form of birefringent octahedral, envelope-shaped calcium oxalate (dihydrate) crystals or needle-shaped calcium oxalate (monohydrate) crystals are highly suggestive of the diagnosis. Additional findings in a urine sample may include renal epithelial cells, proteinuria, and microscopic hematuria. The absence of crystals does not rule out the diagnosis of EG poisoning. The absence of a strong odor of alcohol in a patient who appears intoxicated should raise the suspicion of EG ingestion.

Making a diagnosis of EG toxicity is only one part of investigating such a case. Eyewitness testimony is obviously valuable in such cases, as is evidence of forced entry or unauthorized access to the area frequented by the animal victim. Trace evidence can also be useful, such as when fingerprints or hair of a suspect are found on a container of hamburger meat mixed with EG and placed within reach of the victim. The container should be preserved for testing of any poisonous residue. Stomach contents, excreta, or vomitus not consistent with the victim's usual diet can also provide valuable evidence. This might include remains of hot dogs, meatballs, or other tainted bait that may have been tossed into the victim's yard or enclosure.

Alcohol Poisoning

Many dogs and some cats will ingest alcoholic beverages if given the opportunity and more will do so if encouraged. Occasional reports surface of dogs who suffer fatal alcohol poisoning after being given alcohol to ingest, usually by a person who is similarly intoxicated. The alcoholic component of alcoholic beverages is ethanol (CH_2OH), a short-chain aliphatic alcohol that is the intoxicating agent in fermenting and distilled liquors. Alcohol concentration is expressed as "proof," which is twice the alcohol percentage concentration (200 proof = 100 percent alcohol = 1,000mg/ml). Acute toxicity in animals occurs with ingestion of 5–8 ml/kg of pure alcohol, or 5–8 gm/kg. To calculate the beverage volume necessary to achieve this dose, the proof or percentage of the beverage consumed must be known. Beer is 3–5 percent, wines are 9–12 percent, and whiskey is 50–90 percent. If a 10-kg dog were to ingest beer at 5 percent (50 mg/ml), it would take 1,000 mls to cause acute toxicity: 10 kg x 5 g/kg (toxic dose) = 50 g (toxic dose for 10 kg dog); 50 g x 1,000 mg/g = 50,000 mg; 50,000 mg ÷ 50 mg/ml (alcohol proof) = 1,000 ml.

Blood alcohol concentration determination can aid in assessing the severity and monitoring the progress of toxicosis (Valentine 1990). A venous sample should be collected in a sodium fluoride tube for submission. Swabbing the venipuncture site with isopropyl alcohol may interfere with results and should be avoided. Blood alcohol concentration is measured as millegrams (mg) of alcohol per 100 ml of blood in humans. The same measurement can be performed on animal blood. Blood ethanol concentrations of 2–4 mg/ml in adult dogs produced clinical signs ranging from mild ataxia while climbing stairs to coma (Valentine 1990).

As in humans, ethanol affects animals as a general CNS depressant. Ethanol affects the lipids and proteins of the cell membrane and then reduces sodium and potassium conduction in nerve membranes. Clinical signs are primarily CNS-related and develop within fifteen minutes to two hours, depending on whether the alcohol is ingested on an empty or full stomach, and their duration is typically twelve hours or less (Valentine 1990). Initial stimulation is due to transient depression of inhibitory control, resulting in behavioral changes, excitation, and vocalizing. Clinical signs correlate with blood ethanol concentration. They appear around 1–1.5 g/L as ataxia, drowsiness, polyuria and/or incontinence, mydriasis, vasodilation of conjunctiva, and then stupor and coma. Hypothermia is common and can reduce cardiac output and hepatic blood flow. Death results from respiratory depression (Kammerer, Sachot, and Blanchot 2001). Preexisting disease enhances the appearance and severity of clinical signs.

Alcohol intoxication in which the animal is conscious, ambulatory, and showing only mild to moderate behavioral changes typically requires only symptomatic treatment and observation. Severe intoxication involving profound CNS depression requires immediate attention. Death usually results from respiratory arrest followed by cardiac arrest in alcohol-induced narcosis (Valentine 1990). Hypoglycemia may exacerbate clinical depression and hypothermia.

Like many other forms of animal abuse, proving that alcohol intoxication was intentional rather than accidental will most likely depend on eyewitness testimony, since dogs often readily consume alcoholic beverages, especially beer, and because there are other sources of alcohol intoxication, including ingestion of fermenting substances such as bread dough and rotten apples, and dermal exposure to alcohol-containing products. The examining veterinarian should take care to confirm the diagnosis; differential diagnoses include marijuana intoxication and early stages of EG toxicosis.

Illicit Drugs

Reports of intoxication of animals with illicit drugs are occasionally presented in the scientific literature (Godbold, Hawkins, and Woodward 1979; Bischoff, Beier, and Edwards 1998; Janczyk, Donaldson, and Gwaltney 2004). Animals, particularly dogs, rats, and primates, have been widely used as research models of the effects of illicit drugs on humans (Catravas et al. 1977; Catravas and Waters 1981).

Any situation involving toxicosis of an animal with an illicit or abused drug presents a difficult scenario regarding investigation, diagnosis, and therapy. The person who caused the exposure will not readily admit intentional exposure of an animal to an illicit substance, even if it was not meant to be malicious. Because of the secretive nature of the use and possession of such drugs, a pet owner might not know that a visitor to the home has illicit drugs to which a pet might be exposed, intentionally or not. Another complicating factor is that illicitly manufactured drugs are often of unknown makeup; a dog who is said to have ingested a quantity of cocaine may in fact have ingested a substance that is largely made up of caffeine or an amphetamine substance.

Traditionally, cases of animal exposure to illicit drugs have been treated with humor by the veterinary community, as when a dog ingests his owner's marijuana-laced brownies or eats the owner's "stash" of cut marijuana. Greater gravity is warranted, however, because illicit drugs are illegal substances and because access to such substances by pets in a household might be an indicator that children and other susceptible individuals in the home are at risk for exposure and ingestion as well.

Illicit and abused drugs of concern in animal-cruelty investigation include caffeine, amphetamines, cocaine, marijuana, barbiturates, and opiates (OTC drugs are discussed separately). Most illicit or abused drugs can be classified as one of three pharmacological categories: stimulants (caffeine, amphetamines, and cocaine), hallucinogens (marijuana and phencyclidine), or depressants (primarily barbiturates) (Kisseberth and Trammel 1990).

Caffeine

Caffeine, a methylated xanthine, is often sold on the street as a "look-alike" drug designed in the same size and shape as prescription stimulants such as amphetamines and sometimes combined with phenylpropanolamine. Most tablets or capsules contain 100 to 200 mg. Symptoms of toxicity may result from ingesting as low as 20 mg/kg. The LD50 of caffeine in dogs is 140 mg/kg. The drug is absorbed well orally and affects the central nervous, peripheral nervous, and cardiovascular systems. Typical clinical signs include vomiting, restlessness, hyperactivity, diuresis, tachycardia, and tachypnea. Generalized congestion or hemorrhaging may be seen due to dilation of coronary, pulmonary, and systemic vessels. Hyperthermia may be the result of excessive muscular activity (Gfeller and Messonnier 2004). These signs may be followed by ataxia, tremors, cyanosis, cardiac arrhythmias, seizures, and death. There is no specific antidote, so therapy consists of preventing further absorption and hastening elimination while providing supportive care and symptomatic treatment for any specific clinical signs.

Amphetamines

A 1998 report describes the care and treatment of two English bulldogs thought to have been maliciously poisoned with methamphetamine after their owner testified in court against a neighbor for selling drugs (Bischoff, Beier, and Edwards 1998). Both survived, but a third dog was found dead at the owner's home. Amphetamine, dextroamphetamine, methamphetamine, and their various salts are collectively referred to as amphetamines. Their chemical properties and actions are very similar. Methamphetamine is the most commonly abused drug (*www.dea.gov*). These stimulants are either Class I or II controlled substances that have been used as CNS stimulants in the treatment of conditions such as attention deficit hyperactivity disorder, depression, and narcolepsy (although better alternatives are now available). They are also found in most diet pills. The clinical syndromes caused by amphetamines are similar to those of other stimulants, including caffeine and other methylxanthines and cocaine. Mydriasis, excitement, muscle tremors, ptyalism, hyperthermia, hypo- or hypertension, tachycardia, arrhythmias or heart block, lactic acidosis, and hypoglycemia are possible. Seizures can occur, although infrequently. Acute renal failure associated with rhabdomyolysis is a well-recognized syndrome in humans who have suffered amphetamine overdose. Chlorpromazine and haloperidol are antidotal, and diazepam may be used to control seizures. Additional treatment consists of life support and prevention of absorption.

Cocaine

Cocaine is often diluted, or "cut," with mannitol, lactose, sucrose, cornstarch, inositol, lidocaine, procaine, tetracaine, caffeine, amphetamine, or quinine. The purity of street cocaine averages 12–60 percent or higher, with the "freebase" form (known as "crack" cocaine) as pure as 90 percent. CNS stimulation is the primary effect of cocaine, but the stimulant effect is commonly followed by depression. Cardiovascular effects are also significant, including tachycardia and arrhythmias. Other signs include ataxia, mydriasis, vomiting, salivation, tremors, seizures, tachypnea, dyspnea, pulmonary edema, acidosis, and shock. In the final stages of severe toxicosis, severe hyperthermia, respiratory depression, coma, and respiratory and cardiac arrest are the terminal events. Treatment is supportive, since rapid absorption of cocaine limits the value of efforts to prevent absorption unless large amounts have been consumed.

Marijuana (*Cannabis sativa*)

Animals are usually exposed to marijuana by accidental ingestion, although they can also be poisoned by inhalation. The ASPCA Animal Poison Control Center reports that 96 percent of such cases involve dogs, 3 percent cats, and 1 percent other species (Donaldson 2002). While marijuana does not seem to be a drug that is commonly used to intentionally cause harm to animals, it is worth considering whether allowing an animal access to a toxic quantity of marijuana might constitute negligent endangerment. When considering whether to pursue such a case, investigators should also consider whether there are children in the home who might have similar access to quantities of marijuana.

The active ingredient in marijuana is the alkaloid tetrahydrocannabinol (THC). It is believed that THC acts on several receptors of the CNS such as serotonergic, cholinergic, dopaminergic, GABA, and noradrenergic. It also has antiemetic properties, thereby preventing the animal from vomiting and detoxifying itself. Ninety-nine percent of dogs with oral exposure to marijuana exhibit neurological signs, and 30 percent exhibit gastrointestinal signs. The lowest dose at which signs are reported to occur is 26.8 mg/kg, and the highest reported dose is 84.7 mg/kg. Signs may be seen in dogs who have ingested less than 3 mg/kg; however, the minimum lethal dose is 3 g/kg (Gfeller and Messonnier 2004).

Onset of signs ranges from five minutes to ninety-six hours, with most signs occurring within one to three hours after ingestion and lasting thirty minutes to ninety-six hours. Signs are similar to those seen in humans of early euphoria, hyperexcitement, vocalization, stupor, depression, or somnolence. Ocular signs of conjunctival injection, mydriasis, and nystagmus may be seen. Other signs are tachycardia or bradycardia, hypo- or hyperthermia, hypotension, muscle weakness, ataxia, and, rarely, coma. Management consists of decontamination, sedation (diazepam is the drug of choice), fluid therapy, thermoregulation, and general supportive care, with a good prognosis for full recovery in one to three days. Commercial human laboratories may perform diagnostic testing, and over-the-counter kits for detection of marijuana in urine are available, although their accuracy when using dog urine has not been established (Janczyk, Donaldson, and Gwaltney 2004).

Phencyclidine

Phencyclidine hydrochloride ("PCP" or "angel dust") is a dissociative anesthestic, an easily synthesized chemical analog of the veterinary anesthetic ketamine. It is typically sold in powder, tablet, crystal, liquid, and leaf mixture forms, with purity between 5 percent and 90 percent. Significant clinical signs are observed at an oral dose of 2.5 to 10 mg/kg in dogs, 1.1 to 12 mg/kg in cats (Coppock, Mostrum, and Lille 1989). The primary effect is CNS stimulation or depression, with clinical signs very similar to ketamine anesthesia. Signs include CNS depression or excitement, opisthotonus, ptyalism, mydriasis, nystagmus, sniffing activity, tonic-clonic convulsions, "fly biting" or "jaw snapping," tachycardia, cardiac arrhythmias, hyper- or hypotension, hyperthermia, academia, respiratory failure, and death.

Laboratory findings include acute renal failure, isosthenuria, oliguria to anuria, renal tubular casts, proteinuria, myoglobinuria, glycosuria without hyperglycemia, high AST, high CPK, and hypoglycemia. There is no known antidote, and therapy consists of basic life support, prevention of hyperthermia, and hastening elimination of the drug with intravenous fluid therapy.

Barbiturates

Most barbiturates exposure in animals is due to legal formulations, although perhaps used in an illicit manner. Predominant clinical signs are CNS depression, general anesthesia, and coma. Signs are dose dependent. In moderate toxicity they include hypothermia, ataxia, +/- nystagmus, splenomegaly, +/- hypotension, and +/- hypothermia. More severe cases cause respiratory depression, depressed cardiac contractility, hypothermia, hypotension, splenomegaly, coma, and death. Routine toxicologic screens can detect barbiturates. Emesis is only effective if treatment was within sixty minutes of ingestion and the patient shows no clinical signs. After one hour other decontamination measures are needed. Treatment consists of respiratory and cardiovascular support.

Prescription and Over-the-Counter Medications

Many OTC and prescription medications contain acetaminophen and related compounds. Since it is well known that these drugs are potentially lethal to animals, it is important to consider them as potential sources of intentional poisoning. Some well-mean-ing owners may give these medications to their pets when they are acting "sick," so it is important to determine what symptoms the animal was exhibiting before administration of the now offending agent.

Acetaminophen

Acetaminophen is an analgesic and antipyretic drug that is highly toxic to dogs and cats. It is rapidly absorbed in the bloodstream, reaching peak levels in 30–60 minutes after ingestion. It is metabolized by three different pathways to form intermediate and reactive products that result in hepatotoxicity and methemoglobinemia (brown-colored blood). Methemoglobinemia is more common in cats due to their red blood cells' increased susceptibility to oxidative injury. Dogs are more likely to develop liver injury, though both species can develop either or both. Hepatotoxicity in dogs can be seen when the dose exceeds 75 mg/kg, and methemoglobinemia may be seen when the dose reaches 200 mg/kg. Clinical signs of toxicosis in cats may be seen at doses as low as 10 mg/kg (Gwaltney-Brant and Richardson 2002c). Toxicity may result from a single dose or repeated cumulative doses.

Signs of methemoglobinemia may develop within two to six hours of ingestion and hepatic signs may take twenty-four to forty-eight hours to occur. Clinical signs are dyspnea, cyanosis, chocolate-brown mucous membranes, tachypnea, depression, weakness, tachycardia, vomiting, hypothermia, icterus, coma, and death. Laboratory findings include severely elevated liver enzymes, anemia, hemolysis, and +/- coagulopathy. Facial and paw edema is a hallmark sign of acetaminophen toxicosis in cats and is occasionally seen in dogs. Keratoconjunctivitis sicca (KCS) has been reported in small-breed dogs seventy-two hours after ingestion. A local human hospital can test urine or blood for acetaminophen.

Treatment is aimed at oxygen support, diuresis, and emesis if performed immediately. Treatment with N-acetylcysteine (NAC) should be initiated because it binds acetaminophen metabolites and aids glutathione synthesis. Additional treatment with cimetidine and ascorbic acid in conjunction with NAC further decreases hepatotoxicity and reduces methemoglobin to hemoglobin (Gwaltney-Brant and Richardson 2002c). Veterinarians should avoid using methylene blue as it may cause Heinz body formation and hemolysis. For those with hepatic injury, administration of s-adenosylmethionine may be beneficial. Supportive care may be required for days to weeks.

Ibuprofen

Ibuprofen is a nonsteroidal anti-inflammatory drug (NSAID) that has analgesic, anti-inflammatory, and antipyretic effects. Its mechanism of action is primarily by prostaglandin inhibition, which in turn reduces blood flow to the gastrointestinal (GI) tract resulting in ischemia, ulceration, and possible perforation. Ibuprofen also decreases blood flow to the kidneys, resulting in acute renal failure. Hepatotoxicity is possible in large overdoses as well. Toxicity in dogs can be seen with doses at 50–125 mg/kg. Keep in mind that cats are twice as sensitive as dogs to toxicosis. Signs seen at this dose include vomiting, diarrhea, nausea, anorexia, gastric ulceration, and abdominal pain. In addition to these signs, renal damage can be seen at doses of 175 mg/kg or higher. Oliguric or anuric renal failure may develop within twenty-four to forty-eight hours of ingestion. CNS signs of seizures, ataxia, or coma may occur when the dose reaches or exceeds 400 mg/kg.

Laboratory findings can include anemia, azotemia, hypo- or isosthenuria, renal tubular casts, increased ALT/ALP, acid-base disorders, and possible leukocytosis if peritonitis has developed from perforation. Postmortem lesions associated with ibuprofen toxicosis include gastric perforations, erosions, ulcerations, and GI hemorrhage.

There is no specific antidote for NSAID toxicosis. Treatment is aimed at decontamination for recent exposure, prevention and management of GI ulcerations, perforation, CNS symptoms, and acute renal failure.

Pesticides: Rodenticides, Insecticides, Herbicides, and Molluscicides

Rodenticides are second only to insecticides in the prevalence of pesticide exposure (Murphy 2002). Most insecticide poisonings are accidental and are related to flea products. Herbicide toxicosis is usually from accidental ingestion. There are hundreds of rodenticide products, yet only a handful of them are involved in most toxicosis of companion animals. The most commonly reported toxicosis cases in the United States are those caused by anticoagulant rodenticides, bromethalin, cholecalciferol, strychnine, and zinc phosphide.

Anticoagulant Rodenticides

Anticoagulant rodenticides are vitamin K antagonists. A variety of anticoagulants are used in these baits, with half-lives ranging from less than twenty-four hours to six to seven days. The first-generation group includes warfarin. Second-generation anticoagulants are those that are effective against warfarin-resistant rats and may be longer acting and/or more potent. There is no color coding of the different baits, so the color of the rodenticide provides no clues about the product. Secondary poisoning through ingestion of a poisoned animal is possible, especially with the second-generation class of anti-coagulants. The LD50 of a single dose of warfarin is 5–50 mg/kg, but repeated ingestion of as little as 1 mg/kg may result in severe toxicosis. The LD50 of brodifacoum in dogs is 0.25–3.6 mg/kg and 0.25 mg/kg in cats. As a general guideline, the minimum toxic dose of warfarin is less than 0.5 mg/kg. Other anticoagulants are less than 0.02 mg/kg (Gwaltney-Brant and Richardson 2002b).

Depending on the dose and the type of anticoagulant, signs may develop as soon as one to two days after ingestion, but more commonly they develop in five to seven days. Clinical signs are related to bleeding, such as weakness, depression, and pallor. External signs of hemorrhage may be seen from wounds, gingiva, or the GI tract. Epistaxis, hematuria, and evidence of bleeding into the body cavities and joints may be present as well and are often accompanied by a fever. Brain or spinal hemorrhage may result in neurologic signs. Severe dyspnea may be caused by tracheal constriction from thymic, laryngeal, or peritracheal bleeding. Laboratory findings are anemia, thrombocytopenia, hypoproteinemia, and abnormal coagulation tests (increased PT, then increased APTT and ACT). Commercial laboratories usually offer specific identifying tests.

Treatment is aimed at decontamination if within the first twelve hours, oxygen support, and transfusions. Vitamin K_1 is the antidote and should be given as long as the anticoagulant is present in the body at toxic levels.

Bromethalin

Bromethalin is a potent neurotoxin that causes intramyelinic edema resulting in decreased nerve impulse conduction. The reported minimum toxic dose in dogs is 0.9 mg/kg. Once signs have developed treatment is usually unsuccessful, so it is recommended that decontamination be initiated at doses less than 0.1 mg/kg. Cats are three times more sensitive than dogs, so decontamination should be performed on any cat who has been exposed (Gwaltney-Brant and Richardson 2002b). Secondary poisoning is possible.

The onset and type of clinical signs are variable and dose dependent. Signs may be present within hours or may not begin for as long as two weeks following ingestion. High doses in dogs result in severe tremors, hyperexcitability, hyperreflexia of the hindlimbs, opisthotonus, decerebrate posturing, rigidity, running fits, focal or generalized seizures, hyperthermia, and death within thirty-six hours of ingestion. Lower doses produce depression, anorexia, vomiting, tremors, +/- hyperthermia, progressive paresis originating in the rear, paralysis, progressive CNS signs, miosis, anisocoria, and death. Cats exhibit similar signs, including abdominal swelling. In sublethal exposures signs may arrest at some level of paresis from which the animal may recover over weeks to months or suffer permanent motor impairment.

Postmortem lesions found are spongy degeneration in the white matter of spinal tracts, brainstem, cerebellum, and cerebrum. Electron microscopy demonstrates vacuolation of the myelin sheaths (Gwaltney-Brant and Richardson 2002b). There is no antidote, so treatment is aimed at aggressive decontamination. Supportive care and control of seizures is needed.

Cholecalciferol

Cholecalciferol is a vitamin D analog that increases serum calcium. Prolonged hypercalcemia causes acute renal failure, cardiovascular abnormalities, and tissue mineralization. The minimum toxic dose ranges from 0.5 mg/kg to 3.0 mg/kg, and decontamination is recommended at 0.1 mg/kg. Secondary poisoning is most likely in small dogs or cats.

Clinical signs, which may be delayed in onset as long as eighteen to thirty-six hours after ingestion, can be nonspecific and can include anorexia, lethargy, depression, vomiting, constipation, polyuria and polydipsia, bradycardia, arrhythmias, and shock. In higher doses more severe GI signs may be seen, such as hematemesis and bloody diarrhea. Cats may exhibit anorexia, depression, and renal pain. Severe hypercalcemia may cause muscle twitching, seizures, stupor, and acute renal failure.

Laboratory findings include an initial hyperphosphatemia within the first twelve hours of ingestion accompanied by hypercalcemia within twelve to twenty-four hours of ingestion. Azotemia can occur secondary to hypercalcemia and dehydration.

Postmortem lesions consist of diffuse hemorrhages of the GI tract and possible streaking of the renal cortex. Upon cutting, soft tissues of the GI tract, heart, and kidney tend to have a "gritty" feel to the knife. Mineralization and necrosis of the GI, cardiac, lung and renal tissues are seen histologically, and elevated total kidney calcium concentrations may be detected toxicologically (Gwaltney-Brant and Richardson 2002b).

Treatment is aimed at decontamination, decreasing serum calcium, fluid support, and controlling neurologic and cardiac abnormalities.

Strychnine

Strychnine is an alkaloid extract obtained from the dried ripe seeds of *Strychnos nux vomica*, a small tree of the East Indies. Though not commonly found in the retail market now, strychnine was formerly sold as a pesticide in cracked corn bait to eliminate unwanted bird populations. It was also used to control gopher and mole species by underground application inside artificially created burrows or into natural burrows. It is still often used outside the United States in large-scale animal-control efforts.

Strychnine competitively and reversibly antagonizes glycine, an inhibitory neurotransmitter located in the brain and spinal cord. This results in uninhibited simultaneous contraction of various muscle groups, which results in muscle injury, rhabdomyolysis, and hyperthermia. Respiratory muscles are contracted, resulting in dyspnea, hypoxemia, and, without treatment, death. The LD50 for cats is 2.0 mg/kg, dogs 0.5–1.2 mg/kg.

The onset of symptoms may occur with a prodromal syndrome that includes tonic twitching of the face and neck muscles, muscular cramps in the legs, preceded by restlessness, apprehension, and heightened acuity of perception (hearing, vision, feeling) and hyperreflexia. These are followed by the onset of violent, tetanic muscle contractions. These seizure-like contractions have a characteristic motor pattern that is determined by the most powerful muscles. In most animals the extensor muscles dominate, resulting in a "sawhorse" stance. The contraction of facial muscles results in *risus sardonicus*, known as the "sardonic grin." The frequency and severity of the convulsions is increased by sensory stimulation. These convulsions can begin suddenly after any minor sensory stimulus and last from fifty seconds to two minutes. The patient remains conscious and has intense pain. After the convulsions, all of the muscles relax, and sometimes the patient falls asleep from exhaustion. Convulsions may occur frequently with intermittent periods of depression. Hyperexcitability recurs suddenly after ten to fifteen minutes. The tetanic contractions of respiratory muscles cause dyspnea or apnea. Death is usually caused by asphyxia but may be caused by exhaustion, acute renal failure from myoglobinuria, or complications due to hypoxemia. The animal is fully conscious and lucid until anoxia supervenes.

The urine may be green because commercial preparations of strychnine that are used as rodenticides contain methylene-blue (Bismuth, Pierlot, and Borron 2000). Samples of blood, urine, and gastric fluid should be taken for biomedical analysis and a sample of the product for identification.

Treatment is aimed first at establishing an airway and ventilating the patient, followed by decontamination, treatment to relax the muscles, minimizing sensory stimulation, and supportive care.

Zinc phosphide is a rodenticide that, when ingested, reacts with stomach acid to release phosphine gas. This gas causes respiratory distress and asphyxiation. The reaction is enhanced if the animal has eaten recently, causing an increase in stomach acid. The toxic gas has an odor like rotten fish, rotten eggs, or acetylene. The LD50 is 20–40 mg/kg in most animals, though it depends on the stomach pH. Zinc phosphide is toxic to all species. Special precautions must be taken when treating these animals and handling vomitus or stomach washings to prevent exposure.

Vomiting may occur within fifteen minutes of ingestion and may contain blood. Death may occur in only three to five hours when large doses are consumed. The animal's stomach distends as gas is produced, causing severe abdominal pain. Dogs may exhibit fits of running, baring teeth, biting, and repeated head jerking. Additional signs include respiratory distress, muscle tremors, extensor rigidity, hyperesthesia, hyperthermia, hypoglycemia, and shock. Signs may progress to seizures and death. Delayed renal and/or liver damage may occur as late as five to fourteen days after ingestion. Toxicologic analysis can be performed on frozen stomach contents (Gfeller and Messonnier 2004). Treatment includes decontamination, antacids, and H_2 blockers.

Insecticides

Pyrethrins

Pyrethrins and organophosphates are common insecticides and are present in many flea products for animals and the environment. Most cases of toxicity are accidental but they may be due to intentional pyrethrin poisoning.

Pyrethrins are rapidly metabolized producing neurologic effects due to repetitive nerve firing and sometimes a strychnine-like effect. Cats are much more sensitive to pyrethrins than dogs and symptoms may be seen as soon as one to three hours post exposure. Clinical signs are primarily neurologic and include depression, vomiting, hypersalivation, muscle tremors, ataxia, dyspnea, bradycardia, anorexia, hypo- or hyperthermia, and sudden death due to respiratory failure. Cats may exhibit signs of ear flicking, skin rolling, or shaking their paws (Gfeller 2004). There is no diagnostic test, but an atropine test can help differentiate between pyrethrin and organophosphate toxicity (Gfeller 2004).

Organophosphates

Organophosphates (OPs) are easily absorbed by the skin, orally, or through inhalation. They cause continuous nerve stimulation resulting in a variety of neurologic symptoms. Cats are more sensitive to OP insecticides than are dogs. Clinical signs may include dyspnea, excessive tearing, salivation, miosis, urination, defecation, bradycardia or tachycardia, facial and/or generalized muscle twitching, tremors weakness, ataxia, paralysis, depression, aggression, seizures, respiratory depression, respiratory failure, and death.

Diagnosis is made by clinical symptoms and a blood cholinesterase depression. Another test, though not definitive, is an atropine trial test (Gfeller and Messonnier 2004).

Molluscicides

Metaldehyde is a common ingredient in snail or slug baits, which are available in a variety of forms such as kibble, granules, powder, or liquid. They often contain other toxins in addition to metaldehyde. This bait causes metabolic acidosis and tremors and/or seizures, but the mechanism of action is not precisely known. The LD50 in dogs is 100 mg/kg; however, severe clinical signs are seen at much lower doses (Gfeller and Messonnier 2004).

Clinical signs usually start within fifteen minutes to three hours after ingestion of the bait. Early signs are increased heart rate, anxiety, nystagmus (especially in cats), +/- mydriasis, panting, thick and frothy salivation, stiff-legged gait, ataxia, and +/- vomiting. These are followed by muscle tremors, which may be mild, caused by external stimuli, especially touching. Diarrhea may be seen as well as convulsions. Finally, the animal has continuous convulsions, severe hyperthermia, acidosis, respiratory failure, cyanosis, narcosis, and death. If the animal survives the acute episode, he may eventually die from complications of organ damage in the next three to five days (Gfeller and Messonnier 2004).

Samples of stomach contents, urine, plasma, and tissue may be analyzed for metaldehyde. The samples should be frozen promptly and submitted on ice. Treatment involves decontamination and symptomatic care.

Other Unusual Toxins

The list of the many potential toxins to which companion animals and livestock may be exposed is constantly growing. Although few of these newly recognized sources of toxicity are likely to be used for intentional poisoning, forensic examiners should be aware of all possible sources of poisons in examining suspicious cases. Recent reports have described case histories involving animal poisoning attributed to grapes and raisins (Means 2002), cocoa mulch (Drolet, Arendt, and Stowe 1984); paintballs (Donaldson 2003), flower bulbs (Lieske 2002), macadamia nuts (Hansen 2002), ice-melting chemicals (Hautekeete 2000), coins (Richardson, Gwaltney-Brant, and Villar 2002), potpourri (Richardson 1999), and glow-in-the-dark jewelry (Rosendale 1999).

Domestic animals can and will ingest just about anything, either voluntarily or with human help or maliciousness. This presents special challenges to veterinary and law enforcement professionals, who must use a variety of diagnostic and investigational skills to get an accurate picture of what has entered the animal's system, how it got to be there, and what might have prevented it from happening.

CHAPTER 16 Neglect

nimal-care and -control agencies deal with animal-neglect cases every day. Increasingly, many of the most serious are being prosecuted under felony anti-cruelty laws. The case files compiled by The HSUS provide some recent examples:

- In Oklahoma, a man was convicted of felony animal cruelty for allowing his two dogs to starve and endure cold weather.
- A California woman was convicted of felony animal cruelty and sentenced to six months in jail after locking her dog in a closet to starve to death.
- In Illinois, a former animal breeder pleaded guilty to felony animal cruelty after police found twenty-six living and eight dead cats in his trailer. They were left to starve, but many cats survived by eating their dead companions.
- A Virginia farmer was convicted of one felony count of animal cruelty after scores of cattle were found dead or dying on his property.

Neglect is the most common manifestation of cruelty to animals, yet it is the form veterinarians feel most uncomfortable about addressing. This trepidation is due to vaguely worded anti-cruelty statutes, social and cultural differences and attitudes toward quality of life for both humans and animals, and concerns about how to differentiate intentional neglect from neglect due to ignorance, inattention, or lack of resources on the part of otherwise caring pet owners. The majority of animal-neglect situations are best resolved by education and monitoring of the caretaker. Only a small percentage are candidates for prosecution and mandated resolution, such as court-ordered removal of animals.

Defining Neglect as Cruelty to Animals

State statutes range from very broad to very specific with regard to neglect of animals. Iowa's anti-cruelty code (717B.3) offers a two-tier definition of neglect:

- A person who impounds or confines, in any place, an animal is guilty of animal neglect, if the person does any of the following: fails to supply the animal during confinement with a sufficient quantity of food or water; fails to provide a confined dog or cat with adequate shelter; or tortures, deprives of necessary sustenance, mutilates, beats, or kills an animal by any means which causes unjustified pain, distress, or suffering.
- A person who negligently or intentionally commits the offense of animal neglect is guilty of a simple misdemeanor.
- A person who intentionally commits the offense of animal neglect which results in serious injury to or the death of an animal is guilty of a serious misdemeanor.

The District of Columbia's statute dealing with neglect is unusually comprehensive. It describes neglect as including actions in which someone:

[D]eprives of necessary sustenance...or knowingly causes or procures any animal to be so...deprived of necessary sustenance...and whoever, having the charge or custody of any animal, either as owner or otherwise...unnecessarily fails to provide the same with proper food, drink, air, light, space, veterinary care, shelter, or protection from the weather.

This is the only anti-cruelty law to our knowledge that makes specific mention of animals' needs for proper air, light, and space.

As of mid-2005, Illinois was the only state that specifically recognized the neglect associated with animal hoarding as a distinct form of cruelty to animals. (Because the motives and problems associated with the large number of neglected animals seen in hoarding cases are different from most other neglect investigations, this topic is covered in detail in chapter 17.)

The development of more objective indicators of animal neglect may ease the apprehension of veterinarians. Specific observations and measurements—serum chemistry parameters, precise necropsy findings, and application of scales and body condition scoring systems, for example—all serve to objectify and standardize evaluation of animal-neglect victims, leading to more successful prosecution of offenders and less likelihood of false accusations.

There are many possible manifestations of animal neglect, the most common of which are discussed here.

Starvation

Starvation is a common form of animal neglect. Dogs are the most likely victims of this form of animal abuse, perhaps because they are more likely to be confined than cats. Starvation of dogs is usually accompanied by other aspects of neglect, and the stereotypical victim is a dog tied by rope or chain to a car, a tree, or a dilapidated doghouse who is fed the cheapest dog food available on those occasions when the owner does make the effort to feed the animal.

In 1996 a Durham, New Hampshire, middle-school teacher allowed a two-year-old dalmatian she had adopted from an animal shelter to starve to death in a cage in her basement. She told investigators that she knew the dog was dead, and that it had been the responsibility of her twelve-year-old son to care for Celia. She was convicted of cruelty to animals, a class A misdemeanor, and ordered to pay a $500 fine and obtain mental health counseling. In many other similar cases, prosecutors have declined prosecution due to lack of evidence of "intent" to cause harm, despite the fact that withholding food from a confined animal is an intentional act with the clear ultimate consequence of suffering and death. Starvation of cats, when it does occur, is usually associated with a hoarding situation (see chapter 17) or similar circumstances of confinement.

Starvation is defined as "the prolonged deprival of food, and its morbid effects" (Dorland 1982), but starvation is much more than that. Animals who are not deprived of food can starve when the quantity or quality of that food is not sufficient to meet their metabolic needs. Animals provided with adequate food can suffer the "morbid effects" of starvation when they are unable to use that food due to disease processes. Underlying disease is an acceptable justification for the condition of an animal only when that animal is under the direct and ongoing care of a veterinarian.

Too often, law enforcement officers, investigators, and veterinarians back down from pursuing criminal animal neglect in starvation cases when underlying disease or infection is involved. Veterinarians must insist that such cases are true animal neglect unless ongoing medical care is being provided for the animal. An owner who allows an animal to starve to death due to an undiagnosed malabsorption problem or other disease is just as liable for the starvation of that animal as is the owner who has not provided food.

In general, there are four ways to evaluate whether an animal is starving:

- measurement of the volume and nutritional value of the food the animal is eating;
- body weight of the animal;
- body condition of the animal; and
- body composition of the animal.

Histologic and laboratory changes support a diagnosis of starvation.

Measurement of the Volume and Nutritional Value of the Food the Animal Is Eating

One way to determine whether an animal is being starved is to determine (1) what the dog's nutritional requirements are, and (2) what nutrition the dog is receiving. If the second value does not equal or exceed the first, the animal must be starving.

One of the hardest tasks for an investigator who suspects that an animal is being starved is to determine what the animal is being fed, how much, and how often. Doing so may require actual observation of the animal and her owner's actions for a period of hours, days, or weeks, an impractical task for most animal-control officers and humane investigators. If other evidence warrants seizure of the animal and citation of civil or criminal charges, the tables may be turned and the owner may be required to furnish the information to defend against the charges.

The maintenance energy requirement (MER) of an animal is defined as the amount of energy used by a moderately active adult animal in a thermoneutral environment per day. It includes energy expended for obtaining and using food in amounts necessary to maintain body weight, but it would not support additional physical activity or production, such as growth, gestation, or lactation. The basal energy requirement (BER) of an animal is the amount of energy used when awake but resting and in a postabsorptive (fasting) state in thermoneutral conditions. The resting energy requirement (RER) refers to the energy needed for a normal but fed animal at rest in a thermoneutral environment. It is different from BER in that it includes the energy used for recovery from physical activity and feeding.

Most of the energy used by the body is heat, lost to an animal's surroundings through convection or conduction. Energy expended is directly related to body surface area; therefore, small animals (who have greater body surface area per unit of body mass) have a greater heat loss and greater RER than larger animals do. For dogs and cats weighing 2–45 kilograms, RER (kcal/day) = 30 x (body weight in kg) + 70.

Daily energy requirement (DER) is the average daily energy expended by any animal, depending on life stage and activity. The difference between DER and RER is that DER includes energy used to maintain normal body temperature as well as energy expended in work, gestation, lactation, and growth. To calculate DER, first calculate the RER then multiply by the factor based on the animal's life stage and activity (Figure 16.1a, b) (Hand et al. 2000).

Published values for the nutrient requirements of dogs and cats are available (Committee on Animal Nutrition, National Research Council 1985, 1986), but they are intended to be applied to the "average" dog or cat. These requirements should be used with caution; they cannot be used as absolutes for any individual animal or breed of animal, since needs vary with age, activity, body condition, insulating characteristics of the haircoat, temperature, acclimatization, external environmental circumstances, and psychological temperament.

The only accurate way to determine the nutrient value of a food is by laboratory analysis. The guaranteed analysis of a commercial pet food, required by law on all pet food la-

Figure 16.1a—Calculation of Energy Requirements

Feline Daily Energy Requirements

Maintenance (0.8–1.6 x RER)
Neutered adult......................=1.2 x RER
Inactive adult.......................=1.4 x RER
Active adult ....=1.6 x RER
Obese prone........................=1.0 x RER
Weight loss.........................=0.8 x RER
Critical care ....=1.0 x RER
Weight gain ....=1.2–1.4 x RER at ideal weight

Gestation
Energy requirement increases linearly during gestation in cats. Energy intake should be increased to 1.6 x RER at breeding and gradually increased throughout gestation to 2 x RER at parturition. Free choice feeding of pregnant queens is also recommended.

Lactation
Lactation is nutritionally demanding and the physiologic and nutritional equivalent of heavy work.
Recommended 2 to 6 x RER (depending on number of kittens nursing) or free-choice feeding.

Growth
Daily energy intake for growing kittens should be about 2.5 x RER. Free-choice feeding is recommended.

Source: Hand et al. (2000, 33).

bels, is not the same as the actual analysis of the food. A label analysis only indicates the range of nutrients available, and generic-quality foods may not even meet the guaranteed label analysis due to variability of the quality and content of the ingredients.

Volume of food is one thing, nutritional value of a food is entirely another. To determine the amount of a food that is necessary to meet the caloric needs of an individual animal, it is necessary to determine first the caloric density of the food and the metabolizable energy requirement (MER) of the animal. Some manufacturers specify the energy content of their products; however, this statement is not required and is usually not available.

If the caloric density of a food is not known, it can be calculated using the following formula:

Caloric density = energy provided by each nutrient x the amount of that nutrient in the food.

The gross calories generated when proteins, fats, or carbohydrates are completely oxidized are 5.65, 9.4, and 4.15 kcal/g, respectively. However, it must be remembered that only the portion of these energy nutrients that is digested, absorbed, and retained is available for metabolism. Foods containing protein of such poor quality that it cannot be digested and used by an animal, for example, may not supply the amount of energy indicated by this calculation. Likewise, an animal whose digestive system is diseased and unable to absorb and use nutrients may not be able to obtain the energy contained in the diet.

Body Condition and Composition

In most cases, starvation is defined by the body condition of the animal. Individual variability in the amount of food necessary to sustain the life and health of a dog or cat makes it nearly impossible to use food volume alone to demonstrate that an animal is starving. This information is useful during prosecution, however, and investigators should try as much as possible to determine what, when, and how much an animal is being fed.

The true measure of starvation, however, is the body condition of an animal. Subjective evaluation of body condition is rarely useful. An animal may appear thin to one person but normal to another. Even the testimony of an expert witness—the veterinarian—can be disputed by an expert witness for the defense—*its* veterinarian—whose qualifications to judge an animal's health are the same.

While starvation has many effects on the body, the most recognized one is the loss of fat and muscle, components of which are used to provide energy to sustain the function of the brain and other vital organs. Therefore, clinically apparent loss of fat and muscle mass indicates starvation. Based on this premise, body condition "scales" or scoring systems have been proposed that objectively measure the degree of fat and muscle mass of an animal.

Body condition scoring systems are well recognized for use in evaluating dairy and beef cattle and horses (Henneke 1985; Edmonson 1989; Laflamme 1997b). Pet food manufacturers have circulated body condition scoring systems for dogs and cats, but those systems have focused on obesity of companion animals. A scoring system for the body condition of dogs suffering from malnutrition was developed only recently. The Tufts Animal Care and Condition (TACC) Scales for Assessing Body Condition, Weather and Environmental Safety, and Physical Care in Dogs (appendix C) were developed and published in 1997 to help animal-cruelty investigators and veterinarians assess cases of animal neglect. The TACC scales include a body condition scale for dogs that ranges from ideal body condition to emaciated body condition.

Figure 16.1b—Calculation of Energy Requirements

Canine Daily Energy Requirements

Maintenance (1.0–1.8 x RER)

Neutered adult......................=1.6 x RER
Intact adult........................=1.8 x RER
Obese prone........................=1.4 x RER
Weight loss........................=1.0 x RER
Critical care......................=1.0 x RER
Weight gain ....=1.2–1.4 x RER at ideal weight

Work

Light work.........................=2 x RER
Moderate work ....=3 x RER
Heavy work.........................=4–8 x RER

Gestation

First 42 days: feed as an intact adult.
Last 21 days: use 3 x RER. (This quantity may need to be increased to maintain normal body condition for some dogs, especially larger breeds.)

Lactation

Lactation is nutritionally demanding and the physiologic and nutritional equivalent of heavy work.
Recommend 4–8 x RER (depending on number of puppies nursing) or free-choice feeding.

Growth

Daily energy intake for growing puppies should be 3 x RER from weaning until four months of age.
At four months of age energy intake should be reduced to 2 x RER until the puppy reaches adult size.

Source: Hand et al.(2000, 33).

The amount of body fat an animal has can be determined with dual energy X-ray absorptiometry (DEXA), a technique that has been used for many years to measure bone mineral content (Laflamme 1997a,b). Subjects are scanned with photons at two different energy levels. The ratio of absorbance of the two energy level photons is linearly related to the percentage of fat in the nonbone tissue. Using this ratio, total body fat, fat-free mass, and total body bone mineral can be measured. The clinical definition of starvation is usually based on body condition. An animal who cannot maintain normal body condition is considered to be starving, regardless of how much or what type of food the animal is getting and any disease processes that might be preventing the absorption and use of the nutrients in food.

During starvation the animal will use up his fat stores for energy. This is done in sequence, with the external body fat used first, then the internal body cavity fat preserving the fat around the vital organs, mainly the kidney and heart. The very last area from which the body will consume its fat stores is the bone marrow cavity. During the recovery process from starvation, the bone marrow will also be the last area to be depleted. A bone marrow fat analysis test can be conducted on a deceased animal. The normal value is 60 percent or higher; in starvation cases the levels can be as low as 0–5 percent. A normal value does not rule out starvation.

There are two primary questions to be answered regarding starvation cases. Over what period did starvation of the animal occur? Was there an absence of food, or was there some other reason for starvation, such as unusual metabolic demands due to exposure to extremes of weather or severe parasitism?

Veterinarians testifying in starvation cases no doubt will be called on to offer an opinion about the length of time it took an animal to starve and whether starvation was the actual cause of death. When evaluating a starvation victim, veterinarians must consider not only the period over which starvation has occurred, but also the severity of starvation, and whether accompanying disease conditions (e.g., canine parvovirus infection) contributed to the animal's starvation. For the sake of simplicity, it can be assumed that there are two durations of starvation: acute starvation (sudden food deprivation) and chronic (long-term) starvation. Acute starvation is defined as starvation that occurs when a healthy and properly nourished animal is acutely deprived of all food. Chronic starvation is defined as starvation that occurs when an animal is able to obtain some, but not adequate, nourishment.

In clinical practice, animals frequently are anorexic or are deprived of food for variable periods to facilitate diagnosis or treatment. A review of the changes associated with food deprivation at the enzymatic, organ, and whole-animal levels in the postabsorptive, fasted, and starved states has been published (Allen and Toll 1995).

Important to an understanding of the effects of starvation is the realization that an animal's metabolism does not function as usual under conditions of starvation. During starvation, changes occur in fuel use that permit survival for prolonged periods.

In human beings, prolonged fasting is accompanied by decreased body weight. The extent and rate of weight loss is proportional to initial body weight. The heaviest subjects experience the greatest and most rapid weight loss. Rate of weight loss is hyperbolic, with the rate slowing over time. Initial rapid weight loss is primarily due to loss of body water, and hunger is experienced only for the first two to four days.

The ability to form dilute urine should not be influenced by starvation. Blood urea nitrogen values are expected to be low for the same reasons. Anemia can also be seen in prolonged starvation.

Starvation can have varied effects on individual animals. Very young and very old animals are much less able to withstand food deprivation. Starvation of pregnant animals may retard development of fetuses or result in abortion. In some cases, dehydration may accompany starvation, blurring the diagnostic picture.

Many animals exhibit the behavior of pica when they are in a state of starvation; it is important to look in a live animal's stool for evidence of this. On postmortem exam the stomach contents should be examined for evidence of pica (Plate 14).

Victims of both acute and chronic starvation present with similar physical signs: protrusion of the skeleton and loss of musculature. Loss of the temporal muscles is particularly impressive (Plates 15A and 15B).

Severe dehydration and/or severe atrophy of the muscles of mastication causes retraction of the eyeball and results in protrusion of the third eyelid (the nictitating membrane), which may or may not resolve with nutritional rehabilitation. This symptom is less specific in cats, who may exhibit protrusion of the third eyelid for less specific reasons, including systemic disease or any condition that leads to mental depression (DeLahunta 1983).

Histologically, acute starvation is characterized by serous atrophy of fat, subcutaneous edema, cardiac muscle degeneration, and atrophy of viscera (Cheville 1988). The liver and pancreas are markedly reduced in size, and individual hepatocytes are small. In long-term starvation, fatty degeneration of the liver, anemia, and skin lesions may develop, but these changes often involve mechanisms other than calorie deficiency (Lewis, Morris, and Hand 1987). Cardiac changes associated with chronic starvation in dogs include gross edema, myofibrillar atrophy, and interstitial edema (Allen and Toll 1995). Fatty livers are especially common in animals on low-protein diets, in which total calorie intake is near normal, but the diet is so deficient in protein that body tissues are broken down and the fats and carbohydrates are transported to the liver to be used to synthesize protein. Energy and protein restriction have been implicated in the development of hepatic lipidosis in cats. Although starvation may cause some obese cats to develop hepatic lipidosis, not all obese cats who are starved subsequently develop the condition. The degree and length of starvation can be estimated based on all of the physical findings and laboratory tests. In addition, veterinarians must incorporate evidence other than the condition of the victim—such as witness testimony—to best determine these factors.

Dehydration

Dehydration of an animal occurs when no water is provided, when water is provided but is not potable, or when the method of confinement (a tangled leash, for example) prevents the animal's access to water. Sixty percent of the adult body weight and up to 80 percent of the juvenile body weight of an animal is water. A 10 percent loss of total body water causes serious illness; a 15 percent loss results in death. The water requirement of the dog or cat, expressed in ml/day, is roughly equivalent to the energy requirement in kcal/day. In general, small dogs require approximately 40–50 mls/lb./day, and larger dogs (those weighing twenty pounds or more) require 30–35 mls/lb./day. A cat requires 30–40 mls/lb./day (Lewis, Morris, and Hand 1987). This requirement can vary significantly from one individual to another, however, and depends on such factors as the animal's state of health and level of exercise, the ambient temperature and humidity, and the water content of the animal's diet.

Scales for estimating an animal's level of hydration based on physical examination findings and evaluation of skin turgor are readily available (Schaer 1989). The presence of azotemia in spite of an animal's ability to properly concentrate urine suggests dehydration, as does an elevated hematocrit. These parameters may be of no use in evaluating deceased victims, however, due to the effects of decomposition on skin elasticity and the components of blood and urine. Other indicators must be sought. Because the eyeball is isolated and well protected anatomically, several studies have tried to determine whether the vitreous humor might withstand putrefactive changes and be available for biochemical analysis. Vitreous humor has been found to have relatively stable chemistry and has been used to demonstrate dehydration as the cause of death in cases of child neglect (Spitz 1993d). Although further study is needed to more clearly define such analysis, one study has provided reference values for canine vitreous humor and investigated its usefulness as an indicator of the time of death of the animal (Schoning and Strafuss 1980).

Parasitism

It is no surprise that severely neglected animals are often also severely parasitized animals. This is more likely when more than one animal is involved and is especially true when many (twenty or more) animals are closely confined. The pathophysiology of at least one parasitic disease (demodicosis) is known to have an immunologic component (Muller,

Kirk, and Scott 1989), and animals compromised by malnutrition, dehydration, cramped housing, and an unsanitary environment are likely at greater risk for infestation with common parasites.

Symptoms of parasitic disease are somewhat easier to describe and classify than are other aspects of neglect. For example, due to significant knowledge about the life cycle of the canine heartworm, *Dirofilaria immitis*, it is easy to estimate the length of time an animal has been infected with it. The degree of ectoparasitism can also be quantified somewhat: approximate numbers of fleas or ticks on an animal, for example, or the estimated percentage of body surface area affected by sarcoptic mange. To the extent possible, definite diagnosis of the presence of microscopic parasites is imperative. For court testimony in a criminal case, it is not enough to presume that an itchy dog with encrusted ear margins is suffering from sarcoptic mange. An astute defense attorney will question the validity of a presumptive diagnosis, so the results of skin scraping examinations, heartworm antigen tests, fecal flotation tests, and other laboratory analyses that definitively identify parasites must be presented.

Unsanitary Environment

Neglected animals are often found in the presence of paper and other solid garbage, organic debris (urine, feces, decomposing food, and deceased animals), rotting wood from collapsing fence and housing structures, and metal garbage such as aluminum siding and roofing materials, rusted nails, screws, wires, and fencing materials.

These materials pose a number of hazards to an animal, including ingestion of pathogens collected on decomposing organic materials, puncture wounds and lacerations from sharp objects, and blunt force trauma from falling structures. If an animal is confined by a tether or wearing any type of collar, environmental debris may pose a strangulation hazard. Rotting organic material may emit a toxic concentration of ammoniated gases, especially in indoor confinement situations.

Organic debris also attracts insects and rodents, who may act as fomites or vectors of disease. While it is difficult to quantify the amount of debris present in an animal's environment, the TACC scoring system (appendix C), includes a five-point environmental health scale that can be used to quantify the living conditions in which animals are found. One prosecutor experienced in presenting cases of cruelty to animals recommends collecting samples of such debris (e.g., a section of floor tile and the layer of feces that covers it) for preservation and later presentation to the judge and jury.

Hyperthermia and Hypothermia Due to Environmental Exposure

Both hyperthermia and hypothermia as a result of environmental exposure are common manifestations of animal neglect. While it is thought that the overwhelming majority of heatstroke victims are dogs who have been confined in automobiles and left unattended, it is highly possible that many more cases involve dogs left confined outdoors with little shelter from environmental heat and that these cases are observed less often because their negligent owners are unlikely to present them to a veterinarian after the animals' injury or death. Similarly, most cases of fatal hypothermia probably occur with little public notice.

Heatstroke is a complex pathologic state that results from direct thermal injury to body tissues exposed to excessive temperatures. The critical temperature at which enzyme alterations and cell membrane instability lead to multiple organ deterioration appears to be 109 degrees Fahrenheit. In one study of canine victims of heatstroke, necropsy of euthanized and nonsurviving patients yielded relevant necropsy findings of generalized tissue congestion, hepatic centrolobular necrosis, and pulmonary infarction (Drobatz and Macintire 1996). In some animals a posture of stiffened legs resembling rigor mortis may be seen. Intense heat causes muscle proteins to coagulate, which in turn causes muscle shortening.

Histopathological findings for human victims of hypothermia include intrapulmonary hemorrhages, acute hemorrhagic pancreatitis or focal pancreatitis with fat necrosis, and small myocardial degenerative foci (Spitz 1993d). These findings are presumably applicable to animal victims as well.

Environmental Humidity

Lack of shelter from wet conditions predisposes an animal to hypothermia. Accurate and detailed weather reports from the nearest weather-reporting station should accompany the veterinary report of animals suspected to have succumbed to hypothermia due to neglect. Animals exposed to wet or humid conditions for a period of hours or days may also develop macerated skin, which is attractive to flies and becomes infested with maggot larvae. Forensic entomology is a significant and growing field; references are available that indicate the length of time necessary for maggot infestation to occur and that will allow veterinary examiners to estimate the minimum length of time during which the animal's skin has been exposed to excessive humidity (see discussion of forensic entomology in chapter 8).

Putting It Together

In reporting and giving testimony regarding animal neglect, investigators and veterinary professionals should attempt to provide documented evidence that describes all of the conditions the victim faced in his attempt to survive, including diet, or lack thereof, physical surroundings and environmental pressures, and experiences with disease, parasitism, and injury. These conditions should be contrasted with what the law requires and what a reasonable human being would recognize as necessary to meet these needs. Such evidence will also aid the court in determining if the inability or unwillingness of a defendant to provide adequate care should preclude the individual from having animals returned or should lead to a prohibition of ownership of animals in the future.

CHAPTER 17 Animal Hoarding

Just west of Modesto, California, in August 2000, animal-control officers found themselves facing a horrific scene: 212 cats and kittens and the remains of at least 60 dead cats filled the home of a forty-eight-year-old woman. Litterpans were overflowing, and the stench and filth were so bad that the woman had been living in a small tent in her backyard for some time. Dead cats in plastic bags, strewn among empty cat food containers and a broken freezer, were found in the home's garage. Some of the remains were so entwined that it was difficult for officers to count the bodies. Fined for owning more than 50 cats in 1993, the woman now faced multiple counts of felony cruelty to animals. The officers faced the grim task of removing the live and dead animals and documenting the crime. The victims were so numerous that the county was forced to rent a facility to house the survivors.

The story is gruesome but by no means uncommon and not unfamiliar to most animal-sheltering agencies across the country. Animal shelters have long known about people who are pathological animal collectors and the horrifying situations they can create. The phenomenon of animal collecting—or "hoarding," as it has recently come to be called—is perhaps the most difficult of all types of animal abuse to comprehend because it is so paradoxical. Animal hoarders surround themselves with animals, professing their love for them while at the same time neglecting their basic needs, often to the point of death. Animal-hoarding situations may involve any species of animal, including cats, dogs, small mammals, farm animals such as goats and pigs, reptiles, and small and large exotic animals (including big cats). The majority of prosecuted hoarding situations (over 80 percent) involve cats and/or dogs (Berry, Patronek, and Lockwood 2005). This chapter focuses primarily on cases involving those species.

Veterinarians may play several roles in the investigation, documentation, and resolution of an animal-hoarding case. They may be called on to provide triage decisions at the scene of a hoarding situation, deciding which animals require immediate treatment or euthanasia for humane reasons and which may be treated later or impounded on the premises (if possible). Veterinarians play a central role in working with humane and law enforcement agents to document the condition of the animals and the nature and extent of illness and/or injury of each. They may be asked to outline long-term treatment protocols for the rehabilitation of animals who are malnourished, heavily infested with parasites, or otherwise severely ill, or they may be called on to identify the remains of dead animals found on the property and to offer opinions about cause of death.

Veterinarians are often asked to express an opinion regarding the duration of neglect, so they should pay particular attention to medical problems associated with chronic malnutrition, advanced progression of easily treated ailments, and prolonged exposure to unsanitary conditions. Such information is important in countering the explanation frequently offered by hoarders that the conditions are due to a recent lapse of care. Veterinarians may also be asked to state an opinion about how visible such problems would have been to a reasonable person, what steps could have been taken to prevent these problems, and the degree of pain or suffering experienced by the animals living in these conditions. And although veterinarians are not experts in human mental health, they may be asked to provide an opinion on sentencing or treatment options for hoarders since they can comment on the individual's ability to care for animals based on an understanding of the nature of the conditions of the animals who have been examined and treated.

Animal hoarding can be associated with extreme forms of neglect that are quite different from situations where animals are abandoned or simply cared for improperly. It is important for veterinarians and others responding to these cases to have a basic understanding of the perpetrators and their motivations so that they can offer more informed judgments concerning the possible causes of the illnesses, injuries, and other problems they are likely to find in the animals that are involved.

Until recently, little had been published about animal hoarding; existing information was primarily found in popular, lay, and trade publications, rather than the scientific literature of the veterinary, mental health, or public health communities (Moore 1991; Mullen 1993; Handy 1994a,b; Lockwood 1994; Weiss 1996). Animal hoarding has historically been considered an animal-control problem, but the phenomenon has begun to receive recognition from other groups, including adult protective service and mental health professionals. This recent interest and emphasis has resulted in new publications from the scientific community, several of which include review of the relevant literature about nonanimate hoarding behavior (Patronek 1999, 2001; Hoarding of Animals Research Consortium 2000). An understanding of the relationship that humans have with their possessions and how this relationship may become disarrayed when mental pathology intercedes is essential to understanding the phenomenon of animal hoarding. Human mental health experts have long known about people who hoard objects in an obsessive-compulsive manner. A significant amount of literature regarding this phenomenon has been published (Greenberg 1987; Greenberg, Eitztum, and Levy 1990; Rasmussen and Eisen 1992; Frost et al. 1995; Frost, Krause, and Steketee 1996; Damecour and Charron 1998) and will prove invaluable to any veterinarian who chooses to participate in investigating and prosecuting an animal-hoarding case.

Animal collecting is not, as it would seem at first glance, defined only by the number of animals one keeps. A person with an apparently manageable number of animals may exhibit symptoms characteristic of animal hoarding, while another is capable of providing adequate care for a much larger group of animals. The Hoarding of Animals Research Consortium (HARC) defines an animal hoarder as

> [S]omeone who accumulates a large number of animals; fails to provide minimal standards of nutrition, sanitation, and veterinary care; and fails to act on the deteriorating condition of the animals (including disease, starvation, and even death) or the environment (severe overcrowding, extremely unsanitary conditions) or the negative effect of the collection on their own health and well-being and on that of other household members. (Patronek 1999, 81)

Every animal-hoarding incident has its unique components, but most cases have four characteristics in common that set them apart from the kind of cruelty and neglect situations described in earlier chapters (Handy 1994a,b). They involve an animal abuser whose actions stem from a complex and poorly understood mental condition. They involve a significant number of animals for whom care will be difficult to provide. They attract the attention of the media and the general public, whose responses are often misguided. And they are diffi-cult to resolve completely: animal hoarders have an alarmingly high rate of repeat offenses.

The Animal Hoarder

The stereotype of an animal hoarder is that of the "lonely little old cat lady," a woman who has turned to her cats for affection when the humans in her life have abandoned her. While animal hoarders do tend to be older females who live alone, an analysis of the psy-che and motivations of those who hoard—whether they are hoarding animals or inani-mate objects—paints a more comprehensive picture of the animal hoarder.

Hoarders of objects or animals typically are not distressed by their situation and are not motivated to change unless they are forced either to take action or to risk losing their collection. Hoarders are extremely distressed if their items, no matter how useless they may seem, are taken from them. Their collection of items, although intended to give them control of their lives, often directly results in the loss of that control when the collection becomes so enormous or so hazardous as to require removal by others. While pathologi-cal collecting can be associated with a variety of mental disorders, including borderline personality disorder, schizophrenia, and addiction, most experts consider many cases be a manifestation of obsessive-compulsive disorder. Only recently has it been realized that animal hoarding is yet another expression of hoarding behavior, involving not bits of wood and paper, but living animals.

The relationship between those who hoard animals and the animals themselves can vary. Most animal hoarders claim that their motivation for collecting animals is their love for them or their fear that no one else will care for them. Fear of euthanasia is also a com-mon and distinct factor. Forty-three percent of hoarders are said to know all of their an-imals by name, whereas 33 percent know few, if any, by name (Patronek 1999).

Many animal hoarders attempt to make caring for animals their vocation, professing themselves at some point to be animal shelters or rescue organizations. They may even gain legal nonprofit status from the Internal Revenue Service (IRS), accept donations from the public, and offer some of their animals for adoption. The HARC offers some guide-lines for distinguishing between legitimate rescue groups and animal hoarders. Character-istics of a "rescue hoarder" may include:

- unwillingness to let visitors see the facilities where animals are kept;
- unwillingness or inability to say how many animals are actually present;
- little effort made to adopt and much effort focused on acquisition;
- continued acquisition in the face of declining care for existing animals;
- claims of being able to provide excellent lifetime care for animals with special needs (paralyzed, feline leukemia positive, extreme aggression) without verifiable resources;
- number and staff and/or volunteers inconsistent with the number of animals allegedly being cared for; and
- desire to receive animals at a remote location rather than on-site.

Some cases of mass neglect of dogs or cats may be incorrectly identified as "hoard-ing" situations, when they are in fact simply "puppy mills" or poorly maintained breed-ing facilities. Perpetrators usually have a history of selling or attempting to sell their ani-mals, in contrast to true hoarders, who rarely allow any animals to leave their care. How-ever, this distinction is not always clear-cut. Some hoarding situations have involved breeders who initially bred their animals intentionally and sold them to the public or in-tended to sell them. Commercial animal-breeding establishments are subject to regulation by the U.S. Department of Agriculture (USDA) pursuant to the Animal Welfare Act and must be licensed for commercial sales. Therefore, some animal hoarders have been USDA-licensed breeders. This distinction can be important in understanding the motivations of the individual responsible for the animals' condition.

The Hoarding Site

While hoarders of inanimate objects can create incredible environments of proportions that threaten public health and safety, the addition of animals to such a situation compounds the problems associated with hoarding behavior exponentially. Every animal-hoarding situation is unique, but a typical scene is that of a house in which dozens of animals—usually cats, but also dogs and other species—are kept. The animals may be loose in the building or kept in a labyrinth of makeshift cages and enclosures, or the collector may use a combination of the two methods. The floors of the house and the enclosures are contaminated with anywhere from a few days' to several years' worth of feces and urine. Packages (buckets, bags, and cans) that once held food, water, and cat litter are strewn about or piled in specific areas. Some hoarders, in an attempt to maintain cleanliness, cover each layer of debris with a layer of newspaper, often to the point that the level of the floor has risen several inches. Investigators have reported entering collectors' residences in which they could not stand upright, because the layers of feces and newspaper approached the ceiling.

The residence often has no working water, gas, electricity, or other utilities. Where power is available, it may not be used due to the dilapidated condition of refrigerators, stoves, and other appliances. Furniture is usually covered with feces, urine, animals, and trash. In cases where animals are severely starved, furniture has often been reduced to no more than wooden frames and wire springs, the upholstery and stuffing having been eaten away by the hungry animals. Some animal hoarders block off an area of their home for personal use, prohibiting animals from entering the bedroom or bathroom. Others share these areas with the animals, and sleep, eat, and bathe in rooms contaminated with feces, urine, and other debris. Hoarders may yield to the unsanitary conditions and eventually join the animals in urinating and defecating in areas of the house other than the bathrooms. More than a quarter of animal hoarders reportedly sleep in a bed that has been soiled with human or animal urine or feces or both (Patronek 1999).

Animal hoarders may hoard inanimate objects as well. Accumulations of newspapers and human food items are common, as are large collections of holiday decorations, paperback books, dolls and toys, pornographic materials, plastic milk jugs, medicines, and clothing. The external appearance of the residence of an animal hoarder is often unkempt but nondescript. While some hoarders go unnoticed because their sites are in isolated locations, many have been located in residential neighborhoods. Neighbors may notice that the yard is uncut, and that newspapers and advertising fliers have accumulated on the front porch, but have no inkling of the situation that lies inside. Hoarders often cover the windows of their homes with newspaper or tinfoil or may even paint the windowpanes. Entrances to the residence are carefully controlled so that passersby cannot see inside them. When the power supply is discontinued, the lack of lighting further obscures the interior.

Some hoarders live at the site where they hoard animals, while others may retreat to adjacent trailers or tents. Some hoarders live somewhere else entirely and may have multiple sites at which animals are kept. A common situation is that in which a person has inherited the home of an elderly or deceased parent and then begins keeping animals in that home while continuing to live at her own residence. Neighbors may see this person come and go at irregular intervals but assume this is normal since the home is "uninhabited." Less conventional animal hoarders may keep dogs outdoors, especially in isolated or rural areas. The animals are kept in pens or on tethers, or they may be allowed to run freely. Other hoarders keep animals in barns, mobile homes, old buses, and other structures.

Animal-hoarding sites are usually detected when unsanitary conditions lead neighbors to lodge complaints about odors, leaking water, or fire hazards, or when the animals themselves are observed. In some cases the conditions have been reported by concerned relatives or volunteers who have been helping to care for the animals.

Hoarding Victims

Although any species of animal can be involved, cats—perhaps because they are easily acquired and easily confined and because they reproduce readily with minimal care—are the most common and most numerous victims, followed by dogs. Animals are acquired from various sources, primarily by unplanned breeding, but also as strays, from free-to-good-home ads, and from neighbors and other members of the general public who wish to relinquish their pets but do not want to take them to an animal shelter.

Depending on the severity and duration of the situation, the animals may be in severely compromised condition or may be hardly affected. Veterinarians often find it surprising that animals taken from horrendous hoarding environments may have suffered fewer physical effects than would be expected. Other than some degree of emaciation, mild parasitic infestations, and viral diseases, some of these animals have no other telltale signs of their former plight. In such cases, the criminal charges or other actions must address the unfit environment in which the animals lived and the inability of the caretaker to maintain a sanitary environment. One possible reason for the lack of effect of the hoarding environment on these animals is the adaptability of youth. Surviving animals are young and strong and have not yet succumbed to the stresses of the conditions in which they are living. In other situations, animals rescued from hoarding situations are in dire condition, infected with internal and external parasites, suffering severely from malnutrition and bacterial and viral infections. Complicating the situation may be the fact that these animals have not been socialized to human contact and are difficult to capture, examine, treat, and provide care for.

More often than not, dead animals are found on the premises of animal hoarders (Patronek 1999), and criminal prosecution is much more likely in these cases (Berry, Patronek, and Lockwood 2005). Hoarders may or may not recognize that these animals have died. Some animals are left to decay in the spot where they expired, whereas others are subjected to rituals that mark their death, such as being wrapped and placed in a freezer. At least one case involved a hoarder who also hid human cadavers on the premises (Worth and Beck 1981).

Rarely are animal hoarders able to voluntarily part with any of their animals, living or dead. In death, as in life, they wish to maintain control over the animal. Some hoarders have been known to pick up and carry home "road kill" or other animal remains, complicating the investigative picture.

The Media

One of the most frustrating aspects of animal-hoarding cases is the response of the media and the general public. Television, newspaper, and radio reporters recognize that anything involving animals is a good story and often show up en masse when word of a grisly hoarding scene gets out. But, like much of the general public, they may find the human aspects of the story difficult to understand and often portray the animal hoarder inaccurately.

Despite the horrible conditions they force their animals to live in, animal collectors often appear simply to be animal lovers gone wrong. They are often heartbroken, grandmotherly women with graying hair and glasses and absolute confidence that their love for their pets is more important than the filth and the stench surrounding them. Statements such as, "They're my babies," "I've dedicated my life to them," and "Any life is better than death," are the mantra of animal hoarders, and the sympathy they induce in the media and the general public can be overwhelming. Supporters often rally around an animal collector after the individual's story is portrayed in the local newspaper, offering help and donations of money so the hoarder can keep her animals.

Agencies and individuals involved in the investigation of animal hoarding must be proactive in combating such misguided responses. Being open to working with reporters, and educating them about the phenomenon of animal hoarding, is the key. Despite the chaos that ensues when a large number of severely neglected animals must be captured, transported, processed, and treated in an animal-hoarding case, an individual experienced with the media should be designated to provide details about the case.

Examining Hoarding Victims: Special Forensic Concerns

Effective resolution of an animal-hoarding case, whether through prosecution, mental health evaluation, or negotiated surrender of some or all of the animals involved, requires a clear understanding of the nature of the abuse and neglect inflicted on the animals. Investigators and veterinarians must document the condition of animals removed from hoarding situations in the manner presented in chapters 7 and 8. This task is made more difficult by the large number of animals that may need to be assessed under adverse conditions. Although eventual charges may be based on a sampling of the animals recovered from the scene, it is important to document unique details for every animal victim, dead or alive.

Examination efforts require specific attention to evidence that can be used to substantiate that the condition of the victims is the result of neglect of long-standing duration (weeks or months), was potentially obvious to a reasonably prudent person, was preventable through actions that would normally be undertaken by such a person, and was sufficient to cause extreme discomfort, pain, or suffering. Veterinarians need to carefully document the recovery of the animals, including their appetite on intake, weekly weight gain, and all medical treatment needed. Photographic documentation of the animals' progress is critical. The initial mental status and behavior of the animal should be noted as well as whether there are any changes over time.

Particular attention should be given to identifying evidence related to the following:
- Developmental conditions associated with long-term neglect and/or malnutrition. These might include bone disorders or deformities and other developmental abnormalities.
- Conditions associated with failure to provide routine care. These might include ingrown collars, heavily matted coats, and severely overgrown nails or hooves.
- Problems associated with inadequate monitoring of health, for example, large tumors or severely infected or abscessed wounds. Fights may be common in situations of heavy competition for limited food.
- Problems associated with advanced progression of preventable diseases, for example, enucleation of one or both eyes due to severe upper respiratory infection in cats.
- Conditions brought on by prolonged exposure to unsanitary bedding or flooring, such as urine scald or infection of the skin, feet, or toenails.

- Documentation of variety and extent of parasite loads. It is not uncommon to find nearly hairless dogs due to mange infestation in hoarder cases.
- Evidence of cannibalism and/or starvation and dehydration in any dead animals who are necropsied.
- In cases of a large number of intact cats living in a confined area, evidence of forced matings may be seen. The barbs on the intact male cat's penis can cause vulva and vaginal abrasions from repeated, forced matings.
- Whenever there are intact animals living together there should be puppies or kittens. The lack thereof needs to be explained. Animals who are starving or are under severe stress or those who perceive the environment is unsafe may cannibalize their young.

The Elusiveness of Resolution

Although most prosecuted animal-hoarding cases result in convictions or pleas (Berry, Patronek, and Lockwood 2005), these cases are notoriously difficult to resolve. Hoarders who are required to make restitution for veterinary costs rarely comply, although many agencies are able to recover such costs through public appeals. Those who are ordered to undergo psychological assessment and/or treatment also generally fail to comply. Many agencies have begun to promote a task force approach to respond to hoarding situations. Such groups involve representatives of all stakeholders in the community, including human health and social services, public health, zoning, code enforcement, and animal protection groups to bring a coordinated effort to these cases.

Careful veterinary and investigative documentation that presents a clearer picture of what was allowed to happen to the animals involved and what level of care might be expected if animals are returned to the care of an animal hoarder can aid in successful resolution of these cases.

18 Animal Sexual Assault

I t is ironic that bestiality, one of the rarest forms of cruelty to animals, has the longest history of investigation and prosecution. Proscription of sexual contact with animals dates from at least the time of the Old Testament, which states, "cursed be he that lieth with any manner of beast" (*Deuteronomy* 27:21) and "whosoever lieth with a beast shall surely be put to death (*Exodus* 22:19). The severity of the penalties for such acts had little to do with concern about the harm that might be done to animals but rather was based on the notion that such actions upset the natural order of the universe and led to the production of monstrous offspring who were the work of the devil (Beirne 1997).

The penalty for such activities in many Western cultures was often death for both the human and nonhuman participants. Evans (1906) reviews many well-documented cases of such prosecutions. However, the societal response to bestiality was often inconsistent. Beirne (1997) notes that there were surprisingly few prosecutions for bestiality in Colonial America, despite the strong Puritan presence. In contrast, there were at least seven hundred *executions* for bestiality in Sweden between 1635 and 1778 (Liliequist 1991).

The response of the modern American legal system to sexual contact involving animals has also been inconsistent. Sodomy laws, once on the books in all fifty states, often criminalized a wide variety of sexual behaviors, including oral and anal sex, even between consenting adults, as well as homosexual behavior, "gross lewdness," "gross indecency," pedophilia, necrophilia, and bestiality. Often all of these were included within the catch-all category of "sodomy" or "crimes against nature." Since the 1970s the American Civil Liberties Union (ACLU) (*www.aclu.org*) and other groups have successfully challenged state sodomy laws, usually on the grounds of persecution of individuals based on their sexual orientation and the criminalization of behaviors transpiring between consenting adults. More than thirty states have subsequently repealed their sodomy laws through legislative or court action. It is ironic that, as these antiquated statutes were discarded, the prohibitions against bestiality that were subsumed in these statutes were often thrown out as well. This sometimes has had the effect of essentially decriminalizing animal sexual assault unless the act involved some other crime such as cruelty to animals, indecent exposure, trespass, or breaking and entering. In response to this unintended change, many state legislatures have reenacted provisions specifically targeting bestiality as distinct from other traditional "crimes against nature." As of mid-2005, twenty-nine states had laws specifically prohibiting sexual abuse of animals. Five states provided felony-level penalties with imprisonment for up to twenty years and fines of up to $50,000.

Efforts to restore criminal penalties for bestiality have met with opposition from a contingent of self-described "zoophiles" who maintain a large Internet presence. Any Internet search will quickly produce very graphic and disturbing material describing and promoting the sexual abuse of animals. Detailed how-to guides for the sexual abuse of animals involving a variety of species can be found, along with information on laws, zoonotic diseases, personal advertisements, "pro-zoophile" resources, and even advice about how animal abusers can "come out" to their family and friends. Although such proponents maintain that their behavior constitutes a so-called lifestyle choice, analogous to other nontraditional sexual orientations, this view is countered by the prevailing legal, legislative, and societal view that such contact constitutes "interspecies sexual assault."

Beirne (1997) makes this argument very clearly, noting that sexual abuse of animals parallels that of women and children and is also problematic because (1) human-animal sexual contact is almost always coercive, (2) such practice often causes pain or death for the animal, and (3) animals are unable to consent to or communicate about their abuse. Ascione (1993) notes that bestiality may be considered cruel even in cases when physical harm to an animal does not occur, drawing a parallel to cases of adult sexual activity with a child, where consent is presumed to be impossible.

Defining Animal Sexual Assault

This kind of animal abuse encompasses a wide range of behaviors, including vaginal, anal, or oral penetration; fondling; oral-genital contact; penetration using an object; and killing or injuring an animal for sexual gratification. Animal sexual abuse may or may not include physical violence other than the sexual violation and may or may not result in physical injury to the animal. Animal sexual abuse, like rape, is the eroticization of violence, power, and control. In addition to animal victims, human adult and child victims may be forced or coerced to participate in or observe acts of animal sexual abuse (Walker 1979; Adams 1994, 1995).

The magnitude of the problem of animal sexual abuse is difficult to measure. Although there has been relatively little research on animal sexual abuse and its perpetrators, case reports and anecdotal accounts indicate that men are the primary abusers, although women and children may be forced or coerced into sexual acts with animals or may be abusers themselves. The first attempt to assess the prevalence of bestiality among males was found in Kinsey, Pomeroy, and Martin (1953), who reported that, overall, 8 percent of the total U.S. male population admitted to having had sexual contact with animals, although the incidence was higher in some areas. It may tend to be higher in rural populations (Cerrone 1991). A survey of Iowa college students compared the incidence of sexual contact with animals in data collected in 1974 and 1980. In 1974 5 percent of females and 6 percent of males answered "yes" to "Have you ever had sexual contact with an animal?" In 1980 the incidence was only 2 percent for females and 1 percent for males (Story 1982).

Bestiality, or zoophilia, is not listed as a formal diagnosis in the current *Diagnostic and Statistical Manual of Mental Disorders (DSM-IV-TR)* (American Psychiatric Association 2000) but is listed as an example of "other disorders of sexual preference" or "paraphilia not otherwise specified." Commentary in the previous edition (DSM-IIIR 1987, 405) notes that "zoophilia is virtually never a clinically significant problem by itself." This does not mean that the behavior is insignificant, but rather it suggests that, when present, there are additional significant indicators of other mental disorders. This was documented by Abel et al. (1988), who reviewed 14 cases of bestiality in a larger sample of 561 adult males evaluated or treated for "paraphilia," a broad term referring to sexual arousal in response to sexual objects or situations that are not part of societally normative arousal/activity patterns, or which may interfere with the capacity for reciprocal affectionate sexual activity. Bestiality was most commonly associated with incestuous and non-incestuous female pedophilia, voyeurism, and exhibitionism.

The sexual abuse of animals is often anecdotally linked to the sexual abuse of women and children. This form of domestic violence involves the use of animals for degradation and sexual exploitation of the battered partner. Bestiality may be a part of further tormenting and humiliating the victim (Walker 1979). Child sexual abusers may also sexually abuse animals to enhance, expand, or extend the abuse of the genuinely powerless and unsuspecting victim (Adams 1994). Some case studies of sexual abuse of children include reports of forcing children to interact sexually with animals (Ascione 1993).

Animal sexual contact is higher in some clinical and adjudicated populations. In one study, psychiatric patients exhibited a significantly higher prevalence rate (55 percent) of bestiality than did control groups of medical inpatients (10 percent) and psychiatric staff members (15 percent) (Alvarez and Freinhar 1991). Research also indicates a connection between animal sexual abuse and other types of violent crimes. Forty percent of the perpetrators of sexually motivated *homicides* who had been sexually abused as children report that they had sexually abused animals (Ressler et al. 1986). Duffield, Hassiotis, and Vizard (1998) report on seven young incarcerated psychiatric patients (mean age = 13.4 years) identified as having committed a sexual act with an animal. They characterize this sample as "severely disturbed young persons who may suffer with other psychiatric disorders, such as severe conduct disorder, personality disorder, substance abuse, or psychosis" (303).

Flemming, Jory, and Burton (2002) surveyed 381 institutionalized, adjudicated young male offenders (average age 16.9 years). Twenty-four (6 percent) answered "yes" to the question, "Have you ever done anything sexual to an animal or animals (on your own without being conned or forced to do so)?" All but one of these (96 percent) admitted to having sexually offended against a human, although only 50 percent had been adjudicated as sex offenders, suggesting that many of their sexual assaults had gone undetected. In contrast, the incidence of sexual assaults against humans for the entire study population was 42 percent.

The motivations behind animal sexual assault may be complex. Kolb and Brodie (1982) draw parallels between zoophilia and pedophilia, suggesting that both are driven by heterosexual fearfulness, self-doubt, and expectations of rejection by appropriate partners, leading to a search for sexual gratification from those powerless to resist, namely animals or children.

Adams (1995) goes further, suggesting a variety of motives for animal sexual assault. She suggests that abusers may fall into one or more categories:

- Opportunistic/experimental. This type of abuse is often viewed as the act of a curious youth or a lonely man. These individuals may seek out animals for sexual gratification because animals are accessible, vulnerable, and nonthreatening. They may abuse an animal out of boredom, insecurity, curiosity, or as a substitute for a human partner. This type of abuser becomes accustomed to the idea that it is acceptable to exploit and control others for his own sexual gratification.
- Fixated/primary. In this category of animal sexual abuse, animals are the primary or exclusive focus of a human's sexual desires. These abusers often refer to themselves as "zoophiles." Some individuals may have species or gender preferences and use pornography involving animals. They defend their sexual abuse of animals as "consensual," claiming it benefits their "partners," and characterize their behavior as "loving." The rationalizations used to justify their actions are the same as those used by pedophiles, and, as in the case of victims of pedophiles, the claimed motivations don't matter to the victims. Just as pedophiles may seek employment in child-related fields to have access to numerous potential victims, this type of ani-

mal sexual abuser often seeks out employment in animal-related occupations (veterinary hospitals, animal shelters, boarding stables, etc.).

■ Domineering/sadistic. Batterers, rapists, and pornographers may force women, children, and other vulnerable individuals to have sex with animals to humiliate, dominate, control, and exploit the human and animal victims. Children who have been sexually abused may act out their abuse on animals in an attempt to gain a sense of control; therefore, a child's sexual abuse of an animal may be a cry for help, a sign that the abuser has suffered abuse and is in need of help. Some perpetrators may derive sexual gratification from the pain and suffering inflicted while sexually abusing animals. This type of sadistic abuser will probably injure or kill the animal.

From a variety of clinical, legal, social, and psychological perspectives, animal sexual abuse cannot be considered a harmless lifestyle choice. Its investigation deserves and requires the same care and attention as other forms of sexual assault.

Incidence of Reported Cases of Animal Sexual Assault

Although there is no centralized tracking of animal-cruelty cases, two organizations attempt to get a general picture of the nature of crimes against animals by collecting reports from media and other sources. The HSUS receives daily media clips from Cyberalert®, a service tracking more than thirteen thousand newspapers, magazines, journals, wire services, TV networks, and local TV stations. These clips are drawn from coverage of stories with any mention of animal abuse, cruelty, or neglect. The reports are then reviewed, and data on the specifics of each case are entered into a Microsoft Access® database. A second group, Pet-Abuse.com, uses similar methods but also has merged its data with those compiled by a group specifically concerned about animal sexual assault.

Of the 5,225 cases in the HSUS database for 2002–2004, only forty-six (.88 percent) involved animal sexual assault. The majority of cases involved dogs (36 percent) or horses (21 percent), but reports included incidents involving cats, sheep, cows, rabbits, chickens, pigs, goats, llamas, sea gulls, and an elephant. Criminal charges were filed in 76 percent of cases. A third of these charges were for crimes other than animal sexual assault, including child abuse, theft, breaking and entering, and drug offenses. The incidence of animal sexual assault cases in the Pet-Abuse.com database was low, but it was higher than the HSUS sample: 73 of 4,440 cases, from 1989 to 2005 (1.6 percent). As with the HSUS cases, the majority of the cases recorded involved dogs (52 percent) and horses (18 percent).

A third source of data on incidence of animal sexual abuse is a survey of veterinarians in the United Kingdom seeking information on nonaccidental injury to small animals (Munro and Thrusfield 2001c). Of 448 injuries reported, 28 (6.25 percent) were sexual in nature. The majority of victims (75 percent) were dogs, and injuries ranged from minor to fatal.

Examining an Animal Victim of Sexual Abuse

Physical examination or necropsy of an animal victim of sexual abuse should be performed in the same manner as for any animal abuse victim, as described in chapters 7 and 8. Evidence of any form of injury should be noted, particularly traumatic injury to the anus, rectum, or vulvar/vaginal area (Plates 16 and 17). In addition, if there is any evidence to suggest that there has been sexual contact between the animal and the abuser or with a human victim of the abuser, care should be taken to collect human or animal semen, seminal fluid, vaginal fluids, epithelial cells, pubic hairs, and any other potential evidence. A standard human Sexual Assault Evidence Kit (often referred to as a "rape kit") is a specially sealed box that contains envelopes, bottles, and other containers used primarily to obtain evidence from a human female victim who was assaulted by a male. However, such kits are also used to collect evidence from a male victim or a child and can be useful in processing evidence from animal victims as well.

Such evidence kits can be obtained from any criminal investigation supply company (see appendix B) or, if the need is urgent, from any hospital that deals with human sexual assault victims. A rape kit generally consists of the following items, some of which are not necessary for examination of animal victims:

- evidence envelopes for such things as fingernail scrapings and foreign substances;
- medical history and physical examination forms;
- a sexual assault incident form;
- authorization form;
- oral, vaginal, penile, cervical, and anal swabs;
- smear slides with appropriately labeled mailers;
- blood collection tubes;
- instructions for both male and female victims;
- pubic hair combs and mailers;
- bags for pulled head hair and pubic hair;
- scissors for cutting hair close to root (in the case of victims who object to hair being pulled from the root);
- evidence seals with biohazard labels; and
- paper bags used to collect the victim's clothing or other similar items.

Examination of the genitalia should be a part of the physical examination. Closely examine the perineal area, noting any evidence of edema, abrasions, or tearing of the anal or vaginal orifices. Illuminate and inspect the entire animal with an ultraviolet light source, such as a Woods lamp, which may cause semen stains to fluoresce (pus and urine also fluoresce and must be differentiated). Swab any fluids that are detected and take an additional control swab adjacent to the area of interest. Comb the fur on the body to reveal any human pubic hairs. The animal's head, mouth area, and feet should be inspected for blood or trace evidence in the event the animal bit or scratched the perpetrator. The teeth, gums, and lips should be swabbed for possible DNA testing and scrapings of the nails saved. Full-body radiographs should be taken for related underlying injuries, such as those that might be the result of restraining the animal victim.

Anal swabs for blood and semen testing should be collected before taking the animal's temperature. Suspected liquid semen should be absorbed onto a clean cotton cloth or swab, leaving a portion of the cloth or swab unstained as a control. The cloth or swab should be air-dried and packed in clean paper or an envelope with sealed corners. Plastic containers should not be used. Suspected dried semen stains should be absorbed onto a clean cotton cloth or swab moistened with distilled water and, with a portion of the cloth or swab left unstained as a control, procedures for a liquid semen sample should then be followed.

Rectal palpation may reveal further injuries or the presence of foreign material associated with sodomization with an inanimate object. If blood is found around the anus or inside the rectum, colonoscopy may be indicated. The vaginal walls and cervix should be examined for abrasions, ecchymosis, and lacerations. The vaginal walls and cervix should be swabbed to obtain cultures for gonorrhea and *Chlamydia trachomatis*. If a speculum is used to collect vaginal swabs, it should be lubricated only with sterile saline, since KY Jelly may be spermicidal.

A vaginal washing obtained using normal saline may be observed microscopically for the presence of human sperm. Motile sperm can often be seen up to eight hours postcoitus (Saferstein 1994), and nonmotile sperm may be detected beyond seventy-two hours (Beebe 1991). If sperm are present, the number seen in a high-power field should be documented. The absence of sperm does not exclude the possibility of sexual assault. The assailant may have undergone a vasectomy; 50 percent of assailants of human rape victims experience impotence or ejaculatory dysfunction (Beebe 1991), and this may also be the case in animal sexual abuse cases. The presence of etiologic agents of human sexually transmitted diseases in samples taken from an animal victim is also evidence of animal sexual abuse (Srivastava and Soni 1987).

In some cases perpetrators of animal sexual assault have used condoms. Although condom use may prevent positive suspect identification from DNA, condoms themselves leave exchangeable traces that can provide evidence, including silicon oil lubricants, particulates (such as talc, cornstarch, or lycopodium powder) and spermicides such as nonoxynol-9, which can be recovered from swabs made up to fifty-nine hours after sexual activity (Blackledge 2005).

Conclusion

There are state and federal laws prohibiting animal sexual abuse, and cases may involve extremely violent abuse of both human and animal victims. Yet few cases are identified, investigated, and prosecuted. Participation of veterinarians who know how to evaluate the victims of these cases will increase the likelihood of successful identification and prosecution of animal sexual abuse offenders.

19 Occult and Ritualistic Abuse

The phrase, "occult and ritualistic animal abuse," immediately evokes many disturbing images: a cat nailed to a crucifix and burned, the head of a dog left on the steps of a building with a piece of paper bearing a curse stuck in the animal's mouth, a goat's throat slit as a ritual sacrifice, a dog found hanging in an abandoned building with a railroad spike through the heart, cattle found in a field with their eyes and genitals removed. Few other crimes against animals create such intense concern within a community. Most crimes in which animals are killed or mutilated and left where they will be discovered immediately raise fears of "satanic" or cult activity and justifiable concern about what other crimes the perpetrators of such acts may have committed or be capable of. Yet it is precisely because of the highly emotional nature of these crimes that there is an even greater need for careful, rational, systematic investigation of the evidence.

Background and Definitions

"Occult" literally means "hidden," and occult activity is that which purports to use secret knowledge or rituals connected to supernatural powers. Ritualistic acts are any acts that are carried out repeatedly in a systematic way. Such broad definitions encompass a wide variety of actions, ranging from conventional religious practices to the acts of mentally disturbed individuals.

The 1980s saw rapid growth of public and law enforcement concern about possible criminal activities associated with some occult practices, fueled by widespread claims that occult practitioners were responsible for tens of thousands of human abductions and murders and millions of animal killings. Law enforcement professionals and others (Lanning 1989; Alexander 1990; Hicks 1991a,b; Richardson, Best, and Bromley 1991) later challenged such claims as being without support. Increasingly, law enforcement officials have recognized the need to be familiar with the range of unfamiliar or occult practices one might encounter but, at the same time, they have recognized the need to focus objectively on those *actions* that may constitute a crime and not be distracted by constitutionally protected *beliefs* that are unconventional or even unpopular.

The wide variety of occult-centered beliefs and practices defies simple classification, but most law enforcement discussions (e.g., Olson-Raymer 1990) recognize certain broad categories that depart from Judeo-Christian religious beliefs and practices.

Neopaganism

Neopaganism includes a diverse assortment of beliefs and practices that have evolved from the earliest religions. Although this category encompasses many different practitioners (see Adler 1979), most practice a polytheistic, nature-centered religion. Contemporary followers of such systems have not been associated with animal sacrifice and, in fact, generally promote practices and beliefs that celebrate animals and nature.

Witchcraft

Like neopagans, witches represent many different cultural traditions but have often been perceived as a threat to Judeo-Christian traditions. Many contemporary witches practice a polytheistic religion (witchcraft, Wicca, or the Craft) that generally emphasizes use of "magic" and rituals for healing, personal improvement, or symbolic transformation. Although elements of animals and nature may be used in some rituals (e.g., feathers, fur, bone), animal abuse is not associated with the most prevalent forms of "white" magic. Most modern practitioners of witchcraft emphasize that any harm done in the practice of rituals is reflected onto the practitioner. The few who do undertake harmful rituals that might involve animal maltreatment are usually considered to fall into the category of satanists.

Satanism

Satanism as a formal belief system did not become well known in the United States until the 1960s. Law enforcement authorities generally recognize several categories of satanism.

Religious Satanists

These individuals belong to organized, legally recognized satanic churches. The best known is the Church of Satan, founded in San Francisco in 1966 by former circus animal trainer Anton LaVey. The church advocated egotism, indulgence, and the use of personal and political power. LaVey is best known as the author of *The Satanic Bible* (1969), which specifically mentions criminal acts against children, drug abuse, and harming animals as things absolutely forbidden by the Church of Satan. In fact, LaVey and his daughters assisted humane organizations in the Bay Area and elsewhere in their investigations of animal abuse cases that had "satanic" elements. Several groups subsequently split off from the Church of Satan, most notably the Temple of Set. The fate of the church and its assets was in disarray after LaVey's death in 1997 (Boulware 1998). In 2001 the Church's headquarters were moved from San Francisco to New York City, appropriately in the "Hell's Kitchen" area (Knipfel 2005) and a new edition of *The Satanic Bible* was released (LaVey and Gilmore 2005). Most law enforcement agencies see religious satanists as law-abiding citizens rarely involved in the criminal justice system.

Cult Satanists

Cult satanists allegedly constitute organized groups of individuals practicing deviant and criminal acts, including animal and human sacrifice. They raise the most concern among mainstream religious organizations. Although cults that indulge in illegal practices certainly exist, the extent of such activities has been questioned seriously by many law enforcement officials and others (Lanning 1989; Hicks 1991a; Richardson, Best, and Bromley 1991). As of 2005 The HSUS had yet to encounter a case of animal cruelty attributed to the "satanic" practices of an *organized* group or cult.

Self-styled Satanists

These include young adults or adults often described as "dabblers," who, individually or in small groups, invoke some forms of presumably satanic rituals in the pursuit of power, money, sex, revenge, or other wish fulfillment. The rituals may come from actual occult literature or be inspired by fiction, movies, video games, or the practitioners' own imaginations, and may involve animal sacrifice, torture, or mutilation. This category may also include individuals with a variety of mental disorders (e.g., schizophrenia, nonspecific sadism), who adopt occult rituals as part of the manifestation of their illness.

Youth Subculture Satanists

Similar to adult dabblers are adolescents often seeking to gain power and control over their lives through involvement with or immersion in an occult or satanic subculture. Such individuals usually act alone or in small groups, and they may exhibit a variety of antisocial behaviors consistent with a conduct disorder, including theft, vandalism, arson, and cruelty to animals. Since one motivation for their actions is to distance themselves from mainstream values, they may seek to shock and offend others through actions against easily acquired and valued animals, including pets (often cats), livestock, or "public" animals, including animals in animal shelters or zoos (including petting zoos) or waterfowl at public ponds.

Self-styled and youth subculture satanists generally account for nearly all cases of occult or ritualistic cruelty to animals likely to be investigated by humane or law enforcement authorities and reviewed by veterinary professionals.

Cultural Spiritualism

Cultural spiritualism involves combining two or more different sets of cultural or religious beliefs and practices into a new system. Such practices are often an integral part of the history and culture of the people involved. The types of cultural spiritualism most likely to involve animals and most often encountered by law enforcement agencies are those with their origins in Africa and the Caribbean.

Santeria

Santeria, or "the way of the Saints," had its origins among Yoruba slaves transported from Nigeria to Cuba (Gonzalez-Wippler 1989). A new tradition emerged combining the worship of many gods (orishas) in the guise of Catholic saints. This practice was introduced into Brazil as Candomble and in Trinidad as Shango. Many of the rituals within these traditions involve soliciting the assistance or protection of various gods through offerings, which can include a blood sacrifice (Gonzalez-Wippler 1984). Usually the animals involved are agricultural animals, most commonly chickens and goats, but other rituals may involve doves, pigeons, turtles, opossums, and other animals. Dogs and cats have not traditionally been associated with Santeria ritual sacrifice.

Palo Mayombe

Palo Mayombe shares similar roots with Santeria, having its origins more closely associated with slaves from the Congo. Rituals of Palo Mayombe are more centered on the use of magic to inflict misfortune or death on an enemy. Practitioners make use of a cauldron (nganga) which may contain human or animal bones. Some Palo Mayombe rituals may make use of the body of a dog to "track down" the intended victims of a curse. Other rituals may involve a variety of animals, including lizards, bats, and frogs (Gonzalez-Wippler 1989).

Brujeria

Brujeria represents another fusion of occult traditions from several cultures combining Aztec mythology, European witchcraft, and Santeria with elements of Catholicism. It has its origins in sixteenth-century Mexico and has not been directly associated with cruelty to animals.

Voodoo

Voodoo, or voodoun, had its origins in the practices called Juju by the Ashanti tribes transported as slaves to Haiti. It encompasses the casting of good, bad, or protective spells as well as divination. Voodoo came to America in 1803, when the slave trade from Haiti began. Although animal sacrifice is not an integral part of traditional voodoo practice, certain rituals may use parts of a wide variety of animals, including cats.

The Role of Animals in Ritualistic or Occult Practices

Animals may be used in ritualistic practices for a variety of purposes. For the benign practitioners of neopaganism, witchcraft, and cultural spiritualism, such use may be a celebration of nature and of the animals' spirits. In other contexts, animals may be used as propitiations or offerings or as a source of vital energy or life force. In the most problematic practices, injuring or killing the animal may involve symbolic victimization; be motivated by a desire for revenge; or serve as a way to shock, frighten, intimidate, or offend others. Rituals involving killing pets may also be driven by a desire to bind a group together in its rejection of conventional values. Regardless of the motive, the main objective for investigators is to review the evidence of the treatment or maltreatment of the animal and assist in determining whether a crime has been committed and, if so, by whom.

The use of animal sacrifices within the context of cultural spiritualism has been controversial and divisive in communities where several cultures coexist. As with other forms of ritualistic treatment of animals, the primary concern for humane, veterinary, and law enforcement officials should be whether the housing, care, and treatment of animals used in these activities violate any applicable laws.

The Role of Veterinary Forensic Examination

The significance of veterinary expertise in cases of ritualistic or occult cruelty to animals is essentially the same as that in any other forensic investigation. This includes:

- Assisting in determining the identity of the victim, including species and, in some cases, the individual animal.
- Determining the cause of death and the sequence of injuries and timing of pre- or postmortem mutilations or other treatment (e.g., hanging, burning, or impaling). This may include observations at the scene of the injury as well as necropsy and laboratory analyses.
- Distinguishing between death and injury resulting from human versus nonhuman causes (e.g., predation).
- Identifying evidence that may link the injuries to a particular suspect. This includes recovery of trace materials (e.g., ligatures, adhesives, wax, paint, flammable substances) and analysis of unique injuries such as stab wounds.
- Offering opinion regarding the speed of unconsciousness and/or death and the degree of suffering the victim experienced.

Although the procedures for veterinary examination of evidence in cases of suspected occult or ritualistic cruelty are similar to those of most other veterinary forensic examinations (see chapters 6–8), certain unique precautions should be exercised. Examiners should be alert to the possibility that the victim has been treated with poisons or other potentially toxic substances such as mercury. Some practices may also involve the use of dangerous insects (e.g., scorpions, tarantulas) or venomous snakes. Certain rituals may involve the placement of objects (e.g., coins, paper with inscriptions, cigars) inside or around the body. The placement or arrangement of the animal and the objects on, in, or near the animal may have special significance that provides a link to a particular suspect. A photographic record should be made of any such evidence before it is removed.

Species and Individual Identification

Because animal remains in ritualistic crimes may be decomposed, mutilated, burned, or otherwise incomplete, the first step of an investigation may be to determine the species in question. An example is provided by an account of thirteen mutilated dogs reportedly found in various stages of decomposition in the woods near Lynchburg, Virginia. Their heads had been cut off, all had been eviscerated, most had paws removed, and all but one had been skinned. The local police commander proclaimed that, although there was no evidence indicating that a ritual had occurred at the location, "we are going to investigate whether any satanic activity is involved" (Springston 1991a). The following day it was revealed that the animals were in fact coyotes, not dogs, who had been dissected in a field biology class at nearby Liberty University. Skins and skulls had been removed for use in the university's natural history museum, and the stomachs had been removed for dietary analysis. The carcasses had been left in the woods to decompose for later collection of the bones (Springston 1991b).

The remains of legally trapped or hunted canids such as foxes and coyotes are commonly reported to be dogs when found by the general public. Assistance in identifying such remains can be obtained from local wildlife agencies, university zoology departments, or natural history museums.

Many of the animals victimized in ritualistic crimes, particularly cats, are caught as strays or free-roaming owned animals. In some cases it may be difficult to prosecute a case if no owner is identified, although ownership is not required to prosecute an act of cruelty. Proving ownership can lead to additional charges such as theft or arson. It may be helpful to determine if the remains are in fact those of an animal who has been reported lost or stolen by comparing the remains to blood, tissue, or hair samples obtained previously.

Cause of Death and Sequence of Injuries

If an animal who is victimized in a ritual crime has not been obtained illegally, prosecution of the case under anti-cruelty laws may require demonstrating that the victim was killed inhumanely or subjected to unnecessary pain and suffering. The mutilation of an animal killed instantly may not constitute a crime in many areas, but causing a slow death through torture, followed by mutilation, is likely to be prosecutable in any state. Rituals may use remains of legally killed animals obtained from other sources. These might include parts such as hearts and eyes obtained from butchers or slaughterhouses, improperly disposed of euthanized animals from laboratories or animal shelters, or the remains of animals used for dissection in schools.

Because of the public concern that surrounds suspicions of ritual killings, clarification of the immediate cause of death is a primary objective of the veterinary analysis. Robert Hicks, a criminal justice analyst with the Virginia Department of Criminal Justice Services, has compiled records of many instances in which accurate determination of the cause of animal deaths has rapidly quieted fears of satanic activity. One such typical case included press reports of a mutilated goat found dead, castrated with his horns cut off, in an Illinois river. Local police stated that the goat was "probably the victim of Satanic activity," and noted, "Although both county and city police have received reports of Satanic meetings, rituals, and animal sacrifices, little physical evidence has supported those reports" (Parker 1989a). The next day a new headline appeared in the same paper: "Goat killed in dog attack." The story reported that a local farmer admitted to dumping the goat in the river after the animal had been killed by the man's two German shepherds. The animal's genitals had been damaged in the attack, and he had been routinely dehorned before the incident (Parker 1989b).

Hicks (1991a) reports another case from May 1989 in Allenstown, New Hampshire. Police received reports that six cats were found hanging in a tree not far from a decapitated dog. Drums were heard in a state park, and a woman reported finding the carcass of a mutilated beaver on a "makeshift altar," with another beaver found "surrounded by stakes." Other residents reported dead animals arranged at a roadside "altar." A California police officer noted for conducting cult workshops was consulted and surmised that these sacrifices coincided with Walpurgisnacht, a putative satanic holiday. On closer investigation, however, it was determined that no cats had been found in trees, the beavers had been legally trapped in the park, and the other dead animals reported during the period were roadkill that had been piled up by highway crews for pick up.

When animal remains are clearly the result of malicious killing for ritualistic purposes, it is important to try to identify not only the cause of death, but also the sequence of events. For example, in the case of a cat found burned and nailed to a cross, there are several possible scenarios. Was the cat roadkill that was then treated in a ritualistic, but not necessarily illegal or inhumane, fashion? Was he alive when nailed or when set afire? Which form of assault took place first? Possible actions depend on an accurate determination of the sequence of events. Examination of the victim should seek to clarify which injuries might have been associated with capture (e.g., was the animal stunned by a nonlethal blow, caught in a leghold or body-gripping trap), restraining (e.g., by tying, chaining, binding with wire, or taping), actual killing, and postmortem mutilation. A histologic exam can help determine what injuries occurred antemortem and further define the degree of suffering and possible torture the animal endured before death.

Injury, Death, Mutilation: Human versus Nonhuman Sources

One of the most frequent types of animal abuse cases encountered by humane investigators is that of pets found mutilated on or near their owner's property. Often the public and even local police are quick to attribute such deeds to human action. In very few cases does evidence clearly point to a human perpetrator, such as a threatening note or remains left in areas inaccessible to wildlife, such as in a mailbox or inside a screen door. In many cases veterinary expertise is required to help distinguish between human and nonhuman actions.

In the summer of 1989 in Tustin, California, sixty-seven cats were killed within a three-month period. Most of the carcasses turned up on lawns in this suburban community, many of them described as being dismembered with surgical precision, their blood drained and organs removed. Local residents rejected initial reports from Orange County Animal Control attributing the deaths to predators and were convinced that this was the act of humans, probably satanists. Responding to public pressure, officials undertook a lengthy and costly investigation. Orange County veterinarian Nila Kelly, after conducting or reviewing reports of more than one hundred necropsies, concluded that the cats all showed evidence of animal kills, most probably those of coyotes. Coyotes were common in the surrounding area. New construction had destroyed considerable natural habitat conducive to rabbits and rodents at a time when many juvenile coyotes who were just learning to hunt were forced into the more urban setting in search of relatively abundant and easy prey (Alexander 1990). Kelly noted:

> [C]oyote kills show puncture wounds from the canine teeth, chewing and splintering of bones, signs of which were found in the autopsies....Coyotes prefer the internal organs and can cut a cat in half because they instinctively go for the soft middle section where there are few bones. The lack of

blood at the scene is not surprising...because coyotes kill quickly and the heart stops beating and pumping blood. (Alexander 1990, 14)

Kelly acknowledged that the county had about ten mutilations annually that could be attributed to human intervention, but that there was no evidence of any widespread or organized activity in these killings.

In summer 2003 a similar series of cat mutilations in Denver and Aurora, Colorado, and Salt Lake City, Utah, produced near-hysteria and the formation a multiagency task force to investigate. One of the authors (R.L.) was asked to participate in this task force. One veterinarian involved in examining some of the Denver victims initially suggested in a press briefing that thirty-seven of forty-five cats showed "signs of human involvement," although no cases involved any actions or injuries that could not have been caused by predators. By July investigators in Salt Lake were able to identify tissue found in the claws of some victims in that area as having come from red fox. In Colorado wildlife and animal behavior experts were brought in to reevaluate the evidence and to assess the prevalence of predators in the areas where the killings took place. Local police concluded that all of the incidents were consistent with the actions of coyotes and foxes, who were abundant in the area (Anonymous 2003).

When examining such cases, investigators should contact animal-control and local wildlife agencies to get an idea of what predators occur naturally in the area of the attack. These include not only wild carnivores and free-roaming dogs, but also birds of prey such as eagles or great horned owls, which are capable of killing and dismembering small pets.

Livestock Mutilations: A Special Case

No allegedly ritualistic crime creates more hysteria and generates more forensic misinformation than livestock mutilation. For decades instances of livestock found dead with soft tissue removed have generated a range of hypotheses to explain these findings, including secret military experiments, widespread satanic cults, drunken students, roaming psychopaths, and alien visitations. An apparent surge of cases in the 1970s and 1980s prompted widespread press hysteria, well documented by Kagan and Summers (1984) and requests for federal investigation from former astronaut and New Mexico senator Harrison Schmitt. Such cases continue to appear periodically in the media and often include comments by laymen, law enforcement officers, or veterinarians with little or no forensic or livestock husbandry experience, describing the animals as "drained of blood" or wounds as having been made with "surgical precision."

Such cases are genuinely disturbing and invariably attract media attention, often thrusting police officers, veterinary professionals, ranchers, and others into the limelight. These cases require extra effort to investigate thoroughly and objectively, and veterinary and law enforcement professionals must be prepared for the likelihood that their findings will be rejected by a large element of society that prefers a good story to the truth.

Over that last twenty-five years, considerable veterinary and forensic expertise has gone into the investigation of many instances of livestock death and mutilation. After examining a series of cattle mutilations in eastern Montana, investigators from the Animal Diagnostic Laboratory in Bozeman concluded that *all* of the mutilations could be attributed to predators, primarily coyotes (Cade 1977). Microscopic examination of the wounds debunked the hypothesis that knives or scalpels had been used. The report noted that irregular tears, such as would be expected from predators, take on a smooth appearance as skin decomposes. Likewise, it was noted that blood tends to gravitate to the lower side of the carcass and then decomposes rapidly, giving the impression that the carcass has been "drained."

Perhaps the most extensive objective review of cattle mutilations was conducted under the auspices of a Law Enforcement Assistance Administration grant by retired FBI agent Kenneth Rommel and anthropologist Nancy Owen (Rommel and Owen 1980). They reviewed reports of hundreds of cattle mutilations, including dozens of New Mexico cases in which Rommel personally investigated the alleged crime scene. In many cases he found the carcasses to be covered with bird droppings. Observations of birds such as magpies scavenging cattle indicated that they tend to prefer smooth, exposed soft tissues such as genitalia, rectum, eyes, and tongue, or organs that erupt through orifices with the force of postmortem gas production. The original causes of death for these animals included lightning (as evidenced by finding animals under trees with evidence of a lightning strike), disease, and ingestion of toxic plants. In all of the cases examined, the damage to the carcasses was consistent with predator action and natural postmortem changes.

Rommel described lengthy observations of the fate of several cows found in New Mexico's Carson National Forest soon after they had died from larkspur poisoning. Within three days, blowflies and natural processes of decomposition had reduced each body to the "classic" mutilation victim, including what would appear to be "surgical removal" of the tongue, eyes, and soft tissues (Hitt 1997).

Commenting on several cases of cattle dismemberment widely attributed to "devil worshippers" in 1992 in Arizona, Greg Bradley of the University of Arizona Veterinary Diagnostic Laboratory noted, "It's our feeling that these same kinds of changes can be caused by natural processes, such as scavengers....When you're dead, you don't bleed...the blood pools to the lowest portion of the body and it clots there. When you cut into the body, or when a scavenger works it over, there is no bleeding" (in Pitman 1992). Despite these reassurances, the same paper cited another veterinarian as saying that the injuries were "far too precise to be the work of scavengers."

In 1993 investigators in Arkansas used night vision equipment to continuously observe the carcass of a calf known to have died of natural causes. During a thirty-hour period, the carcass was visited by a skunk, buzzards, a stray dog, and blowflies. As the carcass began to swell, the tongue and other soft tissue protruded. Predators began feeding on these tissues as well as the genitals, udder, and anus. As the carcass cooled, the remains of the tongue and anus retracted, both giving the appearance of have been surgically cut, particularly after blowflies cleaned the edges of the wounds.

Although isolated instances of the killing and mutilation of livestock may be attributed to individual vandals, satanic dabblers, or mentally ill individuals, the most common explanation is likely to be a combination of natural causes. Veterinarians enlisted to assist in field or laboratory analysis of evidence from such cases should be alert to the following considerations to supplement a standard postmortem analysis:

- Possible natural causes of death. A conventional necropsy should allow some conclusions concerning conventional causes of death. These include disease; complications of injuries such as fractures; injuries from fights; poisoning by plants, pesticides, or other man-made toxins; ingestion of foreign objects (e.g., barbed wire); lightning; starvation; predator attack (dog, coyote, eagle); or gunshot.
- Evidence of predator and scavenger activity (bird droppings, animal tracks, scat, fur, scent marks on fences or trees, insect eggs, and larvae, particularly blowflies).
- Evidence of human activity, such as footprints, tire tracks, trash (bottles, cans, shell casings), ritualistic paraphernalia (paint, candles), or evidence of sexual assault of the animal (see chapter 18).
- Wound characteristics associated with possible ritualistic implements (see chapter 11).

Linking Injuries to a Particular Suspect

Ritualistic or occult animal abuse is, by its very nature, highly individualized. Perpetrators are likely to use implements and procedures that are unique. Any materials found on, in, or near the victim should be carefully recorded, catalogued, and preserved for possible comparison with items or substances associated with a particular suspect. Efforts should be coordinated with law enforcement authorities to be sure that significant items are collected if a search warrant is executed. Particular attention should be paid to any notebooks or personal writing that may be seized. Many occult practitioners write detailed accounts of the rituals they have performed or intend to perform, and these descriptions may help clarify what was done to the victim. Particular attention should be given to any evidence associated with the following:

- Knives. Many occult rituals make use of specialized knives, often handmade. These instruments may make unique cuts or leave identifiable cross-sections in tissue. The presence of shallow "hesitation wounds" near deeper injuries may indicate a young, inexperienced, or reluctant assailant or one who has a relationship with the victim or the victim's owner.
- Binding materials. Many victims of ritualistic abuse are restrained with rope, twine, wire, or tape in the course of their abuse. These materials leave fibers, residue, or characteristic injuries that can be linked to materials associated with a suspect. If they are removed from the victim, they should be carefully preserved. Knots should be left tied: such bindings may contain sufficient DNA evidence to identify a possible suspect.
- Clubs. Some victims are stunned or bludgeoned before their ritualistic use, so evidence should be gathered that might be associated with a particular weapon (see chapter 10).
- Vessels. Many rituals use a ceremonial vessel such as the cauldron or *nganga* used in Palo Mayombe. Other rituals may involve collecting blood in a goblet or other container.
- Candles, chalk, oils, herbs. Ritualistic abuse may be accompanied by anointing the victim or burning candles near, on, or in the victim, leaving residues that might be traced.
- Flammable liquids, liquor. If the victim has been burned, accelerants such as gasoline, lighter fluid, or lamp oil may leave a unique residue. Samples of fur or other tissue that might contain such residue should be preserved. Some rituals of Santeria and related groups involve offerings of rum or other liquor as part of the ceremony, which might also leave unique and identifiable residues.
- Other chemicals. Certain rituals use unique chemicals, including mercury, gunpowder, lime, and sea salt. Any chemical residues associated with the victim should be carefully preserved.

Commentary on Degree of Pain or Suffering

One of the unique responsibilities of veterinary experts in cases of ritualistic animal cruelty is to provide insight into the degree of suffering an animal may have experienced. Such testimony may be crucial in meeting the legal definition of "inhumane killing" or "torture" required for prosecution at the highest levels.

It is important to address the suffering in the context of the physical stress, the behavioral responses to the act, and the physiologic responses to pain, fear, and anxiety.

In June 1993, following the U.S. Supreme Court's decision striking down the Hialeah,

Is Animal Sacrifice Legal?

In 1987 the City of Hialeah, Florida, passed an ordinance that banned Santeria Church of Lukumi Babalu Aye practitioners from performing animal sacrifice as part of their ceremonies. The ordinance was upheld by the State Supreme Court and Federal District Court but was overturned by the U.S. Supreme Court—Lukumi Babalu Aye v. City of Hialeah (113 Ct. 2217 [1993])—which argued that the law was too specific in its restrictions of a specific religious organization. Although many feared that this decision might open the door to widespread proliferation of animal sacrifice as a protected religious practice, the Supreme Court unanimously held that governments have the right to enforce more broadly based prohibitions on animal cruelty, livestock keeping, and zoning. The decision did not restrict enforcement of anti-cruelty laws (as in the case of *Florida v. Zamora* described here), nor did it prevent passage of more broadly written regulation or banning of animal sacrifice. However, this case has created a climate in which some prosecutors, unfamiliar with the full court decision, may be reluctant to take action against animal maltreatment allegedly occurring within the context of religious practice.

Florida, ordinance banning ritual sacrifice, Rigoberto Zamora, a Miami Santeria practitioner, held a press conference where he performed a Santeria ritual that involved sacrificing three goats and one sheep by slitting their throats. Videotaped evidence showed that one goat continued to bleat after the first knife cut, although the cut appeared to enter the animal's trachea. A second goat was clearly conscious after being stabbed in the neck and struggled while Zamora made more cuts in a haphazard sawing fashion. The sheep required seven cuts to the throat before he was killed.

Detailed veterinary testimony was provided by Michael W. Fox, D.V.M., and Melanie Adcock, D.V.M., of The HSUS and by livestock handling and slaughter expert Temple Grandin, Ph.D. Each reviewed the videos and other detailed reports of the sacrifice. Their affidavits concluded that the slaughter had been cruel and unnecessarily painful. Zamora was charged with four counts of cruelty to animals in July 1995. His motion to have the charges dismissed on the grounds of religious freedom was denied. In July 1996 he pleaded no contest to the charges and received two years' probation and four hundred hours of community service. (He appealed this conviction to the circuit court, which upheld the conviction in October 1997.)

Conclusion

In many instances in the examination of animal evidence of allegedly occult or ritualistic crimes, veterinarians may be the first and last voice of reason in the investigation. Through careful application of sound medical and forensic methods, they are in an ideal position to allay unwarranted public fears and, when a crime actually has been committed, clarify evidence that may bring the perpetrator to justice.

20 Dogfighting and Cockfighting

Dogfighting and cockfighting are both violent crimes that, according to many humane investigators, continue to grow in popularity. Although cockfighting is a serious concern for humane and law enforcement officials, prosecution of cockfighting is generally based on direct observation and/or the presence of fighting birds and implements for training and fighting of the birds. Unlike dogfighting prosecutions, action against cockfighting has not usually been based on detailed information on the conditions of animals seized at the scene. However, it is always advisable to have veterinary evaluation of a sampling of the animals. This has become more important as cockfighting was implicated in the spread of exotic Newcastle disease in California in 2002 and 2003.

In 1975 no states had felony provisions that addressed dogfighting. By 2005 dogfighting was illegal in all fifty states and the District of Columbia, and the federal Animal Welfare Act (AWA) prohibited interstate transportation of dogs for fighting purposes. As of March 2005, forty-eight states had made dogfighting a felony offense. Since the penalties associated with the AWA's dogfighting violations have been almost universally weaker than state laws, few federal charges have been filed in such cases. In mid-2005, however, both houses of Congress unanimously passed the Animal Fighting Prohibition Enforcement Act to establish felony-level penalties for violations of the federal animal-fighting law and to prohibit interstate and foreign commerce in knives and gaffs used for cockfighting.

As these laws continue to be strengthened, humane and law enforcement officials increasingly seek the assistance of veterinarians in responding to dogfighting. Although animal injuries associated with dogfighting share many of the characteristics of blunt and sharp force trauma reviewed in chapters 10 and 11, the unique characteristics of dogfighting evidence deserve more detailed review. Veterinary professionals in several states (including Arizona, California, Illinois, Minnesota, Wisconsin, and West Virginia) are currently *mandated* to report suspected dogfighting activity involving animals they have treated. Reporting mandates are likely to increase as law enforcement and animal-care and -control agencies attempt to deal with the proliferation of this brutal practice. As with other mandated reporters of suspected illegal activity, veterinary professionals typically receive immunity from any civil action that might result from a good-faith report of suspicions of fighting activity.

Arizona State Law (32-2239A and B) is typical of most of these mandates. It states:

> Veterinarians have a duty to report in writing...within 5 days of examining or treating a dog he reasonably suspects of having participated in an organized dog fight. He or she is also immune from civil liability for any report made in good faith.

One might easily believe that an individual engaged in illegal dogfighting would not seek the services of a veterinarian. This is often true. Many dogfighters attempt to treat their animals themselves, collecting a relatively sophisticated assortment of drugs, instruments, and veterinary supplies for this purpose. They may try to obtain some of these supplies from a veterinarian under false pretenses, or they may simply use mail-order or Internet supply sources to establish their own "clinic." These supplies are likely to be seized if a search warrant is executed in the case of a suspected dogfighter. Veterinarians can play a key role in identifying such items for the court and in describing their potential legal or illegal use.

Background

A detailed discussion of the history, conduct, and investigation of dogfighting is provided in Dantzler et al. (2000), which is available to law enforcement agencies through The HSUS. It is important for anyone involved in the care and assessment of animals who have been used in this activity to be familiar with the some of the current practices.

The Dogfighters

Dogfighting participants are generally divided into three categories, each presenting different challenges to law enforcement and to veterinary professionals who may assist in the investigation:

Serious (Professional) Dogfighters. These participants are very active in breeding, conditioning, training, and fighting their animals, often on a national or even international level. They participate in high-stakes matches and place great importance on maintaining winning bloodlines. They may use sophisticated diet and exercise regimens, called "keeps," to maintain their dogs in good physical condition. They are the most likely to be involved in medically treating their own animals. A large portion of their income may be from stud fees for champion animals and the sale of pups, so they are more likely to seek help for the care of valuable animals who have been injured. Pups who fail to show good fighting potential may be culled, often by shooting, and disposed of on or near the breeder's property.

Hobbyists. These individuals are usually more involved in the gambling aspects of dogfighting. Their animals are often poorly bred and relatively untrained, and they are likely to provide only as much care for injured animals as might be necessary to recoup their investment.

Street Fighters. These are often juveniles, sometimes with gang affiliations. Their dogs may be stolen or obtained from shelters lacking strong adoption policies. "Conditioning" is often limited to subjecting animals to abusive practices such as feeding them gunpowder, spraying them with pepper spray, force-feeding them hot sauce, or beating them to encourage aggressiveness. "Training" often consists only of giving the dog an opportunity to attack other animals, including stolen dogs and cats. Dogs who lose are considered an embarrassment and are often killed or left to die at the scene of an impromptu fight, such as in an alley or abandoned building.

The Dogs

Many breeds have been developed primarily for the purpose of dogfighting. These include the Neapolitan mastiff, the Japanese Akita and Tosa Inu, the Chinese shar-pei, the dogo Argentino, the fila Brasileiro and the Presa Canario. In the United States, fighting dogs are almost exclusively American Pit Bull Terriers. If a fighting dog is registered, it is usually with the American Dog Breeders Association (ADBA) or the United Kennel Club (UKC). The American Kennel Club (AKC) American Staffordshire Terrier, derived from some of the same early bloodlines as today's fighting dogs, is not seen in fighting circles, although fighters may describe their dogs as American Staffordshires to veterinarians, animal-control officials, and the general public to avoid the stigma and/or restrictions associated with dogs identified as "pit bulls."

For more than a century, fighting dogs have been selected for a collection of characteristics dogfighters generally term "gameness." These include a strong predisposition for aggression against dogs and other animals, physical strength and stamina, persistence in aggressive behavior, and apparent tolerance of pain. Because these dogs have been bred for success in the pit, the aggressive behaviors of animals from recent fighting lineages are often considerably different from those of other wild and domestic canines, including individuals from fighting breeds who have a history of selection for "pet" qualities rather than for combat (Lockwood and Rindy 1987; Lockwood 1995).

Most canine aggression is highly ritualized. Dogs fight to establish dominance and to control access to resources such as food, territory, or mates, and they cease fighting when one of the combatants withdraws or displays submission. Most dogs, like their wild counterparts, have good bite inhibition and display damaging aggression only in extreme conditions. Submissive behaviors, such as whining or rolling over, normally act as "cut-off" signals, ending the attack.

In fighting dogs, this inhibition has been removed through generations of selection. Such dogs routinely ignore "normal" displays of submission and continue to attack, leading to injuries to the opponent's abdominal and inguinal areas. Such injuries are rare in fights between dogs without a fighting background. Fighting animals have been bred to inflict maximum damage on their opponents rather than to simply drive them away. The style of attack is more like predation than typical intraspecific fighting; it is more likely to include grabbing, shaking, and tearing. Dogfighters may select for a specific style of attack and may describe their dogs as "face dogs," "leg dogs," or "belly dogs," in reference to their preferred target.

Normal dogs usually have a very expressive repertoire of signals that communicate their mood and intention. It is a disadvantage for a fighting animal to signal his emotional state or intentions and, as a result, such animals can be very difficult to "read," for both people and other dogs. This is one reason why such dogs are often described as "attacking without warning." Cropping the dog's ears and tail, often to an extreme degree, helps the dogfighter create an animal who is less likely to communicate his mood or telegraph an imminent attack. Cropping also reduces areas that an opponent can easily grab and injure.

This history has also influenced fighting dogs' response to people. Until relatively recently, fighting dogs posed relatively little threat to people. Since dogs often fight in close proximity to at least three people (the handlers of opposing dogs and a referee), fighters argue that such dogs have actually been selected *against* showing aggression to people, noting that attacks on people in the pit are grounds for elimination. (Many of the dogs seized from professional fighters can be surprisingly easy for law enforcement, humane agents, or veterinary staff to handle. However, this tractability can be limited to people similar to those to whom the dogs have been socialized—usually adult males. Fighting dogs may, in fact, react to unfamiliar people, especially small children, as if they were canine opponents.) Dogs involved in fights conducted by hobbyist and street fighters often do not come from lineages in which there has been selection against aggression toward people. These animals have often been bred and trained to serve as guard or attack dogs. Stable, well-bred, socialized, people-friendly examples of all fighting breeds are abundant, but animals from a known recent fighting background should be handled with caution.

Conditioning and Training

Dogfighters vary widely in the kinds of training and conditioning they use. Serious fighters may establish a daily regimen of diet, vitamins, and exercise. Dogs may be exercised on a treadmill or jenny, resembling a miniature horse walker. Grip strength may be enhanced by encouraging the animal to grab onto and hang from a tire, animal hide, or other lure. Actual fight training may involve a series of "rolls," brief bouts with other dogs, sometimes while muzzled. Hobbyists and street fighters are less likely to engage in a lengthy training and conditioning program. They may train their dogs for fights using smaller animals such as cats, rabbits, or small dogs. These "bait" animals are often stolen pets or animals obtained through "free to good home" advertisements. Some, like serious fighters, may give their dogs various drugs to try to achieve rapid results. These can include androgenic hormones, amphetamines, and diuretics.

The Nature of Dogfighting

Procedures used in conducting dogfights are reviewed in Dantzler et al. (1997). Points most relevant to veterinary forensics are reviewed here.

Dogfights are conducted in a variety of situations, from elaborate, permanent "pits" constructed of wood, hay bales, or makeshift materials to impromptu street fights with no formal pit. The more professional fights use specific rules, but the general procedures are similar for most fights. Serious fights often begin with weighing and washing the dogs (the latter is to guarantee that the dog's fur has not been treated with a poisonous or caustic "rub" that could injure the opponent).

Most fights match dogs by weight and sex. Some fights involve females against females, and street fights involving males against females do occur. Handlers "face" their dogs in opposite corners and release them. Handlers are permitted to touch their dogs only if it is necessary to separate them, for example, if one animal's tooth becomes caught on the opponent's lip or other area. Dogs may be separated with a "break stick," often a pointed piece of axe or hammer handle used to pry the animals apart. Less sophisticated fighters may use screwdrivers or other implements for this purpose, producing additional injuries.

The fight continues until one animal appears to be unwilling to continue. The animals are separated and released: if one dog is then unable or unwilling to cross the "scratch line" and continue the fight, the match ends. Although most dogfights are not fought to the death, according to most humane organizations, at least half of the animals involved die as a result of their injuries. Among professional fighters, a dog who has won three contract matches is considered a champion; five victories define a dog as a grand champion.

The Role of the Veterinary Professional

Veterinary professionals may play a variety of roles in responding to the needs of the victims of dogfight activity.

Participation in Search and Seizure

Humane and law enforcement organizations usually want at least one veterinarian on the scene in any operation in which injured, dead, or dying dogs are likely to be encountered. A veterinarian is needed to provide treatment for injured animals and to assist in documenting injuries and collecting and properly preserving any dead animals. In cases involving a large number of animals, the veterinarian will be needed to assist in triage and may be called on to euthanize severely injured dogs.

If a seizure is being conducted at a location where many dogs are housed, the veterinarian should, if possible, conduct a basic health check of all dogs present at the scene. In one instance the evidence of a suspect's involvement in organized fighting was weak, but the presence of dogs with serious untreated injuries, including one with an infected compound leg fracture, was sufficient to prosecute the suspect for gross neglect, leading to the surrender of all of his animals to animal-control authorities.

Treatment of Fighting Dogs

Veterinarians may be called on to provide treatment to dogfighting injuries in ways other than direct participation in a raid. They may receive such animals from humane or law enforcement officials following a raid or seizure, or they may receive dogs from an owner or breeder they may suspect is involved in illegal fighting.

In caring for dogs suspected of involvement in dogfighting, veterinarians should pay particular attention to thorough documentation of all injuries and to safe and secure housing of the animals. Fighting dogs, even if they are seriously injured, can be extremely aggressive toward other animals. During transport and recovery they should be housed in strong, secure enclosures that do not permit any access to other animals. They should be separated from other animals by a solid, secure partition and, whenever possible, should not be able to see other dogs. Dogs seized from a fight may be extremely valuable and could be the target of theft, so added security may be necessary.

Dogs who have been rescued from a fighting situation may suffer from multiple forms of trauma, including blood loss, dehydration, puncture wounds, infection, crushing injuries, and broken bones. The examination of each dog should proceed as described in chapters 7 and 8, with each injury carefully noted. Wounds should be photographed and recorded on a data sheet. It is helpful to characterize bite wounds as "fresh" (e.g., open and bleeding), "recent" (e.g., new, pink scar tissue), or "healed" (e.g., older, whitish scar tissue). This will help document the history of the animal's injuries.

Identifying Suspicious Injuries

Dogfighters often provide veterinarians with an interesting variety of explanations for the injuries their animals have suffered. Most frequently the injuries will be characterized as the result of a regular fight between two of the owner's dogs, either in the course of a dominance or territorial dispute or while attempting to mate dogs unfamiliar with one another. If the other dog does not belong to the client or is reportedly uninjured or unavailable for examination, it may be cause for increased suspicion. Other clients have reported that their dogs' injuries were the result of encounters with other animals, including raccoons, opossums, and wild pigs. Although pit bulls are often used in pig hunting and are frequently injured in the process, their injuries are distinctively different from those sustained in a dogfight. Dogfighting injuries have also been attributed to cuts from barbed wire or rosebushes and collisions with glass doors. These explanations may change or become extremely elaborate upon retelling. Veterinarians should make note of any evidence that might support or call into question the possibility of injuries from other sources, for example, the presence or absence of foreign matter, glass shards, or vegetation. One of the primary indications of nonaccidental injury is that the nature of the wound is simply inconsistent with the explanation.

Several distinctive characteristics are suggestive of injuries sustained in a staged dogfight. The dog often has multiple injuries on parts of the body not usually injured in "normal" intraspecific aggression. Most dogs engage in highly ritualized combat in which most of the bites are directed to the scruff, shoulder, and haunches. These types of bites are usually inhibited, and few bites produce puncture wounds to the full depth of the canine teeth. The abdomen and inguinal areas are rarely bitten. Bites to the face and legs are also relatively uncommon. In contrast, fighting dogs frequently bite the face and legs repeatedly. The face often receives multiple puncture wounds over much of the surface of the muzzle and cheek. Such dogs continue to attack an opponent who is submitting and thus may injure the belly and groin regions. Often, in the course of a fight, one dog firmly seizes the lower leg of its opponent, who tries to pull away. This produces a ringing or degloving injury that encircles the entire limb. Scars from such ringing injuries are often found on one or more limbs of fighting dogs.

Since most fighting dogs have engaged in more than one fight, they typically show signs of multiple injuries at various stages of healing, including multiple puncture wounds to the face and bite and "ring" wounds to the legs. Noting wounds in different stages of healing helps to document a history of injury and may be helpful in countering assertions that injuries were the result of a single accident. Fighting dogs may have been subjected to amateur cropping of ears and docking of tails, leaving characteristic scarring in these areas as well. All wounds should be carefully photographed from a distance, showing their location on the body, and at close range, to indicate the type of injury and its stage of healing.

Injuries from animals other than dogs are generally distinctively different. Opossums and raccoons have smaller canines and generally deliver a small number of bites only to the muzzle or chest. Injuries from wild pigs are typically delivered by the tusks, which produce slashing lacerations to the face or side, with no puncture wounds.

Careful documentation of the atypical nature of the dog's injuries will be reinforced by other documentation of physiological stresses associated with combat, such as signs of dehydration, abnormal hematocrit, and elevated blood CPK levels. Toxicology and drug testing—for steroids, diuretics, analgesics, and illegal drugs such as amphetamine or cocaine—should be conducted on any dog suspected of being used for dogfighting.

Reporting Suspected Dogfighting

Veterinarians in several states are mandated to report suspicions of dogfighting activity to the appropriate authorities. It is not the veterinarians' responsibility to confront the client with their suspicions, but clients should be given an opportunity to explain any suspicious injuries, and veterinarians should include these statements in the clinical record. Even if veterinarians are not mandated to do so, reporting suspected criminal activity may not be considered a breech of confidentiality. Veterinarians should check with their local veterinary medical association for guidance on reporting policies and procedures in their state. Anonymous reports to law enforcement or humane agencies can be made, but they will not be as effective without the veterinarian's full participation in describing and interpreting the suspicious nature of the injuries.

Review of Evidence

In addition to documenting injuries to fighting dogs, veterinarians can play an important role in the prosecution of dogfighting cases by helping the court to identify and interpret medical evidence seized at the scene, including supplies, surgical instruments, and drugs. The mere presence of a veterinarian on the prosecution's witness list may be sufficient to prompt a plea bargain.

Many of the substances or supplies found in a suspect's possession may be legal and not unusual for a kennel (e.g., vitamins, topical ointments and antibiotics, deworming medications). Other materials may be legal but unusual for those caring for pets or working dogs (e.g., lactated Ringer's solution or other electrolytes fluids, sutures, IV kits, blood hemoglobin test kits, forceps, scalpels, and surgical scissors). Some of the material may be Schedule IV drugs under the U.S. Controlled Substance Act. The Act, passed in 1970 and enforced by the U.S. Drug Enforcement Administration, classifies drugs into five major categories according to their potential for abuse.

Restricted items that might be found can include:

- amphetamines (capsule or injectable) for stimulating a tired dog;
- dexamethasone, a potent anti-inflammatory steroid used to reduce swelling, delay shock, and relieve pain;
- anabolic steroids (e.g., testosterone propionate, Equipoise) to build muscle mass and increase aggression;
- painkillers;
- prednisone or NSAID anti-inflammatory agents; or
- epinephrine.

The standard of evidence in prosecuting a felony dogfighting case is usually "beyond a reasonable doubt." Defendants often try to introduce such doubt by claiming that evidence seized was related to the legitimate care of working dogs. Veterinary testimony on the use of this evidence in dogfighting, when coupled with other evidence (injuries to the dogs, presence of other dogfighting paraphernalia), helps to build a comprehensive picture of the nature of the enterprise and may remove any doubt about the suspect's involvement in illegal activity.

21 The Future of Veterinary Forensics

The public has always loved a good mystery, from the first detective stories of Edgar Allan Poe and the exploits of Sherlock Holmes to the modern-day forensic thrillers of writers such as Patricia Cornwell and the popularity of the television show *CSI* and its several spin-offs. Interest in using emerging scientific methods to solve crimes and bring wrongdoers to justice is not new, but it is significantly changing the way modern crimes are investigated and prosecuted. Stockwell (2005) describes the impact this interest has had on courtrooms nationwide. Juries have come to expect a high level of forensic expertise and appropriate use of such evidence, even in relatively minor cases. If no advanced forensic methods have been used, prosecutors feel they must explain why such evidence was not collected. Criminal justice professionals have dubbed this phenomenon "the CSI effect." Stockwell notes that this is not just a case of the public confusing reality and entertainment. There is genuine concern among jurors about exoneration of innocent prisoners through new DNA evidence and greater awareness of the unreliability of eyewitness testimony.

As most states adopt felony-level penalties for egregious animal-cruelty offenses, the requirement for successfully prosecuting those cases will be "proof beyond a reasonable doubt." For most juries and judges, this necessitates a level of investigative expertise beyond what has usually been practiced in animal-cruelty cases. There are many reasons why such evidence might not be gathered or used. Since this field is still in its infancy, there simply may be no appropriate forensic models that apply to the case. Animal-cruelty investigators may be unaware of the forensic possibilities in animal cases or of laboratories that can perform necessary analyses. Animal-related evidence may have been mishandled by humane investigators, law enforcement personnel, or veterinarians untrained in appropriate forensic methods. The added cost of such tests may be considered too great, particularly if the attitude is that the victim "was only an animal."

These issues need to be addressed. If they are not, problems are likely to arise in prosecuting animal abuse cases, as they already have in many human cases. The veterinary community has recognized this need. In 2003 the American Animal Hospital Association issued its position statement on animal abuse reporting, which includes the following mandate:

> In order to encourage veterinarians and practice team members to be responsible leaders in their communities and to assist in the detection and reporting of animal abuse, the profession should educate its members to recognize, document, and report animal abuse, develop forensic models, promote legislation concerning reporting by veterinarians, and collaborate with other animal and human welfare groups and professionals within communities to eliminate the incidence of animal abuse. (American Animal Hospital Association 2003)

We offer a few suggestions for advancing the field of veterinary forensics to the point where animal-cruelty cases are treated with the precision and professionalism they deserve:

1. Enhance the development of centralized data and information resources relevant to crimes against or involving animals—particularly companion animals and livestock, the most frequent victims of serious, prosecutable abuse and neglect.

Although there are resources, such as the U.S. Fish and Wildlife Service Forensic Laboratory (Stroud 1998) and the many state veterinary diagnostic laboratories, these focus almost entirely on disease control and prevention and crimes involving threatened or endangered species. A wealth of data is being gathered on the canine and feline genomes, on unique fur characteristics of different species, on incidence and effects of exposure to different toxins, and so on. Such data need to be made more accessible to the investigative community.

Establishment of a national animal-cruelty forensic center would offer a much needed resource for animal-cruelty investigations. Ideally, a center of this kind would consult with veterinarians, law enforcement, and prosecutors on animal-cruelty cases. Veterinarians would have a lifeline for their animal examinations and testing; photographs from cases could be analyzed to assist the prosecution; expert-witness testimony would be available; and deceased animals could be submitted for full examination and testing. Such a center would provide a database of findings in animal abuse cases and would offer training to veterinarians in veterinary forensics.

2. Establish a comprehensive database of serious crimes against animals that is accessible by law enforcement and animal-care and -control professionals.

Although attempts have been made to collect and analyze such data by a number of nonprofit organizations such as The HSUS and *Pet-Abuse.com*, these efforts are very time-consuming and have depended on press reports as a primary source of data. Even when prosecuted at the felony level, animal-cruelty cases are not formally tracked by the U.S. Department of Justice and do not comprise any existing crime index, even though lesser "property" crimes are included. A uniform record of such crimes would aid greatly in tracking and preventing such crimes.

3. Introduce training on animal cruelty into standardized veterinary and law enforcement curricula.

Society has recognized the importance of animal abuse, and some states have laws passed requiring veterinarians to report animal cruelty. This mandates the need for education and training in this area. Veterinary forensics needs to be taught at continuing education seminars to reach practicing veterinarians. In addition, it is imperative that it become part of the veterinary curriculum at all veterinary colleges. Not only would students benefit from learning the pathology associated with abuse, but such knowledge would also serve to heighten their awareness of animal abuse itself. These graduating students could then go on to share their knowledge with their future colleagues.

In the same way, basic training in recognizing and handling animal-related evidence should be part of standardized police officer training nationwide. Such evidence may be crucial in investigating crimes not only against animals but against people as well. For example, officers must recognize that an injured animal is potentially a key piece of evidence in an investigation of domestic violence or child abuse.

4. Encourage continuing education and career development related to veterinary forensics.

Veterinarians who want to become involved with animal-cruelty investigations have a wide variety of options. They can work with their local animal investigators and become their animal-cruelty veterinarians on a contract or consulting basis. Some shelters have a list of veterinarians who are on call to assist at the scene. Veterinarians may be asked to consult on cases from other jurisdictions as well. It is important for veterinarians to communicate with the prosecutor's and solicitor's office regarding their skills and their willingness to be involved with these cases and to offer their services.

It is important, too, to be properly prepared to investigate, examine, and testify in animal-cruelty cases. Veterinarians need to have the proper tools to identify, retrieve, and store evidence. They need to maintain an evidence log and chain of evidence forms, and secure storage areas are needed to hold evidence. Veterinary staff need to be trained in how to assist and handle evidence properly. In addition, a standard operating procedure is needed on how to handle cases of suspected abuse and the media.

All veterinarians will see at least one case of cruelty to animals in their lifetimes and, most likely, many more once they know what to look for. To assist the veterinarian, more resources and more training need to be made available.

The future of animal-cruelty work has been established on the legal side: animal law is now being taught in prestigious law schools, states are enhancing their anti-cruelty statutes, and more cases are being prosecuted. There is an increasing need for veterinary forensics to assist in these cases. The future holds tremendous possibilities, but there is much work to be done.

Literature Cited

Abel, G.G., J.V. Becker, J. Cunningham-Rathner, M. Mittelman, and J.L. Rouleau. 1988. Multiple paraphilic diagnoses among sex offenders. *Bulletin of the American Academy of Psychiatry and the Law* 16(2): 153–168.

Adams, C.J. 1994. Bringing peace home: A feminist philosophical perspective on the abuse of women, children, and pet animals. *Hypatia: A Journal of Feminist Philosophy* 9: 63–84.

_____. 1995. Bestiality: The unmentioned abuse. *Animals Agenda* 15: 29–31.

Adler, M. 1979. *Drawing down the moon: Witches, druids, goddess worshippers, and other pagans in America today.* New York: Viking.

Aksu, M.N., and J.P. Gobetti. 1996. The past and present legal weight of bite marks as evidence. *American Journal of Forensic Medical Pathology* 17(2): 136–140.

Alexander, D. 1990. Giving the devil more than his due. *The Humanist* 50: 5–14.

Allen, T.A., and P.W. Toll. 1995. Medical implications of fasting and starvation. In *Kirk's current veterinary therapy XII: Small animal practice,* ed. J.D. Bonagura and R.W. Kirk, 53–59. Philadelphia: W.B. Saunders Company.

Almirall, J.R., J. Wang, K. Lothridge, and K.G. Furton. 2000. The detection and analysis of ignitable liquid residues extracted from human skin using solid phase microextraction (SPME)/gas chromatography (GC). *Journal of Forensic Science* 45: 453–461.

Alvarez, A.A., and J.P. Freinhar. 1991. A prevalence study of bestiality (zoophilia) in psychiatric in-patients, medical in-patients, and psychiatric staff. *International Journal of Psychosomatics* 38: 45–47.

American Animal Hospital Association. 2003. Position Statements. *http://www.aahanet.org/About_aaha/About_Position.html#abuse.*

American Psychiatric Association. 1987. *Diagnostic and statistical manual of mental disorders,* 3d ed., rev. Washington, D.C.: American Psychiatric Association.

_____. 2000. *Diagnostic and statistical manual of mental disorders,* 4h ed. (text rev.). Washington, D.C.: American Psychiatric Association.

American Veterinary Medical Association (AVMA). 2001. Report of the AVMA Panel on Euthanasia. *Journal of the American Veterinary Medical Association* 218(5): 669–696.

Andrews, J.J., W.G. Van Alstine, and K.J.U. Schwartz. 1986. A basic approach to food animal necropsy. *Veterinary Clinics of North America: Food Animal Practice* 2: 1–29.

Anonymous. 2003. Animal predators suspected in Colorado cat mutilations. July 30. Associated Press. *http://news4colorado.com/topstories/local_story_211200815.html.*

Arkow, P. 1999. Initiating an animal abuse reporting policy at a veterinary hospital. In *Child abuse, domestic violence, and animal abuse: Linking the circles of compassion for prevention and intervention,* ed. F.R. Ascione and P. Arkow, 257–259. W. Lafayette, Ind.: Purdue University Press.

Ascione, F.R. 1993. Children who are cruel to animals: A review of research and implications for developmental psychopathology. *Anthrozoös* 6: 226–246.

Ascione, F.A., and R. Lockwood. 2001. Cruelty to animals: Changing psychological, social, and legislative perspectives. In *The State of the Animals: 2001,* ed. D.J. Salem and A.N. Rowan, 39–53. Washington, D.C.: Humane Society Press.

Associated Press. 2005. Las Vegas man loses appeal in arson case. *http://www.krnv.com/Global/story.asp?S=4040010&nav=8faO.* October 31.

Barton, V.R., and F.W. Oehme. 1981. The incidence and characteristics of animal poisonings seen at Kansas State University from 1975 to 1980. *Veterinary and Human Toxicology* 23: 101–102.

Beasley, V.R., and W.B. Buck. 1980. Acute ethylene glycol toxicosis: A review. *Veterinary and Human Toxicology* 22: 225–263.

Beaver, B.V. 1992. *Feline behavior: A guide for veterinarians.* Philadelphia: W.B. Saunders.

_____. 1999. *Canine behavior: A guide for veterinarians.* Philadelphia: W.B. Saunders.

Beebe, D.K. 1991. Emergency management of the adult female rape victim. *American Family Physician* 43: 2041–2046.

Beirne, P. 1997. Rethink bestiality: Towards a concept of interspecies sexual assault. *Theoretical Criminology* 1(3): 317–340.

Berry, C., G. Patronek, and R. Lockwood. 2005. Animal hoarding: A study of case outcomes. *Animal Law* 11: 167–194.

Bevel, T., and R.M. Gardner. 1997. *Bloodstain pattern analysis with an introduction to crime scene reconstruction (Practical aspects of criminal and forensic investigations).* Boca Raton, Fla.: CRC Press.

Biourge V.C., J.M. Groff, R.J. Munn, C.A. Kirk, T.G. Nyland, V.A. Madeiros, J.G. Morris, and Q.R. Rogers. 1994. Experimental induction of hepatic lipidosis in cats. *American Journal of Veterinary Research* 55: 1291–1302.

Bischoff, K., E. Beier, and W.C. Edwards. 1998. Methamphetamine poisoning in three Oklahoma dogs. *Veterinary and Human Toxicology* 40: 19–20.

Bismuth, C., P. Pierlot, and S.W. Borron. 2000. Are poisonings inflicted upon others always criminal? *Veterinary and Human Toxicology* 42: 104–107.

Blackledge, R. 2005. Condom trace evidence: The overlooked traces. *Forensic Nurse,* May/June. *www.forensicnursemag.com/articles/311feat6.html.*

Blitzer, H.L., and J.L. Jacobia. 1997. *Digital documentation of domestic violence.* Presented at the Federal Bureau of Investigation special seminar on digital imaging in law enforcement. Las Vegas, Nev. *www.ifi-indy.org/ifi%20publications/DomoVilo.html.*

Borchelt, P.L., R. Lockwood, A.M. Beck, and V.L. Voith. 1983. Attacks by packs of dogs involving predation on human beings. *Public Health Reports* 98(l): 57–65.

Boulware, J. 1998. A devil of a time: How is the Church of Satan getting along? Not so hot. *Washington Post,* August 30, F1.

Bowers, C.M., and G. Bell, eds. 1995. *Manual of forensic odontology.* Saratoga Springs, N.Y.: American Society of Forensic Ontology.

Boxall, B. 2001. Proved guilty by a hair. *Los Angeles Times,* December 21.

Brinker, W.O., D.L. Piermattei, and G.L. Flo. 2000. *Handbook of small animal orthopedics and fracture treatment,* 2d ed. Philadelphia: W.B. Saunders.

Brouardel P. 1897. *La pendasion, la strangulation, la suffocation, la submersion.* Paris: J.B. Baillere.

Brown, L.J. 1995. Necropsy techniques in small animal medicine. *Veterinary Technician* 16: 409–419.

Budge, R.C., J. Spicer, B.R. Jones, and R. St. George. 1996. The influence of companion animals on owner perception: Gender and species effects. *Anthrozoös* 9: 10–18.

Byrd, J.H., and J.L. Castner, eds. 2000. *Forensic entomology: The utility of arthropods in legal investigations.* Boca Raton, Fla.: CRC Press.

Cade, L. 1977. Cattle mutilations: Are they for real? *Montana Farmer-Stockman.* March 3, 6–11.

California Energy Commission. 1995. *Avian collision and electrocution: An annotated bibliography.* Publication No.: P700-95-001.

Campbell, D. 2000. Remarks to the Professional Animal Workers of Maryland education and training conference. Ocean City, Md., March 15.

Catravas, J.D., and I.W. Waters. 1981. Acute cocaine intoxication in the conscious dog: Studies on the mechanism of lethality. *Journal of Pharmacology and Experimental Therapeutics* 217: 350–356.

Catravas, J.D., I.W. Waters, J.P. Hickenbottom, and W.M. Davis. 1977. The effects of haloperidol, chlorpromazine, and propranolol on acute amphetamine poisoning in the conscious dog. *Journal of Pharmacology and Experimental Therapeutics* 202: 230–243.

Cerrone, G.H. 1991. Zoophilia in a rural population: Two case studies. *Journal of Rural Community Psychology* 12(1): 29–39.

Cheville, N.F. 1988. *Introduction to veterinary pathology.* Ames: Iowa State University Press.

Clutton-Brock, J. 1993. *Cats ancient and modern.* Cambridge, Mass.: Harvard University Press.

Committee on Animal Nutrition, National Research Council. 1985. *Nutrient requirements of dogs,* rev. ed. Washington, D.C.: National Academy Press.

_____. 1986. *Nutrient requirements of cats,* rev. ed. Washington, D.C.: National Academy Press.

Conn, A.W., K. Miyaska, M. Katayama, M. Fujita, H. Orima, G. Barker, and D. Bohn. 1995. A canine study of cold water drowning in fresh versus salt water. *Critical Care Medicine* 23: 2029–2037.

Connally, H.E., M.A. Thrall, S.D. Forney, G.F.

Grauer, and D.W. Hamar. 1996. Safety and efficacy of 4-methylpyrazole for treatment of suspected or confirmed ethylene glycol intoxication in dogs: 107 cases (1983–1995). *Journal of the American Veterinary Medical Association* 209: 1880–1883.

Copeland, A.R. 1985. An assessment of lung weights in drowning cases. The Metro Dade County experience from 1978 to 1982. *American Journal of Forensic Medical Pathology* 6(4): 302–304.

Coppock, R.W., M.S. Mostrum, and L.E. Lille. 1989. Ethanol and illicit drugs of abuse. In *Current Veterinary Therapy X*, ed. R.W. Kirk, 171–176. Philadelphia: W.B. Saunders.

Curtis, P. 1984. *The animal shelter.* New York: E.P. Dutton.

Damecour, C.L., and M. Charron. 1998. Hoarding: A symptom, not a syndrome. *Journal of Clinical Psychiatry* 59: 267–272.

Dantzler, F., K. Johnson, R. Lockwood, M. Paulhus, and E. Sakach. 1997. *Illegal animal fighting ventures: A law enforcement primer for the investigation of cockfighting and dogfighting.* Washington, D.C.: The Humane Society of the United States.

Davies, J.W.L. 1997. Interactions of heat with tissues. In *Scientific foundations of trauma*, ed. G.J. Cooper, H.A.F. Dudley, D.S. Gann, R.A. Little, and R.L. Maynard, 479–483. Boston: Butterworth-Heinemann.

Davis, L.E. 1963. Thermal burns in the dog. *Veterinary Scope* 8: 2–16.

Deedrick, D.W. 2000. Hairs, fibers, crime, and evidence. *Forensic Science Communications* 2(3). Online ed. *www.fbi.gov/hq/lab/fsc/backissu/july2000/deedrick.htm.*

Deedrick, D.W., and S.L. Koch. 2004. Microscopy of hair, Part II: A practical guide and manual for animal hairs. *Forensic Science Communications* 6(3).*www.fbi.gov/hq/lab/fsc/backissu/july2004/research/2004/_3_research02.htm.*

DeLahunta, A. 1983. *Veterinary neuroanatomy and clinical neurology*, 2d ed. Philadelphia: W.B. Saunders Co.

Di Maio, V.J.M. 1999. *Gunshot wounds: Practical aspects of firearms, ballistics, and forensic techniques*, 2d ed. Boca Raton, Fla.: CRC Press.

———. 2000. Homicidal asphyxia. *The American Journal of Forensic Medicine and Pathology*, 21(1): 1–4.

DiMillo, G. 1996. *Children and fire: A bad match.* Portland, Me.: Portland Fire Department Public Education Office.

Dimski, D.S., and J. Taboada. 1995. Feline idiopathic hepatic lipidosis. *Veterinary Clinics of North America: Small Animal Practice* 25: 357–373.

Dix, J., M. Graham, R. Hanzlick. 2000. *Asphyxia and drowning: An atlas.* Boca Raton, Fla.: CRC Press.

Dolensek, E.P. 1971. Necropsy techniques in reptiles. *Journal of the American Veterinary Medical Association* 159: 1616–1617.

Donaldson, C.W. 2002. Marijuana exposure in animals. *Veterinary Medicine* 97(6): 437–439.

———. 2003. Paintball toxicosis in dogs. *Veterinary Medicine* 98(12): 995–997.

Donley, L., G.J. Patronek, and C. Luke. 1999. Animal abuse in Massachusetts: A summary of case reports at the MSPCA and attitudes of Massachusetts veterinarians. *Journal of Applied Animal Welfare Science* 2: 59–73.

Dorland, W.A.N. 1982. *Dorland's pocket medical dictionary*, 23d ed. Philadelphia: W.B. Saunders Company.

Drobatz, K.J., and D.K. Macintire. 1996. Heat-induced illness in dogs: 42 cases (1976–1993). *Journal of the American Veterinary Medical Association* 209: 1894–1899.

Drobatz, K.J., L.M. Walker, and J.C. Hendricks. 1999a. Smoke exposure in dogs: 27 cases (1988–1997). *Journal of the American Veterinary Medical Association* 215: 1306–1311.

———. 1999b. Smoke exposure in cats: 22 cases (1986–1997). *Journal of the American Veterinary Medical Association* 215: 1312–1316.

Drolet, R., T.D. Arendt, and C.M. Stowe. 1984. Cacao bean shell poisoning in a dog. *Journal of the American Veterinary Medical Association* 185(8): 902.

Duckett, W.M. 1995. Acute care of burn victims. *Journal of Equine Veterinary Science* 15: 157–159.

Duffield, G., A. Hassiotis, and E. Vizard. 1998. Zoophilia in young sexual abusers. *Journal of Forensic Psychiatry* 9(2): 294–304.

Duncan, J.R., and K.W. Prasse. 1986. *Veterinary laboratory medicine*, 2d ed. Ames: Iowa State University Press.

Edmonson A.J., L.D. Lean, T. Weavs, T. Farver, and G. Webster. 1989. A body condition scoring chart of Holstein dairy cows. *Journal of Dairy Science* 72: 68–78.

Eliopulos, L.N. 1993. *Death investigator's handbook: A field guide to crime scene processing, forensic evaluations, and investigative techniques.* Boulder, Colo.: Paladin Press.

Evans, C. 1996. *The casebook of forensic detec-

tion. New York: John Wiley and Sons.

Evans, E.P. 1906 (reprinted 1987). *The criminal prosecution and capital punishment of animals.* London: Faber and Faber.

Fackler, M.L. 1988. Wound ballistics: A review of common misconceptions. *Journal of the American Veterinary Association* 259(18): 2730–2736.

Favre, D., and V. Tsang. 1993. The development of anti-cruelty laws during the 1800's. *Detroit College of Law Review,* Spring: 1–35.

Feigin, G. 1999. Frequency of neck organ fractures in hanging. *The American Journal of Forensic Medicine and Pathology* 20: 128–130.

Fisher, B.A.J. 2000. *Techniques of crime scene investigation.* Boca Raton, Fla.: CRC Press.

Flemming, W.M., B. Jory, and D.L. Burton. 2002. Characteristics of juvenile offenders admitting to sexual activity with nonhuman animals. *Society and Animals* 10(1). *www.psyeta.org/sa/sa10.1/flemming.shtml.*

Frost, R.O., T.L. Hartl, R. Christian, and R. Williams 1995. The value of possessions in compulsive hoarding: Patterns of use and attachment. *Behaviour Research and Therapy* 33: 897–902.

Frost, R.O., M.S. Krause, and G. Steketee. 1996. Hoarding and obsessive-compulsive symptoms. *Behavior Modification* 20: 116–132.

Furlington, R.J., and C.M. Otto. 1996. Characteristics and management of gunshot wounds in dogs and cats: 84 cases (1986–1995). *Journal of the American Veterinary Medical Association* 210(5): 658–662.

Gaynor A.R., and N. Nishi-Dupha. 1999. Acute ethylene glycol intoxication. Part I. Pathophysiology and clinical stages. *Compendium on Continuing Education for the Practicing Veterinarian* 21: 1014–1023.

Geberth, V.J. 1996. *Practical homicide investigation: Tactics, procedures and forensic techniques (Practical aspects of criminal and forensic investigations).* Boca Raton, Fla.: CRC Press.

Gfeller, R.W., and S.P. Messonnier. 2004. *Handbook of small animal toxicology and poisonings,* 2d ed. St. Louis, Mo.: Mosby.

Giertsen, J. 2000. Drowning. In *The pathology of trauma,* 3d ed., ed. J.K. Mason and B.N. Purdue, 253–264. New York: Oxford University Press.

Gilbert, F.F., and N. Gofton. 1982. Terminal dives in mink, muskrat, and beaver. *Physiology and Behavior* 28: 835–840.

Godbold, J.C., B.J. Hawkins, and M.G. Woodward. 1979. Acute oral marijuana poisoning in the dog. *Journal of the American Veterinary Medical Association* 175: 1101–1102.

Goff, M.L. 2000. *A fly for the prosecution.* Cambridge, Mass.: Harvard University Press.

Gonzalez-Wippler, M. 1984. *Rituals and spells of Santeria.* New York: Original Publications.

———. 1989. *Santeria: The religion.* New York: Harmony Books.

Gordon, L.E., C. Thacher, and A. Kapatkin. 1993. High-rise syndrome in dogs: 81 cases (1985–1991). *Journal of the American Veterinary Medical Association* 202: 118–122.

Gourbiere, E. 1999. Lightning injuries to humans in France. Presented at the Conference on Atmospheric Electricity, Guntersville, Ala., June 7.

Graham, D.L. 1984. Necropsy procedures in birds. *Veterinary Clinics of North America: Small Animal Practice* 14: 173–177.

Green, P.D. 1980. Protocols in medicolegal veterinary medicine II. Cases involving death due to gunshot and arrow wounds. *Canadian Veterinary Journal* 21: 343–346.

Greenberg, D. 1987. Compulsive hoarding. *American Journal of Psychotherapy XLI:* 409–416.

Greenberg, D., E. Eitztum, and A. Levy. 1990. Hoarding as a psychiatric symptom. *Journal of Clinical Psychiatry* 51: 417–421.

Gruspier, K.L., and M.S. Pollanen. 2000. Limbs found in water: Investigation using anthropological analysis and the diatom test. *Forensic Science International* 112(l): 1–9.

Guglich, E.A., P.J. Wilson, and B.N. White. 1993. Application of DNA fingerprinting to enforcement of hunting regulations in Ontario. *Journal of Forensic Science* 38(1): 48–59.

Gwaltney-Brant, S.M., and J.A. Richardson. 2002a. Defrosting the dog: Antifreeze toxicity. *Proceedings 8th International Veterinary Emergency and Critical Care Symposium:* 579–583.

———. 2002b. Not all rodenticides are alike! *Proceedings 8th International Veterinary Emergency and Critical Care Symposium:* 574–578.

———. 2002c. Acetaminophen and NSAID overdoses. *Proceedings 8th International Veterinary Emergency and Critical Care Symposium:* 584–588.

Hand, M.S., C.D. Thatcher, R.L. Remillard, and P. Roudebush. 2000. *Small Animal Clinical Nutrition,* 4h ed. Topeka, Kan.: Mark Morris Institute.

Handy, G.L. 1994a. Handling animal collectors, Part 1: Interventions that work. *Shelter Sense,* May/June: 3–10.

———. 1994b. Handling animal collectors,

Part 2: Managing a large-scale animal rescue operation. *Shelter Sense*, July: 3–12.

Hannah, H.W. 1999. For what may damages be awarded in a malpractice action against a veterinarian? *The Journal of American Veterinary Medical Association* 214: 335–336.

Hansen, S. 2002. Macademia nut toxicosis in dogs. *Veterinary Medicine* 97(4). *http://www. aspca.org/site/DocServer/toxbrief_0402.pdf?do cID=115*.

Harris, W., A. Luterman, and P.W. Curreri. 1983. BB and pellet guns: Toys or deadly weapons? *The Journal of Trauma* 23: 566–569.

Haskell, N.H., and R.E. Williams. 1990. Collection of entomological evidence at the death scene. In *Entomology and death: A procedural guide*, ed. E.P. Catts and N.H. Haskell, 82–97. Clemson, S.C.: Joyce's Print Shop.

Hautekeete, L.A. 2000. Ice melts are health hazards. *Veterinary Medicine* 95(2): 110–112.

Heath, G.A., V.A. Hardesty, and P.E. Goldfine. 1984. Fire setting, enuresis, and animal cruelty. *Journal of Child and Adolescent Psychotherapy* 1: 97–100.

Hellman, D.S., and N. Blackman. 1966. Enuresis, firesetting, and cruelty to animals: A triad predictive of adult crime. *American Journal of Psychiatry* 122: 1431–1435.

Henneke, D.R. 1985. A condition score system for horses. *Equine Practice* 7: 13–15.

Hetts, S., and D. Estep. 2000. *Canine behavior: Body postures and evaluating behavioral health*. Denton, Tex.: Animal Care Training Programs.

_____. 2002. Assessing behavioral health. Presented at the Colorado Veterinary Medical Association meeting, Keystone, Colo., September 9.

Hicks, R.D. 1991a. *In pursuit of Satan*. Buffalo, N.Y.: Prometheus Books.

_____. 1991b. The police model of Satanic crime. In *The satanism scare*, ed. J.T. Richardson, J. Best, and D.G. Bromley, 175–189. Hawthorne, N.Y.: Aldine De Gruyter.

Hitt, J. 1997. Operation moo. *Gentlemen's Quarterly*, February, 153–159.

Hoarding of Animals Research Consortium. 2000. People who hoard animals. *Psychiatric Times* 17: 25–29. *http://www.tufts.edu/vet/ cfa/hoarding.html*.

Holt, D.E., and G. Griffin. 2000. Bite wounds in dogs and cats. *Veterinary Clinics of North America: Small Animal Practice* 30: 669–679.

Hornfeldt, C.S., and M.M. Murphy. 1992.

1990 Report of the American Association of Poison Control Centers: Poisonings in animals. *Journal of the American Veterinary Medical Association* 200: 1077–1080.

_____. 1997. Poisonings in animals: The 1993–1994 report of the American Association of Poison Control Centers. *Veterinary and Human Toxicology* 39: 361–365.

_____. 1998. American Association of Poison Control Centers report on poisonings of animals, 1993–1994. *Journal of the American Veterinary Medical Association* 212: 358–361.

Houston, J. 2001. Man pleads guilty to animal-cruelty felony. Columbus (Ga.) *Ledger Enquirer*, December 11, 1.

Humber, K.A. 1988. Near drowning of a gelding. *Journal of the American Veterinary Medical Association* 192: 377–8.

Icove, D., and J. Estepp. 1987. Motive-based offender profiles of arson and fire-related crimes. *FBI Law Enforcement Bulletin* 56: 17–23.

James, S.H. 1998. *Scientific and legal applications of bloodstain pattern interpretation*. Boca Raton, Fla.: CRC Press.

James, S.H., F. Eckert, and W.G. Eckert. 1998. *Interpretation of bloodstain evidence at crime scenes (Practical aspects of criminal and forensic investigations)*. Boca Raton, Fla.: CRC Press.

Janczyk, P., C.W. Donaldson, and S. Gwaltney. 2004. Two hundred and thirteen cases of marijuana toxicosis in dogs. *Veterinary and Human Toxicology* 46: 19–21.

Kagan, D., and I. Summers. 1984. *Mute evidence*. New York: Bantam Books.

Kammerer, M., R. Sachot, and D. Blanchot. 2001. Ethanol toxicosis from the ingestion of rotten apples by a dog. *Veterinary and Human Toxicology* 43: 349–350.

Karlsson, T. 1997. A multivariate approach to the interpretations in homicidal and suicidal sharp force fatalities. Doctoral diss., Karolinska Institutet.

Keatinge, W.R., and J.A. Nadel 1965. Immediate respiratory response to sudden cooling of the skin. *Journal of Applied Physiology* 20: 65–69.

Kempe, C.H., F.N. Silverman, B.F. Steele, W. Droegemueller, and H.K. Silver. 1962. The battered-child syndrome. *Journal of the American Medical Association* 181: 105–112.

Khan, S.A., M.M. Schell, H.L. Trammel, S.R. Hansen, and M.W. Knight. 1999. Ethylene glycol exposures managed by the ASPCA National Animal Poison Control Center from July 1995 to December 1997. *Veterinary and Human Toxicology* 41: 403–406.

King, M. 1998. Red flag: Signs of animal abuse. *Veterinary Product News* 10: 1, 18–21.

King, J.M., and D.C. Dodd. 2000. *The necropsy book*. Gurnee, Ill.: Charles Louis Davis, DVM, Foundation.

Kinsey, A., W.B. Pomeroy, and C.E. Martin. 1953. *Sexual behavior in the human male*. Philadelphia: W.B. Saunders.

Kisseberth, W.C., and H.L. Trammel. 1990. Illicit and abused drugs. *Veterinary Clinics of North America: Small Animal Practice* 20: 405–418.

Knipfel, J. 2005. Alas, Babylon. *New York Press* 18(34). *www.nypress.com.18/23/news&columns/knipfel.cfm*.

Koehler, W.R. 1986. *The Koehler method of dog training*. New York: Howell Book House.

Kolata, R., and D.E. Johnston. 1975. Motor vehicle accidents in urban dogs: A study of 600 cases. *Journal of the American Veterinary Medical Association* 167: 938–941.

Kolata, R.J., N.H. Kraut, and D.E. Johnston. 1974. Patterns of trauma in urban dogs and cats: A study of 1,000 cases. *Journal of the American Veterinary Medical Association* 164: 499–502.

Kolb, L.C., and H.K. Brodie. 1982. *Modern clinical psychiatry*, 10h ed. Philadelphia: W.B. Saunders Co.

Kornblum, R.N., and S.K. Reddy. 1991. Effects of the Taser in fatalities involving police confrontation. *Forensic Sciences* 36(2): 434–448.

Laflamme, D. 1997a. Development and validation of a body condition score system for cats. *Feline Practice* 25: 13–18.

_____. 1997b. Development and validation of a body condition score system for dogs. *Canine Practice* 22: 10–15.

Landau, R. 1999. The veterinarian's role in recognizing and reporting abuse. In *Child abuse, domestic violence and animal abuse: Linking the circles of compassion for prevention and intervention*, ed. F.R. Ascione and P. Arkow, 241–249. W. Lafayette, Ind.: Purdue University Press.

Lanning, K.V. 1989. Satanic, occult, ritualistic crime: A law enforcement perspective. *Police Chief* 46(10): 62–83.

Lauridson, J.R., and L. Myers. 1993. Evaluation of fatal dog bites: The view of the medical examiner and animal behaviorist. *Journal of Forensic Sciences* 38(3): 726–731.

LaVey, A. 1969. *The Satanic bible*. New York: Avon.

LaVey, A., and P. Gilmore. 2005. Reissue of 1969 ed. *The Satanic bible*. New York: Avon.

Leonard, A.E. 1999. Identifying the physical evidence of animal cruelty and violence. American Humane Association shelter veterinarian educational program. Minneapolis, Minn., October 12.

Lewchanin, S., and E. Zimmerman. 2000. *Clinical assessment of juvenile animal cruelty*. Brunswick, Me.: Biddle Publishing Company.

Lewis, L.D., M.L. Morris, and M.S. Hand, eds. 1987. *Small animal clinical nutrition III*. Topeka, Kan.: Mark Morris Associates.

Lieske, C.L. 2002. Spring-blooming bulbs: A year-round problem. *Veterinary Medicine* 97(8): 580–588.

Liliequist, J. 1991. Peasants against nature: Crossing the boundaries between man and animal in seventeenth- and eighteenth-century Sweden. *Journal of the History of Sexuality* 1(3): 393–423.

Lockwood, R. 1985. The role of animals in our perception of people. *Veterinary Clinics of North America: Small Animal Practice* 15(2): 377–385.

_____. 1994. The psychology of animal collectors. *Trends* 9: 18–21.

_____. 1995. The ethology and epidemiology of canine aggression. In *The domestic dog: Its evolution, behaviour and interactions with people*, ed. J. Serpell, 132–138. New York: Cambridge University Press.

_____. 1997. The abused dog: Recognizing and responding to its special needs. Association of Pet Dog Trainers educational conference, Memphis, Tenn., November 21.

_____. 1999. Animal cruelty and societal violence: A brief look back from the front. In *Child abuse, domestic violence and animal abuse: Linking the circles of compassion for prevention and intervention*, ed. F.R. Ascione and P. Arkow, 3–8. W. Lafayette, Ind.: Purdue University Press.

Lockwood, R., and F.R. Ascione, eds. 1998. *Cruelty to animals and interpersonal violence: Readings in research and application*. W. Lafayette, Ind.: Purdue University Press.

Lockwood, R., and K. Rindy. 1987. Are pit bull terriers different? An analysis of the pit bull terrier controversy. *Anthrozoös* 1(1): 2–8.

Ludders, J.W., R.H. Schmidt, F.J. Dein, and P.N. Klein. 1999. Drowning is not euthanasia. *Wildlife Society Bulletin* 27: 666–670.

Mader, D.R. 1996. Euthanasia and necropsy. In *Reptile medicine and surgery*, ed. D.R. Mader, 277–281. Philadelphia: W.B. Saunders.

Marder, A., and J. Engle. 1998. Are there behavioral indicators of animal abuse? Presented at the meeting of the Veterinary Society of Animal Behavior, Baltimore, Md., July 25.

Marquis, J. 1996. The Kittles case and its aftermath. *Animal Law* 2: 197–201.

Martinez, D., and K. Lohs. 1987. *Sorcery and science. Poison. Friend and foe.* Leipzig, GDR: Edition Leipzig.

Means, C. 2002. The wrath of grapes. *ASPCA Animal Watch* 22, 2.

Melzack, R. 1968. The role of early experience in emotional arousal. *Annals of the New York Academy of Science* 159: 720–730.

Meuten, D.J. 1985. Necropsy procedure. *Veterinary Clinics of North America: Food Animal Practice* 1: 609–620.

Meyer, G. 1992. Nonlethal weapons vs. conventional police tactics: Assessing injuries and liabilities. *Police Chief* 59(8): 10–18.

Miller, E. 2000. Creatine kinase. In *The 5-minute veterinary consult*, 2d ed., ed. L.P. Tilley and F.W.K. Smith, Jr., 258. Baltimore: Lippincott Williams and Wilkins.

Miller, L., and S. Zawistowski, eds. 2004. *Shelter medicine for veterinarians and staff.* Ames, Iowa: Blackwell.

Molony, V.J., E. Kent, and I.S. Robertson. 1993. Behavioural responses of lambs of three ages in the first three hours after three methods of castration and tail docking. *Research in Veterinary Science* 55: 236–245.

Moore, E. 1991. Addicted to animals. *Texas*, July 21: 8–11.

Moore, T.D. 1999. Animal hair identification. In *Wildlife forensic field manual*, ed. W.J. Adrian, 32–48. Denver, Colo.: Association of Midwest Fish and Game Law Enforcement Officers.

Mullen, S. 1993. Too many cats. *Cat Fancy*, October 36: 50–53.

Muller, G.H., R.W. Kirk, and D.W. Scott. 1989. *Small animal dermatology.* Philadelphia: W.B. Saunders.

Munro, H.M. 1999. The battered pet: Signs and symptoms. In *Child abuse, domestic violence and animal abuse: Linking the circles of compassion for prevention and intervention*, ed. F. Ascione and P. Arkow, 199–208. W. Lafayette, Ind.: Purdue University Press.

Munro, H.M., and M.V. Thrusfield. 2001a. "Battered pets": Features that raise suspicion of non-accidental injury. *Journal of Small Animal Practice* 42(5): 218–226.

_____. 2001b. "Battered pets": Non-accidental physical injuries found in dogs and cats. *Journal of Small Animal Practice* 42(6): 279–290.

_____. 2001c. "Battered pets": Sexual abuse. *Journal of Small Animal Practice* 42(7): 333–337.

Munro, R. 1998. Forensic necropsy. *Seminars in Avian and Exotic Pet Medicine* 7: 201–209.

Murphree, O.D., R.A. Dykman, and J.E. Peters. 1967. Genetically determined abnormal behavior in dogs: Results of behavioral tests. *Conditional Reflex* 1: 199–205.

Murphy, M.J. 2002. Rodenticides. *Veterinary Clinics of North America: Small Animal Practice* 32: 469–84.

National Oceanic and Atmospheric Administration. 1998. Forensic analysis finds 10 Texas sea turtle mutilations likely caused by shark bites. *www.noaanews.noaa.gov/stories/s57.htm.*

Nickell, J., and J.F. Fischer. 1999. *Crime science: Methods of forensic detection.* Lexington: University Press of Kentucky.

Orlowski, J.P., M.M. Abulleil, and J.M. Phillips. 1989. The hemodynamic and cardiovascular effects of near-drowning in hypotonic, isotonic, or hypertonic solutions. *Annals of Emergency Medicine* 18: 1044–1049.

Olson-Raymer, G. 1990. *Occult crime: A law enforcement primer.* Sacramento: Calif.: State of California Office of Criminal Justice Planning.

Overall, K.L. 1997. *Clinical behavioral medicine for small animals.* St. Louis, Mo.: Mosby.

Parent, J. 1999. Neurologic disorders. In *Small animal clinical diagnosis by laboratory methods*, 3d ed., ed. M.D. Willard, H. Tvedten, and G.H. Turnwald, 285–286. Philadelphia: W.B. Saunders Company.

Parker, T. 1989a. Goats near Pontiac possibly a sacrifice. *The Pantagraph* (Pontiac, Ill.), July 28, 3.

_____. 1989b. Goat killed in dog attack. *The Pantagraph* (Pontiac, Ill.), July 29, 8.

Patronek, G.J. 1997. Tufts animal care and condition (TACC) scales for assessing body condition, weather and environmental safety, and physical care in dogs. In *Reporting and recognizing animal abuse: A veterinarian's guide.* Denver: American Humane Association.

_____. 1999. Hoarding of animals: An under-recognized public health problem in a difficult-to-study population. *Public Health Reports* 114: 81–87.

_____. 2001. The problem of animal hoarding. *Municipal Lawyer*, May/June: 6–9, 19.

Pavletic, M.M. 1985. A review of 121 gunshot wounds in the dog and cat. *Veterinary Surgery* 14: 61–62.

_____. 1986a. Gunshot wounds in veterinary medicine: Projectile ballistics—Part I. *Compendium on Continuing Education* 8(1): 47–60.

_____. 1986b. Gunshot wounds in veterinary medicine: Projectile ballistics—Part II. *Compendium on Continuing Education* 8(2): 125–133.

_____. 1996. Gunshot wound management. *Compendium on Continuing Education* 18(12): 1285–1299.

Penn and Schoen Associates. 1997. *Americans support tougher laws, enforcement, tracking of animal abuse.* Press release. The Humane Society of the United States, Washington, D.C., March 3.

Perper, J.A. 1993. Time of death and changes after death. In *Spitz and Fisher's medicolegal investigation of death: Guidelines for the application of pathology to crime investigation,* 3d ed., ed. W.U. Spitz, 14–49. Springfield: Charles C. Thomas.

Peterson, M.E. 2000. Smoke inhalation. In *The 5-minute veterinary consult,* ed. L.P. Tilley and F.W.K. Smith, Jr., 1202–1203. Baltimore: Lippincott, Williams, and Wilkins.

Petrites-Murphy, M.B. 1998. User's guide to pathology services. *Journal of the American Veterinary Medical Association* 212: 362–364.

Pitman, D. 1992. Satanists blamed for mutilations. *Tucson Citizen,* October 10, 1992, 1.

Pollanen, M.S. 1998. *Forensic diatomology and drowning.* New York: Elsevier.

Pollanen, M.S., and D.A. Chiasson. 1996. Fracture of the hyoid bone in strangulation: Comparison of fractured and unfractured hyoids from victims of strangulation. *Journal of Forensic Science* 41: 110–113.

Pollard, R.E., C.D. Long, R.W. Nelson, W.J. Hornof, and E.C. Feldman. 2001. Percutaneous ultrasonographically guided radiofrequency heat ablation for treatment of primary hyperparathyroidism in dogs. *Journal of the American Veterinary Medical Association* 218: 1106–1110.

Ponder, C., and R. Lockwood. 2000. Recognizing the connection: Law enforcement's response to animal cruelty and family violence. *The Police Chief* 67(11): 31–36.

_____. 2001. Cruelty to animals and family violence. Training Key #526, Arlington, Va. *International Association of Chiefs of Police* 1–6.

Rasmussen, S.A., and J.L. Eisen. 1992. The epidemiology and clinical features of obsessive compulsive disorder. *Psychiatric Clinics of North America* 15: 743–758.

Ratliff, C. 2000. Introductory remarks to attendees of the Animal Control Officer/Personnel Training course provided by Howard Community College, Columbia, Md., September 14.

Rauch, A. 2003. Overview of the use of veterinary forensics in animal-cruelty investigations. Presented at the American Veterinary Medical Association Annual Convention, Denver, Colo., July 23.

Reimschuessel, R. 2000. Necropsy techniques in aquarium fish. In *Kirk's Current Veterinary Therapy XIII,* ed. J. Bonagura and R. Kersey, 1198–1203. Philadelphia: W.B. Saunders.

Ressler, R.K., A.W. Burgess, C.R. Hartmen, J.E. Douglas, and A. McCormack. 1986. Murderers who rape and mutilate. *Journal of Interpersonal Violence* 1: 273–287.

Richardson, J.A. 1999. Potpourri hazards in cats. *Veterinary Medicine* 94(12). http://www.aspca.org/site/DocServer/toxbrief_1299.pdf?docID=129.

Richardson, J.A., S.M. Gwaltney-Brant, and D. Villar. 2002. Zinc toxicosis from penny ingestion in dogs. *Veterinary Medicine* 97(2). http://www.aspca.org/site/DocServer/toxbrief_0202.pdf?docID=112.

Richardson, J.T., J. Best, and D.G. Bromley, eds. 1991. *The satanism scare.* Hawthorne, N.Y.: Aldine De Gruyter.

Robinson, G.W. 1976. The high rise trauma syndrome in cats. *Feline Practice* 6: 40–43.

Rohrer, E.S. 1996. Proper preparation of specimens for diagnostic laboratories. *Veterinary Technician* 17: 587–593.

Rollin, B. 1994. An ethicist's commentary on whether veterinarians should report cruelty. *Canadian Veterinary Journal* 35: 408–409.

Rollins, C.E., and D.E. Spencer. 1995. A fatality and the American mountain lion: Bite mark analysis of the offending lion. *Journal of Forensic Sciences* 40(3): 486–489.

Rommel, K.M., and N. Owen. 1980. *Operation animal mutilation.* Report of the District Attorney, First Judicial District, State of New Mexico, Santa Fe.

Rosendale, M.E. 1999. Glow jewelry (dibutyl phthalate) ingestion in cats. *Veterinary Medicine* 94(8): 703.

Rowan, A.N. 1993. Cruelty to animals (editorial). *Anthrozoös* 6: 218–220.

Saferstein, R. 1994. *Forensic science handbook.* Vol. 2. Englewood Cliffs, N.J.: Prentice Hall.

Samorini, G. 2002. *Animals and psychedelics: The natural world and the instinct to alter consciousness.* Rochester, Vt.: Park Street Press.

Sartin, E.A., J.S. Spano, and T.L. Hathcock. 1999. A practitioner's guide to necropsy. *Compendium on Continuing Education for the Practicing Veterinarian* 21: 954–960.

Saxon, W.D., and R. Kirby. 1992. Treatment of acute burn injury and smoke inhalation. In *Kirk's current veterinary therapy XI*, ed. R.W. Kirk, 146–154. Philadelphia: W.B. Saunders Company.

Scarlett, J.M., S. Donoghue, J. Saidla, and J. Wills. 1994. Overweight cats: Prevalence and risk factors. *International Journal of Obesity* 18: S22–S28.

Schaer, M. 1989. General principles of fluid therapy in small animal medicine. *Veterinary Clinics of North America: Small Animal Practice* 19: 203–212.

Schaefer, J.M., R.D. Andrews, and J.J. Dinsmore. 1981. *Recognizing and reducing sheep predator losses.* Ames: Iowa State University cooperative extension service report. Pm-989-10.

Schoning, P., and A.C. Strafuss. 1980. Determining time of death of a dog by analyzing blood, cerebrospinal fluid, and vitreous humor collected at postmortem. *American Journal of Veterinary Research* 41: 955–957.

Schwartz, L.D., and A.A. Bickford. 1986. Necropsy of chickens, turkeys, and other poultry. *Veterinary Clinics of North America: Food Animal Practice* 2: 43–60.

Scientific Working Group on Digital Evidence (SWGDE). 2000. Digital evidence: Standards and principles. *Forensic Science Communications* (2): 3. *www.fbi.gov/hq/lab/fsc/backissu/april2000/swgde.htm.*

Sharpe, M.S. 1999 A survey of veterinarians and a proposal for intervention. *In Child abuse, domestic violence and animal abuse: Linking the circles of compassion for prevention and intervention,* ed. F.R. Ascione and P. Arkow, 250–256. W. Lafayette, Ind.: Purdue University Press.

Sherman, R.T., and R.A. Parrish. 1963. Management of shotgun injuries: A review of 152 cases. *The Journal of Trauma* 3: 76–86.

Siegel, R.K. 1989. *Intoxication: Life in pursuit of artificial paradise.* New York: Dutton.

Smith, Jr., W.K., and R.L. Hamlin. 2000. Heart murmurs. In *The 5-minute veterinary consult, canine and feline,* 2d ed., ed. L.P. Tilley and F.W. K. Smith, Jr., 114–115. Baltimore: Lippincott, Williams, and Wilkins.

Spackman, C.A., D.D. Caywood, D.A. Feeney, and G.R. Johnston. 1984. Thoracic wall and pulmonary trauma in dogs sustaining fractures as a result of motor vehicle accidents. *Journal of the American Veterinary Medical Association* 185(9): 975–977.

Spitz, W.U. 1993a. Blunt force injury. In *Spitz and Fisher's medicolegal investigation of death: Guidelines for the application of pathology to crime investigation,* ed. W.U. Spitz, 199. Springfield, Ill.: Charles C. Thomas.

_____. 1993b. Thermal injuries. In *Spitz and Fisher's medicolegal investigation of death: Guidelines for the application of pathology to crime investigation,* ed. W.U. Spitz, 413–443. Springfield, Ill.: Charles C. Thomas.

_____. 1993c. Drowning. In *Medicolegal investigation of death: Guidelines for the application of pathology to crime investigation,* ed. W.U. Spitz, 498–515. Springfield, Ill.: Charles C. Thomas.

Spitz, W.U., ed. 1993d. *Medicolegal investigation of death,* 3d ed. Springfield, Ill.: Charles C. Thomas.

Spraker, T.R., and R.B. Davies. 1999. Differentiation of wounds in carcasses. In *Wildlife forensic field manual,* ed. W.J. Adrian, 131–141. Denver, Colo.: Association of Midwest Fish and Game Law Enforcement Officers.

Springston, R. 1991a. Dog carcasses puzzle police in Lynchburg. *Richmond Times-Dispatch,* January 14, 4.

_____. 1991b. Coyote carcasses were used in lab. *Richmond Times-Dispatch,* January 15, 10.

Srivastava, D.N., and J.L. Soni. 1987. *Clinical veterinary toxicology and jurisprudence.* Jabalpur, India: Anubha Prakashan.

Staggs, S. 1997. *Crime scene and evidence photographer's guide.* Temecula, Calif.: Staggs Publishing.

Sternberg, S. 2002. *Great dog adoptions: A guide for shelters.* Alameda, Calif.: The Latham Foundation.

Stockwell, J. 2005. Defense, prosecution play to new "CSI" savvy. *Washington Post,* May 22, 1.

Story, M.D. 1982. A comparison of university student experience with various sexual outlets in 1974 and 1980. *Adolescence* 17(68): 737–747.

Strafuss, A.C. 1988. *Necropsy: Simplified procedures and basic diagnostic methods for practicing veterinarians.* Springfield, Ill.: Charles C. Thomas.

_____. 1997. Necropsy. In *Laboratory procedures for veterinary technicians,* ed. P.W. Pratt, 505–534. St. Louis, Mo.: Mosby.

Stroud, R.K. 1998. Wildlife forensics and the veterinary practitioner. *Seminars in Avian and Exotic Pet Medicine* 7: 182–192.

Surrell, J.A., R.C. Alexander, S.D. Cohle, F.R.

Lovell, Jr., and R.A. Wehrenberg. et 1987. Effects of microwave radiation on living tissues. *The Journal of Trauma* 27: 935–939.

Swaim, S.F. 1990. Burns. In *Handbook of veterinary procedures and emergency treatment*, 5h ed., eds. R.W. Kirk, S.I. Bistner, and R.B. Ford, 29–30. Philadelphia: W.B. Saunders Company.

Swanson, C.R., N.C. Chamelin, and L. Territo. 1999. *Criminal investigation*. New York: McGraw-Hill Higher Education.

Sweet, D., and C.M. Bowers. 1998. Accuracy of bite mark overlays: A comparison of five common methods to produce exemplars from a suspect's dentition. *Journal of Forensic Sciences* 43(2): 362–367.

Tams, T.R. 1994. Environmental injury. In *The cat: Diseases and clinical management*, 2d ed., ed. R.G. Sherding, 251–256. New York: Churchill Livingstone.

Taser International. 2002. *Taser International technical support information*. August.

Thornton, P.D., and A.E. Waterman-Pearson. 1999. Quantification of the pain and distress responses to castration in young lambs. *Research in Veterinary Science* 66: 107–118.

Tremayne, J. 2005. Veterinarians reporting abuse stuck between ethics, self-preservation. *DVM Newsmagazine*, February 1, 1.

Unti, B.O. 2002. *The quality of mercy: Animal protection in the United States, 1866–1930*. Doctoral diss., American University.

U.S. Department of Agriculture. 1994. *A producers guide to preventing predation of livestock*. Agricultural information bulletin number 650.

U.S. Department of Justice. 1996. *Photodocumentation in the investigation of child abuse*. Washington, D.C.: U.S. Department of Justice, Office of Juvenile Justice and Delinquency Prevention.

U.S. Department of Justice, Office of Justice Programs, National Institute of Justice. 2000. *Fire and arson scene evidence: A guide for public safety personnel*. (The full text of this report, NCJ 181584, may be downloaded free of charge from the website of the U.S. Department of Justice: *http://www.ojp.usdoj.gov/nij/pubs-sum/181584.htm*.)

Valentine, W.M. 1990. Short-chain alcohols. *Veterinary Clinics of North America: Small Animal Practice* 20: 515–523.

Van der Borg, J.A.M., W.J. Neto, and D.J. Planta. 1991. Behavioural testing of dogs in animal shelters to predict problem behavior. *Applied Animal Behaviour Science* 32: 237–251.

Vermeulen, H., and J.S.J. Odendaal. 1993. Proposed typology of companion animal abuse. *Anthrozoös* 6: 248–257.

Wade, D.A., and J.E. Browns. 1985. Procedures for evaluating predation on livestock and wildlife. Texas Agricultural Extension Service publication B-1429.

Walker, L.E. 1979. *The battered woman syndrome*. New York: Springer Publishing.

Wax, D.E., and V.G. Haddox. 1973. Sexual aberrance in male adolescents manifesting a behavioral triad considered predictive of extreme violence: Some clinical observations. *Journal of Forensic Sciences* 19: 102–108.

Weiss, L.E. 1996. Dealing with collectors: A cautionary tale. *C.H.A.I.N. (California Humane Action and Information Network) Letter*. Summer: 15–16.

Whitney, W.O., and C.J. Mehlhaff. 1987. High-rise syndrome in cats. *Journal of the American Veterinary Medical Association* 191: 1399–1403.

Williams, C.L., K. Blejwas, J.J. Johnston, and M.M. Jaeger. 2003. A coyote in sheep's clothing: Predator identification from saliva. *Wildlife Society Bulletin* 31(4): 926–932.

Wilson, J.F. 1988. *Law and ethics of the veterinary profession*. East Longmeadow, Mass.: Priority Press Ltd.

Wilson, J.F., B.E. Rollin, and J.L. Garbe. 1993. *Law and ethics of the veterinary profession*. East Longmeadow, Mass.: Priority Press Ltd.

Wise, S. 1999. Animal thing to animal person: Thoughts on time, place, and theories. *Animal Law* 5: 61–87.

Worth, D., and A.M. Beck. 1981. Multiple animal ownership in New York City. *Transactions and Studies of the College of Physicians of Philadelphia* 3: 280–300.

Wright, J.C., and R. Lockwood. 1987. Behavioral testing of dogs implicated in a fatal attack on a young child. Paper presented at Animal Behavior Society, Williamstown, Mass., June 12.

Yoffe-Sharp, B., and L. Sinclair. 1998. *Recognizing and reporting animal abuse: A veterinarian's guide*.

Glossary

Abbreviations

Bw	Body weight
cc	Cubic centimeter; same measurement as millimeter, e.g., 1cc = 1ml
g	gram
kg	kilogram
L	liter
LD50	median lethal dose; lethal dose of 50 percent of the test subjects
ml	millimeter; same measurement as cubic centimeter, i.e., 1ml = 1cc
ACT	activated clotting time
ALP	alkaline phosphatase
ALT	alanine transferase
APTT	activated partial thromboplastin time
AST	aspartate transferase
BUN	Blood Urea Nitrogen
CBC	Complete Blood Cell count
CNS	Central Nervous System
CPK/CK	Creatine Kinase
ECG	electrocardiogram
EEG	electroencephalogram
NSAID	non-steroidal anti-inflammatory drug
PT	a test for prothrombin time

Definitions

Abrasion—an area of body surface denuded of skin or mucous membrane by some unusual or abnormal mechanical process

Acidemia—a decreased pH of the blood

Acidosis—a pathologic condition resulting from accumulation of acid or depletion of the alkaline reserve in the blood and body tissues

Alveolar-capillary barrier—barrier between the pulmonary alveoli and the corresponding capillaries

Ambulatory—able to walk

Ammoniated—combined with ammonia

Anabolic—the constructive phase of cellular metabolism in which simple molecules are assembled in stepwise reaction into more complex nutrient substances by living cells

Analgesics—agents that alleviates pain without causing loss of consciousness

Anaphylaxis—the systemic or generalized anaphylaxis, anaphylactic shock; a manifestation of immediate hypersensitivity in which exposure of a sensitized individual to a specific antigen or hapten results in life-threatening respiratory distress, usually followed by vascular collapse and shock

Androgenic hormones—hormones that produce masculine characteristics

Anemia—condition of low erythrocytes (red blood cells)

Anisocoria—inequality in the diameter of the pupils

Anoxia—the total lack of oxygen

Ante mortem—before death

Anterior—situated in front of or in the forward part of an organ toward the head end of the body

Anticoagulant—any substance that prevents clotting of the blood

Antiemetic—an agent that prevents or alleviates nausea and vomiting

Antipyretic—an agent that relieves or reduces fever

Anuria—complete suppression of urine secretion by the kidneys

Apnea—cessation of breathing

Arrhythmia—any variation in the normal rhythm of the heart beat

Asphyxia—condition due to lack of oxygen in respired air, resulting in impending or actual cessation of apparent life

Aspiration—the act of inhaling

Ataxia—failure of muscular coordination; irregularity of muscular action

Azotemia—an excess of urea or other nitrogenous compounds in the blood

Bestiality—sexual connection with an animal

Blepharospasm—tonic spasm of the orbicularis oculi muscle, producing more or less complete closure of the eyelids

Body condition score—an assessment of an animal's relative proportions of muscle and fat using both visual assessment and palpation and comparing the animal under examination with a stereotyped animal on a chart

Bradycardia—slowness of the heart beat

Bronchi—the bronchial tree of the lungs

Bronchospasm—spasmodic contraction of the smooth muscle of the bronchi

Buccal—pertaining to or directed toward the cheek

Callus—an unorganized network of woven bone formed about the ends of a broken bone which is absorbed as repair is competed and ultimately replaced by true bone

Capillary—one of the minute vessels connecting the arterioles and venules

Cardiovascular—pertaining to the heart and blood vessels

Catecholamines—any of a group of sympathomimetic amines, such as epinephrine

Caudal—situated more towards the posterior end of an animal's body

Cerebral—pertaining to the cerebrum, the main portion of the brain

Cerebrospinal—pertaining to the cerebrum and the spinal cord

Cervical—pertaining to the neck

Coagulation—formation of a clot

Coagulopathy—any disorder of clot formation

Comminuted—broken or crushed into small pieces

Congested/congestion—abnormal accumulation of blood in a part

Conjunctiva (Conjunctival)—the delicate membrane lining the eyelids and covering the eyeball

Consolidated—the condition of being solid

Contusion—bruise; injury to a part with a break in the skin

Coronary—referring to vessels related to the heart

Cranial—pertaining to the anterior end of the body

Cremains—the ashes that remain after a body has been cremated

Crystalluria—crystals present in urine

Cyanosis a—bluish discoloration of skin and mucous membranes due to excessive concentration of reduced hemoglobin in the blood

Cystocentesis—aspiration of urine from the bladder via a needle and syringe

Cytotoxic—having deleterious effect upon cells

Decerebrate posturing—rigidity of limb extensor muscles, usually indicating a severe midbrain lesion in comatose animals

Decompose—to break down organic matter from a complex to a simply form, mainly through the action of fungi and bacteria, or to undergo this process

Degloving injury—An injury in which skin is peeled back, uniformly exposing an area of underlying tissue

Demodicosis—skin disease caused by the Demodex mite

Dermatitis—inflammation of the skin

Dermis—the thick sensitive layer of skin or connective tissue beneath the epidermis that contains blood, lymph vessels, sweat glands, and nerve endings

Diastolic—the rhythmic expansion of the chambers of the heart at each heartbeat, during which they fill with blood

Digestive—associated with or aiding in the digestion of food

Distal—remote; farther from any point of reference

Diuresis—increased excretion of urine

Diuretics—an agent that promotes urine secretion

Dorsal—directed toward or situated on the back surface

Dyspnea—labored or difficulty breathing

Ecchymosis—small hemorrhagic spot, larger than a petechia

Echocardiography—recording the position and motion of the heart walls or internal structures of the heart and neighboring tissue by the echo obtained from beams of ultrasonic waves directed through the chest wall

Ectoparasite—parasite living on the outside of the body

Edema—abnormal accumulation of fluid in intercellular spaces of the body

Emaciated—extremely thin, a wasted condition of the body, especially because of starvation or illness

Embedded—to become deeply and solidly lodged in something

Emesis—the act of vomiting

Endocrine—relating to glands that secrete hormones internally directly into the lymph or bloodstream

Enteritis—inflammation of the intestine, especially the small intestine

Entomology—the branch of zoology that deals with the study of insects

Epidermis/Epidermal—the thin outermost layer of the skin, itself made up of several layers, that covers and protects the underlying dermis

Epinephrine—the hormone adrenaline

Epiphysis—the end of the long bone, usually wider than the shaft and either entirely cartilaginous or separated from the shaft by a cartilagionous disk

Epistaxis—hemorrhage from the nose

Epithelialization—healing by the growth of epithelium over a denuded surface

Erythema—redness of the skin due to congestion of the capillaries

Euphoric—extremely happy or excited

Euthanasia—an easy or painless death

Excision—removal by cutting

Excreta—waste material produced by the body

Exogenous—originating outside or caused by factors outside the organism

Exploratory laparotomy—a examination of the internal abdominal cavity for diagnostic purposes via an incision through the abdominal wall

Exsanguination—excessive blood loss due to internal or external hemorrhage

Extensor rigidity—the rigid condition of a muscle that extends a joint

Fascia—a sheet or band of fibrous tissue such as lies deep to the skin or invests muscles and various body organs

Fasciculation—a small local involuntary muscular contraction visible under the skin

Faux—fake

Feral—used to describe untamed or undomesticated animals

Fluoresce—to exhibit fluorescence: the property of emitting light while exposed to light

Fomite—an inanimate object or material on which disease-producing agents may be conveyed

Forensic—pertaining to or applied in legal proceedings

Fracture—the breaking of a part, especially bone

Frenulum—a small fold of integument or mucous membrane that limits the movements of an organ or part

Gastric mucosa—the internal lining of the stomach

Gastrointestinal/GI—pertaining to the stomach and intestinal tract

Gestation—the period of development of the young in viviparous animals from the time of ovum fertilization to birth

Glycosuria—the presence of glucose in the urine

Granulation—the formation in wounds of small, rounded masses of tissue during healing

Hapten—a substance not inducing antibody formation but able to combine with a specific antibody

Hard palate—the portion of the palate covering the bony surface of the skull

Heart block—impairment of conduction in heart excitation

Heart murmur—abnormal heart sound

Heinz body—when oxidative toxins damage hemoglobin, causing it to precipitate within the red blood cell

Hematemesis—the vomiting of blood

Hematocrit—the volume percentage of erythrocytes in whole blood

Hematuria—the presence of blood in the urine

Hemoconcentration—decrease of the fluid content of the blood with resulting increase in concentration of its formed elements

Hemodilution—increase in fluid content of blood, resulting in diminution in the concentration of formed elements

Hemodynamics—the study of the movements of the blood and of the forces concerned therein

Hemoglobin—the oxygen-carrying pigment of the erythrocytes

Hemolysis—the liberation of hemoglobin by destruction of the red blood cells

Hemoperitoneum—blood in the peritoneal cavity

Hemorrhage—the escape of blood from the vessels; bleeding

Hepatocytes—liver cells

Hepatic—referring or pertaining to the liver

Hepatic lipidosis—fatty liver; disease that causes excessive fat deposition into the liver

Hepatotoxicity—the condition where a toxin has destroyed liver cells

Histologic—referring to a branch of anatomy concerned with the study of the microscopic structures of animal and plant tissue

Histopathology—the microscopic study of diseased tissue

Hydrolyzed—to make a substance undergo hydrolysis, the cleavage of a compound by the addition of water

Hypercarbia/hypercapnia—an excess of carbon dioxide in the blood

Hypercalcemia—an excess of calcium in the blood

Hyperesthesia—an increased sensitivity to stimulation

Hyperglycemia—an excess of glucose in the blood

Hyperkalemia—an excess of potassium in the blood

Hyperphosphatemia—an excess of phosphorous in the blood

Hyperreflexia—exaggeration of reflexes

Hyperthermia—greatly increased body temperature

Hypertonic—denoting increased tone or tension; denoting a solution having greater osmotic pressure than the solution with which it is compared

Hyperventilation—unusually deep or rapid breathing, caused by extreme anxiety or an organic disease, that leads to loss of carbon dioxide from the blood and often faintness

Hypocalcemia—lack of calcium in the blood

Hypoglycemia—lack of glucose in the blood

Hypoperfusion—decreased blood flow through an organ, as in circulatory shock; if prolonged, it may result in permanent cellular dysfunction and death

Hypoproteinemia—deficiency of protein in the blood

Hypotension—abnormally low blood pressure

Hypothermia—low body temperature

Hypotonic—denoting decreased tone or tension; denoting a solution having less osmotic pressure than one with which it is compared

Hypoxemia—reduction of oxygen supply to a tissue below physiological levels despite adequate perfusion of the tissue by blood

Icterus—jaundice

Immunologic—pertaining to the science dealing with all aspects of immunity, including allergy, hypersensitivity, etc.

Ingesta—material taken into the body by mouth

In situ—in its natural or original place

Integumentary—pertaining to or composed of skin

Interstitial—pertaining to or situated between parts or in the interspaces of a tissue

Intervertebral—between two contiguous vertebrae

Intramyelinic—within the lipid substance surrounding nerves and various normal and pathologic tissues

Intrathoracic—within the thorax

Ischemia—deficiency of blood in a part due to functional constriction or actual obstruction of a blood vessel

Isosthenuria—maintenance of a constant osmolality of the urine regardless of changes in osmotic pressure of the blood

KCS/Keratoconjunctivitis sicca—inflammation of the cornea and conjunctiva due to dryness, usually lack of tear production

Laceration—a torn, ragged, mangled wound

Laryngospasm—spasmodic closure of the larynx

Larynx—the organ of voice; the air passage between the lower pharynx and the trachea, containing the vocal cords and formed by cartilages

Lateral—denoting a position farther from the median plane or midline of the body or a structure; pertaining to a side

Lesion—a pathologic or traumatic discontinuity of tissue or loss of function of a part

Leukocytosis—an increase in the number of white blood cells (leukocytes)

Livor mortis—discoloration of dependent parts of the body after death

Lucid—of clear mind

Lymph—a transparent, usually slightly yellow, often opalescent liquid found within the lymphatic vessels and collected from tissues in all parts of the body; chiefly composed of lymphocytes

Malabsorption—impaired intestinal absorption of nutrients

Mandibular—pertaining to the mandible

Mastication—the process of chewing food

Medial—situated toward the midline of the body or a structure

Mesentery—a membranous fold attaching various organs to the body wall; especially the peritoneal fold attaching the small intestine to the dorsal body wall

Metabolic acidosis—a disturbance in which the acid-base status shifts toward the acid because of loss of base or retention of noncarbonic or fixed acids

Metaphysis—the wider part at the end of the shaft of a long bone, adjacent to the epiphyseal disk

Methemaglobinemia—the presence of methemoglobin in the blood

Miosis—contraction of the pupil

Mucoid—any group of mucus-like conjugated proteins of animal origin, differing from mucin in solubility

Mucous membranes—a moist lining in the body passages of all mammals that contains mucus-secreting cells and is open directly or indirectly to the external environment

Mummified—to dry out and shrivel

Musculoskeletal—pertaining to the muscular and skeletal system

Mydriasis—dilation of the pupil

Myocardial—pertaining to the heart muscle, myocardium

Myofibrillaratrophy—the shrinking in size of the myofibril, a slender thread of muscle fiber

Myoglobin—the oxygen-transporting pigment of muscle

Myoglobinuria—the presence of myoglobin in the urine

Narcosis—reversible depression of the central nervous system, marked by stupor or insensibility

Necropsy—examination of the body after death

Necrosis—the death of cells in a tissue or organ caused by disease or injury

Nephrotoxicosis—condition of destruction to the kidney caused by a toxin

Neurologic—pertaining to the nervous system

Neurotoxin—a substance that is poisonous or destructive to the nerve tissue

Neurotransmitter—a substance released from the end of a nerve which diffuses across to the target cell causing either excitement or inhibition

Norepinephrine—a catecholamine

Nystagmus—involuntary rapid movement of the eyeball

Oliguric—diminished urine secretion in relation to fluid intake

Opisthotonus—a form of spasm in which the head and feet are bent backward and the body bowed forward

Oropharynx—the part of the pharynx between the soft palate and the upper edge of the epiglottis

Orthopedic—relating to or marked by disorders of the bones, joints, ligaments, or muscles

Osmolality—the concentration of a solution in terms of osmoles of solutes per kilogram of solvent

Ossification—formation of or conversion into bone or a bony substance

Pallor—paleness

Palpation—the act of feeling with the hand

Panniculus—a layer of membrane

Paresis—slight or incomplete paralysis

Parturition—the act or process of giving birth

Pathogens—any disease-producing agent or microorganism

Pathognomonic—specifically distinctive or characteristic of a disease or pathologic condition

Pathology—the structural and functional manifestations of disease

Pathophysiology—the physiology of disordered function

Perforate—to make a hole or penetrate through something

Pericardium—the fibroserous sac enclosing the heart and the roots of the great vessels

Perimortem—around the time of death

Perineal—pertaining to the perineum, which is the region of the anus and genital areas

Periorbital—around the eye socket

Peritonitis—inflammation of the peritoneum

Peritracheal—around the trachea

Petechia—a minute red spot due to the escape of a small amount of blood

Pharyngeal—pertaining to the pharynx, which is the cavity behind the nasal cavities, mouth and larynx, communicating with them and with the esophagus; the throat

Pica—craving for unnatural articles as food; a depraved appetite

Pinna (Pinnae)—the part of the ear outside the head

Pleura—a serous membrane investing the lungs and lining the walls of the thoracic cavity, the two layers enclosing a potential space, the pleural cavity

Pneumothorax—air or gas in the pleural space

Polydipsia—excessive thirst

Polyuria—excessive secretion of urine

Posterior—directed toward or situated at the back

Postmortem—after death

Preaural—in front of the ears

Prodromal—a symptom indicating the onset of disease

Proteinuria—the presence of protein in the urine

Proximal—nearest point of reference, as to the center or median line or to the point of attachment or origin

Ptyalism—excessive drooling

Pulmonary—pertaining to the lung

Punctate—spotted; marked with points or punctures

Purulent—containing or forming pus

Putrefaction—enzymatic decomposition, especially of proteins, with the production of foul-smelling compounds

Radiograph—a film produced by radiography

Rancid—having a musty, rank taste or smell

Renal—pertaining to the kidneys

Replete—amply, completely or fully supplied with something

Respiratory—pertaining to respiration

Retina—the innermost tunic of the eyeball, containing the neural elements for reception and transmission of visual stimuli

Rhabdomyolysis—disintegration of striated muscle fibers with excretion of myoglobin in the urine

Rigor mortis—the stiffening of a dead body accompanying depletion of adenosine triphosphate in the muscle fibers

Sarcoptic mange—a skin disease caused by the Sarcoptic mite

Scleral—pertaining to the sclera of the eye

Sepsis—the presence in the blood or other tissues of pathogenic microorganisms or their toxins

Septicemia—blood poisoning; systemic disease associated with the presence and persistence of pathogenic microorganisms or their toxins in the blood

Signalment—a detailed physical description

Skin turgor—referring to the normal rigidity of the skin

Slough—necrotic tissue in the process of separating from viable portions of the body

Sodomy—anal intercourse

Solute—the substance dissolved in solvent to form a solution

Somnolence—sleepiness; also, unnatural drowsiness

Splenomegaly—enlarged spleen

Stupor—partial or nearly complete unconsciousness

Subcutaneous—beneath the skin

Suppurative—containing pus

Synchondroses—a type of cartilagionous joint in which the cartilage is usually converted into bone before adult life

Systolic—associated with the contraction of the heart, usually the ventricles

Tachycardia—abnormally rapid heart rate

Tachypnea—very rapid respiration

Tetanic—pertaining to tetanus, which is a continuous tonic contraction of a muscle without distinct twitching

Thermoneutral—neutral environment

Thoracic—related to the chest

Thoracocentesis—aspiration of fluid from the chest cavity

Thrombocytopenia—low platelet count in the blood

Thrombosis—the formation or presence of a thrombus

Toxicology—the science and study of poison

Tracheitis—inflammation of the trachea

Tympanic membrane—the ear drum

Ulceration—the formation or development of an ulcer

Urogenital—pertaining to the urinary and genital system

Vasodilation—dilation of the blood vessels

Vector—a carrier which transfers an infective agent from one host to another

Venipuncture—surgical puncture of the vein

Ventral—pertaining to the abdomen

Ventricular fibrillation—an often fatal heartbeat irregularity in which the muscle fibers of the ventricles work without coordination, resulting in loss of effective pumping action of the heart

Vestibular—related to the vestibular nerve

Visceral/Viscera—the large internal organs

Vomitus—matter vomited

Vulvar—pertaining to the vulva

Zoonotica—disease of animals transmitted to humans

Appendix A
Forensic Laboratories

Visit www.aavld.org, *The American Association of Veterinary Laboratory Diagnosticians: from here you can access the full list of accredited laboratories in the United States.*

List Current as of March 2005

Veterinary Diagnostic Laboratories

Arkansas Livestock and Poultry Diagnostic Laboratory
P.O. Box 8505
Little Rock, AR 72215
Director: Paul E. Norris
Phone: 501-907-2430
Fax: 501-907-2410
Website: *www.arlpc.org*

Arizona Veterinary Diagnostic Lab
2831 N. Freeway
Tucson, AZ 85705
Director: Robert D. Glock
Phone: 520-621-2356
Fax: 520-626-8696
Website: *http://microvet.arizona.edu*

Animal Health Centre
1767 Angus Campbell Rd.
Abbotsford, BC V3G2M3
Canada
Director: Ronald J. Lewis
Phone: 604-556-3003
Fax: 604-556-3010
Website: *www.agf.gov.bc.ca/croplive/anhlth/ahc/ahcweb.htm*

California Animal Health and Food Safety Lab System
P.O. Box 1770
University of California, Davis
Davis, CA 95617
Director: Alex Ardans
Phone: 530-752-8700
Fax: 530-752-5680
Website: *http://cahfs.ucdavis.edu*

Colorado State University
Veterinary Diagnostic Lab
Fort Collins, CO 80523
Director: Barbara E. Powers
Phone: 970-491-1281
Fax: 970-491-0320
Website: *www.cvmbs.colostate.edu/dlab*

Department of Pathobiology and Veterinary Science
University of Connecticut
Unit 3089
61 N. Eagleville Rd.
Storrs, CT 06269-3089
Director: Herbert Van
Phone: 860-486-3736
Fax: 860-486-2794
Website: *www.patho.uconn.edu*

Animal Disease Laboratory
Florida Dept. of Agriculture
P.O. Box 458006
Kissimmee, FL 34745
Phone: 407-846-5200
Fax: 407-846-5204
Website: *http://doacs.state.fl.us*

Athens Diagnostic Laboratory
College of Veterinary Medicine
University of Georgia
Athens, GA 30602
Director: Doris Miller
Phone: 706-542-5568
Fax: 706-542-5977
Website: *www.vet.uga.edu*

University of Georgia Veterinary Diagnostic
and Investigational Laboratory
43 Brighton Rd.
Tifton, GA 31793-3000
Director: Charles A. Baldwin
Phone: 229-386-3340
Fax: 229-386-3399
Website: *http://hospital.vet.uga.edu*

Veterinary Diagnostic and Production
Animal Medicine
Iowa State University
1600 S. 16th St.
Ames, IA 50011
Director: Bruce H. Janke
Phone: 515-294-1950
Fax: 515-294-3564
Website: *www.vdpam.iastate.edu*

Illinois Department of Agriculture
Centralia Animal Disease Laboratory
9762 Shattuc Rd.
Centralia, IL 62801
Director: Gene Niles
Phone: 618-532-6701
Fax: 618-532-1195
Email: gniles@agr.state.il.us
Website: *www.agr.state.il.us*

Illinois Department of Agriculture
Galesburg Animal Disease Laboratory
2100 South Lake Storey Rd.
P.O. Box 2100X
Galesburg, IL 61402
Director: Dale M. Webb
Phone: 309-344-2451
Fax: 309-344-7358
Email: dwebb@agr.state.il.us
Website: *www.agr.state.il.us*

College of Veterinary Medicine
Veterinary Diagnostic Laboratory
2001 S. Lincoln
Urbana, IL 61802-6199
Director: John J. Andrews
Phone: 217-333-1620
Fax: 217-244-2439
Website: *www.cvm.uiuc.edu*

Purdue Animal Disease Diagnostic
Laboratory
Purdue University School
of Veterinary Medicine
406 S. University St.
West Lafayette, IN 47907
Director: Linda Hendrickson
Phone: 765-494-7448
Fax: 765-494-9181
Website: *www.addl.purdue.edu*

Veterinary Diagnostic Laboratory
Kansas State University
College of Veterinary Medicine
Manhattan, KS 66506
Director: M.M. Chengappa
Phone: 785-532-5650
Fax: 785-532-4039
Website: *www.vet.ksu.edu/depts/dmp/*

Veterinary Diagnostic and Research Center
Murray State University
P.O. Box 2000 North Dr.
Hopkinsville, KY 42240
Director: M. Douglas Cox
Phone: 270-886-3959
Fax: 270-886-4295
Website: *www.murraystate.edu/cit/bvc/
service.html*

Livestock Disease Diagnostic Center
1429 Newtown Pike
Lexington, KY 40512
Director: Lenn Harrison
Phone: 859-253-0571
Fax: 859-255-1624
Website: *www.uky.edu/Agriculture
/VetScience/lddc.htm*

Louisiana Veterinary Medical Diagnostic
Laboratory
P.O. Box 25070
Baton Rouge, LA 70894
Director: H.W. Taylor
Phone: 225-578-9777
Fax: 225-578-9784
Website: *www.vetmed.lsu.edu/lavmd*

Diagnostic Center for Population
and Animal Health
Michigan State University
P.O. Box 30076
Lansing, MI 48909-7576
Director: Willie M. Reed
Phone: 517-353-0635
Fax: 517-353-5096
Website: *www.ahdl.msu.edu*

Veterinary Diagnostic Laboratory
1333 Gortner Avenue
St. Paul, MN 55108
Director: James E. Collins
Phone: 612-625-8707
Fax: 612-624-8707
Email: mvdl@umn.edu
Website: *www.vdl.umn.edu*

Veterinary Medical Diagnostic Laboratory
University of Missouri
P.O. Box 6023
Columbia, MO 65205
Director: Stan W. Casteel
Phone: 573-882-6811
Fax: 573-882-1411
Website: *www.cvm.missouri.edu/vmdl*

Mississippi Veterinary Diagnostic Laboratory
P.O. Box 4389
Jackson, MS 39296
Director: Lanny W. Pace
Phone: 601-354-6089
Fax: 601-354-6097
Website: *www.mbah.state.ms.us*

State of Montana Diagnostic
Laboratory Division
Box 997
Bozeman, MT 59771
Director: A.W. Layton
Phone: 406-994-4885
Fax: 406-994-6344

North Carolina Department of Agriculture
Rollins Animal Disease Diagnostic
Laboratory
2101 Blue Ridge Rd.
Raleigh, NC 27607
Phone: 919-733-3986
Fax: 919-733-0454
Website: *www.ncagr.com/vet/lab/index.htm*

Veterinary Diagnostic Laboratory
North Dakota State University
Van Es Hall
Fargo, ND 58105
Director: Neil Dyer
Phone: 701-231-8307
Fax: 701-231-7514
Website: *www.ndsu.nodak.edu/ndsu/
veterinary_science/vetdiag/index.htm*

Veterinary Diagnostic Center
Fair Street, E. Campus Loop
University of Nebraska
Lincoln, NE 68583-0907
Director: David Steffen
Phone: 402-472-1434
Fax: 402-472-3094
Website: *http://nvdls.unl.edu/*

New Mexico Department of Agriculture
P.O. Box 4700
Albuquerque, NM 87106
Director: R.F. Taylor
Phone: 505-841-2580
Fax: 505-841-2518

New York State College of Veterinary Medicine
Veterinary Diagnostic Laboratory
Cornell University
Ithaca, NY 14853
Director: Alfonso Torres
Phone: 607-253-3900
Fax: 607-253-3943
Website: *http://diaglab.vet.cornell.edu*

Animal Disease Diagnostic Laboratory
8995 E. Main St., Building 6
Reynoldsburg, OH 43068
Director: Beverly Byrum
Phone: 614-728-6220
Fax: 614-728-6310
Website: *www.state.oh.us/agr/addl*

Oklahoma Animal Disease Diagnostic Laboratory
Oklahoma State University, College of Veterinary Medicine
P.O. Box 7001
Stillwater, OK 74074-7001
Director: William C. Edwards
Phone: 405-744-6623
Fax: 405-744-8612
Website: *www.cvm.okstate.edu/ Depts/ADL/oaddl/oaddl.htm*

University of Guelph, Animal Health Laboratory
P.O. Box 3612
Guelph, ON N1H 6R8
Canada
Director: Maxie Grant
Phone: 519-824-4120
Fax: 519-821-8072
Website: *http://ahl.uoguelph.ca/*

Oregon State Veterinary Diagnostic Laboratory
Oregon State University
P.O. Box 429
Corvallis, OR 9733-0429
Director: Jerry R. Heidel
Website: *www.vet.orst.edu*

Department of Agriculture
Pennsylvania Veterinary Laboratory
2305 N. Cameron St.
Harrisburg, PA 17110-9408
Director: Helen M. Acland
Phone: 717-787-8808
Fax: 717-772-3895

Clemson Veterinary Diagnostic Center
P.O. Box 102406
Columbia, SC 29224-2406
Director: Pamela G. Parnell
Phone: 803-788-2260
Fax: 803-788-8058
Website: *www.clemson.edu/LPH/index.htm*

Animal Disease Research and Diagnostic Laboratory
South Dakota State University
P.O. Box 2175, North Campus Dr.
Brookings, SD 57007
Director: David Henry Zeman
Phone: 605-688-5171
Fax: 605-688-6003
Website: *http://vetsci.sdstate.edu/*

C.E. Kord Animal Disease Diagnostic Laboratory
P.O. Box 40627
Nashville, TN 37204
Director: Ronald B. Wilson
Phone: 615-837-5125
Fax: 615-837-5250
Website: *www.state.tn.us/agriculture/ regulate/labs/kordlab.html*

Texas A&M University
Veterinary Medical Diagnostic Laboratory
P.O. Box 3200
Amarillo, TX 79106
Director: Robert W. Sprowls
Phone: 806-353-7478
Fax: 806-359-0636
Website: *www.tvmdl.tamu.edu*

Texas Veterinary Medical Diagnostic Laboratory
Drawer 3040
College Station, TX 77841
Phone: 979-845-9000
Fax: 979-845-1794
Website: *www.tvmdl.tamu.edu*

Washington State University
Animal Disease Diagnostic Laboratory
P.O. Box 2037
Pullman, WA 99165-2037
Director: Terry McElwain
Website: *www.vetmed.wsu.edu/depts_waddl*

Wisconsin Veterinary Diagnostic
Laboratory
University of Wisconsin
6101 Mineral Point Rd.
Madison, WI 53705
Director: Robert Shull
Phone: 608-262-5432
Fax: 608-262-5005
Website: *www.wvdl.wisc.edu*

Wyoming State Veterinary Laboratory
1174 Snowy Range Rd.
Laramie, WY 82070
Director: Donald O'Toole
Phone: 307-721-2051
Website: *wyovet.uwyo.edu*

Animal Forensic Laboratories

U.S. Fish and Wildlife Service
National Fish and Wildlife
Forensics Laboratory
1490 E. Main
Ashland, OR 97520
Director: Richard K. Stroud, D.V.M., M.S.
Senior Veterinary Medical Examiner
Phone: 541-482-4191
Email: Dick Stroud@fws.gov

Bone Marrow Fat Analysis
Diagnostic Center for Population and Animal Health
Michigan State University
P.O. Box 30076
Lansing, MI 48909-7576
Director: Willie M. Reed
Phone: 517-353-0635
Fax: 517-353-5096
Website: *www.ahdl.msu.edu*

Animal DNA Testing

DNA Diagnostics
P.O. Box 455
626 Bear Dr.
Timpson, TX 75975
Phone: 936-254-2228
Email: info@dnadiagnostics.com

QuestGen
29280 Mace Blvd.
Davis, CA 95616
Phone: 530-758-4254
Website: *questgen@zoogen.biz*

Therion International, LLC
35 Phila St.
Saratoga Springs, NY 12866
Phone: 518-584-4300
Email: therion@theriondna.com

Veterinary Genetics Laboratory
Forensic DNA Testing
Old Davis Rd.
Davis, CA 95616
Phone: 530-752-2211
Website: *forensics@vgl.ucdavis.edu*

Board Certified Forensic Entomologists

Gail S. Anderson, Ph.D.
School of Criminology
Simon Fraser University
Burnaby, BC V5A 1S6 Canada
Phone: 604-291-3589
Fax: 604-291-4140
Pager: 604-252-5785
Email: ganderso@sfu.ca

Jason H. Byrd, Ph.D.
Director of Operations
Office of the Medical Examiner
1360 Indian Lake Rd.
Daytona Beach, FL 32124
Phone: 386-258-4060
Fax: 352-392-0190
Email: jhbyrd@forensic-entomology.com

Val Cervenka, M.S.
Invasive Species Unit
Minnesota Department of Agriculture
90 West Plato Blvd.
St. Paul, MN 55107
Phone: 651-296-0591
Fax: 651-296-7386
Email: valerie.cervenka@state.mn.us

M. Lee Goff, Ph.D.
Chair, Forensic Sciences Program
Chaminade University of Honolulu
3140 Waialae Ave.
Honolulu, HI 96833
Phone: 808-948-6741
Email: lgoff@chaminade.edu

Robert D. Hall, Ph.D., J.D.
Associate Vice Provost for Research
Office of Research
205 Jesse Hall
University of Missouri
Columbia, MO 65211
Phone: 573-882-9500
Email: HallR@missouri.edu

Neal H. Haskell, Ph.D.
425 Kannal Ave.
Rensselaer, IN 47978
Phone: 219-866-7824
Fax: 219-866-7628
Email: blowfly@technologist.com

K.C. Kim
Department of Entomology
501 ASI Building
Pennsylvania State University
University Park, PA 16802
Email: kck@psuvm.psu.edu

Wayne D. Lord, Ph.D.
Forensic Science Unit
Laboratory Division
FBI Academy
Quantico, VA 22135
Phone: 703-640-6131

Richard W. Merritt, Ph.D.
Department of Entomology
Michigan State University
East Lansing, MI 48824
Phone: 517-355-8309
Fax: 517-353-4354
Email: merrittr@msu.edu

Veterinary Toxicology

Several diagnostic laboratories offer toxicology testing on-site. Check with your local laboratory for more information.

Analytical Sciences Laboratory
University of Idaho
2222 W. Sixth St.
Moscow, ID 83844-2203
Phone: 208-885-7900
Fax: 208-885-8937
Email: asl@uidaho.edu

ASPCA Animal Poison Control Center
Urbana, IL
Director: Steve Hansen, D.V.M.
Phone: 217-337-9751, 888-426-4435
Website: *www.apcc.aspca.org*

Veterinary Diagnostic & Production
Animal Medicine
Iowa State University
1600 S. 16th St.
Ames, IA 50011
Director: Bruce H. Janke
Phone: 515-294-1950
Fax: 515-294-3564
Website: *www.vdpam.iastate.edu/*

Diagnostic Center for Population
and Animal Health
Michigan State University
P.O. Box 30076
Lansing, MI 48909-7576
Director: Willie M. Reed
Phone: 517-353-0635
Fax: 517-353-5096
Website: *www.ahdl.msu.edu*

Appendix B

Forensic Investigation Supplies Reference List

www.barnsteadthermolyne.com: From this site can be ordered the ERT 600 thermometer for approximately $16.00. It has a digital display, is waterproof, can switch from °C to °F, and has a 5" probe. This thermometer can measure from -58 °F–302 °F. The company can be reached via telephone: 800-446-6060 or by mail at: P.O. Box 797, 2555 Kerper Blvd., Dubuque, IA 52004.

www.crime-scene-investigator.net: This site has links to articles regarding crime scene investigation and related information.

www.evidentcrimescene.com: This is the site from which to order crime scene and evidence collection products.

www.fitzcoinc.com: This is the site from which to order forensic collection and labeling supplies, specializing in material for collection of DNA evidence.

www.sirchie.com: This is the site from which to order forensic collection and labeling supplies.

Appendix C

Tufts Animal Care and Condition Scales

Source: Tufts Center for Animals and Public Policy

Tuft's Animal Care and Condition* (TACC) scales for assessing body condition, weather and environmental safety, and physical care in dogs

*Patronek, GJ. In: A manual to aid veterinarians in preventing, recognizing, and verifying animal abuse. American Humane Association, 1997.

I. Body condition scale (Palpation essential for long-haired dogs; each dog's condition should be interpreted in light of the typical appearance of the breed)

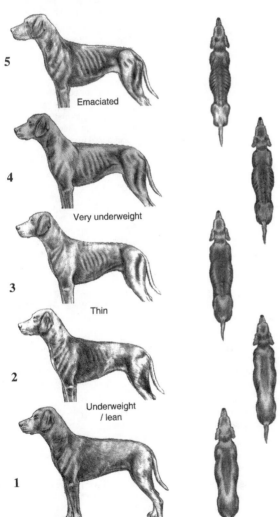

5 — Emaciated
- All bony prominences evident from a distance
- No discernible body fat
- Obvious loss of muscle mass
- Severe abdominal tuck and extreme hourglass shape

4 — Very underweight
- Ribs, lumbar vertebrae, and pelvic bones easily visible
- No palpable body fat
- Some loss of muscle mass
- Prominent abdominal tuck and hourglass shape to torso

3 — Thin
- Tops of lumbar vertebrae visible, pelvic bones becoming prominent.
- Ribs easily palpated and may be visible with no palpable fat
- Obvious waist and abdominal tuck
- Minimal loss of muscle mass

2 — Underweight / lean
- Ribs easily palpable with minimal SQ fat
- Abdominal tuck evident
- Waist clearly visible from above
- No muscle loss
- May be normal for lean breeds such as sighthounds

1 — Ideal
- Ribs palpable without excess SQ fat
- Abdomen tucked slightly when viewed from the side
- Waist visible from above, just behind ribs

Body condition scale adapted from Laflamme, DP. Proc. N.A. Vet Conf 1993, 290-91; and Armstrong, PJ., Lund, EM. Vet Clin Nutr 3:83-87; 1996. Artwork by Erik Petersen.

The Tufts Animal Care and Condition (TACC) scales were designed by Gary Patronek, VMD, to help animal control officers, cruelty investigators, veterinarians, and others more accurately determine the condition of a potentially neglected dog. First printed in the manual, Recognizing and Reporting Animal Abuse: A Veterinarian's Guide, published by the American Humane Association (AHA), the TACC scales were field-tested by officers with the Massachussets SPCA and are now used by Fort Wayne (Ind.) Animal Care and Control and other agencies.

With these guidelines in hand, an officer can objectively assess an animal's physical condition and determine the degree of neglect or level of care being provided by the owner. After the officer has evaluated the dog's health, he may simply offer the owner some care guidelines and discuss the potential health risks posed to the animal. But in more extreme cases, the officer might seize an animal, record the TACC score in his report, and submit the evaluation as evidence in a court case.

The TACC system helps field officers prioritize return visits while tracking the progress of cases, teaches new field personnel how to look for signs of neglect, and ensures consistent reporting throughout the agency. The objective scoring system also gives veterinarians a reliable way to corroborate their decision to seize or treat an animal in the event that a lawsuit arises afterward.

(continued)

II. Weather safety scale

Read score off diagonal bars, by dog size:

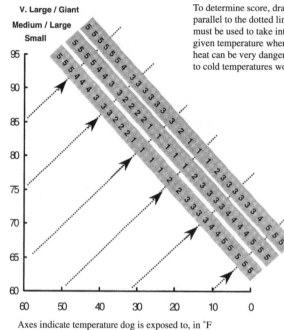

To determine score, draw a line up from the current temperature and parallel to the dotted lines, and read score on bars. Common sense must be used to take into account the duration of exposure to any given temperature when assessing risk; even brief periods of high heat can be very dangerous, whereas a similar duration of exposure to cold temperatures would not be life-threatening.

In warm or hot weather:

- Subtract 1 pt. if water is available
- Subtract 1 pt. if dog is in a shaded area protected from full sun
- Add 1 pt. if dog is brachycephalic
- Add 1 pt. if dog is obese

In cool or cold weather:

- Add 1 pt. if toy dog
- Add 2 pts. if dog out in rain/sleet
- Subtract 1 pt. if dog is a northern or heavy-coated breed
- Subtract 1 pt. if dog has good shelter and bedding available
- Subtract 1 pt. if dog has been acclimated to cold temperatures

In all weather conditions:

- Add 1 pt. if dog is <6 months of age or elderly

Axes indicate temperature dog is exposed to, in °F

III. Environmental health scale

5   **Filthy**—many days to weeks of accumulation of feces and / or urine. Overwhelming odor, air may be difficult to breathe. Large amount of trash, garbage, or debris present; inhibits comfortable rest, normal postures, or movement and / or poses a danger to the animal. Very difficult or impossible for animal to escape contact with feces, urine, mud, or standing water. Food and / or drinking water contaminated.

4   **Very unsanitary**—many days of accumulation of feces and / or urine. Difficult for animal to avoid contact with waste matter. Moderate amount of trash, garbage, or clutter present that may inhibit comfortable rest and/or movement of the animal. Potential injury from sharp edges or glass. Significant odor makes breathing unpleasant. Standing water or mud difficult to avoid.

3   **Unsanitary**—several days of accumulation of feces and urine in animal's environment. Animal is able to avoid contact with waste matter. Moderate odor present. Trash, garbage, and other debris cluttering animal's environment but does not prohibit comfortable rest or normal posture. Clutter may interfere with normal movement or allow dog to become entangled, but no sharp edges or broken glass that could injure dog. Dog able to avoid mud or water if present.

2   **Marginal**—As in #1, except may be somewhat less sanitary. No more than 1-2 days' accumulation of feces and urine in animal's environment. Slight clutter may be present.

1   **Acceptable**—Environment is dry and free of accumulated feces. No contamination of food or water. No debris or garbage present to clutter environment and inhibit comfortable rest, normal posture and range of movement or pose a danger to or entangle the animal.

"Environment" refers to the kennel, pen, yard, cage, barn, room, tie-out or other enclosure or area where the animal is confined or spends the majority of its time. All of the listed conditions do not need to be present in order to include a dog in a specific category. The user should determine which category best describes a particular dog's condition.

IV. Physical care scale

5   **Terrible**—extremely matted haircoat, prevents normal motion, interferes with vision, perineal areas irritated from soiling with trapped urine and feces. Hair coat essentially a single mat. Dog cannot be groomed without complete clipdown. Foreign material trapped in matted hair. Nails extremely overgrown into circles, may be penetrating pads, causing abnormal position of feet and make normal walking very difficult or uncomfortable. Collar or chain, if present, may be embedded in dog's neck.

4   **Poor**—substantial matting in haircoat, large chunks of hair matted together that cannot be separated with a comb or brush. Occasional foreign material embedded in mats. Much of the hair will need to be clipped to remove mats. Long nails force feet into abnormal position and interfere with normal gait. Perineal soiling or irritation likely. Collar or chain, if present, may be extremely tight, abrading skin.

3   **Borderline**—numerous mats present in hair, but dog can still be groomed without a total clip down. No significant perineal soiling or irritation from waste caught in matted hair. Nails are overdue for a trim and long enough to cause dog to alter gait when it walks. Collar or chain, if present, may be snug and rubbing off neck hair.

2   **Lapsed**—haircoat may be somewhat dirty or have a few mats present that are easily removed. Remainder of coat can easily be brushed or combed. Nails in need of a trim. Collar or chain, if present, fits comfortably.

1   **Adequate**—dog clean, hair of normal length for the breed, and hair can easily be brushed or combed. Nails do not touch the floor, or barely contact the floor. Collar or chain, if present, fits comfortably.

All of the listed conditions do not need to be present in order to include a dog in a specific category. The user should determine which category best describes a particular dog's condition. This scale is not meant for assessment of medical conditions, e.g., a broken limb, that clearly indicate a need for veterinary attention.

Interpretation of the TACC score from scales I–IV

The Tufts Animal Condition and Care (TACC) score is assessed from the number of points read off either the **Body Condition, Weather Safety, Environmental Health,** or **Physical Care** Scale. When multiple scales are evaluated, the highest score on any scale should be used to determine the risk of neglect. Multiple high scores are indicative of greater neglect, risk, or inhumane treatment than a single high score.

Score	Body condition, physical care, environmental health scales	Weather safety scale
≥ 5	Severe neglect and inhumane treatment. An urgent situation that justifies an assertive response to protect the animal.	Potentially life-threatening risk present. Immediate intervention to decrease threat to the animal required (provide water, shelter).
4	Clear evidence of serious neglect and / or inhumane treatment (unless there is a medical explanation for the animal's condition). Prompt improvement required.	Dangerous situation developing. Prompt intervention required to decrease risk (e.g. provide water, shade, shelter, or bring indoors). Warn owner of risk and shelter requirements.
3	Indicators of neglect present. Timely assessment; correction of problems and/or monitoring of situation may be required.	Indicators of a <u>potentially</u> unsafe situation, depending on breed, time outdoors. Inform owner of risk and proper shelter requirements.
2	A lapse in care or discomfort may be present. Evaluate, and discuss concerns with owner. Recommend changes in animal husbandry practices, if needed.	Risk unlikely, but evaluate the situation, and if warranted, discuss your concerns and requirements for proper shelter with the owner.
≤1	No evidence of neglect based on scale(s) used.	No evidence of risk.

Disclaimer: The TACC score is intended to be a simple screening device for determining when neglect may be present, for prioritizing the investigation of reported animal cruelty cases and as a system for investigative agencies to use to summarize their case experience. The TACC score is not intended to replace definitive assessment of any animal by a veterinarian or law enforcement agent. A low TACC score does not preclude a diagnosis of abuse, neglect, or a dog requiring veterinary care upon more careful examination of an animal and its living situation.

About
the Authors

Leslie Sinclair, D.V.M., is a principle with Shelter Veterinary Services in Columbia, Maryland. She is the former director, Companion Animal Veterinary Issues, for The Humane Society of the United States, where she oversaw HSUS programs related to veterinary issues and animal behavior. She is a graduate of the Texas A&M University College of Veterinary Medicine and is the former chief veterinarian for the Houston (Texas) SPCA. She is a member of the American Veterinary Medical Association, Maryland Veterinary Medical Association, American Animal Hospital Association, American Veterinary Society of Animal Behavior, and the American Veterinary Medical Law Association. She has served on the scientific advisory committee to the National Council on Pet Population Study and Policy and the Maryland Veterinary Medical Association's human-animal bond committee. She is the author of *Ask the Vet About Dogs* (BowTie Press) and currently teaches Humane Society University's "Humane Euthanasia by Injection" course.

Melinda Merck, D.V.M., is the veterinary forensic consultant for the Fulton County District Attorney's Office in Atlanta, Georgia. She also conducts veterinary forensic examinations for Gwinnett County (Georgia) Animal Control and Cobb County (Georgia) Animal Control. She is vice president of veterinary and forensic affairs for Georgia Legal Professionals for Animals and grand prize winner of the ASPCA 2003 Pet Protector Award. She is a graduate of Michigan State University and owner of The Cat Clinic of Roswell (Georgia). She has served on the board of directors for Good Mews Animal Foundation and volunteered with Cherokee County Humane Society and numerous rescue organizations. She is a member of the American Veterinary Medical Association, American Animal Hospital Association, American Association of Feline Practitioners, and the Georgia Veterinary Medical Association, among others. She lectures on veterinary forensics to veterinarians, law enforcement personnel, and legal professionals across the United States.

Randall Lockwood, Ph.D., is senior vice president for anti-cruelty initiatives and training for the American Society for the Prevention of Cruelty to Animals in New York City. In this position he assists in integrating projects of humane law enforcement, veterinary services, shelter outreach, and national programs that relate to cruelty prevention and response and training. He is the former vice president, Research and Educational Outreach, for The Humane Society of the United States. He is a fellow of the American College of Forensic Examiners, a member of the American Psychological Association, and an Animal Behavior Society-certified applied animal behaviorist. He is the co-editor (with Frank Ascione) of *Cruelty to Animals and Interpersonal Violence* (Purdue University Press).

Index

Page numbers in *italics* refer to tables or figures

Arsenic
   characteristic odor, 141
Arson. *See* Thermal injuries
Asphyxia. *See also* Drowning
   binding and, 107
   chemical, 126, 129–130
   compared with drowning, 131
   definition of, 125
   dogs and cats as victims, 125
   dragging and, 102
   examination for, 126
   generalization of violence to other
      victims and, 130
   intimate nature of, 130
   mechanical, 125, 126–129
   multiple abuse and, 125
   petechial hemorrhages and, 126, 128,
      129
   steam inhalation and, 90
Aspirin
   characteristic odor, 141
ATP. *See* Adenosine triphosphate
Atropine test
   organophosphate poisoning, 153
   pyrethrin poisoning, 153
Atwood, Edward
   murder of, 91
AVMA. *See* American Veterinary Medical
      Association
AVMA Report on Euthanasia
   drowning as an unacceptable form of
      euthanasia, 131
AWA. *See* Animal Welfare Act

B
Ballard, Elizabeth
   dog hairs as forensic evidence in the
      murder of, 53
Barbiturates
   clinical signs of poisoning and
      treatment for, 148
Bartonella henselae
   examining surviving victims and, 63
Basal energy requirement
   starvation and, 157
BB guns
   mechanics of injury, 122
   used as discipline, 120

Beating
   "battered child syndrome" and,
      107–108
   client behavior and, 108
   clinical signs and pathology of, 108
   kicking injury characteristics, 108
Behavioral assessment
   animal's eventual recovery or
      placement and, 67
   examination of the surviving victim
      and, 67–68
   individual variations in reactions and,
      68
   purposes of, 67
Beirne, P.
   animal sexual abuse parallel to abuse
      of women and children, 174
   review of prosecutions for animal
      sexual assault in Colonial
      America, 173
Benzene
   characteristic odor, 141
BER. *See* Basal energy requirement
Bestiality. *See* Animal sexual assault
Binding
   asphyxiation and, 107
   "body gripping" conibear traps, 107
   crushing effects, 106
   leghold traps, 107
   materials for, 106
   rubber bands for castration or tail
      docking, 106–107
   snares, 107
Biological specimens
   collection and preservation of, 51
   crime scene examination and, 57
   orifice samples taken during
      necropsies, 77–78
Birds. *See also* Cockfighting
   elimination of unwanted populations
      with strychnine, 151
   high-voltage electrical wire contact
      injuries, 95
   microwave irradiation court case, 92
   necropsy techniques, 79
Bite injuries. *See also* Dogfighting
   analysis of, 113–114
   "forelimb stab" behavior of dogs, 107

Forensic Investigation of Animal Cruelty: A Guide for Veterinary and Law Enforcement Professionals

Contact wounds
    characteristics of, 119–120
    mechanics of injury, 119
    star-shaped appearance, 119
    tattooing and, 120
Contusions or bruises
    color changes, 100
    hanging and, 127
    inflammatory action around the time
        of death, 99
    mechanism of injury, 99
    as the most common blunt force
        trauma, 99
    patterns of, 99
    photographs of, 99
CPK. *See* Serum creatine phosphokinase
Creosote
    characteristic odor, 141
Crime scene examination
    assault scenes, 58
    attempts to hide the crime, 59
    bodily fluid samples, 57
    canvassing the neighborhood, 60
    chain of evidence preservation, 60
    drawings, diagrams, and sketches,
        60–62
    entomological evidence, 57
    establishing the perimeter of the scene,
        55–56
    ever-widening circle search, 57
    footprint evidence, 59
    guarding the scene and recording all
        persons coming and going, 55
    hazardous conditions reporting, 58
    identification and individualization of
        weapons, 59
    initial examination of the body, 56–57
    license tags of vehicles in the area, 60
    livor mortis degree, 57
    media interest and, 55
    mutilated animals, 57
    neglect scenes, 58
    newspapers and postmarked mail, 60
    photographic evidence, 56
    position and location of the deceased
        animal, 57
    projectile injuries, 59
    prosecuting attorney's role, 56

releasing the scene, 60
    rigor mortis degree, 57
    routes of access or visual contact
        opportunities, 58
    sector or zone search, 57
    special personnel and, 56
    straight line search, 57–58
    strip search, 58
    time frame of the incident, 60
    trace evidence, 56
    unsupervised or free-roaming animals
        and, 58
    veterinarian's role, 55
*Crime Scene Investigation: A Guide for
    Law Enforcement*, 62
Criminal law
    classification of act as misdemeanors
        or felonies, 2
    combined civil and criminal charges in
        severe abuse cases, 3
    crime investigation procedure, 2
    cruelty to animals cases, 3
    location of state criminal anti-cruelty
        laws, 5–6
Cruelty to animals
    definition, 1
    prevalence of, 19
    range of harmful behaviors, 1, 2
Cuba
    Santeria and, 181
Cult satanists, 180
Cultural spiritualism
    Brujeria, 181
    Palo Mayombe, 181
    Santeria, 181, 187–188
    use of animals in rituals, 182
    voodoo, 181–182
Cutaneous myiasis, 73
Cyanide
    "bitter almonds" or musty aroma and,
        130, 141
    cherry red or red-pink skin coloring
        and, 130
Cyberalert®
    tracking of animal sexual assault cases,
        176

Fox, Michael W., D.V.M.
 veterinary testimony in the *Florida v. Zamora* Santeria ritual case, 188
Fractures
 examination of the surviving victim and, 66
 "high-rise syndrome" and, 103, 104
Freeman, Mark
 Eddie Knowles animal-cruelty case and, 117
Frostbite
 neglect and, 84
"Furious" drowning
 as an act of punishment or intimidation, 131
 dog training method, 133
 domestic violence situations and, 133
 restraint equipment and, 133
Furlington, R.J.
 review of gunshot wound cases, 118
 treatment of low-velocity gunshot wounds, 119
 types of dogs usually seen as gunshot wound victims, 121–122
Future of veterinary forensics
 continuing education and career development related to, 199
 development of centralized data and information resources, 198
 establishment of a national animal-cruelty forensic center, 198
 impact of modern-day forensic thrillers on juries, 197
 need for a standard operating procedure to handle cases of suspected animal abuse, 199
 need for education and training, 198
 suggestions for advancing the field, 198–199

G

Garroting. *See* Ligature strangulation
Gas accelerants, 88
Gas chromatography
 liquid accelerant analysis, 89
Gasoline, 88, 91

Georgia
 aggravated felony animal anti-cruelty law, 117
Gillett's 100-percent Lye®, 91
Glow-in-the-dark jewelry
 poisoning from, 153
Goff, M.L.
 forensic entomology, 74
Government animal-control agencies
 authority of, 22
 jurisdiction issues, 22
 variation in resources of, 22
Grandin, Temple, Ph.D.
 testimony in the *Florida v. Zamora* Santeria ritual case, 188
Grapes
 poisoning from, 153
Green, P.D.
 entrance and exit wound characteristics, 119
 forensic interpretation of gunshot wound characteristics, 121
 necropsies of gunshot wounds, 120–121
Guglich, E.A.
 DNA fingerprinting, 52
Gunshot injuries
 cats and, 118
 close-range wounds, 120
 contact wounds, 119–120
 earlier wounds found on examination of, 120
 expert witnesses and, 117
 high-velocity wound treatment, 119
 "humane" or euthanasia scenarios, 121
 long-range wounds, 120
 low-velocity wound treatment, 118–119
 mechanics of injury, 118
 misdiagnosing as bite wounds or vehicular trauma, 118
 necropsies, 120–121
 situations in which injuries may occur, 118
 trajectory of the bullet and, 121

H

Hypothermia
  alcohol poisoning and, 145
  neglect and, 163
  role in drowning, 134

I

Iams
  body condition scoring system, 65
Iatrogenic wounds
  potential problems associated with, 114
Ibuprofen
  clinical signs of poisoning from, 149
  laboratory findings of poisoning with, 149–150
  mechanism of action, 149
  minimum toxic dose, 149
  treatment for poisoning from, 150
Ice-melting chemicals
  poisoning from, 153
Idaho
  anti-cruelty law, 4
Iguanas
  investigation of neglect and, 30, 33
Illicit drugs
  amphetamines, 147
  animal research and, 139, 146
  barbiturates, 148
  caffeine, 146
  cocaine, 147
  marijuana, 147–148
  phencyclidine, 148
  secretiveness of owners who possess illicit drugs, 146
  unknown makeup of, 146
Illinois
  felony animal-cruelty conviction for neglect, 155
  recognition of hoarding as a distinct form of cruelty to animals, 156
Immersion burns, 94
Incised wounds
  characteristics of, 111–112
  "hesitation" wounds, 111–112
  personalization of the attack and, 112
Indiana
  definition of "animal," 4
  felony penalty provision for animal-cruelty offenses, 5

Insecticides
  molluscicides, 153
  organophosphates, 153
  pyrethrins, 152–153
Insects
  collection of, 73
  colonization of wounds on living victims, 73
  colonization patterns, 73
  combing of the body and, 78
  cutaneous myiasis, 73
Instant photography
  advantages and disadvantages, 49
Internet
  "crush videos," 16
  federal crime for depictions of animal cruelty, 16
  state websites with texts of state laws, 6
  supply source for dogfighters, 190
  zoophile postings, 173–174
Investigation and prosecution of cruelty to animals. *See also* Veterinarians as investigators of cruelty to animals
  concerned citizens' role, 23
  government animal-control agencies, 22
  law enforcement agencies and their officers, 21
  private, nonprofit animal shelters, 21–23
  private individuals and professionals, 23
  responsibility for prosecution, 21
  violent acts of cruelty and, 23
Iowa
  prosecution of animal cruelty using unrelated laws, 19
  survey of college students on sexual contact with animals, 174
  two-tier definition of neglect, 155
Isopropyl alcohol
  characteristic odor, 141

J

Jory, B.
  survey of juvenile male offenders on animal sexual assault, 175

K

Kagan, D.
    livestock mutilation cases, 185
Kansas
    prosecution of animal cruelty using
        unrelated laws, 19
Karlsson, T.
    stab wounds and the relationship
        between the perpetrator and
        the victim, 112
Kelly, Nila
    case of cats killed by coyotes rather
        than satanists, 184–185
Kempe, C.H.
    clinical signs and pathology of
        "non-accidental" injury, 108
Keratoconjunctivitis sicca
    acetaminophen and, 149
Kerosene, 88, 91
Kicking injuries, 108
Kinsey, A.
    prevalence of bestiality among men, 174
Knife wounds. *See* Stab wounds
Knowles, Eddie
    animal-cruelty case, 117

L

Laboratory tests. *See also* Forensic
        laboratories
    availability of samples and, 66
    financial considerations, 66
    neglect cases, 66–67
Lacerations
    force and direction of the trauma and
        appearance of, 100
    stab wounds compared with, 111
    "tissue bridging" and, 100, 111
Lactic acid
    rigor mortis and, 72
Landau, R.
    survey of veterinarian involvement in
        animal-cruelty cases, 25
Laryngospasm
    dry drowning and, 134
LaVey, Anton
    The Satanic Bible, 180
Law enforcement agencies and their
        officers

investigation and prosecution of
        cruelty to animals, 21
    searches of the scene of a crime with a
        search warrant, 41–42
    use of stun guns for dangerous
        animals, 96
Leghold traps, 107
Lesions
    diagrams and outlines of, 65
    measuring, 80–81
    necropsies and, 78, 79, 80–81
    photo evidence scale for, 65
    specific characteristics of, 65
    Woods light test, 67
Lewis Red Devil Lye®, 91
Liability issues
    reporting suspected animal abuse or
        neglect, 30
Ligature strangulation
    knot preservation, 129
    mechanics of injury, 129
Lightning-related burns, 95
Liquid accelerants, 88, 89
Listeriosis
    examining surviving victims and,
        63–64
Livestock
    bite wound analysis and, 113
    development of centralized data and
        information resources relevant
        to crimes against or involving,
        198
    mutilations of, 185–186
Livor mortis
    carbon monoxide and, 129
    crime scene examination and, 57
    differentiating from antemortem
        bruising, 73
    hanging and, 128
    time of death and, 72–73
    uses in forensic examination, 72–73
Locard's Exchange Principle, 52
Louisiana
    maximum sentences and fines for felony
        animal-cruelty offenses, 5
Luminol
    blood trace identification at the scene
        of the crime, 59

Forensic Investigation of Animal Cruelty: A Guide for Veterinary and Law Enforcement Professionals

Nevada
    felony penalty provision for animal-
        cruelty offenses, 5
New Hampshire
    felony penalty provision for animal-
        cruelty offenses, 5
    starvation court case, 156
    state animal-related law handbook, 6
New Mexico
    review of livestock mutilation cases, 186
New York
    felony penalty provision for animal-
        cruelty offenses, 5
Newspapers
    crime scene examination and, 60
NSAIDs. *See* Ibuprofen

O

Occult and ritualistic abuse
    background and definitions, 179
    cultural spiritualism, 181–182
    degree of pain or suffering and,
        187–188
    emotional nature of, 179
    evidence considerations, 187
    Hialeah, Fla., Santeria case, 187–188
    human *versus* nonhuman sources of
        injury, death, and mutilation,
        184–185
    identifying the cause of death and
        sequence of injuries, 183–184
    linking injuries to a particular suspect,
        187
    livestock mutilations as a special case,
        185–186
    neopaganism, 179, 182
    role of animals, 182
    satanism, 180–181
    species and individual identification,
        183
    supplemental postmortem analysis, 186
    unique precautions in the examination
        of victims, 182
    veterinary forensic examination role,
        182
    witchcraft, 180, 182
Ocular fluid
    obtaining during necropsies, 78

Oedema aquaosum
    drowning and, 135
Office of Justice Publications
    *Crime Scene Investigation: A Guide
        for Law Enforcement,* 62
Ohio
    maximum sentences and fines for felony
        animal-cruelty offenses, 5
    state animal-related law handbook, 6
Oklahoma
    felony animal cruelty conviction for
        neglect, 155
OP poisoning. *See* Organophosphate
    poisoning
Organophosphate poisoning
    clinical signs and diagnosis, 153
Organophosphates
    characteristic odor, 141
Otto, C.M.
    review of gunshot wound cases, 118
    treatment of low-velocity gunshot
        wounds, 119
    types of dogs usually seen as gunshot
        wound victims, 121–122
Over-the-counter medications. *See*
    Prescription drugs and over-the-
    counter medications
Overall, K.L.
    behavioral assessment of dogs, 67
Owen, Nancy
    review of livestock mutilation cases, 186

P

Paintballs
    poisoning from, 153
Palo Mayombe
    description, 181
Parasitism
    closely confined animals and, 161–162
    symptoms and diagnosis, 162
Parrish, R.A.
    classification of shotgun wounds, 120
Pavletic, M.M.
    basic ballistics review, 118
    "projectile" definition, 117
    radiographs of projectile injuries, 120
    survey of gunshot injuries treated at
        Boston's Angell Memorial

liability issues, 27, 29–30
partial commitment to assisting with
an investigation, 33–34
perceived ability to evaluate cases, 30,
33
personal safety issues, 34–35
policies for signs suggestive of abuse or
neglect, 26–27
preparation necessity, 26
reporting procedures, 26
reporting suspected abuse or neglect, 27
responsibilities of participating in an
investigation, 33–34
surveys of involvement, 25
time commitment, 34
unowned or abandoned animals, 26
veterinarian reporting laws for animal
cruelty and animal fighting,
April 2005, *31–32*
ways a practitioner may be involved,
25–26
Veterinary diagnostic laboratories
contact information, 219–223
Veterinary toxicology laboratories
contact information, 224
Videography
establishing the location of the crime
scene and the identification of
victims, 56
narration of the crime scene and
procedures being used, 50
Virginia
felony animal-cruelty conviction for
neglect, 155
state animal-related law handbook, 6
Vitamin K_1
anticoagulant rodenticide antidote, 150
Vitiated atmosphere
mechanics of injury, 126
Vizard, E.
psychiatric disorder link with animal
sexual assault, 175
Voodoo
description, 181

W

Warfarin. *See* Anticoagulant rodenticides
Washington, D.C.
felony penalty provision for animal-
cruelty offenses, 4
statute defining neglect, 155–156
Washington (D.C.) Humane Society
authority for the enforcement of anti-
cruelty laws, 22
Weather conditions
crime scene examination and, 56, 58
entomological evidence and, 57
TACC weather safety scale, 228
Wet conditions
neglect and, 163
White, B.N.
DNA fingerprinting, 52
WHS. *See* Washington (D.C.) Humane
Society
Wildlife
"disposal" drowning and, 131, 132
Williams, R.E.
entomological evidence collection and
preservation, 57, 74
Wilson, P.J.
DNA fingerprinting, 52
Wisconsin
anti-cruelty law, 3
Witchcraft
use of animals in rituals, 180, 182
Woods light test
ethylene glycol poisoning, 144
lesions and, 67
ringworm and, 67
Work animals
history of legal protection, 3
state anti-cruelty laws, 3
Wright, Dwayne
Edward Atwood murder case and, 91

X

Xylene
characteristic odor, 141

Y

Yoking
mechanics of injury, 129

Z

Other Books from Humane Society Press

The Use of Animals in Higher Education: Problems, Alternatives, and Recommendations, by Jonathan Balcombe

Fund-Raising for Animal Care Organizations
edited by Julie Miller Dowling

Compassion Fatigue in the Animal-Care Community
by Charles R. Figley, Ph.D., and Robert G. Roop, Ph.D.

Volunteer Management for Animal Care Organizations
by Betsy McFarland

The Humane Society of the United States Euthanasia Training Manual, by Rebecca H. Rhodes, D.V.M.

Humane Wildlife Solutions: The Role of Immunocontraception
edited by Allen R. Rutberg, Ph.D.

The State of the Animals: 2001
edited by Deborah J. Salem and Andrew N. Rowan

The State of the Animals II: 2003
edited by Deborah J. Salem and Andrew N. Rowan

The State of the Animals III: 2005
edited by Deborah J. Salem and Andrew N. Rowan

Community Approaches to Feral Cats: Problems, Alternatives and Recommendations, by Margaret R. Slater, D.V.M.

Protecting All Animals: A Fifty-Year History of The Humane Society of the United States, by Bernard Unti